Caring for Children With Neurodevelopmental Disabilities and Their Families

An Innovative Approach to Interdisciplinary Practice

Caring for Children With Neurodevelopmental Disabilities and Their Families

An Innovative Approach to Interdisciplinary Practice

Edited by

Claudia María Vargas
Patricia Ann Prelock
University of Vermont

LAWRENCE ERLBAUM ASSOCIATES, PUBLISHERS
2004   Mahwah, New Jersey   London

Lawrence Erlbaum Associates, Inc., Publishers
10 Industrial Avenue
Mahwah, New Jersey 07430

Cover design by Kathryn Houghtaling Lacey

Cover photo: James Cipriano is now a 42-year-old adult with Down Syndrome working full-time and living in his home community in Ohio.

Library of Congress Cataloging-in-Publication Data

Caring for children with neurodevelopmental disabilities and their
    families : an innovative approach to interdisciplinary practice.
        p. cm.
    Includes bibliographical references and index.
ISBN 0-8058-4476-7 (cloth : alk. paper)
ISBN 0-8058-4477-5 (pbk. : alk. paper)
1. Developmental disabilities—Case studies. 2. Developmentally
    disabled children—Case studies. 3. Developmental disabilities—
    Patients—Family relationships. 4. Developmental neurobiology.
    5. Children—Diseases—Treatment.   I. Vargas, Claudia María.
    II. Prelock, Patricia A.
RJ506.D47C376 2004
362.196'8—dc22   2004040372
                                                              CIP

Books published by Lawrence Erlbaum Associates are printed on acid-
free paper, and their bindings are chosen for strength and durability.

Printed in the United States of America
10 9 8 7 6 5 4 3 2 1

*To the children and families
who guided our learning process.*

Contents

Preface

The annals of medicine, anthropology, and history are filled with hor-rific stories of the inhumane treatment of persons with disabilities. Even the most advanced societies have skeletons in the closet: maltreat-ment, abuse, and, yes, even experimentation, as during the Holocaust. Although institutionalization was advanced to provide a safe place for persons with disabilities who, until then, were imprisoned in jails, this too, was recognized as cruel for children who were condemned to an isolated life from family and community. Yet, de-institutionalization is a recent phenomenon even in the state of Vermont, where we write, and institutionalization continues to be practiced in other states and in other countries. Nationally, parents of children with disabilities, inspired by the Civil Rights movement of the 1950s and 1960s, came to realize that their children were also victims of segregation.

The field of disabilities has evolved in leap and bounds in the last 30 years in the United States with the passage of Public Law 94-142 in 1975 and the Individuals with Disability Education Act (IDEA). Although much has been accomplished, more remains to be done in this country as well as internationally.

The intent of this book is to demonstrate the importance of interdisci-plinary practice in addressing the needs of children with neurodevelop-mental disabilities and their families by sharing the experiences and lessons learned from the Vermont Interdisciplinary Leadership Educa-tion for Health Professionals (VT–ILEHP) Program, one of the 35 Lead-ership Education in Neurodevelopmental Disabilities (LEND) programs throughout the country funded by the United States govern-ment through the Maternal and Child Health Bureau (MCHB). The mis-sion of the MCHB is to train health professionals who will become instrumental, as leaders, in improving the health of children with dis-abilities. One of the goals in the VT–ILEHP Program is to prepare current and future professionals for their roles as future leaders in maternal and child health by inculcating an interdisciplinary as opposed to a solo approach to practice in which each discipline operates independent of the others. Another goal is to prepare them to become catalysts in the various systems in which they will be employed, to facilitate clients' working through a maze of separate service systems for families and children with disabilities. Infusing systems with the spirit of family-centered care is critical to this goal.

Although the VT–ILEHP model is based on the experience of a small state, mainly rural, with a population of about 608,000 and over 244 small towns under 2,500 inhabitants, it has taught the trainees and fellows and faculty members important lessons that may be helpful to others nationally and internationally. Until recently, Vermont was considered the "Whitest" state in the nation. The 2000 Census suggests that the ethnocultural, racial tapestry of Vermont has become culturally rich. Over 30 languages are spoken in the state and the refugee community last year included 50 Sudanese, Lost Boys of Sudan, and this year will welcome 200 Bantu families from Somalia.

The intent of the editors was to make the chapters easily accessible yet clinically sound. The book was written for undergraduate and graduate students, health care professionals, educators, administrators, policymakers, and leaders in the field of disabilities as well as for families with children with disabilities. We tried to make the style clear without compromising the substantive knowledge, highlighted evidenced-based practice, and avoided cumbersome jargon characteristic of each discipline involved. A glossary of terms and diagnoses to which the reader can easily refer is provided to facilitate understanding. To help parents and professionals, a list of pertinent resources is provided at the end of each chapter.

The structure of the book was sculpted by real stories of the children and families with whom we have been so fortunate to work. The book introduces each component of the clinical process through a story of a child with complex health needs. Thus, the contributors focus attention on the challenges, hopes, and dreams of these families and children. They then interweave the perspective of child, family, and that of service providers as they struggle through the health care system maze to obtain specialized services for their child with neurodevelopmental disabilities.

The experience captured in the book has been profoundly touching for the editors and collaborators. It presents not only the clinical experience of each but also the personal histories of children with disabilities—sons, daughters, cousins, sisters, brothers, relatives, or friends. The book invites the reader to embark on a journey we have traveled together with the families who graciously allowed us into their lives.

The model advanced by VT–ILEHP is anchored by five competencies: family-centered care, cultural competence, interdisciplinary practice, leadership, neurodevelopmental disabilities, and policy and leadership. The program provides advanced graduate training for health professionals in 12 disciplines: pediatrics, speech and language pathology (SLP), nursing, physical therapy, occupational therapy, psychology, social work, nutrition, audiology, policy and public law, family support, and education. The interdisciplinary model is applied to practitioners serving infants to young adults. Each chapter illustrates how the program put into practice the five core competencies while working with individual families and systems of care. The chapters are designed to invite the reader, as a member of the interdisciplinary team, to put into practice each of the components of the program. The book begins with an introduction to the entire program, specifically, a definition of the five competencies, a description of each curricular and clinical component, and the frameworks that guide clinical and leadership practice. Although the program focuses on training, its goal is to change the systems in place by modeling directly not only to the trainees and fellows but also to the community and school teams that may already be in place.

We hope the book constitutes a useful addition to current theory and research, but, further, that it provides a model clinicians, policymakers, and parents can apply to their own efforts. It is intended, above all, to help parents and professionals develop the potential of children with disabilities and to live as normal lives as possible. We, the editors, owe a debt to the contributors, but most of all, to the families that were willing to embark on this journey with us as a training endeavor.

One last word about the photos in the book. First, the photos of the children are intended to counter misconceptions of these children as somehow different from other children in negative ways. These children are beautiful. Second, as some of the photos portray, family members are affected by the disability of a child but, at the same time, parents, siblings, and children with developmental disabilities engage in each other's lives in ways that offer tremendous opportunities for growth and maturity. Last, the photos are intended to capture their strengths as well the joy that these children bring to their families and to their communities.

ACKNOWLEDGMENTS

Over the past eight years we have been privileged to be part of an interdisciplinary expedition that has taught us much about the value of collaboration and teaming, the meaning of family-centered care, commitment to cultural competence, the complexities of neurodevel-

opmental disabilities, and the importance of leadership. On our journey, we have partnered with family support organizations, school
districts, pediatric practices, developmental service agencies, and others to make a difference in the lives of children with special health care
needs and their families.

We are indebted to our faculty collaborators at the University of Vermont, the families who have taught us so much, their children who
have given us new ways of thinking about disability, and the community professionals who serve them across the state of Vermont.

We are also grateful to the Maternal and Child Health Bureau for its
funding of the Vermont Interdisciplinary Leadership Education for
Health Professionals (VT–ILEHP) Program that has allowed us to
train new leaders committed to the care of children and families with
special needs.

The partnerships with colleagues to outline, draft, revise, and draft
again the chapters of this book was a focused, rewarding, and sometimes
challenging adventure. It served an important purpose in producing a
quality product. We are ever thankful to our faculty collaborators for following through on the assigned tasks and completing a quality product.
A special thank-you to the VT–ILEHP Program Assistant, Kerstin
Hanson, for her computer expertise, support, encouragement, and calm-
ness, especially the final days before completing the document when we
pleaded for multiple tasks all at the same time.

Finally, we want to express our sincere appreciation to Susan
Milmoe, Senior Consulting Editor, LEA, for believing in our project at
its inception and for trusting that we would bring it to fruition as well
as for her continuous encouragement. Tina Hardy, we thank you for
scrutinizing the manuscript in page edits. We particularly want to extend our sincere appreciation to Marianna Vertullo, Production Editor,
for her patience in answering all our questions and willing to help us
through the production process.

Most important, we thank our spouses, Phillip and Bill. Without their
love, understanding, and support, we could not have managed the extended workdays, the sleepless nights, and the canceled social and family events. We are forever grateful and indebted to them both.

—*Claudia María Vargas*
—*Patricia A. Prelock*

About the Contributors

Jean Beatson is research assistant professor of Nursing at the University of Vermont. She earned a master's degree in nursing from the University of Vermont and is currently a doctoral candidate in the Educational Leadership Program. Ms. Beatson is the Clinical Director and Associate Training Director for the Vermont Interdisciplinary Leadership Education for Health Professionals (VT–ILEHP) Program and serves as its core nursing faculty.

Sara N. Burchard is associate professor of Psychology at the University of Vermont where she received her doctorate in Developmental Psychology. Dr. Burchard is a licensed practicing psychologist and a member of the Behavior Therapy and Psychotherapy Clinic in the Psychology Department at the University of Vermont where clinical doctoral students receive training. Dr. Burchard serves as the core psychology faculty.

Stephen Contompasis is a developmental pediatrician and associate professor of Pediatrics at the University of Vermont. He earned his MD at Tufts Medical School and did his residency training at Dartmouth-Hitchcock Medical Center and his post-residency training at Children's Hospital in Boston. He is board certified in pediatrics, developmental and behavioral pediatrics, and neurodevelopmental disabilities. Dr. Contompasis is Program Director for the VT–ILEHP Program. He serves as its core pediatrics faculty.

Phillip J. Cooper is Gund Chair Professor in Public Administration in the Department of Political Science at the University of Vermont. He received his doctorate in political science from Syracuse University. Dr. Cooper serves as the core faculty member in public administration, public law and policy for the VT–ILEHP Program. A Fellow of the National Academy of

Public Administration, he has authored numerous books and articles on public law, public administration, the Supreme Court, sustainable development, refugee services, and health policy.

Ruth Dennis is a certified occupational therapist and research assistant professor of Education at the University of Vermont. She earned her doctorate from the University of Vermont in Educational Leadership. She is also a member of the State of Vermont Interdisciplinary Team (VT-I Team) through the Center for Disability and Community Inclusion. Dr. Dennis serves as the core occupational therapy faculty member for VT–ILEHP.

Marty Dewees is a social worker and associate professor of Social Work at the University of Vermont. She received her doctorate in social welfare from State University of New York-Albany. Dr. Dewees serves as the core faculty member in social work for VT–ILEHP.

Nancy DiVenere is executive director of Parent to Parent of Vermont and adjunct faculty in the Department of Pediatrics at the University of Vermont. She received her bachelor of science degree in sociology from St Michael's College in Vermont. Ms. DiVenere served as VT–ILEHP core faculty member in family support.

Priscilla Douglas is a certified clinical audiologist at The Audiology Center, Fletcher Allen Health Care in Burlington, Vermont. She has a master of science degree in audiology from the University of Vermont. Ms. Douglas serves as the core VT–ILEHP Program faculty member in audiology.

Malai Holland is a registered and certified dietician and the State Nutritionist for the Children with Special Health Needs Program in the state of Vermont. She has a master's degree in public health nutrition from the University of Minnesota. Ms. Holland serves as the VT–ILEHP consulting faculty member in nutrition.

Deborah A. O'Rourke is a licensed physical therapist and assistant professor in the Department of Physical Therapy at the University of Vermont. She received her doctorate in Experimental-Developmental Psychology from the University of Vermont. Dr. O'Rourke serves as one of the VT–ILEHP core faculty members in physical therapy.

Patricia A. Prelock is a certified speech-language pathologist and a professor in the Department of Communications Sciences which she currently chairs at the University of Vermont. She has a secondary appointment in the Department of Pediatrics. She received her doctorate in child language with a concentration in cognitive psychology at the University of Pittsburgh. She is Board recognized as a child language specialist. Dr. Prelock serves as the VT–ILEHP training director and as one of its core faculty members in speech-language pathology.

Claudia María Vargas is research assistant professor in the Department of Pediatrics and director of intercultural programs at the University of Vermont. She earned her doctorate from the University of Southern California in education with a focus in educational administration, organizational leadership, and counseling. She co-edited a book for the United Nations on sustainable development (1995), was guest editor for the *Refuge* journal on refugee service delivery and partnerships (2000), and co-authored *Implementing Sustainable Development: From Global Policy to Local Action* (2004). She serves as a VT-ILEHP core faculty member in education.

Jo Yoder was family faculty coordinator for Parent to Parent of Vermont and an adjunct faculty member in the Department of Pediatrics at the University of Vermont. She has a master's degree in education from Iowa State University, Ames, Iowa. Ms. Yoder served as a VT–ILEHP core faculty member in family support.

List of Case Stories and Disorders

tion (impaired bowel and bladder function), musculoskeletal deformities, and a latex allergy

Chapter 6

Carolina's Story: attention deficit hyperactivity disorder (ADHD, receptive and expressive language delays, hypernasality, articulation problems, chronic Otitis Media, fluctuating conductive hearing loss, and a surgically repaired submucous cleft palate

Chapter 7

Jacques's Story: autism, developmental delays, and seizure disorder

Chapter 8

Nicole's Story: Down Syndrome and celiac disease

Chapter 9

Sam's Story: autism spectrum disorders (ASD)

Chapter 10

Allison's Story: cerebral palsy, spastic quadriplegia, and seizure disorder

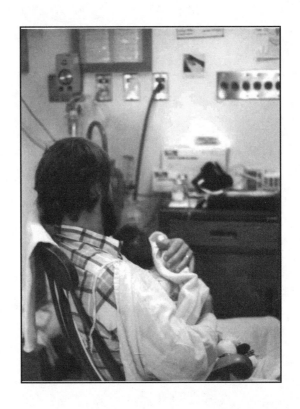

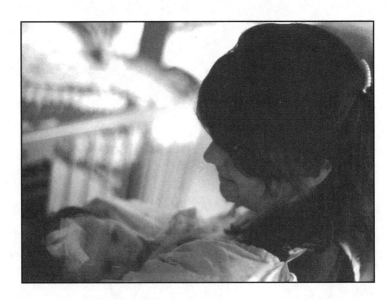

A Different Kind of Challenge

Patricia A. Prelock
Claudia María Vargas
University of Vermont

The chapters in this book have evolved through participant observation and the interdisciplinary practice of health professionals over the last 8 years as conducted by the Vermont Interdisciplinary Leadership Education for Health Professionals (VT–ILEHP) Program. The cases developed for each chapter have been carefully selected to represent a range of disabilities affecting infants, children, and youth, and their families, as well as diverse family structures, socioeconomic, racial, and ethnocultural backgrounds. An interdisciplinary model for training and service delivery is the approach used to respond to the cases presented.

> The federal Maternal and Child Health Bureau (MCHB) funds the VT–ILEHP Program. The MCHB mission is to provide national leadership and to work in partnership with states, communities, public–private partners and families to strengthen the maternal and child health infrastructure, assure the availability and use of medical homes and build the knowledge and human resources in order to assure continued improvement in the health, safety and well-being of the MCH population. (MCHB, 2003, p. 2)

As one of several vehicles used to address the leadership mission of MCHB, funding is available for both public and private nonprofit institutions of higher education that offer interdisciplinary training and education opportunities to individuals working in the maternal and child health professions. One of the funded training programs is Leadership Education in Neurodevelopmental Disabilities, also known as LEND. The VT–ILEHP Program is one the 36 LEND programs in the country that are currently funded by MCHB. The primary goal of the LEND programs is to train future leaders in a variety of disciplines (e.g., pediatrics, nursing, occupational therapy, physical therapy, psychology, speech–language pathology, audiology, dentistry, nutrition, social work, public health administration, special education) to improve the health of children who have, or are at risk of, developing neurodevelopmental disabilities or other similar conditions such as autism and mental retardation. In concert with the MCHB mission and goal for interdisciplinary training, individuals are recruited in the VT–ILEHP Program who show promise in becoming leaders in the MCH field through their teaching, research, clinical practice, and administration and policymaking. Faculty within the VT–ILEHP Program mentor students in providing exemplary public health practice and develop curricula that will enhance trainees' knowledge of MCH and public health. Frustration in the fragmentation of services for children with special health needs across the state was an impetus for the pursuit of leadership training in Vermont. The overall purpose of the VT–ILEHP Program is to prepare culturally competent, family-centered and community-based care and develop leadership skills in professionals to improve the health of infants, children, and adolescents, with or at risk for, neurodevelopmental and related disabilities and their families (VT–ILEHP Program, 2003). The program is committed to translating these principles into action. Specifically, it focuses on providing quality services for families, children, and adolescents with complex health needs who require a different kind of clinical practice. The training integrates every pillar into the curriculum but, equally important, it ensures that clinical practice is truly interdisciplinary, family-centered, and culturally responsive.

Comprehensive care for children with special health or developmental concerns requires coordination across education, health, and developmental service systems. These systems often lack a common model and language for establishing coordinated efforts. Leaders trained in our program utilizing collaborative teaming models and procedures adapted by the VT–ILEHP Program can promote meaningful change toward integrating these systems, and thus improve health outcomes for children and their families. The VT–ILEHP Program is entering its 9th year of leadership training. Over the last 8 years we have trained nearly 50 trainees. Our former trainees occupy a number of diverse positions in service, training, and academia. Our program has also provided continuing education both on campus through our interdisciplinary leadership and research seminar, as well as through a number of presentations to the community by faculty and trainees. Further, program faculty and trainees provide technical assistance and consultation to community and state or regional agencies and programs, including active and ongoing collaboration with the Vermont Children with Special Health Needs (CSHN) programs. The work of the VT–ILEHP Program relates directly and indirectly to a number of the Vermont State Team outcomes (e.g., families, youth, and individuals are engaged in their community's decisions and activities; children are ready for and succeed in school and live in stable, supported families; and, youth choose healthy behaviors and successfully transition to adulthood), and to federal Health and Human Services "Critical Indicators: Measuring Success for Healthy People 2010" (e.g., children with special health needs receive coordinated ongoing comprehensive care within a medical home and their families have adequate private or public insurance to pay for services; children will be screened early and services for CSHN and their families will be organized in ways that families can use them easily; families of CSHN will partner in decision making; and, youth with special needs will receive the necessary services to support later transitions).

There are three purposes to this chapter. First, the interdisciplinary model used to serve children with neurodevelopmental disabilities and their families is described. The model emphasizes five pillars or competencies: family-centered care, cultural competence, interdisciplinary teaming and collaboration, neurodevelopmental disabilities, and developing leadership in maternal and child health. The model is driven by a strengths perspective and incorporates the most recent classification system created by the World Health Organization (WHO), which was field-tested internationally (WHO, 2001). In line with the WHO, the interdisciplinary model developed through the VT–ILEHP Program serves children with multiple, complex disabilities affecting their function, activity, and participation in all aspects of life. Second, the curriculum is introduced as well as each of its components: orientation, training, seminars and the various required assignments, interdisciplinary practicum experience, and implementation of interdisciplinary practice. Third, this chapter provides a description of each of the remaining chapters to share the highlights and unique features that are addressed by the interdisciplinary model to respond to the challenges of individual case studies.

MODELS OF PRACTICE FOR NEURODEVELOPMENTAL DISABILITIES, NEW AND OLD

Historically, two models of practice have been used to explain disability. The medical model or deficit perspective considers disability as an individual problem created by an organic dysfunction, a congenital syndrome or disease or a nonspecific impairment. Intervention practices are often directed at persons affected who are expected to make personal adjustments and behavior changes. In contrast, a more social model or strengths perspective sees the problem as society's challenge integrating individuals with disabilities and the need to recognize the abilities, skills, and talents of individuals with disabilities and their families. In contrast to the deficit perspective, intervention practices are directed toward building the strengths of children in the context of their family and community, social encounters, and environmental change.

The deficit view certainly has the advantage of providing a diagnosis and clarifying the reasons for a child's specific challenges. Such a view can also identify the limitations to which a family and service system must respond and may allow greater access to services. Yet the advantages can also be perceived as disadvantages. A deficit perspective focuses on limitations and fails to recognize the unique strengths and abilities of children with neurodevelopmental disabilities. It may also ignore or deny the capacity of the family and community to respond to a child's needs and often fails to guide service delivery. Further, it is likely to result in a narrow view of the child, missing the "whole" of the child because the focus tends to be primarily on the disability. For example, consider the following scenario of a child with autism who has extreme sensitivities to loud noises and is challenged by unpredictable changes in his environment.

> As a fifth grader who is enrolled in an inclusive educational setting, Halsey participates in all the activities of his classmates. On one occasion, an unexpected music assembly was announced and Halsey proceeded to follow his peers to the gymnasium. When Halsey approached the gym, the noise exceeded what he was accustomed to because all children in the school (kindergarten through sixth grade) were filing in. Halsey initially responded by bolting and when directed back to the classroom, he bit his instructional assistant and threw himself on the floor.

As a result, the team decided that Halsey would no longer attend assemblies at school and would instead stay in the classroom with his instructional assistant because of his inability to handle the situation. The team failed to consider, however, that the environment and not the child could be adjusted so that Halsey could participate in future assemblies. Allowing Halsey to get to the gym before everyone else or after everyone was seated may decrease the impact of noise on his ability to process what was happening. Because visual supports facilitate Halsey's understanding of an event, showing a calendar of upcoming assemblies or designing a story to be read to him ahead of time about what was going to happen could have primed him for the event. *Capitalizing* on his interest in music, a strong motivator for him, the team might explain what is going to happen and how he could meet the musicians once the assembly was completed. The team knew the deficits Halsey experienced (e.g., sensory problems, difficulty with transitions), but the solution was limited to responding to his challenges, seeing him alone as the reason for the outburst that occurred, and failing to recognize and tap some of his strengths.

The strengths perspective, on the other hand, recognizes and celebrates a child's potential (Saleebey, 1997, 2002). Although a child's challenges are identified, disability is seen as only one aspect amidst a whole realm of the child's being. Such a view allows service providers to *capitalize* on the person's strengths and support his or her challenges. Disadvantages, however, are also characteristic of the strengths perspective. A lack of diagnosis or emphasis on disability could jeopardize access to services or compromise ongoing service needs. Service providers, overzealous in accentuating strengths, may fail to recognize the impact of a child's challenges at two critical levels, a personal service level and a funding or policy-making level (see Chapter 10).

Both the deficit and strengths perspectives require careful consideration in the assessment and intervention practices implemented for children with special health needs. Hence, it is important in clinical practice to integrate considerations from both views to address the multiple, complex needs of children with neurodevelopmental disabilities and their families.

The World Health Organization: International Classification of Function, Disability, and Health (ICF)

The ICF has synthesized the polarized views of the deficit and strengths perspectives to create an understanding of health on both the biological and social level (WHO, 1999, 2001). It serves a valuable purpose in collecting data that can be used to assess the consequences of a person's health condition and, equally important, to identify an individual's intervention needs. The WHO ICF presents three dimensions of disability: impairments (function and structure at the body level), activities (performance at the person level), and participation (at the societal level). These dimensions can be used alone or in relation to each other to describe the experiences, attributes, and circumstances of individuals with disabilities (WHO, 1999).

The impairment dimension, or the function and structure of the body of the ICF, requires clinicians to sift through a person's physical capabilities. For example, if a child is diagnosed with cerebral palsy, at the impairment or body level there are external signs of the disorder such as a child who is not able to walk or a child who wears leg braces. Although the impairment dimension considers potential physical limitation, the activities dimension guides the clinician in determining what types of events, social or physical, in which the child can engage. For example, the same child with cerebral palsy might have limitations in his ability to participate in gym class or play ball with his peers at recess. At the handicap or societal level, restriction in participation is considered. For example, the child in a wheelchair cannot attend a birthday party of a classmate or participate in a "sleepover," because the classmate's home is not handicap accessible.

The ICF also requires consideration of the dimensions of disability affected by contextual factors. An interdisciplinary assessment that considers contextual factors that influence how a person perceives both the medical and social aspects of his or her life can improve and add depth to any evaluation. Contextual factors, both personal and environmental, broaden the scope of traditional assessment beyond a deficit focus toward a more holistic and dynamic view of the individual's experience, especially when conducted in his or her natural setting. Personal factors include age, gender, other health conditions, past and current experiences, educational level, fitness, lifestyle, habits, and coping styles. Environmental factors comprise societal attitudes, cultural norms, laws, educational and health systems, and architectural characteristics, for example, a ramp or elevators for wheelchair access.

The WHO classification framework has important implications for assessment at all levels of function, activity/participation, and context (WHO, 2001). This framework provides the theoretical foundation for the interdisciplinary assessment model described throughout this book.

A Competency-Based Framework for Training and Best Practice

The interdisciplinary model developed by the VT–ILEHP Program has integrated the classification concepts of the WHO and the strengths perspective while considering five pillars or core competency areas as the foundation for the training. Each of these, neurodevelopmental and related disabilities, interdisciplinary process and collaborative teaming, family-centered care, cultural competence, and leadership in maternal and child health, is summarized below and is demonstrated through the discussion of cases in the remaining chapters. The specific criteria under each of the five competency areas that guide the interdisciplinary model described throughout this book are listed in Appendix A.

Neurodevelopmental and Related Disabilities.   Although clinicians and health administrators can resort to the WHO classification framework as their counterparts in other countries, health professions in the United States are bound by U.S. federal and state mandates regarding services to persons with disabilities including the 1997 Individuals With Disabilities Education Act (IDEA; Individuals With Disabilities

Act Amendments of 1997). Disabilities, according to IDEA, are defined as the following:

> ... mental retardation, hearing impairment (including deafness), speech or language impairments, visual impairments (including blindness), serious emotional disturbance (hereafter referred to as 'emotional disturbance'), orthopedic impairments, autism, traumatic brain injury, other health impairment or specific learning disabilities; and ... who, by reason thereof, needs special education and related services.

> ... the term 'child with a disability' for a child aged 3 through 9 include(s) a child ... experiencing developmental delays, as defined by the state and as measured by appropriate diagnostic instruments and procedures, in one or more of the following areas: physical development, cognitive development, communication development, social or emotional development, or adaptive development, and who ... by reason thereof, needs special education and related services. (Individuals With Disabilities Act Amendments of 1997, p. 7)

Faculty, students, and professionals in training work to increase their awareness and knowledge of primary, secondary, and tertiary aspects of prevention and health promotion for children and families with special health needs. Increased awareness and knowledge is also developed in the areas of incidence and prevalence and new, or newly recognized morbidities such as HIV, abuse and neglect, head injury, and the sequelae of neonatal intensive care. Knowledge and skill in service provision is focused on genetic syndromes, autism spectrum disorders, attention deficit hyperactivity disorder, traumatic brain injury, learning disabilities, mental retardation, neuromotor disorders, vision and hearing impairments, and normal versus disordered development in cognition, language, social–emotional, and motor development. According to the ICF, IDEA, and the pillars espoused by the VT–ILEHP Program, these disabilities are considered in the context of families and communities for infants, children, and youth.

Interdisciplinary Process and Collaborative Teaming. The training program also focuses on increasing awareness and knowledge of various models of teaming in health care practice and interdisciplinary approaches to service provision (Bagnato & Neisworth, 1991; McGonigel, Woodruff, & Roszmann-Millican, 1994). Over the last several years, models of teaming for children with neurodevelopmental disabilities and their families have evolved. Three primary teaming models, multidisciplinary, interdisciplinary, and transdisciplinary, are described in the literature (Brown, Thurman, & Pearl, 1993; Foley, 1990). Practitioners working on multidisciplinary teams generally function independently of one another. For example, each service provider individually assesses a child and reports to the "leader" of the team or case manager (Brown et al., 1993; Foley, 1990). The role of parents is minimal and there is no requirement for group consensus. As teaming models have evolved, interdisciplinary teams have been formed to recognize the role of families and seek group consensus. Practitioners work cooperatively. For example, practitioners on interdisciplinary teams typically provide discipline-specific assessment although some cross disciplinary activity may occur. Team members meet to discuss their findings and to develop action plans together (Brown et al., 1993; Foley, 1990). Interdisciplinary models of teaming recognize that children and adults with complex health and educational needs require a comprehensive, holistic assessment and intervention model that cannot be managed by a single discipline (Guralnick, 2000; Prelock, Beatson, Contompasis, & Bishop, 1999; Prelock, Beatson, Bitner, Broder, & Ducker, 2003). As teaming models move forward in response to the ever growing needs of children with complex health conditions and their families, transdisciplinary teams have formed. In an effort to provide cost-effective services while maintaining service quality, practitioners on transdisciplinary teams pool their knowledge and skills (Woodruff & McGonigel, 1988). In a transdisciplinary model, team members work collaboratively, cross discipline boundaries, and develop trusting relationships (Brown et al., 1993). Parents are recognized as core members of the team with key points of information and knowledge to share.

Interdisciplinary process and collaborative teaming competencies require development of skills in effective listening and speaking, cooperative learning, team problem solving and team decision making, conflict resolution, and brainstorming. A collaborative teaming process is especially important in collaborative assessment, design, delivery, and evaluation and, community-based coordination of services. The interdisciplinary process is particularly relevant in serving children and families with complex health needs requiring services from multiple health practitioners but in an integrated approach.

Family-Centered Care.   Over the last several decades, family-centered care has been redefined several times (Pellegrino & Meyer, 1998). The literature has outlined several key principles that guide best practice using a family-centered model (Filer & Mahoney, 1996; Prelock et al., 1999; Shelton & Stepanek, 1994), including recognizing the family as a constant in the child's life, using a strengths perspective, and attending to cultural diversity. Family-centered care also requires practitioners to think about children with disabilities as children first (Rappo, 1997), and to be collaborative with families in a way that is responsive to their needs and that of their children (Leviton, Mueller, & Kauffman, 1992).

To ensure providers recognize the critical role of families in the health care of children with neurodevelopmental and related disabilities, competencies are emphasized that require increased knowledge and skill at developing parent-professional partnerships. This family-professional partnership model recognizes children as members of families within communities and acknowledges personal biases and beliefs of health practitioners without imposing those beliefs or values on children and families with special health needs. Clinicians become competent in their collaboration with families to facilitate service systems and supports in the assessment, design, delivery, and evaluation of service to these children and families.

Cultural Competence. This area of competence focuses on increased awareness and knowledge of the beliefs, values, patterns of behavior, language, and attitudes, whether overt or subtle, that have an impact on the health care provided to children and families with diverse needs and from diverse—racial, ethnocultural, linguistic, religious, and gender—backgrounds. The training model promotes the development of skills to help clinicians not only to translate but also to mediate their increased cultural sensitivity into culturally competent behavior as they interact with children and families. Specifically, clinicians enhance their understanding of the social environment (family, community, school) as it intersects with culture affecting the health of children and families. The worldview is also considered specifically as it relates to a family's concept of health and illness, attribution of the illness or etiology of the disability, the curative or healing process, and perception of the family unit. The training program emphasizes how socioeconomic status, occupation, education level, and geographic location influence culture. It attends to cultural values that may influence access to or quality of provision of services to children and their families as well as the quality of the interaction between the provider and the family, ultimately affecting the health outcomes of children. Chapter 3 delves into a discussion of these issues.

Leadership in Maternal and Child Health. This competency focuses on increasing awareness, knowledge, and skills in several areas. Among these are current technologies for the acquisition and processing of information, examination of public policy problems and health care reform affecting the health care and services to families and children with special health needs. The training program examines the successes of and barriers to implementation of systems of health care (e.g.,

Managed Care, Medicaid, nongovernmental organizations or NGOs, and other third-party reimbursement systems). Further, the program emphasizes advocacy for children and families with neurodevelopmental and related disabilities, creation and implementation of the "medical home" concept, research in maternal and child health, and demonstrating leadership in the policy arena.

Leadership regarding policy is demonstrated by the application of a feasibility framework for policy implementation, administration, or decision-making processes (Cooper & Vargas, 2004; Cooper, 2000; Cooper & Vargas, 1995). This framework, developed by Cooper and Vargas, is comprised of seven elements intended to help practitioners analyze their decision environment. The first element is "technical feasibility," in which an organization asks whether it has the technical know-how to respond to a problem or a demand. "Legal feasibility" is the second element in which potential decisions are considered in terms of whether they are permitted by law. The third element, "fiscal feasibility," requires questioning the availability of funds to do what is in question. "Administrative feasibility" is the fourth element and it begs the following question: Does the team have the organization and the people in place to carry out what is proposed? The fifth element is "political feasibility," which examines whether the public supports the proposed decision or whether it is politically possible to move forward as planned. The sixth element, "cultural feasibility," requires consideration of the cultural values or beliefs that may affect a decision or proposed treatment. A decision or treatment may be great, but if it goes against cultural beliefs it may be totally disregarded. The last element is "ethical feasibility," which requires practitioners to assess whether a treatment or decision violates personal, professional, or organizational ethics or places a child at risk. The feasibility framework is explored further in Chapter 10.

The competencies described here are developed throughout the remaining chapters. They guide the practice of our interdisciplinary faculty and the mentoring and training of graduate students (trainees) and community-based health professionals (fellows) who are seeking a more comprehensive approach and model for delivering services to children with special health care needs and their families.

TRAINING A DIFFERENT CADRE OF HEALTH PROFESSIONALS: ESSENTIAL ELEMENTS AT WORK

The faculty members participating in the interdisciplinary model represent several disciplines. The core disciplines include developmental pediatrics, nursing, social work, nutrition, psychology, speech–language pathology, audiology, occupational therapy, physical therapy, public administration, family support, and education. Representatives from each of these disciplines have made a commitment to children with neurodevelopmental disabilities and have determined that an interdisciplinary approach to service delivery best meets the needs of this population. They are committed to social justice in their practice and to ethical standards based on the civility, respect, equity, and equality of participation for all individuals with developmental differences.

The training curriculum in which the faculty model their practice standards and mentor students and community professionals is tailored according to the five pillars or competencies the VT–ILEHP Program established to develop community-based, culturally-competent care. It also trains clinicians to become leaders in interdisciplinary practice committed to improving the health care of infants, children, and adolescents and their families, with neurodevelopmental disabilities. There are several required components of the core curriculum used to prepare health professionals as community leaders: (a) a 2-day orientation, (b) fall training, (c) Interdisciplinary Leadership and Research Seminars, (d) interdisciplinary practicum experiences, and (e) interdisciplinary clinical practice and interdisciplinary teaming.

Orientation

The VT–ILEHP Program begins with a 2-day orientation as an overview. This includes a description of the mission, goals, and objectives of the program (see Appendix B) as well as an explanation of interdisciplinary practice and the various roles of the core disciplines as explained by the interdisciplinary faculty. Participants, both faculty and trainees and fellows, in the program assess their level of confidence in the criteria under each of the five competencies that serve as pillars for the interdisciplinary model. Based on this assessment, trainees and fellows begin to develop an interdisciplinary leadership training plan (ILTP) with their faculty mentor.

Fall Training

Orientation is followed by approximately 4 weeks of training. This training is intended to increase the trainees' and fellows' awareness and knowledge of the following areas: community agencies and programs, models of teaming and collaborative practice, the role of families in service delivery, the need for cultural responsiveness in assessment and intervention, and the role of public policy and leadership in making a difference in the lives of children with complex health, educational, and mental health needs and their families.

Interdisciplinary Leadership and Research Seminars

Faculty and trainees and fellows also participate in two, 3-credit graduate seminars offered across two semesters to enhance their knowledge
of a variety of neurodevelopmental disabilities as well as legal, policy,
health, and education systems, cross-cultural perceptions of disability,
and family systems theory. Although both seminars have been transformed over the last 8 years to better prepare interdisciplinary professionals, trainees and fellows in the VT–ILEHP Program, and those who
attend as students with a specific interest in this area are required to
complete a number of assignments. These assignments have been developed and expanded over the years to enhance the students' application of their knowledge. A description of each of these assignments is
provided in the following paragraphs.

Critical Article Review.   Students are required to reflect, in writing,
on the required readings for one of the topics presented during the semester. Students are to integrate the information from the readings and
compare and contrast the theoretical or conceptual frameworks espoused in each article in their review. They are expected to determine
whether any of the theoretical or conceptual frameworks presented in
the articles led to evidence-based practice as described in the article or
in their own discipline. Finally, they are to identify the implications for
interdisciplinary practice with children with neurodevelopmental disabilities and their families based on the articles they read.

Evidence-Based Practice Critique.   Students are required to select
one research article from the readings listed in the course syllabus or in
their discipline-specific area that focuses on evidence-based practice.
Students are to determine through a comprehensive critique of the research presented in the article if, in fact, the findings would be considered valid. Students may select a quantitative or qualitative research
article to review. Students choosing to review a quantitative research article are asked to answer questions about the type of evidence identified, the assignment of participants to groups, concealment of group
membership to evaluators, and group composition prior to, during, and
following intervention. The students also evaluate the validity of the research based on their own understanding. Students choosing to review
a qualitative research article are asked to address evidence in the areas
of feasibility (how practical the research is and the level of training or resources required), appropriateness (level of acceptability and how jus-
tifiable the research is in consideration of ethical guidelines),
meaningfulness (how the research leads to advocating change, local, regional, and national reform, or practice development), and effective-

ness (the process used to determine the validity of the research and the existence of contradictory findings).

Book Review. To increase students' awareness and understanding of the specific challenges and joy experienced by individuals with disabilities and their families as well as to reflect on the theoretical health perspectives affecting individuals with chronic conditions, students are required to read a book about a child or family affected by a chronic health condition or developmental disability. Students prepare a book review that provides a description of the child with the chronic health condition or special need and the child's family, an explanation of the different health perspectives that affected the care of the child, and the interaction with the child's family. Last, students include a reflection on the most important lesson they learned while reading the book which is likely to change their practice for children with chronic health conditions or special needs and their families.

Cross-Cultural Analysis. This is a new assignment added to the course curriculum to enhance the students' application of their knowledge in cultural competence in serving children and families with complex health needs whose ethnocultural, racial background is diverse. Students, for example, complete an assignment exploring what specific factors affect access and quality of care for children and families of diverse backgrounds—e.g., race and ethnicity. The assignment also requires trainees and fellows to consider how they may need to adapt their clinical practice to be culturally responsive in assessment and intervention and to adapt their communication style when working with families and children of diverse ethnocultural and racial backgrounds.

Policy Assignments. Students complete a series of assignments in the policy realm (described in more detail in Chapter 10) that move them from awareness of the issues affecting their practice at a local, state, and national level to enhancing their knowledge as they work to understand and navigate the systems that are likely to impact the services they provide or seek for the children they serve with neurodevelopmental disabilities. The policy assignments emerged as activity needed to facilitate the students' comfort with and recognition of the importance of policy to their practice.

Interdisciplinary Practicum Experiences

In addition to enhancing the trainees' and fellows' content knowledge, the VT–ILEHP Program established several practica to facilitate the application of their knowledge across the five competency areas. Four major activities have been used to model and support interdisciplinary practice and leadership skills. Each of these is briefly described below and are developed further in the chapters that follow.

Parent to Parent of Vermont Family Match.   This practicum experience offers the trainees' and fellows' a unique opportunity to develop a relationship with a family. This family match experience involves a 40-hour expectation for trainees and fellows. These 40 hours include learning to know a family by spending time with them in life activities (school, health, community) and providing them with 15 to 20 hours of respite. The specific objectives include gaining a comprehensive understanding of the daily lives of children with special needs and their families, identifying and showing growth in family-centered competencies, and learning how existing systems and policies can become more responsive to family strengths, concerns, and priorities. For a more comprehensive description of this practicum and the trainees' and fellows' experiences, see Chapter 8.

Community Assessment.   During the community-based assessment practicum, trainees and fellows engage directly with children having a variety of neurodevelopmental disabilities, their families, and community providers. The community assessment is founded in an interdisciplinary model that has incorporated an ecological, dynamic assessment framework (Haney & Cavallaro, 1996; Notari-Syverson & Losardo, 1996; Pena, 1996). There are six components or steps in the model: intake, preassessment planning meeting, community-based assessment, postassessment planning meeting, report writing, and community-based follow-up meeting and care coordination or community assessment follow-up. Each of these components is illustrated through a family story in Chapter 3.

Community Assessment Follow-Up.   The provision of coordinated care for children with neurodevelopmental disabilities and their families is critical. Often, assessment teams provide a comprehensive evaluation and report with recommendations, yet the family and community-based team are left to follow up and carry out a number of complex tasks that require coordinated efforts among several agencies and programs. The purpose of this practicum, originally defined as care coordination, is to support, not supplant, the efforts of in-place teams working to meet the needs of children with neurodevelopmental disabilities and their families. Initially, the VT–ILEHP team attempted to support community teams and families addressing the complex health needs of children through coordinated care among health, education, and mental health without first engaging in a comprehensive, interdisciplinary assessment. Over the last few years, however, this practicum has focused on ensuring that the recommendations that have been made and actions that have been established following an interdisciplinary community assessment are implemented in a timely and coordinated fashion. A trainee or fellow, assigned as assessment coordinator during the community assessment practicum, continues to work with the family, the primary health care provider, and the educational case manager, following the assessment. During the community assessment follow-up practicum, the assessment coordinator works diligently to facilitate understanding of the interrelations among education, health, developmental services, and the community to establish and maintain community and agency connections. The successes and challenges experienced in this practicum are highlighted in Chapter 4.

Leadership and Research. Trainees and fellows engage in several activities to expand their experience and exposure to research and to facilitate their involvement in community teams designed to foster leadership in maternal and child health. These activities are selected to provide opportunities for collaboration, to pursue an area of interest that requires further investigation, to observe the struggles and successes of community leaders in action, and to be able to teach what they know.

Trainees and fellows participate in a journal study presentation that requires them to identify and review literature in a topic area that crosses discipline boundaries and provides an opportunity to respond to varying levels of evidence-based practice. Trainees and fellows select articles for the interdisciplinary faculty to read and then lead a scholarly discussion on the selected topic, for example, sexuality education of youngsters with disabilities, focusing on the research articles that were reviewed. This is a collaborative team activity in that the trainees and fellows work together to select the readings, review the literature, and facilitate the discussion. Often the trainees and fellows select a topic area that is not part of the core seminar content or is an expansion of a particular content area. Some of the journal topics that have been selected in the past include the validity of auditory integration therapy, parents with developmental disabilities who have children with complex health needs, nutrition challenges, and interventions for children with autism spectrum disorders, as well as others. Trainees and fellows are evaluated on the quality of the selected readings, their understanding of the literature reviewed, the quality of the process for facilitating a critical discussion, their organization of the journal study discussion, and their use of quality audiovisual and other instructional materials. For team planning meetings in preparation for the journal study, agendas and minutes are kept. Trainees and fellows evaluate the effectiveness with which they work and collaborate as a team.

All trainees and fellows are involved in research activities with faculty or peers in the program, which are related to neurodevelopmental disabilities in children or other MCH issues. In addition, trainees and fellows prepare a presentation to the program on their research in the forms of a poster presentation. For trainees enrolled in a graduate program, their research may be tied to a project they are completing as part of their discipline-specific requirements. For community fellows, the research may be part of an action research project in collaboration with other community professionals. Using a poster session format, each trainee and fellow presents their research, which is then followed by a question and answer session with faculty and peers. Their research project and presentation is evaluated in consideration of the following: (a) relation of the research activity to improving knowledge or practice in the area of maternal and child health, (b) inclusion of appropriate literature to support the research activity, (c) appropriateness of the project's design, (d) clarity of the results or implications, and, (e) quality of the presentation, including preparation of the poster, summary of the project, and ability to address questions asked.

Trainees and fellows are encouraged to participate in the meetings of at least one committee or council in the community that serves an important function in the care of or advocacy for children with special health needs and their families. Trainees and fellows keep a log of their participation in any committee or council in which they become involved to provide both a professional and personal reflection of their experience. They are also required to identify implications they gleaned from their participation on a committee or council in at least two of the competency areas emphasized for the VT–ILEHP Program.

Last, trainees and fellows are required to participate in the planning of one seminar in collaboration with one or more of the interdisciplinary faculty. The seminar chosen is based on their particular interests or competency needs so they can increase the learning opportunities they have in a particular content area.

Interdisciplinary Practice at Work

Team approaches have gained widespread acceptance as best practice for serving children with special needs and their families (Bagnato & Neisworth, 1991; McGonigel et al., 1994). Teaming requires that individuals are "on the same side" and are organized and committed to work together for a joint purpose, for example, serving a family and a child with special health needs. The collaboration that must occur within a team for it to be successful is an interactive process. It enables individuals with different backgrounds and expertise to define and creatively solve problems. The premise of a collaborative team is that no single person alone can produce the necessary solutions to complex problems. A collaborative team approach recognizes that children with complex health needs require a comprehensive, interdisciplinary assessment and intervention model that cannot be managed by a single discipline. There is also increased attention to the benefits of providing preservice coursework and field-based practica that address team structure and function for students enrolled in preservice early assessment and intervention programs (Lamorey & Ryan, 1998).

Over the past 10 years, there has been a paradigm shift from the professional as expert to the professional as partner with families—valuing the expertise both bring to service delivery (Johnson & Lindschau, 1996; Prelock et al., 1999; Shelton, Jeppson, & Johnson, 1987; Vincent, 1985). Evidence suggests that not only service delivery but also assessment approaches which are family-centered and interdisciplinary offer promising practices for meeting the needs of children with neurodevelopmental disabilities (Brewer, McPherson, Magrab, & Hutchins, 1989; Dunst, Trivette, & Deal, 1988; Roberts-DeGennaro, 1996; Shelton & Stepanek, 1994).

As members of collaborative interdisciplinary teams, practitioners need to understand their own cultural biases if they are to develop the flexibility needed to establish successful family–professionals partnerships. Practitioners must also recognize the team culture within which they practice. Team culture considers the values and beliefs that reflect the team's history and learning over time (Briggs, 1997). For example, a team culture may be based on operating from a discipline-specific perspective or the team culture may dictate having a single leader as opposed to shared leadership. Understanding team culture provides insight into the attitudes and beliefs of a team, acknowledges current practice patterns, helps to frame roles and responsibilities, and creates a context in which team members interpret what is and what will occur (Briggs, 1997; Westby & Ford, 1993b). It allows a group to differentiate between those who are members and those who are not. It also informs team members of what is valued and how individual members are supposed to act. Interdisciplinary professionals need to examine the level of congruence between those values espoused by a particular team and the underlying assumptions that appear to be guiding the team's actions (Westby & Ford, 1993a). Interdisciplinary teaming also requires recognition of the unique contributions individual disciplines and team members can make as well as the overlaps that often exist among practitioners in their delivery of services. Each of these factors is an important indicator of team health that can facilitate or hinder the development of partnerships with families.

Rationale for Interdisciplinary Teams

Think for a moment about a group of practitioners who are invited to take a trip and are asked to bring with them all of their favorite things. When each of them arrives at the requested location, however, they find that they are sharing space in a van with other providers and a family who has a child with a disability. They learn that they must make some decisions about what they can take on the trip because everyone is limited in what they can bring. Also, they learn that no one speaks the same language and there is no road map to follow, but they embark on the task anyway. So, what are all these busy people doing in the same place? Where will they go? What will they do?

Children with neurodevelopmental disabilities have multiple, complex, long-term challenges which affect not only their health but their integration into their home communities (Nagi, 1991). Professionals from a number of disciplines have specific knowledge and skills in areas such as growth, development, health, and family support, yet no one has all the answers or information they need. It becomes important, therefore, to access the expertise of individuals who have had numerous experience with families and children with similar challenges and needs, and at the same time include the family's knowledge and expertise on the child.

To improve the quality of life of families and their children with neurodevelopmental disabilities, practitioners need to work as a team, expanding their view of intervention and services (Dennis, Williams, Giangreco, & Cloninger, 1993). Also, practitioners can learn from each other through interdisciplinary practice as they gain a better sense of each other's discipline (Johnson & Johnson, 1994). For instance, interdisciplinary teaming can provide insights into how assessment and interventions in one discipline affect the others. Most important, it allows practitioners to see the impact on the family when any one discipline prescribes interventions for the child.

Team Approaches.   If we return to the busy people who find themselves on the van without a shared language or a road map, they must find a way to organize themselves, particularly as they find they are working within different models of service delivery. Following up with the busy people in the van who have now decided on an organizational structure, that is, a team approach, the next question is, how will they relate to each other? A team involves more than one person, usually organized to work together for a joint purpose. The benefits of teaming are well documented (Bagnato & Neisworth, 1985; Villa, Thousand, Stainback, & Stainback, 1992) and several team approaches have been described in the literature. A multidisciplinary team approach is most often used in clinical settings, engaging individual disciplines in the assessment and intervention of children with disabilities. Although the individual disciplines meet as a team at some point, most of their work is done in isolation. In contrast, an interdisciplinary team involves team members in, among other activities, sharing information to address common goals. There are a couple of variations of this model. A transdisciplinary team approach is one that has been adapted for assessment and involves team members in not only exchanging information but sharing and releasing their discipline-specific roles (McGonigel et al., 1994) across disciplines to more directly and consistently address the needs of a child and family. The second variation is an interdependent team approach. It is adapted for intervention in natural settings providing special services that are necessary. Like the transdisciplinary approach, it also involves role release and role support among professionals. Relationships among team members vary depending on the team approach selected and where along the continuum the team appears to be functioning. There may be a time for each model of practice, depending on the team's goals and the context in which they are working. For the VT–ILEHP Program, an interdisciplinary team approach that utilizes aspects of both the transdisciplinary and interdependent approach to service delivery best addresses the children and families we serve.

Lessons to Be Learned.   So how do those busy people in the van move to a better place—one that can help them address their language barriers, work as a team, make decisions about the road to take, and support the needs of the family? First, practitioners need to recognize that families are in the driver's seat. The involvement of family in both assessment and intervention is critical. Team members change whereas the family is usually constant. Families have the greatest stake in service outcomes for their children. Children also need to learn to drive on this long trip—first with guidance, but then independently. The team needs to recognize the child's self-determination and support his or her development of self-advocacy skills as he or she grows and matures.

The group also needs to work together to read the map and plot the course that will be taken. This requires that the team members work on their collaborative teaming skills and develop and refine models of creative problem solving and conflict resolution. The team also needs to define its norms, plan its meeting agendas, establish roles, develop action plans, and determine ways to evaluate what the team is doing. These are the collaborative principles that guide the interdisciplinary teaming and collaborative process of the VT–ILEHP Program, which apply to both trainees and fellows, and faculty.

Practitioners must also understand that the trip is for the children and family. Goals belong to the child and family and not the team. The team needs to identify discipline-free goals and provide the needed supports and services. Decisions about what is to be done are based on the map followed and the skills and resources of others. Interdependent decision making limits the gaps and overlaps in services and helps practitioners determine precisely what support is necessary. Everyone does his or her part to ensure that the van keeps moving to a better place. It is not any one person's job to be the leader. Instead, everyone shares in the leadership by doing what it takes to accomplish the desired goals and to maintain the relationships that have been formed. Everyone needs to do what he or she agrees to do. Each practitioner is personally accountable, and when a problem occurs, the team needs to seek the appropriate supports.

It is also suggested that "groceries" and "gas" are purchased locally, that is, the team should utilize community-based services that are familiar and accessible to families. Communities provide natural supports over time. Practitioners should also share their "toys." This will provide opportunities for professional development along the way as practitioners engage in role release and role support to teach one another and learn new skills.

Vans are also different, with different models and people. It is important to acknowledge cultural diversity and support and strengthen families' cultural resources. Practitioners need to understand the role and challenge of different professional organizations and community cultures. Finally, the team needs to know the "rules of the road" and watch for changes in speed limits, one-way streets, construction, and so forth. The trip also requires practitioners who know the policies and procedures that dictate services as well as help families negotiate the services they need.

THE PRACTICE OF THE FIVE PILLARS
IN VARIOUS CONTEXTS

The VT–ILEHP Program has worked diligently to apply the five competencies that serve as the pillars of our training program. Throughout this book the reader will experience several examples of our practice through child and family stories across a number of contexts. The interdisciplinary, community-based assessment process developed through the VT–ILEHP Program is guided by the principles of family-centered care and has at its core the belief that families define what they need for themselves and their children. In the assessment process, families are recognized as an integral component of the assessment and their participation in all assessment aspects is ensured.

During the intake process, we take our first step in looking at the family as a system interacting with providers in the community. Specifically, the family participates in a face-to-face intake interview at the family's home or other comfortable location. The family also participates in the preassessment planning meetings, the actual assessment, and the follow-up planning meetings. Family members are not only included as participants, they are also key decision makers in their child's assessment. The methods for assessment are designed specifically to incorporate best practice principles in family-centered care. The community assessment considers the child within his or her family and his or her educational and social community. It challenges us to "see" the child and family on their "turf" in their home and school community. These natural contexts for observation and assessment allow for a more authentic perspective on who the child and family are and what they need. The community assessment follow-up helps trainees and fellows learn the importance of follow-through and empowering families and community providers to take the lead in coordinating the care of children with complex health needs. The assessment process and follow-up on action plans provide an initial scaffold for the family and the community team, preparing them to take the lead.

Clinical experience in the neonatal intensive care unit follow-up clinic allows trainees and fellows and faculty to practice a variation of our interdisciplinary assessment team. In this clinic, a transdisciplinary approach to assessment is emphasized in which cross-disciplinary training and supervision allows trainees and fellows and faculty to release their discipline-specific roles.

Finally, the parent to parent practicum allows our trainees and fellows to really put family-centered principles into practice. They do this not as discipline-specific providers but as individuals trying to gain insight into the experiences of families affected by children with complex health and educational needs.

INITIATING A JOURNEY OF THE MODEL IN PRACTICE

In writing this book, the editors envisioned the reader as an active participant in the interdisciplinary model, in other words, as a member of the interdisciplinary team. As such, the reader is invited to join the team in all aspects of the process as challenging and complex cases of children with neurodevelopmental disabilities are presented.

Chapter 2 introduces the model of family-centered care and its application through a complex case study of a child with brain injury secondary to cancer. The challenges of a team attempting to address a child's developmental needs is raised while responding to the family's fears of their child's health status. Various lenses are used to address cultural competence in Chapter 3. The authors address what culture is and how it affects conceptions of what constitutes a family and who makes the decisions. This chapter also presents cross-cultural perceptions of disability. It contrasts traditional medicine with Western or biomedicine and suggests ways these approaches to health can be integrated without compromising the well-being of the child. Last, it analyzes ways culture affects assessments, diagnoses, and interventions.

A proactive approach to responding to the sequelae of neonatal intensive care is explored in Chapter 4. Through the discussion of three separate cases, each of an infant with mild, moderate, and severe sequelae, the reader will recognize the value of utilizing interdisciplinary screening tools that require clinicians to cross-train and step out of their discipline-specific role to assess infants with tools from other disciplines. Chapter 5 invites the reader into an essential element of the interdisciplinary model, the community assessment process. The authors describe the interdisciplinary model used to evaluate the complexities of a child with spina bifida, limited family resources, and inadequately trained community personnel. Chapter 6 presents some of the challenges of community assessment follow-up. Although some successes occurred for this child, many more challenges existed in meeting the needs of a single parent with disabilities living in poverty who ultimately loses custody of her child with language learning disabilities, attention deficit hyperactivity disorder, and hearing impairment.

Chapter 7 delves into transition from high school to adulthood and independent living, a difficult process for the individual with a disability, the family, and the service providers. This is particularly challenging when there are communication issues characteristic of persons with autism and when a controversial method is the individual's primary communication means. Family and community team tensions around transition needs complicates the application of the interdisciplinary model. Chapter 8 presents a model for innovation in expanding competency in family-centered care. A service provider is invited to join the day-to-day joys and struggles of a family managing the challenges of a child with Down syndrome complicated by celiac disease. In Chapter 9, a model for collaboration among programs with a shared vision for interdisciplinary training is presented. The community-based focus of the Vermont Rural Autism Project is integrated with the interdisciplinary assessment process of the VT–ILEHP Program to address the challenges of differential diagnosis for an adolescent with autism and a genetic bone growth disorder. The role of health care administration in best practice is developed in Chapter 10 as the interdisciplinary model is applied to a system of care for a child with significant motor, learning, communication, and medical challenges. The authors respond to the need for creating leaders to build capacity in systems where policy, law, and management are critical factors affecting clinical practice.

The book ends with a chapter designed to integrate what applications the reader might make to his or her own interdisciplinary practice. Chapter 11 provides an analysis of the first 10 chapters and proposes a new approach, based on a critical analysis of the model, to training for health professionals. It also raises the nagging challenges facing new leaders committed to family-centered, culturally competent, interdisciplinary care for children with neurodevelopmental disabilities and their families. Finally, it explores the evolving and dynamic policy and legal environments affecting services to children with disabilities and their families.

Let us now enter the lives of those families that have allowed us to share their experiences, to learn from them and to lead the way to best practice for children with complex health needs. Because issues of confidentiality and ethical practice are central to our interdisciplinary model, the names and circumstances of the children and families discussed in the chapters that follow have been changed to protect their privacy.

Appendix A
VT–ILEHP Program Competencies

COMPETENCY AREA I:
NEURODEVELOPMENTAL AND RELATED DISABILITIES

Knowledge of:

1. Etiology, epidemiology, and natural history of neurodevelopmental and related disabilities across the lifespan.
2. Primary, secondary and tertiary prevention of neurodevelopmental and related disabilities.
3. Disablement frameworks and the dimensions of health, disability, and functioning (activity and participation) such as the U.S. Institute of Medicine and the World Health Organization International Classification of Functioning, Disability, and Health.
4. Current approaches to defining and assessing neurodevelopmental and related disabilities.
5. Current evidence-based and accepted clinical practices as well as alternative/complementary therapies and treatment of neurodevelopmental and related disabilities.

6. Typical development in infants, children, and adolescents and variations of development associated with neurodevelopmental and related disabilities.
7. The effects of socioeconomic disadvantage on health and development in children with and without neurodevelopmental and related disabilities.
8. Current and emerging issues challenging the health and well being of children such as HIV, fetal alcohol, violence, and environmental toxins.
9. Current issues and practices in the field of genetics impacting the diagnosis and treatment of children with neurodevelopmental and related disabilities and their families.
10. The impact of nutrition on health and development in children with and without neurodevelopmental and related disabilities.
11. Children's understanding of their condition or diagnosis and the importance of promoting self-advocacy and self-management skills.
12. Current understanding of physiological and psychological aspects of pain and implications for pain assessment and management in infants and children with neurodevelopmental and related disabilities.

Skill in:

13. Identification of issues related to differential diagnosis of health conditions impacting children and adults with neurodevelopmental and related disabilities.
14. Accessing local, national and international resources and services related to neurodevelopmental and related disabilities.
15. Distinguishing information from evidence, and the ability to critically analyze information and qualitative and quantitative evidence related to standard, emerging and alternative approaches to intervention.

COMPETENCY AREA II: INTERDISCIPLINARY PROCESS AND COLLABORATIVE TEAMING

Knowledge of:

1. Individual learning and communication style which impact on interaction with others.
2. Characteristics of effective and non-effective teams (e.g. understand team culture, team roles, resolving conflict, etc.).

3. Models of teaming in educational and health care practice (e.g. multidisciplinary, interdisciplinary and transdisciplinary) and advantages and disadvantages of each model.
4. Interdisciplinary approaches to service provision.

Skill in:

5. Accommodating differences in learning styles, redirecting conversation and speaking at a level that meets the needs of different audiences.
6. Cooperative group process (e.g., establishing mutual goals, assigning roles, brainstorming, etc.).
7. The VT–ILEHP process for assessment and follow-up (e.g., establishing a relationship with the family, collaborating with community providers, intake, interdisciplinary planning and report writing, home and school visits, information dissemination, etc.).
8. Identifying and networking with community resources.
9. Building partnership with other professionals and establishing mentor relationships.
10. Considering consequences of possible solutions, accepting responsibility for implementing solutions and evaluating.

COMPETENCY AREA III: FAMILY-CENTERED CARE

Awareness of:

1. Children as members of families within a community.
2. Personal biases and beliefs regarding family, parenting and disability so not to impose them on children and families with special health needs.
3. The relationships between family members and family subsystems.
4. The sequence of challenges, growth, and changes that occur in families as they progress through a family's life cycle.
5. The family as a constant in the life of a child with a disability, and the impact of the family on health of all family members.
6. The family as the locus of decision-making related to their child with a disability and that each family member has strengths and abilities that impact decision making.

Knowledge of:

7. The impact of family contexts (including family resources, characteristics of the family and methods for meeting individual needs) on all family members.

8. The range of effects on families (parents, grandparents, siblings and others) who have a child with a neurodevelopmental or related disability.
9. The tensions that exist in the practice of family-centered care, e.g., professional or friend, child or parent voice, definition of family, discipline specific best practice vs. family needs.
10. The family's right to ask questions and challenge professionals.

Skill in:

11. Listening to the concerns and priorities of families.
12. Creating opportunities for families to share concerns, priorities, and resources on an ongoing basis during assessment, planning, implementation, and coordination of services.
13. Assuring families' access to relevant information for decision making.
14. Providing opportunities for family members to acquire new knowledge, skills and confidence in promoting the health of their children and to share this knowledge with others who interact with their children.
15. Working with a family to identify their strengths and resources and to help them develop new capacities.
16. Communicating with families in a culturally competent manner, respecting educational, ethnic, and economic differences.
17. Obtaining information from a family and conveying information (both orally and in writing) to families in a professional manner, which is comfortable for all family members.
18. Responding to family needs by providing information regarding the availability and location of community-based support services and activities.
19. Demonstrating respect for the confidentiality of families.
20. Recommending and providing services that minimize disruptions to family schedules.
21. Strengthening family-to-family linkages and linkages between families and their community to encourage natural, informal, support systems.
22. Providing program evaluation opportunities for families to evaluate and modify the services they receive and the manner in which they receive them.
23. Seeking input from families regarding program policies and practices that govern health care related services.
24. Advocating for families and the health needs of their children.
25. Creating parent/professional partnerships.

26. Facilitating collaborative team practice where the family voice is honored.

COMPETENCY AREA IV: CULTURAL COMPETENCE

Knowledge of:

1. Diverse beliefs, world views, attitudes and cultural values that affect the health care provided to children and families.
2. Socioeconomic, political, historical, and cultural values that affect access and the quality of health care for children and families.
3. The social environment (family, community, and school) and its impact on the health of infants, children, and adolescents with or at risk for neurodevelopmental and related disabilities, and their families.
4. Cultural differences in the health practices and concepts of health, illness, and etiology of disabilities.
5. Differences in traditional healing practices of diverse ethnocultural, racial groups and how these can be integrated with biomedicine.
6. How communication, or lack thereof, affects the quality of health services for families who are English-language-learners.
7. Multilingual and multicultural resources for children and families.
8. Need to adapt assessment tools and intervention materials to meet the needs of children from diverse linguistic and ethnocultural backgrounds who have neurodevelopmental disabilities.

Skill in:

9. Applying knowledge of diverse belief systems, cultural values, cosmology, and attitudes and interactions with children and families of diverse backgrounds.
10. Applying knowledge of how communication affects the quality of health services for families who are English-language-learners.
11. Recognizing the need for cultural interpretation in health care settings and awareness of basic techniques employed in cultural interpretation.
12. Providing services, including assessment, intervention, and coordination in a culturally respectful manner.
13. Adapting assessment tools and intervention materials to meet the needs of children from diverse linguistic and ethnocultural backgrounds who have neurodevelopmental disabilities.

14. Obtaining multilingual and multicultural resources for children and families.

COMPETENCY AREA V: LEADERSHIP

Knowledge of Policy

1. Policy concepts & processes, including global, national, & state contexts, policy. Instruments (legislation to regulations to contracts), decision-making models, & stages of the policy process (agenda setting to policy termination).
2. Techniques for assessment of one's decision environment, including dimensions from the fiscal to the political to the cultural that are essential to understand the context of leadership and policy action.
3. Advocacy and consultation skills, including role awareness, consultation challenges, techniques of advocacy, and preparation of option packages.
4. Substantive policy knowledge, including federal Maternal and Child Health programs (the MCH Pyramid), federal education programs, particularly IDEA and FIT, ADA, Medicaid, and their state counterparts.
5. The development and implementation of federal and state legislation, including legislative process and politics and accessing and interpreting statutes.
6. Administrative rulemaking at the federal and state levels, including the rulemaking process and accessing and interpretation of regulations.

Knowledge of Law

7. Basic legal concepts and processes, including structure and function of courts and differences between public law and private law processes.
8. Fundamentals of legal research, including the ability to access, read, and analyze judicial opinions.
9. Relationship between ethics and law, including similarities, differences, and potential tension.

Knowledge of Budget and Finance

10. Public finance, including awareness of the use of and challenges in government revenue forecasts and basic awareness of revenue sources and limits.
11. Budget process, including the federal and state budget cycles.
12. Techniques for reading and understanding budget documents.

Knowledge of Management and Leadership

13. Relationship between management and leadership.
14. Inter-organizational issues, including boundary spanning, "silo" problems, and coalition building.
15. NGOs and their relationships with other groups and public agencies.

Appendix B
VT–ILEHP Mission Statement

The mission of the Vermont Interdisciplinary Leadership Education For Health Professionals (VT–ILEHP) Program is to improve the health of infants, children, and adolescents, with or at risk for, neurodevelopmental and related disabilities and their families through the development of culturally competent, family-centered, community-based leadership professionals.

Goals & Objectives

The VT-ILEHP Program:

- develops culturally competent leadership professionals committed to improving the health status of infants, children and adolescents, with, or at risk for, neurodevelopmental and related disabilities, and their families.
- promotes the use of interdisciplinary approaches in the provision of family-centered, community-based services for infants, children and adolescents, with, or at risk for, neurodevelopmental and related disabilities, and their families.
- collaborates with State Title V Programs, the Agency of Human Services, and the Department of Education, at both state and local levels, and private providers, to ensure family-centered, community-based leadership experiences in the provision of services for infants, children and adolescents, with, or at risk for, neurodevelopmental and related disabilities, and their families.
- continues to improve the quality of its interdisciplinary leadership education program including both curriculum and community-based practicum experiences, through implementation of a comprehensive project evaluation plan.

- disseminates information locally, regionally, and nationally, related to family-centered community-based, culturally competent health promotion, for infants, children and adolescents, with, or at risk for, neurodevelopmental and related disabilities, and their families.

REFERENCES

Bagnato, S. J., & Neisworth, J. (1985). Efficacy of interdisciplinary assessment and treatment for infants and preschoolers with congenital and acquired brain injury. *Analysis and Intervention in Developmental Disabilities, 5,* 107–128.

Bagnato, S. J., & Neisworth, J. T. (1991). *Assessment for early intervention: Best practices for professionals.* New York: Guilford.

Brewer, E. J., McPherson, M., Magrab, P. R., & Hutchins, V. L. (1989). Family-centered, community-based, coordinated care for children with special health care needs. *Pediatrics, 83,* 1055–1060.

Briggs, M. H. (1997). *Building early intervention teams: Working together for children and families.* Gaithersburg, MD: Aspen.

Brown, W., Thurman, S. K., & Pearl, L. (1993). *Family-centered early intervention with infants and toddlers: Innovations in cross-disciplinary approaches.* Baltimore: Brookes.

Cooper, P. J. (2000). *Public law and public administration.* Itasca, IL: Peacock.

Cooper, P. J., & Vargas, C. M. (Eds.). (1995). *Implementing sustainable development.* New York: United Nations.

Cooper, P. J., & Vargas, C. M. (2004). *Implementing sustainable development: From global policy to local action.* Lanham, MD: Rowman & Littlefield Publishers.

Dennis, R., Williams, W., Giangreco, M., & Cloninger, C. (1993). Quality of life as a context for planning and evaluation of services for people with disabilities. *Exceptional Children, 59,* 499–512.

Dunst, C. J., Trivette, C. M., & Deal, A. (1988). *Enabling and empowering families.* Cambridge, MA: Brookline Books.

Filer, J. D., & Mahoney, G. J. (1996). Collaboration between families and early intervention service providers. *Infants and Young Children, 9,* 22–30.

Foley, G. M. (1990). Portrait of the arena evaluation: Assessment in the transdisciplinary approach. In E. D. Gibbs & D. M. Teti (Eds.), *Interdisciplinary assessment of infants: A guide to early intervention professionals* (pp. 271–286). Baltimore: Brookes.

Guralnick, M. J. (2000). Interdisciplinary team assessment for young children: Purposes and processes. In M. J. Guralnick (Ed.), *Interdisciplinary clinical assessment of young children with developmental disabilities* (pp. 3–15). Baltimore: Brookes.

Haney, M., & Cavallaro, C. C. (1996). Using ecological assessment in daily program planning for children with disabilities in typical preschool settings. *Topics in Early Childhood Special Education, 16,* 66–81.

Individuals with Disabilities Education Act, 20 U.S.C. § 1400. (1997).

Johnson, A., & Lindschau, A. (1996). Staff attitudes toward parent participation in the care of children who are hospitalized. *Pediatric Nursing, 22,* 99–102.

Johnson, D. W., & Johnson, F. W. (1994). *Joining together: Group theories and skills* (5th ed.). Englewood Cliffs, NJ: Prentice Hall.

Lamorey, S., & Ryan, S. (1998). From contention to implementation: A comparison of team practices and recommended practices across service delivery models. *Infant–Toddler Intervention. The Transdisciplinary Journal, 8,* 309–331.

Leviton, A., Mueller, M., & Kauffman, C. (1992). The family-centered consultation model: Practical applications for professionals. *Infants and Young Children, 4,* 1–8.

Maternal and Child Health Bureau. (2003). MCHB Vision and Mission Statement and Strategy Plan 1998–2003, Final Draft. Retrieved December 1, 2003, from http://www.mchb.hrsa.gov/

McGonigel, M. J., Woodruff, G., & Roszmann-Millican, M. (1994). The transdisciplinary team: A model for family-centered early intervention. In L. J. Johnson, R. J., Gallagher, M. J. LaMontagne, J. B. Jordan, J. J. Gallagher, P. L. Hutinger, & M. B. Karnes (Eds.), *Meeting early intervention challenges: Issues from birth to three* (pp. 95–131). Baltimore: Brookes.

Nagi, S. Z. (1991). Disability concepts revisited: Implication for prevention. In Institute of Medicine, Committee on a National Agenda for the Prevention of Disabilities (Eds.), *Disability in America: Toward a national agenda for prevention* (pp. 309–237).

Notari-Syverson, A., & Losardo, A. (1996). Assessing children's language in meaningful contexts. In K. N. Cole, P. S. Dale, & D. J. Thal (Eds.), *Assessment of communication and language* (pp. 257–280). Baltimore: Brookes.

Pellegrino, L., & Meyer, G. (1998). Interdisciplinary care of the child with cerebral palsy. In J. P. Dormans & L. Pellegrino (Eds.), *Caring for children with cerebral palsy* (pp. 55–70). Baltimore: Brookes.

Pena, E. D. (1996). Dynamic assessment: The model and its language applications. In K. N. Cole, P. S. Dale, & D. J. Thal (Eds.), *Assessment of communication and language* (pp. 281–307). Baltimore: Brookes.

Prelock, P. A., Beatson, J., Bitner, B., Broder, C., & Ducker, A. (2003). Interdisciplinary assessment for young children with Autism Spectrum Disorders. *Language, Speech and Hearing Services in Schools, 34,* 194–201.

Prelock, P. A., Beatson, J., Contompasis, S., & Bishop, K. K. (1999). A model for family-centered interdisciplinary practice in the community. *Topics in Language Disorders, 19*(3), 36–51.

Rappo, P. (1997). The care of children with chronic illness in primary care practice: Implications for the pediatric generalist. *Pediatric Annals, 26,* 687–695.

Roberts-DeGennaro, M. (1996). An interdisciplinary training model in the field of early intervention. *Social Work in Education, 18,* 20–29.

Saleebey, D. (Ed.). (1997). *The strengths perspective in direct practice, second edition.* New York: Longman.

Saleebey, D. (Ed.). (2002). *The strengths perspective in direct practice, third edition.* Boston: Allyn & Bacon.

Shelton, T. L., Jeppson, E. S., & Johnson, B. H. (1987). *Family centered care for children with special health care needs.* Washington, DC: Association for the Care of Children's Health.

Shelton, T. L., & Stepanek, J. S. (Eds.). (1994). *Family-centered care for children needing specialized health and developmental services* (3rd ed.). Washington, DC: Association for the Care of Children's Health.

Vermont Interdisciplinary Leadership Education for Health Professionals Program. (2003). The VT–ILEHP Program Goals and Objectives and Mission Statement. Retrieved December 1, 2003, from http://www.uvm.edu/~vtilehp

Villa, R. A., Thousand, J. S., Stainback, W. C., & Stainback, S. B. (1992). *Restructuring for caring and effective education: An administrative guide to creating heterogeneous schools*. Baltimore: Brookes.

Vincent, L. J. (1985). Family relationships. *Equals in this partnership: Parents of disabled and at-risk infants and toddlers speak to professionals* (pp. 33–41). Washington, DC: National Center for Clinical Infant Programs.

Westby, C. E., & Ford, V. (1993a). Professional communicative paradigms in family-centered service delivery. *American Speech and Hearing Association Monograph*, *30*, 50–59.

Westby, C. E., & Ford, V. (1993b). The role of team culture in assessment and intervention. *Journal of Educational and Psychological Consultation, 4*, 319–341.

Woodruff, G., & McGonigel, M. J. (1988). Early intervention team approaches: The transdisciplinary model. In J. B. Jordan, J. J. Gallagher, P. L. Hutinger, & M. B. Karnes (Eds.), *Early childhood special education: Birth to 3* (pp. 163–181). Reston, VA: Council for Exceptional Children.

World Health Organization. (1999). *ICIDH-2: International classification of functioning, disability and health*. Geneva, Switzerland: Author.

World Health Organization. (2001). *ICF: International classification of functioning, disability and health*. Geneva, Switzerland: Author.

2

Family-Centered Care and the Family's Perspective: Traumatic Brain Injury, Cancer, and Co-Morbid Learning Challenges

Jo Yoder
Nancy DiVenere
Parent to Parent of Vermont

Questions to Consider

1. How might you describe and support the strengths of a family?
2. In what ways might individual health care providers respond to a family's identified needs?
3. In what ways might a systems approach be most helpful to a family?

KARLA'S STORY: TRAUMATIC BRAIN INJURY

Karla's family planned a wonderful celebration for her 13th birthday, a day 5 years ago they feared they would never see. They would celebrate with Karla's 15-year-old brother Will, a protective big brother who doted on Karla, and her 7-year-old brother, Jason. In turn, Karla loved to care for her younger brother, too. Karla had been a healthy newborn and a bright, spirited, affable, and independent child until she was diagnosed with a brain tumor 5 years ago, at age 8. The diagnosis of cancer had been difficult for her entire family, but today, as they prepare for her 13th birthday celebration, they are feeling optimistic about her future.

Michael and Anne, Karla's parents, had learned a great deal about cancer and its treatment during the 18 months following Karla's diagnosis. They had rearranged their lives around doctor's appointments, surgery, radiation, and chemotherapy treatments. Although they had kept a watchful eye on her development, compromised temporarily due to her treatment protocol, they had remained hopeful that Karla would someday be cancer free. Now, 5 years later, they are still in regular contact with specialists and her teachers at school. They are determined to give Karla every opportunity again to be the active, independent girl she had been as a small child.

Anne, a nurse with a BSN degree, had changed her full-time, day schedule to a part-time, night rotation at a medical center in Vermont so she could be available for Karla during the days when appointments and therapies occurred. She believes medical science offers the possibility of permanent remission and wants to leave no stone unturned in finding and accessing the best interventions and therapies for Karla. Anne's parents are Quebecois and live in Montreal, Canada, where her father is a professor at a university and her mother is a bank vice president. Given the Canadian health care system they are used to, Anne's parents don't really understand the financial drain that Karla's illness is putting on the family. Although Anne's family is concerned that Karla gets the best care possible, they are unable to adjust their busy schedules to offer daily support.

Michael, the oldest of six children in his family, grew up on the family farm. He met Anne during the year he was studying for a computer science degree at the University of Vermont. Although he had earned a full scholarship, he had to drop out after his freshman year when his father had a heart attack and needed help on the family dairy farm. When his two brothers were old enough to take over the farm work, Michael pursued his first love and started a small, computer consulting business. He works long hours to keep his business financially sound and to prove to his family that he can provide for his wife and children, away from the farm, without accepting financial help. Michael knows all about financial stress. He was brought up with traditional values of hard work and independence—values reinforced in his family's daily struggle as they worked together to keep the family farm going. They could not afford health insurance and became proudly self-sufficient, using alternative remedies whenever possible. Unlike Anne, Michael, even now, is wary of depending on doctors and other health care providers.

One of Michael's siblings, at age 10, died as a result of peritonitis from a perforated appendix. Michael remembers long talks with his family about the importance of quality of life, the cycle of life, and inevitability of death. His current thinking about health care is influenced by his memories of these family discussions.

Karla's family lives in a rural area of Vermont, where housing costs are low. They travel over an hour to the nearest tertiary hospital where most of the specialists who treat Karla practice.

Karla's Current Medical Status

After her initial diagnosis and treatment—surgery, chemotherapy, and radiation—at age 8, Karla exhibited some global developmental delays. With the help of a speech–language pathologist, she showed noticeable improvement in speech fluency, vocabulary, and language comprehension. She still has some motor planning challenges and a decrease in upper body strength, so her Individualized Education Plan (IEP) lists accommodations and recommendations that are carried out by a physical therapist and an occupational therapist. Although Karla is performing slightly below grade level academically, she is making progress. Michael is concerned about Karla's emotional health as well and wonders if the treatments that have caused some of Karla's delays might also be having an impact on her relationships with friends and on her interactions with her brothers.

As Karla approaches puberty and even as her family is looking forward to celebrating her 13th birthday, some delays have become more noticeable to them and to her teachers. She appears to be less attentive, her speech has slowed and lost some oral fluency, and she has become more aggressive in her interactions with Jason. Now Karla's entire family has been thrown into an emotional upheaval, having learned that not only was she experiencing symptoms of a traumatic brain injury (TBI) secondary to brain cancer and partial removal of brain tissue, but new tumor growth has been found.

Although terribly worried about Karla's developmental problems, her family felt they could cope, believing once she was cancer free she would regain lost skills. Now, with the news of a reoccurrence, they once again experience the overwhelming stress and worry about her very survival (Melnyk & Alpert-Gillis, 1998). They are reliving their initial treatment decision to have both chemotherapy and radiation therapy, and rethinking the information they were given at that time. Could they have done something differently? And, would it have made a difference now, 5 years later? They remember their struggles with the health care system and dread the necessity of going down that path once more. Jason and Will are both frightened about the return of the cancer but are often left to deal with their feelings individually as Anne and Michael, once more, focus their energy on Karla. Karla just longs for the normalcy of the planned celebration to launch her into her teenage years.

Although each family member is experiencing Karla's illness in an individual way, they have an unwavering devotion to each other as a family. They are in this together and whatever affects one of them affects all of them in some way. Satir (1972) used the analogy of a mobile to illustrate this idea:

> In a mobile all the pieces, no matter what size or shape, can be grouped together and balanced by shortening or lengthening the strings attached or rearranging the distance between the pieces. So it is with the family. None of the family members is identical to any others; they are all different and at different levels of growth. As in a mobile, you can't arrange one without thinking of the other. (pp. 119–120)

The distance Anne feels from her extended family is more than just geography. Both she and Michael realize the support they need should not have strings attached and should come without advice. The support should also be available when needed or refused without judgment. This is the kind of support they have had from church friends, neighbors, and community members—their new definition of "family."

Families who have children with special health care needs have not always been recognized and respected as invaluable members of their child's health care team. Medical decisions were the purview of the physician and there was an expectation that medical advice would be accepted as dispensed. Health care providers worked in isolation from each other and from the family, each one expertly caring for a child from the knowledge base of his or her specific discipline. Conferencing among primary care physicians, specialists, and the family to coordinate information and care was an exception. The advance of family-centered care as a philosophy that recognizes and supports the knowledge and experience of families in the care of their child has given health care providers a framework to assure a holistic approach to care.

This chapter explains how families deal with complex health issues in the context of their unique family definition and situation. It discusses the philosophy of family-centered care, and then looks specifically at how family-centered care can be practiced in the context of families with complex needs. The chapter explores examples of what does and does not work for Karla's family and other families as they enter this "maze" of new information and interactions with health care practitioners. In so doing, it becomes evident how crucially important a family-centered, interdisciplinary, community-based, and culturally appropriate model is in meeting both the family and child's needs. The chapter ends with lessons learned and implications for practice.

A FAMILY-CENTERED CARE PHILOSOPHY

Although the term "family-centered care" has been used for nearly 40 years, the eight key elements of this philosophy were first articulated in

1987, in a monograph funded by the Maternal and Child Health Bureau (MCHB), U.S. Department of Health and Human Services, and published by the Association of Children's Health (Shelton & Stepanek, 1994). Incorporating these key elements into policy and practice for children needing specialized health and developmental services became the agenda for the MCHB, families, and professional organizations in the following 15 years.

Polly Arango, the mother of a son with cerebral palsy, reflected on the changes that have happened in our country:

> About 10 years ago, Surgeon General C. Everett Koop challenged the healthcare community and families to develop systems of care for children who have special healthcare needs. Why? Because this country's 12.6 million youngsters who have special healthcare needs use health systems more intensely and more frequently than most. In many ways, our children test the way in which pediatric healthcare is delivered in this country. If health systems and services work for our children, they will work for all children. (Arango, 1999, p. 30)

The impetus for C. Everett Koop's agenda came from meetings with families whose children had significant health care needs and the cogent and compelling monograph, written in 1987, defining the elements of family-centered care. That monograph has undergone three revisions, and although the eight key elements, as seen in Table 2.1, have been slightly reworded for clarity, and the order has been revised, the intent of each remains the same (Shelton & Stepanek, 1994). Following is a discussion of these core elements.

Family Is the Constant

Whatever the family configuration and however families define themselves, the family is the constant in a child's life. Some families have two parents; others have a single father or mother. For some families, friends, significant others, grandparents, or aunts and uncles are primary or secondary caregivers. These individuals provide the constellation of support. Their knowledge and experience comprise a collective wisdom that informs decision making. It is important for professionals to recognize that how families evolve and support one another will be unique to different family situations.

In Karla's life, Michael, Anne, Will, and Jason have been the constant. Teachers, therapists, doctors, and counselors move in and out of Karla's life, sometimes monthly, but it is her family who knows the intimate details of her life. They have lived her medical history, they recognize the changes that have occurred since the beginning of her illness and they recognize the importance of conveying this information to those caring

TABLE 2.1

Key Elements of Family-Centered Care

• Incorporating into policy and practice the recognition that the family is the constant in a child's life, while the service systems and support personnel within those systems fluctuate.

• Facilitating family/professional collaboration at all levels of hospital, home, and community care: care of an individual child; program development, implementation, evaluation, and evolution; and, policy formation.

• Exchanging complete and unbiased information between families and professionals in a supportive manner at all times.

• Incorporating into policy and practice the recognition and honoring of cultural diversity, strengths, and individuality within and across all families, including ethnic, racial, spiritual, social, economic, educational, and geographic diversity.

• Recognizing and respecting different methods of coping and implementing comprehensive policies and programs that provide developmental, educational, emotional, environmental, and financial supports to meet the diverse needs of families.

• Encouraging and facilitating family-to-family support and networking.

• Ensuring that hospital, home, and community service and support systems for children needing specialized health and developmental care and their families are flexible, accessible, and comprehensive in responding to diverse family-identified needs.

• Appreciating families as families and children as children, recognizing that they possess a wide range of strengths, concerns, emotions, and aspirations beyond their need for specialized health and developmental services and support.

---

for Karla. And, they understand how important it is for Karla to plan her birthday celebration.

Family–Professional Collaboration

Family-centered practice ensures that family–professional collaboration happens at all levels of care. Jeppson and Thomas (1995) suggested that a professional commitment to the idea that families can and should be an essential part of evaluation, planning, and the delivery of services is critical to family–professional collaboration. Professionals learn to respect the expertise and knowledge that families contribute to an understanding of health care problems. Family members interact in all situations of daily living and have the broad perspective essential to planning care for a child. They become partners in the design, implementation, and evaluation of their child's services (Bishop, Woll, &

Arango, 1993). This partnership will be ensured if the following six elements are diligently practiced.

Exchanging Complete and Unbiased Information

Families are the experts on their child and hold a wealth of information that will affect care. Practitioners are experts in their discipline and families depend on them to have the technical information needed for decision making. Some children and adolescents, like Karla, ask to be involved in the information-sharing process. The importance of keeping an open, honest communication flow, involving all family members, as defined by the family, and all providers involved in the care of a child, cannot be overemphasized. The model of the Johari Window illustrates this exchange of complete information. Four windows show different portions of shared information. One window contains information shared by all. Two windows show information known by one person and hidden from others, whereas the fourth window contains information unknown to all parties (Luft, 1970). The implication is that opening up the area of shared information assures that more common knowledge is available to facilitate greater understanding and collaboration.

Honoring Cultural Diversity

Cultural competence is a requirement in the practice of family-centered care. Families from many racial, ethnic, and social backgrounds bring diverse experiences and interpretations of health. Dunn (2002) defined cultural competence as the ability to communicate between and among cultures and to demonstrate skill outside one's culture of origin; and becoming culturally competent requires changing the way people think about, understand, and interact within the world around them. This is illustrated in the story of a Hmong family from Laos who settled in the United States. Communication between the family and health care providers was challenging, and not just due to language differences. The family's wish to participate in ceremonies and rituals associated with their beliefs about healing and honoring their child's spirit did not fit with the understanding of western medical practitioners, creating a clash of cultures (Fadiman, 1997). (See Chapter 3 for further discussion.)

Karla's parents are both totally committed to improving their daughter's quality of life, but they have different, and very individual values and beliefs guiding their approach to illness, health care, and death. Karla's health care providers may have an entirely different set of values and beliefs. However, for all involved, Karla's well-being is primary. McCubbin, Thompson, Thompson, McCubbin, and Kaston (1993) described it this way: "Thus, for the sake of the child, it behooves practitioners to understand their own prejudices, beliefs, and behavior and how these 'fit' or do not 'fit' with the family's schema and paradigms" (p. 1070).

Different Methods of Coping

Families make choices based on their values, beliefs, coping styles, and needs. Families reprioritize their needs when their child is diagnosed with a critical or chronic illness. When individual family members' priorities are understood and when helpful programs and policies are in place, families are better able to cope.

Recognizing and responding to individual coping styles builds on family strengths and reinforces each family member's ability to support one another. Karla prefers to be in control of the information she shares with friends about her health and her parents have their own preferences about gathering, holding, and sharing information.

Anne's method of coping is to find out all she can about Karla's diagnosis. Her family tends to intellectualize issues, to ponder options in an organized manner, drawing logical conclusions and then moving forward with a plan. In her family, feelings are internalized while each person presents himself or herself as able to handle almost anything.

Michael grew up in a family that discussed issues in detail, rehashing a topic, problem solving, and trying out different solutions before deciding on one course of action. These discussions were usually accompanied by tears, laughter, and angry outbursts—but all feelings were on the table. Michael finds it comforting to share Karla's struggles with his family, friends, and church community.

Initially, Michael and Anne struggled when working together with professionals, but they have learned to clearly state their differences at the outset, and their wish to be treated as individuals regarding their information-processing needs. They look for family-centered practitioners who respect different ways of coping and treat family members as individuals.

Family-to-Family Support

In a five-state research study completed between 1995 and 1998, parents related that the support they received from another parent who shared a similar situation was a unique kind of support that they did not typically find within a formal service system (Singer et al., 1999). Some parents find individual support is most helpful whereas others seek out support groups or more social situations such as topical parent evenings. Families, however, are not automatically a part of such networks before they have a child with special needs. Hence, it is the responsibility of the family-centered professional to make helpful referrals to family support organizations such as Parent to Parent programs (see www.p2pusa.org for more information).

Flexible, Accessible, and Comprehensive Hospital, Home, and Community Service and Support Systems

Where, when, how, and by whom services are provided are decisions best made in concert with the family. For some families, home-based services are most helpful whereas others look for services to be provided at schools or child-care settings. Although Karla's specialty care is provided at the tertiary care hospital, her family relies on their community for emotional and physical support.

It was Karla's pediatrician, after conferring with the pediatric oncologist, who first explained the implications of Karla's diagnosis and who offered to coordinate the multiple appointments necessary to determine and begin treatment. Karla's pediatrician is committed to providing the kind of care described by the American Academy of Pediatrics (AAP) as necessary for all children but critical for children with complex health care needs—a "Medical Home." In noting the characteristics that define a Medical Home, AAP (2002) stated the following:

> ... the medical care of infants, children, and adolescents ideally should be accessible, continuous, comprehensive, family centered, coordinated, compassionate, and culturally effective. It should be delivered or directed by well-trained physicians who provide primary care and help to manage and facilitate essentially all aspects of pediatric care. The physician should be known to the child and family and should be able to develop a partnership of mutual responsibility and trust with them. (p. 184)

This emerging concept of care is the result of families and pediatricians working together to determine how best to coordinate care. In "medical home" practices, families, as trusted advisors to pediatric office practices, identify and prioritize strategies to meet their child and family's needs more effectively and efficiently; for children who have complex health care needs, it might simply be color-coded charts alerting office staff to the need for extended time. Or, there might be a separate waiting area for children with complex needs coming in for routine care and hoping to avoid contracting other illnesses.

Karla's pediatrician practices in a multiphysician group (more than one physician providing care for a child) where Karla and her family are well known by two of the physicians who are available whenever the family calls. After hearing from Anne and talking with Karla's oncologist, Karla's physician pulls together an interdisciplinary team including the family, teachers, and school administrators, the school nurse, therapists, specialists, and community service providers. Part of the strength of a Medical Home is the collaboration among physicians, school staff, and families to ensure that learning is accessible to the child who is receiving regular medical treatments and that educational teams understand the medical needs of the child.

Appreciating Families as Families and Children as Children

Families and professionals often note that a child with special needs is more like his or her peers than different. They understand that a child and family have full lives aside from the medical need that is the impetus for interactions with providers. In a number of collaborative programs with the University of Vermont and its School of Medicine, students have opportunities to spend time with families in their homes. They learn that each family is, first and foremost, a family, and that the medical needs of a child are only one part of their lives. One medical student explained it this way: "I found ... in that wonderful house ... the one thing I did not anticipate. I found a family .... They had hopes and dreams for themselves and their children" (Leonard, 2003, p. 1). The medical students begin to understand that it would be impossible for them to practice as an "expert in isolation" without acknowledging families for the broader picture they hold, beyond the disability or chronic illness that brings them to the physician.

ENTERING THE MAZE: DEALING WITH COMPLEXITY

As families like Karla's enter the "world" of disability, they learn to navigate complex systems that have been developed and implemented to meet some of the needs of families in this position. They meet people they would never have met and gain knowledge they did not know they would want or need (Kingsley, 1987). They embark on a very steep learning curve as their time becomes consumed with medical appointments, therapy sessions, phone calls, and research. They are required to learn new skills, for example, tube feeding, chest physical therapy, or administering medication or treatments around the clock. These additional responsibilities in a family's daily life can sometimes be overshadowed by the mixed emotions of fear, guilt, confidence, incompetence, hope, and hopelessness—an ever-changing, sometimes mind-numbing, turmoil. Well-trained, family-centered professionals will ensure optimal outcomes for children and families in this situation.

Family-centered care is one of the five strands of the interdisciplinary model at the University of Vermont's Interdisciplinary Leadership Education for Health Professionals (VT–ILEHP) Program. The convergence of knowledge, experience, and research among faculty members and others working with children with complex health care needs and their families was responsible for the design and implementation of Vermont's Leadership Education in Neurodevelopmental Disabilities (LEND) program as a training model in family-centered care. The key elements of family-centered care are woven into every aspect of the process, from the orientation of trainees and fellows to assessment and program evaluation. From the outset, families have been an integral part of this interdisciplinary model. Their needs and concerns for their children with complex health needs continue to be a driving force behind each decision made by the interdisciplinary team. Faculty members are trained and knowledgeable about the philosophy of family-centered care, and are committed to challenge each other to be family-centered in all interactions.

The Diagnosis: Breaking the News to the Family

Just before Karla's thirteenth birthday, Anne took her for a routine visit with her pediatrician. He asked Karla about a hesitancy he noticed in her speech and she told him that sometimes the "words don't come out right" although she knows exactly what she wants to say. When Anne agreed and also expressed concerns about Karla's lack of attention, and her decreased patience for and sometimes aggression toward her friends and Jason, her pediatrician suggested scheduling an MRI, just to rule out concerns other than typical changes of puberty.

Anne and Karla went for the MRI on the following Friday, planning to do some birthday shopping after the appointment. Instead, the radiologist sent the reading immediately to Karla's pediatrician, at his request, and the pediatrician suggested Anne, Michael, and Karla stop at his office on their way home. Anne tried to call Michael to join them at the pediatrician's office, but had to leave a message and hoped he would receive it in time to come.

Their anxiety was high as they drove toward the pediatrician's office—they had forgotten about shopping. Michael was not there and the pediatrician asked if they would like to wait for him, but by this time their concern was so great, they decided to go ahead without him. They were devastated to hear that changes had occurred since the last MRI—Karla's tumor was growing again. The pediatrician offered to talk to Michael directly when he got home and to meet with all of them again on the following day. Anne appreciated his offer and knew she could rely on him in the coming weeks, but she recognized that only the strength of their nuclear family would get them through the coming hours. The ride home was difficult as Anne swallowed her own fears and tried to offer comfort and support to Karla's outburst of anger. They could not begin to think of how they would share this news with Michael, Will, and Jason.

Anne knew Karla's pediatrician would help keep their medical world together in the next months. He would want to talk to the oncologist immediately, just as she did. After their first experience 5 years ago, she and Michael had learned what questions to ask and what support and information they needed for Karla and for themselves. This time they had a context for the new diagnostic information and would be able to act immediately.

Most families do not have this background knowledge when their child receives an initial diagnosis and they may have little experience with the internal operation of health care systems. In addition, families feel vulnerable, and they may be overwhelmed by other information and not process anything but the diagnosis.

They may be unfamiliar with medical "jargon" and not know to whom they should address their questions or even what questions to ask. It is important to provide ongoing opportunities for families to ask questions and for providers to continually offer information. It may be necessary for health care providers to repeat information shared during past visits.

Test results are not always so quickly and readily available as they were at Karla's appointment. Some parents await confirmation, knowing something is wrong. One parent waited for weeks to learn about test results, only to find out that the physician's schedule did not allow the mother to call immediately when the results were available. The physician's lack of urgency did not match the parent's stress, anxiety, and desperate need to know. Families endure long, excruciating hours, days, and weeks while waiting to hear results of medical tests or developmental assessments. During this time they contemplate "what if" scenarios, even while they continue to hope for positive outcomes. Fialka and Mikus (1999) wrote about the emotions and reactions experienced by parents and professionals throughout a lengthy assessment process: "All too often, however, these feelings, concerns, and hopes remain unarticulated and unaddressed—hidden voices. The power of unspoken worries and reactions should not be underestimated as they shape relationships and determine outcomes for the children involved" (p. 16). Family-centered practice compels professionals to share unbiased information in a timely, responsive, honest manner during difficult diagnostic times and throughout the treatment process.

An interdisciplinary care team can help to eliminate the frustration families often feel when they first learn about their child's diagnosis and must see an array of professionals—each time retelling and reliving their illness story. By contrast, when an interdisciplinary care team is immediately organized, a family's story only needs to be told once.

Anne is a practicing nurse and very knowledgeable about health and medicine. Sometimes, she is acknowledged for the medical expertise she has. At other times, however, because of her nursing background, she is expected to understand everything. Often in this situation, Anne just wants to be a parent—Karla's mother. It is a careful dance, for both the parent and the professional, and can be successfully "choreographed" only through open, honest communication.

Parents Respond as Individuals

Because Anne thought she was taking Karla for a routine MRI and would not hear results until some days later, as had always happened previously, she discouraged Michael from taking time off from work to go along. After her surprise and sadness at the news she and Karla heard, and following a long, emotional trip home, she was unprepared for the anger Michael expressed at not having been present to hear the news directly. All of his emotions and sadness were misplaced and directed toward the "bearer of bad news." Michael and Anne, with the support of Karla's pediatrician, renewed their determination to be together at any appointments where news of any kind was shared and discussed.

The critical role of fathers is often forgotten or ignored in the North American society where a mother is often the parent who takes a child to appointments. The practice of family-centered care supports and expects flexibility in responding to the expressed needs of a family, however they define their family membership. Family-centered care also considers participation and input from the mother as well as the father, a dual parent family. At the same time, many health care providers find it impossible to make schedule adjustments, unlike Karla's pediatrician who recognized the importance of calling Michael immediately, was willing to wait with Anne and Karla, and then reiterated the offer to call and meet the next morning. Too often, news is given at the convenience of the provider, with little sensitivity to the needs of the family.

There is great variability in parents' desire for information about a diagnosis. For example, one parent may want up-to-date research articles whereas another will be comfortable with a minimum of information. Some will spend hours reading on the Internet whereas others will want to spend their time talking through what they know and feel. The health care provider must be prepared to hear respectfully a parent's questions and to respond in diverse ways. Providers need to consider when a face-to-face conversation is important, how resource materials including books, videotapes, audiotapes, research articles, and Web sites might be offered, and if connections with other parents would be helpful.

Michael and Anne, fortunately, have flexible schedules and feel equally responsible for participating in Karla's appointments and procedures. However, although Michael wants to participate fully, he worries about the lost work time, which translates to less income. He struggles with the knowledge that Anne contributes as much to the family income as he does; although he intellectually has shifted from some of the traditional values with which he was raised, it is not as easy to change his practice.

Some families, because of earning power or nonflexible schedules, have fewer choices, potentially leading to resentment. Financial issues are exacerbated with loss of work time and when a child's needs are extremely complicated, it can become impossible to hold a full-time or even a part-time job. Parents who rely on nursing care for their child cannot leave for their job until the nurse arrives at the house. If the nurse is late, their job reliability suffers. Children with special health needs might need shortened school days and a parent's available hours for work become fewer. A single parent has no partner to share the load of appointments and therapy sessions. Providers who are unaware of a family structure might be critical of an absent parent, or of the parent who may appear uncooperative. A family-centered provider is aware of diverse family configurations and responses. Such a provider is skilled in supporting parents in a variety of circumstances.

Siblings Are Pained, Too

Jason and Will knew that something was wrong the minute Anne and Karla arrived at home following the pediatric appointment. Anne wanted to wait for Michael to get home, but Karla felt comfortable and seemed even eager to tell her brothers what was going on. Will was immediately concerned and afraid that the return of Karla's cancer meant that she could die but he did not want to say that out loud; that would make the concept much too real to deal with at that moment. In contrast, when Jason saw that both Karla and Anne were very sad and upset, he reacted by clinging to both of them, wanting to reassure and be reassured.

Anne recalls that when Karla was first diagnosed, she was offered information on a continuum of care plan that included resources on coping and grief. She did not want to entertain the possibility of Karla's dying at that time, but, in retrospect, feels this information would have been helpful to her family, including her two sons. She plans to contact the oncology social worker for this information and to encourage her to give families information multiple times, as it is hard to retain all of the information given at times of crisis. Good communication within families is vitally important at times like this when it is hard to speak openly with a sick child or with healthy siblings (Eiser & Kopel, 1997). Health care providers can help facilitate that communication by providing information and resources.

Siblings experience a range of emotions although they may be unable to recognize or express them. Guilt, a sense of loss, anger, loneliness, and worry are some of the experiences and feelings Meyer and Vadasy (2000) discussed in their book, based on personal experiences of siblings living with brothers and sisters with special needs. This is evidenced in the reflection of a sibling of a child with cancer:

> Every time I thought about the stress I was experiencing, and complained to myself, I immediately felt incredibly guilty. How could I complain when Maddy was going through so much? Guilt became a big part of my life. Why did Maddy have the cancer, not me? How could I be so petty as to complain about anything? And worst, I was haunted by everything mean or cruel I'd ever done to Maddy. Every punch, hair pull, kick, pinch, prank, every time I'd teased her or taken her favorite cookie or snapped at her took on mammoth proportions. (Kemp, 2002, p. 2)

Most siblings want clear, honest information. One wrote, "Sometimes, instead of telling them the truth, parents and doctors tell siblings a lot of baloney. It is easier to handle when at least you have all the facts" (Murray & Jampolsky, as cited in Meyer & Vadasy, 2000, p. xvii). Considering the experience of siblings is part of family-centered care.

Honoring the Child's Decision About Involvement in His or Her Care

Children with complex needs are part of families and depending on age or temperament it is important to honor their personal wishes. Sometimes the children's wishes are congruent with those of their parent and sometimes they are different. A practitioner's sensitivity to and honoring of children's wishes is integral to embracing family-centered care. In this context, children can speak honestly regarding their feelings about their own illness (Stevenson, 1998).

Karla tells Anne and Michael that she would like to be the one to tell her family members and friends that her tumor has returned. She uses a phrase heard commonly in self-determination groups: "I don't want you to talk about me without me there." She also clings to as much "normalcy" as possible and does not want to bring up the subject of her illness until it is necessary. This is a struggle for Michael and Anne, who want to honor her wishes but feel it is important that the school know soon. They also need support and encouragement from their friends in the community, on whom they depend. At the same time, they are tremendously proud of Karla's determination to be a part of the decisions about her life. They feel it is this "gutsy" attitude that keeps her from becoming discouraged about her health situation.

Karla does not want cancer to "define" who she is, limit expectations, alter friendships, or further restrict her from experiencing a typical adolescence. Her parents feel it is important for Karla's classmates to know what is keeping her out of school, and what is causing some of the changes her friends are witnessing. Psychologically, some parents find labels helpful as they can tell people "why" their child acts differently, has challenges, and so forth. Behaviors become attributed to the "label" rather than the child—neither the child nor the parent is to blame (Hastings & Remington, 1993). But labels can take on an insidious life of their own. They lead to stereotyping, which is hurtful and unfair. Labels can lead to assumptions and inappropriate information, potentially leading to attributions about individuals that may turn out to be inaccurate and biased (Baroff, 1991; Gilman & Heyman, 1999; Rosenhan, 1973). This, in turn, leads to expectations, both positive and negative, that can influence behavior and opportunities for the children (Hastings, 1994; Rosenthal, 1994; Rosenthal & Jacobson, 1968). Nevertheless, labeling a disability through proper assessment and testing is often the way to get needed services, particularly after age 3. There are many variables to consider when sharing personal health information. For the moment, Karla's parents honor her decision about when and how to disclose her illness.

There are many issues to take into account in determining a child's level of involvement in medical decision making, including developmental, clinical, and informed consent issues. (McCabe, 1996). Although involvement will vary depending on a child's developmental stage, even the simple choice of having blood drawn with or without first applying EMLA cream (anesthetic) will encourage independence and cooperation from a child. A 16-year-old with epilepsy made the difficult decision to change his medication of choice because of the weight gain it caused and the resultant daily impact a restricted diet had on his life. Although the medication switch was a frightening process, his parents were supportive of his decision to think about long-term consequences. Children and adults often resist taking medication when difficult side effects affect their quality of life. Shared decision making between parents and a child are important at such times.

Because Karla has been in the same school throughout her life, the librarian and school nurse have worked together to make information about TBI and brain cancer available to teachers and students. When children are very young, either a teacher or a member of the family can read picture books aloud to the class and initiate a discussion to engage the children. Books can be available for personal perusal, in libraries and in individual classrooms. Older children, either the ones who have the illness or their classmates, might be more interested in writing a report or giving a presentation about an illness. Karla has decided to speak to her class to explain why she will be absent for a number of days in the coming months.

Families feel differently about how personal information is shared in a school setting. Sometimes teachers are given detailed information and research articles by parents, and others spend hours gathering and reading information so they can best support a child in their class. In all instances it is important to share information in a manner that entails sensitivity to the wishes of the child and family.

Supports in Times of Difficult News

Having a child with a chronic illness can be a lonely time for a family, particularly when first hearing a diagnosis. They have built their social network around other common life experiences and, suddenly, have an experience that is exclusive to them.

Parent to Parent programs all over the country share a common mission of helping parents find one-on-one support from another parent and are also a source of information about diagnosis, community resources, and funding possibilities (Santelli, Poyadue, & Young, 2001). Anne and Michael were not referred to their local Parent to Parent program by Karla's pediatrician but fortunately learned about this resource during one of Karla's hospital stays. Michael appreciated talking with other parents and through the Parent to Parent organization he found out about a local support group for families who had children with TBI. He and Anne learned of a sibling support program that would give Will and Jason an opportunity to meet other siblings of children with special needs. Anne was interested in learning about the TBI waiver as a way to help pay for some of the supports Karla now needs. However, she was discouraged to find that it was unavailable for Karla. The services were only for individuals 16 years of age or older who had experienced a recent, moderate to severe TBI and were at risk for being in and out of rehabilitation centers (Parent to Parent of Vermont, 2002). Although they do not feel the need for it just now, Anne and Michael heard from other parents about funding possibilities for respite care which would allow them to take time for themselves, as a couple, to reconnect with a bit of the illusive "normalcy" in their own lives.

WORKING THROUGH THE MAZE:
HEALTH, EDUCATION, AND COMMUNITY

After the diagnosis of a chronic illness, as families learn to cope on a daily basis, they find numerous paths through this maze. They become intimately involved in the worlds of health care and education. They learn to advocate for sensitive and respectful delivery of care and discover that their advocacy makes a difference, not only for their family, but also for long-term system change. A sense of community is discovered anew in caring and supportive neighbors and friends.

The Health Care System: The Perspective of Families

Anne remembered how difficult previous chemotherapy treatments had been for Karla and the numerous hospitalizations due to the treatments, pneumonia, and septicemia (blood poisoning). She had carried antiseptic wipes with her to clean equipment in the rooms where Karla stayed and even with a quarantine had been worried about all of the germs floating around on the children's ward which could so easily invade Karla's already compromised immune system. She ached, remembering the uncomfortable chair she fell asleep in every night because she was so exhausted. She thought about the day that Karla was so sick; she did not eat all day because she was afraid to leave her alone.

Hospitals can change over time and this particular children's hospital had convened a focus group of families who had children with chronic illnesses to hear how they could provide a more family-centered environment. They listened to the families and planned changes that would offer more comfort and better care. A family space was created including a kitchen, shower, and laundry facilities. Recliners were purchased so parents could sleep more comfortably, some old equipment was replaced, and parents could wear a hospital beeper when they went to the cafeteria. The hospital also allowed food delivery to the child's room. Parents were given a list of names and phone numbers to call when they had questions or concerns (Hanson, Johnson, Jeppson, Thomas, & Hall, 1994). This alleviated the sense of isolation they felt when staying with their child in a hospital room for long hours each day. If Karla needed another period of time in the hospital, Anne was in for a welcome surprise.

When Karla was in the hospital a number of times 5 years ago, Michael and Anne had observed a group of older children who offered support to each other around their cancer diagnosis. Karla is a social child and has no problem talking about her cancer or her TBI, so Michael and Anne were hopeful that a peer group like this might offer a venue for her to express some of her feelings. Anne wished someone on staff would offer this opportunity to Karla but she knew it would be up to her to contact the social worker to ask about groups for teens. Some children may be less inclined to talk about themselves. Child Life specialists at hospitals, who understand that children have unique needs, offer a variety of opportunities for children to express themselves.

Anne knows that she will tap into the expertise and support of the comprehensive team, as she did 5 years ago. Along with the Child Life specialist, this team consists of an oncologist, a nurse practitioner, a psychologist, a social worker, and a parent liaison. Michael may be interested in joining the support group for parents run by the parent liaison (S. Billadou, personal communication, May 8, 2002).

Health care is expensive and finances become a stressor in many families' lives when their child is diagnosed with a critical illness (Melnyk & Alpert-Gillis, 1998). Anne's health plan at the small, rural hospital where she works includes the entire family. They have recently learned that Karla can additionally receive Medicaid coverage through the Dr. Dynasaur program, the State of Vermont's expanded Child Health Insurance Program (VCHIP). They found out about qualification for Medicaid through a booklet, *Six Ways to Access Medicaid/EPSDT* (Parent to Parent of Vermont, 2002), that Michael picked up at his support group one evening. Anne does the family paperwork, but the applications for Medicaid were a difficult process, although she had received help from her pediatrician's office, their Medical Home. Hospitals or medical offices committed to family-centered practice will need to have someone available to help families with paperwork, insuring that the process is accessible for all.

Although Karla's family felt fortunate that insurance covered most of their medical needs, they struggled with nonmedical expenses: lost income when Michael and Anne spent fewer hours working, gas and car expenses for so many appointments, restaurant food costs when they were away from home, and paying for numerous activities to occupy Jason and Will's time when Anne and Michael were caring for Karla's needs. Some families find that insurance does not consider all of a child's needs as medically necessary. Families with young children often spend a good deal of their income on child care when they have to be away from home with another child for long periods of time. No one wants money to be the basis of a decision about a child's health, but many parents are forced into difficult compromises.

Family-centered providers are familiar with resources and funding choices to offer families. They assure that parents know about small amounts of flexible dollars given through family support and advocacy organizations for incidental needs not covered by typical insurance plans. Pediatric social workers are often aware of small amounts of discretionary funds for similar needs. These options can be offered sensitively and respectfully, letting families make the decision about what is most helpful. It is also important to be sensitive when talking about financial concerns in front of the child.

After her initial discouragement, Anne tapped into her problem-solving skills and began researching treatment options for a recurrence of cancer. When she called the specialists she had previously known, asking about new treatment options and research, she often heard about new specialists. A difference this time was that Karla was more independent and asked to be included in the decisions about her treatment and care. Anne carefully explained different possibilities and relied on the specialists to give Karla specific information. She realized that Karla's reasoning capacity was compromised because of the TBI and she wanted to be sure that Karla was fully informed and capable of making decisions regarding her care (McCabe, 1996). She planned to talk with Karla's pediatrician about her concerns. It was clear that Karla needed some opportunities to feel in control of her life, despite the limited choices she faced. Family-centered physicians are aware of the developmental aspects of care; they ask questions to understand family choices in including children in conversations regarding treatment plans.

The Educational System: The Perspective of Families

Karla and her family have been working within the special education system for 5 years. Michael and Anne prepare for IEP meetings by listing questions to ask and finding research to support the program suggestions they want to make. The team has come to depend on the books and articles on TBI that Anne shares with them. Two neuropsychological assessments provided recommendations. The pediatric neuropsychologist arranged her schedule so she could attend one of Karla's IEP meetings to discuss teaching adaptations to accommodate some of her specific needs. With Karla's new diagnosis, the team decided to invite the VT–ILEHP Program team to define components of Karla's educational program by doing a COACH (Choosing Outcomes and Accommodations for Children; Giangreco, Cloninger, & Iverson, 1998).

Anne spends hours reading special education regulations, talking with Michael, and consulting with their local Parent Information Center representative (see Resources, Technical Assistance Alliance for Parent Centers, PACER Center). The Vermont Parent Information Center is a nonprofit organization with a mission to empower families to become effective advocates for improving the education and quality of life of the child who has a special need. Together with families, the organization is committed to finding a way to negotiate with schools. Karla's school is equally committed to developing the best program for her needs. Not all families experience such respect and partnership in school interactions. Too often a relationship can become adversarial and a child is caught in the middle of conflict (for further discussion, see Chapters 6, 7, and 10 of this book). Karla's family is fortunate in having a Medical Home and a pediatrician who is familiar with the special education process. Indeed, this is a key function of the Medical Home provider (American Academy of Pediatrics, 2000).

Karla knows whom she can depend on at school. She checks in with the school nurse each day when she takes her thyroid medication. It was natural that she chose to speak with the nurse first about the recurrence of her cancer. The nurse listened carefully to Karla and called on their mutual respect and shared humor to encourage her when they had this difficult conversation.

Karla loves her classroom teacher and wishes she did not have to ride the school bus so she could stay after school to talk with her. Her classroom teacher knows that Karla learns best using visual cues and hands-on experience. Based on her concern about Karla's social development, she designs many small-group learning activities that encourage Karla's involvement with her classmates. The teacher takes time to respond to concerns that come up during the Medical Home team meeting, and again in the IEP meeting.

Karla resents her instructional assistant (IA) who follows her too closely and discourages her from going to her "real" teacher with questions. She is also in the way when Karla initiates interactions with her classmates. In fact, she wonders sometimes if her classmates avoid her because they do not want an adult hearing everything they say. When she yelled at her IA one day to just leave her alone, it seemed like her classmates backed off, rather than the IA. It is difficult to express her feelings in situations like this.

Karla is enthusiastic about participating with her peers in all school programs and she wishes that her schoolwork would not be such a daily struggle so she would have more time to do other fun, teenage things. She knows that she is struggling to keep up with her assigned work and wonders if her classmates think she is "dumb." It is difficult to hear other girls in her class talk about boys and sleep-overs when she is not included in their conversations or invitations. Karla's mother tells her honestly that she is not always easy to be around. Although moodiness is a part of Karla's illness, it may be difficult for others. Anne recognizes that Karla is having a hard time and looks for ways to deal with this by constantly setting up meetings with people at school who can provide support to Karla. Sometimes Karla thinks her mother expects too much of her. In contrast, her teacher always points out the things she does well and makes Karla feel that whatever she accomplishes is praiseworthy.

The Community Connection

In a number of surveys and focus groups facilitated by Parent to Parent of Vermont between 1997 and 2002, a recurring theme is parents' wishes for services and supports in their communities (Parent to Parent of Vermont, 1999, 2001–2002). Karla's paternal grandparents live nearby but they are not well and lack the physical strength to care for Karla, or to keep track of Jason. It is important for family-centered providers to understand that they cannot assume that having a geographically close family translates to support, either physical or emotional. Families find that neighbors, school acquaintances, work colleagues, and church family are often their support system. Sometimes families look for others in similar circumstances through organizations that can help facilitate that type of connection (Santelli et al., 2001). (See Resources at the end of this chapter for more information.)

There are instances when communities come together around a family cause and wonderful things happen. In one small, rural community, a child with multiple disabilities was unable to maneuver his wheelchair within the small spaces in his home. He had become too heavy to lift into a regular bath and there was not enough space to do physical therapy in the cramped living room. After reading a letter from this child's grandmother to the editor of a local newspaper, a community member called the child's mother with her idea of building a room onto the family's home. This community member, who did not know the family initially, began to recruit contractors, an architect, a job foreman, and a bathroom designer. Her church became the depository of donated funds. A benefit concert was planned locally with donations going to the fund. The new room—built entirely from donated funds, labor, and materials—has a handicapped accessible bedroom and bathroom and space for physical therapy and recreation (O'Neil, 2001). Such community support contributes immeasurably to a child and family's quality of life.

There are other instances when communities rally around families: ramps are added to houses, child care is volunteered, and meals are cooked and delivered. Karla's family has a church friend who organizes meals to be brought to their home every evening following appointments at the tertiary hospital, an hour away. One neighbor offered to have Jason come to her home after school on those days and Will's computer teacher asked him to stay after school some evenings to help keep the computer lab in good order. Friends offered to transport Will and Jason to and from sports practices when needed. Anne and Michael feel privileged to have this ongoing support from their community.

However, this is not the case for all families. Having a child with a chronic illness or a disability can become a very isolating situation.

Families experience limitations in their lives when natural supports are not available. One mother in the Parent to Parent survey had not left her child with anyone else since her child's birth 3 years earlier. Two-parent families might take turns staying home with a child, unable to join community activities as a family. An invitation to dinner is declined if the child is not also invited; however, meeting a child's dietary needs discourages friends from extending that invitation. Local, summer camps may not be accessible to a child with physical or behavioral challenges and special camps are prohibitively expensive. These challenges are more complex for single parents.

A medical student who spent one summer in a community writes compellingly about two boys with chronic illnesses who live in the same community but receive very different responses. He felt that a community's ability to be supportive depended on a number of things: awareness of the child's illness, parents' connections, parents' advocacy skills, and language and cultural differences. There are cases in which community members are judgmental, especially when they think they know a family too well (Maslow, 2002).

The practice of family-centered care allows many options for services within a child and family's local community. Within these supportive communities families cope and thrive.

LESSONS LEARNED AND IMPLICATIONS FOR PRACTICE

The philosophy of family-centered care becomes real in families' lives as the key elements are put into practice, within the unique context of each family. Family-centered responses to a child's complex medical situation positively impact a family's ability to navigate the maze of medical and educational systems. As children become involved in their own health care decisions and as families become adept within supportive systems, their expert knowledge becomes the impetus for positive change. Coordinated care for children assures that the professionals who work on their team will be able to provide mutual support for each other as family-centered practitioners.

Core Support for Individuals and Their Families

All families define themselves differently. Whereas some families enjoy a large, supportive family network, others reach out into communities to create their family. The Task Force on Young Children and Families, New Mexico Legislature, defined "family" in the following way:

> Families are big, small, extended, nuclear, multi-generational, with one parent, two parents, and grandparents. We live under one roof or many. A

family can be as temporary as a few weeks, as permanent as forever. We
become part of a family by birth, adoption, marriage, or from a desire for
mutual support ... A family is a culture unto itself, with different values
and unique ways of realizing its dream; together, our families become the
source of our rich cultural heritage and spiritual diversity ... Our families
create neighborhoods, communities, states and nations. (Hanft, as cited
in Webster & Johnson, 1999, p. 34)

It is important for health care professionals and educators to listen
carefully as families and individuals talk about what they would find
most helpful: medical advice, educational support, respite, support for
siblings, or an opportunity to talk with another parent or individual.
They must ensure that systems are in place to refer individuals and families to community resources and supports. When families' choices are
heard and respected, their level of coping is increased. Concrete suggestions include the following:

- Ask individuals and family members to list those whom they
  would want present when sharing diagnostic or treatment information, or when developing an educational plan.
- Provide flexibility, including evening hours, when difficult information needs to be shared, or changes in an educational plan are
  being considered.
- Contact family support organizations such as Parent to Parent
  programs or Parent Information Centers to provide staff in-ser-
  vices to learn about the resources and supports that are available
  and how to make referrals.
- Provide ongoing opportunities for families to learn about the resources and supports in their community.

Involvement of Adolescents in Their Own Health Care

Critical questions in the practice of family-centered care are when and
how to involve adolescents in decisions about their own treatment. Although adolescents are part of their family structure, they are individuals as well and their voices must be heard in decisions that directly affect
them. Rushforth (1999), in writing about communication with hospitalized children, placed major responsibility on practitioners:

... it is essential for all practitioners working in the field of child health
to be well informed about contemporary issues pertaining to child development, communicating with children, and ways in which children
conceptualize the world. More importantly, it will be increasingly be-

holden on practitioners to apply these principles to their practice, in order to ensure that the children for whom they care are truly given a voice, and that voice is listened to and taken account of. (p. 690)

Using Families as Advisors to Insure Child/Family Needs Are Heard

Families' experiences can help change health care systems. It is essential to incorporate family input into policy and practice to ensure family needs are considered. Families are serving on advisory boards across the country, teaching health care professionals and educators, providing testimony, and developing policies that exemplify best practice in the care, education and support of individuals with chronic illness or disability (Jeppson & Thomas, 1995; Ruder, 2002). Clearly each family is unique and it is important to have diverse representation on committees and advisory groups. Family-centered providers find ways to support family participation, through flexible scheduling of meetings, to providing stipends for participation, transportation, and child-care needs (Jeppson & Thomas, 1995).

The Need for a Medical Home for Children With Special Health Needs

Healthy People 2010 describes one of the six core outcomes for children with special needs: "All children with special health care needs will receive ongoing comprehensive care within a medical home" (Weissman, n.d.). A child's special services will be coordinated within that "home" and teams, which include parents and the child when appropriate, will meet to develop care plans. A workgroup has been convened to develop this core outcome, which will become part of a monograph that will direct the work of the MCHB with children with special health care needs in the next 10 years.

The American Academy of Pediatrics (AAP) (2000) provides guidelines regarding a pediatrician's role in supporting educationally-related services for children with special needs. As part of the primary care, physicians provide medical management, supervision, and program planning. A physician can also serve as an advocate based on the child's special needs and realistic expectations for changes in health, performance, and behavior. These important services are not mandated through IDEA but those practitioners in a Medical Home practice find ways to provide this care to families.

Becoming a Medical Home is a process for a pediatrician's office. Physicians and parents work together, not only in the care of their children, but also in making changes and improvements to the practice. According to one practice that has experienced this process, "The payoff ... is healthier children and stronger families" (Wehr, 2002, p. 74). All families deserve this choice.

Ultimately, the AAP is moving toward providing medical care for infants, children, and adolescents that is family-centered, compassionate, comprehensive, continuous, accessible, and coordinated. This means that practitioners are expected to develop trusting relationships with families, honoring their diversity and recognizing their constancy in their children's lives; to provide ongoing primary care, including acute, chronic, and preventive care; to identify the need for consultation and referral; to interact with educational and community programs to ensure the needs of children and their families are being addressed; to maintain records that are relevant, accessible, and comprehensive; to provide assessment and counseling that is developmentally and culturally appropriate; and, to implement a coordinated care plan (American Academy of Pediatrics, 2002).

Mutual Support for Professionals

It is imperative to provide professional development opportunities to learn about and incorporate the philosophy and practice of family-centered care in every professional work setting. One way to do this is to identify mentors or form a mentoring group to encourage and celebrate movement toward best practices in family-centered care. Clinicians and families can learn about the Maternal and Child Health/Academy of Pediatrics Medical Home Project (The National Medical Home Mentorship Network at the American Academy of Pediatrics, n. d.) as well as other initiatives aimed at developing comprehensive, coordinated systems of care for children with special health needs and their families. Last, a long-term and important goal is to invite faculty members, health care professionals, and family members to conduct research to validate and advance the practice of family-centered care.

CONCLUSION

A diagnosis of an illness or disability alters the life of each member of a family. For individuals and family members to restore balance in their lives, families need information to make critical decisions and emotional supports to sustain them during various phases in the cycle of life, even death. Healing for all family members begins within an environment of mutual respect and honesty, created when health care professionals provide complete, accurate, unbiased information, sustained by opportunities for ongoing questions to be answered, information clarified, and decisions honored.

Family stories inform practice choices. There is a need for core supports and involvement of all family members, including the child with the disability, particularly when that child is an adolescent. It is imperative to insure opportunities to hear from families at all levels, from initial questions and concerns to advocacy and input into system policies and processes. As professionals partner with families and commit to family-centered practice, they become adept at sharing these best practices with colleagues, who in turn provide mutual encouragement in finding consistent ways to support families.

When families are connected to the resources and supports they need, they can continue to live their lives in the comfort of their community of choice, among those whom they have identified as "family." In this way, the practice of family-centered care is infused throughout the health and education system and, to this end, training programs embrace this philosophy and ensure that all those entrusted to them learn and practice family-centered care.

STUDY QUESTIONS

1. In what ways might the systems in which you practice or hope to practice actualize best practice in family-centered care?
2. How might the interdisciplinary team of the Medical Home support Karla in her school setting? In what ways might this same team support the needs of the family?
3. What are some practice changes that can be accomplished individually by providers?
4. What are the areas where a partnership between a provider and family and child are crucial for achieving the best outcomes?
5. List specific areas where providers must be involved at the system level to ensure family-centered services.

GLOSSARY

COACH—Choosing Outcomes and Accommodations for CHildren is a family-centered process that helps educational teams, in collaboration with families, to identify valued life outcomes that can be used to guide the Individual Education Plan process for children with special needs.

EMLA cream—A topical ointment used to numb an area and decrease the potential for discomfort when experiencing a shot or blood draw.

IEP—An Individual Education Plan is a planning document required by the Individuals with Disabilities Education Act that educational teams use, in collaboration with families, to determine, monitor, and evaluate the services children with special needs require to be successful in school.

Medical Home—A concept put forward by the American Academy of Pediatrics to ensure that infants, children, and adolescents receive medical care that is family-centered, compassionate, comprehensive, continuous, accessible, and coordinated.

Neuropsychologist—Someone who specializes in the understanding and assessment of the mental and intellectual state of individuals and the relation of the functions of the human mind to the brain.

Oncologist—A physician who specializes in the study of tumors and other cancerous conditions.

Tertiary facility—Hospital.

TBI—traumatic brain injury is a condition in which an individual suffers a sudden assault to the brain that can cause difficulty in cognitive (thinking), motor, and language function.

RESOURCES

Beach Center on Families and Disability
3111 Haworth Hall
University of Kansas
Lawrence, KS 66045
Telephone: (785) 864-7600
Fax: (785) 864-7605
http://www.beachcenter.org

Center for Medical Home Improvement
Hood Center for Children and Families
Children's Hospital at Dartmouth–Hitchcock Medical Center
One Medical Center Drive
Lebanon, NH 03756-1479
Telephone: (603) 653-1480
Fax: (603) 653-1479
http://www.medicalhomeimprovement.org

Division of Children With Special Needs
Medical Home Web site
www.medicalhomeinfo.org

The Family Village
Waisman Center
University of Wisconsin—Madison
1500 Highland Avenue
Madison, WI 53705-2280
E-mail: familyvillage@waisman.wisc.edu
http://www.familyvillage.wisc.edu (See "community resources" for
international and diverse cultural and lifestyle resources.)

Family Voices
P.O. Box 769
Algodones, NM 87001
Telephone: (505) 867-2368
Fax: (505) 867-6517
http://www.familyvoices.org

Grassroots Consortium on Disabilities
P.O. Box 61628
Houston, TX 77208
Telephone: (713) 734-5355
Fax: (713) 643-6291
http://www.GCOD.org

Institute for Family-Centered Care
7900 Wisconsin Avenue, Suite 405
Bethesda, MD 20814
Telephone: (301) 652-0281
Fax: (301) 652-0186
http://www.familycenteredcare.org

Parent to Parent USA
http://www.p2pusa.org
Parent to Parent of Vermont
600 Blair Park Road, Suite 240
Williston, VT 05495-7549
Telephone: (802) 764-5290
Fax: (802) 764-5297
http://www.partoparvt.org

The Sibling Support Project
Children's Hospital and Medical Center
P.O. Box 5371, CL-09
Seattle, WA 98105
Telephone: (206) 527-5712

Fax: (206) 527-5705
dmeyer@chmc.org

Technical Assistance Alliance for Parent Centers
PACER Center
8161 Normandale Boulevard
Minneapolis, MN 55437-1044
Telephone: (952) 838-9000, (800) 537-2237
TTY: (952) 838-0190
Fax: (952) 838-0199
http://www.PACER.org
http://www.taalliance.org

Vermont Department of Education
www.state.vt.us/educ/

Vermont Parent Information Center.
1 Mill Street, Suite 310
Burlington, VT 05401
Telephone: (802) 658-5315
Fax: (802) 658-5395
www.vtpic.com

REFERENCES

American Academy of Pediatrics: Committee on Children with Disabilities. (2000). Provision of educationally-related services for children and adolescents with chronic diseases and disabling conditions. *Pediatrics, 105,* 448–449.

American Academy of Pediatrics: Medical Home Initiative. (n.d.). *The National Medical Home Mentorship Network at the American Academy of Pediatrics.* Washington, DC: Author.

American Academy of Pediatrics: Policy Statement. (2002). The medical home. *Pediatrics, 110,* 184–186.

Arango, P. (1999). No one does it alone: Families and professionals as partners for our children. *Exceptional Parent Magazine, 29,* 30–35.

Baroff, G. S. (1991). What's in a name: A comment on Goldfarb's guest editorial. *American Journal of Mental Retardation, 96,* 99–100.

Bishop, K. K., Woll, J., & Arango, P. (1993). *Family/professional collaboration for children with special health needs and their families* (with support from the Division of Services for Children with Special Health Needs, Maternal and Child Health Bureau, U.S. Department of Health and Human Services). Burlington, VT: University of Vermont Department of Social Work.

Dunn, A. M. (2002). Culture competence and the primary care provider. *Journal of Pediatric Health Care, 16,* 105–111.

Eiser, C., & Kopel, S. (1997). Children's perception of health and illness. In K. J. Petrie & J. A. Weinman (Eds.), *Perceptions of health and illness: Current research and applications* (pp. 47–76). London, England: Harwood Academic Publishers.

Fadiman, A. (1997). *The spirit catches you and you fall down: A Hmong child, her American doctors, and the collision of two cultures.* New York: Farrar, Straus & Giroux.

Fialka, J., & Mikus, K. C. (1999). *Do you hear what I hear? Parents and professionals working together for children with special needs.* Ann Arbor, MI: Proctor Publications, LLC.

Giangreco, M. F., Cloninger, C. J., & Iverson, V. S. (1998). *Choosing outcomes and accommodations for children: A guide to educational planning for students with disabilities* (2nd ed.). Baltimore: Brookes.

Gilman, S. A., & Heyman, G. D. (1999). Carrot-eaters and creature-believers: The effects of lexicalization on children's inferences about social categories. *Psychological Science, 10,* 489–493.

Hanson, J. L., Johnson, B. H., Jeppson, E. S., Thomas, J., & Hall, J. H. (1994). *Hospitals moving forward with family-centered care.* Bethesda, MD: Institute for Family-Centered Care.

Hastings, R. P. (1994). On good terms: Labeling people with mental retardation. *Mental Retardation, 32*(5), 363–365.

Hastings, R. P., & Remington, B. (1993). Connotations of labels for mental handicap and challenging behavior. A review and research evaluation. *Mental Handicap Research, 6,* 237–249.

Jeppson, E., & Thomas, J. (1995). *Essential allies: Families as advisors.* Bethesda, MD: Institute for Family-Centered Care.

Kemp, C. (2002). Stay attuned to needs of seriously ill patients' siblings. *AAP News, 20,* 99.

Kingsley, E. P. (1987). Welcome to Holland. In S. D. Klein & K. Schive (Eds.), *You will dream new dreams: Inspiring personal stories by parents of children with disabilities* (pp. 216–217). New York: Kensington Publishing Corp.

Leonard, D. (2003). *Reflection paper.* Williston, VT. Medical Education Project; Parent to Parent of Vermont.

Luft, J. (1970). *Group processes: An introduction to group dynamics* (2nd ed.). Palo Alto, CA: National Press Books.

Maslow, G. (Summer). Lost boys. *Dartmouth Medicine,* 40–43, 59.

McCabe, M. A. (1996). Involving children and adolescents in medical decision making: Developmental and clinical considerations. *Journal of Pediatric Psychology, 21,* 505–516.

McCubbin, H. I., Thompson, E. A., Thompson, A. I., McCubbin, M. A., & Kaston, A. J. (1993). Raising children with disabling conditions in a culturally diverse world: Culture, ethnicity, and the family: critical factors in childhood chronic illnesses and disabilities. *American Academy of Pediatrics, 91,* 1063–1070.

Melnyk, B. M., & Alpert-Gillis, L. J. (1998). The COPE program: A strategy to improve outcomes of critically ill young children and their parents. *Pediatric Nursing, 24,* 521–526.

Meyer, D., & Vadasy, P. (2000). *Living with a brother or sister with special needs: A book for sibs* (2nd ed.). Seattle: University of Washington Press.

O'Neil, L. (2001, August 16). Community unites for 'Nicky's Room.' *The Burlington Free Press,* p. 4B.

Parent to Parent of Vermont. (1999). [Parent focus groups/surveys]. Unpublished raw data.

Parent to Parent of Vermont. (2001–2002). [Parent phone surveys]. Unpublished raw data.

Parent to Parent of Vermont. (March, 2002). *6 ways to access Medicaid/EPSDT for Vermont's children.* Williston, VT: Author.

Rosenhan, D. L. (1973). On being sane in insane places. *Science, 179,* 250–258.

Rosenthal, R. (1994). Interpersonal expectancy effects: A 30-year perspective. *Current Directions in Psychological Science, 3,* 176–179.

Rosenthal, R., & Jacobson, L. (1968). *Pygmalian in the classroom.* New York: Holt, Rinehart & Winston.

Ruder, D. (2002). Patients and families make a difference at Dana-Farber. *Paths of Progress,* 26–29.

Rushforth, H. (1999). Practitioner review: Communicating with hospitalised children: Review and application of research pertaining to children's understanding of health and illness. *Journal of Child Psychology and Psychiatry, 40,* 683–691.

Santelli, B., Poyadue, F., & Young, J. (2001). *The Parent to Parent handbook: Connecting families of children with special needs.* Baltimore: Brookes.

Satir, V. (1972). *Peoplemaking.* Palo Alto, CA: Science and Behavior Books.

Shelton, T. L., & Stepanek, J. S. (1994). *Family-centered care for children needing specialized health and developmental services* (3rd ed.). Bethesda, MD: Association for the Care of Children's Health.

Singer, G. H. S., Marquis, J., Powers, L. K., Blanchard, L., DiVenere, N., Santelli, B., et al. (1999). A multi-site evaluation of Parent to Parent programs for parents of children with disabilities. *Journal of Early Intervention, 22,* 217–229.

Stevenson, M. J. (Producer & Director). (1998). *Families and health: "A child's voice"* [motion picture]. Available from Department of Film and Television, College of Communication, Boston University, Boston, MA.

Webster, P. D., & Johnson, B. H. (1999). *Developing family-centered vision, mission, and philosophy of care statements.* Bethesda, MD: Institute for Family-Centered Care.

Wehr, E. (June). Vermont parent doctor team designs a medical home for children with special healthcare needs. *The Exceptional Parent, 32*(6), 72–78.

Weissman, G. (n.d.). *Achieving and measuring success for children with special health care needs by 2010.* Rockville, MD: Division of Services for Children with Special Health Needs, U.S. Department of Health and Human Services, Health Resources and Services Administration, Maternal and Child Health Bureau.

3

Cultural Competence in Differential Diagnosis: Posttraumatic Stress Disorder and Reactive Attachment Disorder

Claudia María Vargas
Jean Beatson
University of Vermont

Questions to Consider

1. How can we apply cultural competence in clinical practice?
2. What are potential problems in the use of standardized assessment tools and evaluation when children are from multicultural groups?
3. What ethnocultural and linguistic factors should be considered in differential diagnosis?
4. What factors may lead to conflict between the cultural concepts of health and disability when working with children and families from diverse backgrounds?
5. What complexities can arise in the application of the strengths model and family-centered care model when working with multicultural children and families?

NATASHA'S STORY

Natasha was a 4½-year-old girl living with her adoptive mother. This beautiful child was adopted from an orphanage in Rumania at 2 years of age. Little is known of her health history except from the orphanage staff and some brief medical reports. Her biological mother was 28 years old and it was her fifth pregnancy. At birth, the mother left Natasha at the hospital where she remained for her 1st year of life until transferred to an orphanage.

Although the orphanage was clean and light, the space was very confined. The staff did not bring toys out of the shelves for the children to play with and took the children for walks only occasionally. The orphanage served 150 children, and had a 1:35 staff–child ratio. The adoptive mother believes babies were tightly swaddled for the 1st year of life and that this may have affected Natasha's gross motor development. Natasha did not walk independently until she was 2 years old. The children were kept in only one room during the day whereas the sleeping area was separate. The opportunity for interaction among children was sparse.

The adoptive mother believes that the diet at the orphanage was limited to potato bread, some meats, and milk as major staples. Fruits and vegetables were rarely available; therefore, there was a concern about possible rickets. Natasha was undernourished but not malnourished. Her height was at the 25th percentile and her weight at the 5th percentile. Natasha was described as having flat feet, although they appeared to have improved since her arrival at her new home. She exhibited a mild outward bulging around the midabdomen, indicative of weak or low muscle tone.

Since her arrival in Vermont, Natasha has enjoyed generally good and unremarkable health, except for a few colds without ear infections. The pediatrician in Vermont discovered a deep sacral dimple in the spine and prescribed a magnetic resonance imaging (MRI) of her lower spine to test for spina bifida. The MRI revealed a deep sinus but did not involve spinal nerves.

Natasha did not exhibit difficulties with reasoning, memory, or thinking. Her attention span was variable, depending on the environment and situation. At home, in solitary play, or with her mother, she exhibited adequate attention span. For example, she would play for a period of 5 to 10 minutes with puzzles or develop imaginary schemes with dolls. Similarly, she engaged with her imaginary friend, Tatiana, for about the same time. She enjoyed having someone read to her and had memorized certain parts of books. Group settings, however, presented challenges, such as in Sunday school, where she had more difficulty staying engaged in activities. Her mother attributed this to her attachment style with adults, originating from her experience in the orphanage where she interacted primarily with adults. For instance, she has sought generally the attention of adults instead of peers. The staff had concerns especially regarding Natasha's "frozen watchfulness," assuming a fetal position on the floor and rocking, repeating language spoken to her, and sensory challenges, such as difficulty playing with finger paint. Although the mother observed that her child was more distractible in certain circumstances, she was not seeking out a specific diagnosis such as attention-deficit hyperactivity disorder (ADHD) or autism spectrum disorder (ASD).

Attachment Concerns

The adoptive mother had noticed great improvements in attachment to Natasha's new family despite the challenges. Natasha is an attractive and engaging child, characteristics that have played against her development of a sense of social boundaries especially with adult strangers. In the past, it was not uncommon for her to approach adult strangers with hugs and questions. The mother interpreted this as a direct result of the types of attachments afforded her in the orphanage and hospital settings. The mother has had to politely ask strangers not to respond to Natasha's behavior to avoid reinforcing. Over time, this behavior pattern occurred less frequently, although Natasha continued to gravitate to adults rather than peers.

Natasha's mother wanted the staff at her child-care program to take into consideration Natasha's unique history and style. Specifically, Natasha's mother wanted the interdisciplinary team to address educational support and issues of transition to kindergarten because Natasha was going to be 5 years old by the end of the academic year. The mother was seeking, in particular, recommendations and ideas on the types of supports her daughter would require to promote success in educational settings as well as with peers.

Natasha's mother is highly educated, with a doctorate degree in international relations and is fluent in three foreign languages. She is a single mother by choice. The mother speaks to the child in two languages, English and French, previously unknown to the child. Because she does frequent, work-related travel, she leaves the child with an employee of the child-care center, a French–Canadian woman who speaks to the child in French. This dual, simultaneous language exposure was also a factor in her language development in English.

Clearly, when the Vermont Interdisciplinary Leadership Education for Health Professionals (VT–ILEHP) team came to work with Natasha and her mother, trainees, fellows, and faculty members engaged in a range of cultural factors that shaped not only Natasha's reality but also the team's perceptions.

INTRODUCTION

For minority groups, First Nations Peoples (indigenous or Native Peoples), refugees, and new immigrants, health care has either not been accessible, or, when available, has been of less quality than that of the majority of the population (Smedley, Stith, & Nelson, 2003). Specifically, research findings indicate marked disparities in diagnosis and treatment (Geiger, 2003). On July 8, 2003, United States General Accounting Office (GAO) testimony asserted the following:

> A recent report by the Institute of Medicine [Smedley, Stith, & Nelson, 2003], a branch of the National Academy of Sciences, found that racial and ethnic minority groups tend to receive a lower quality of health care than nonminorities, even when access-related factors such as income and insurance coverage are controlled. It concluded that the elimination of racial and ethnic health care disparities is a major challenge in the United States. Racial and ethnic minority groups identified by the federal government—American Indians or Alaska Natives, Asians, Blacks or African Americans, Hispanics or Latinos, and Native Hawaiians or other Pacific Islanders—are expected to make up an increasingly large portion of the U.S. population in coming years. (p. 1)

A number of mediating factors attest to these disparities. Past ethnic and racial segregation, including that which occurs at medical facilities, and socioeconomic inequalities ubiquitous in all aspects of American life, inevitably affect access and quality of health care.

However, even when these groups do have access, the quality of health care may be compromised by discrimination (Smedley, Stith, & Nelson, 2003). Indeed, discriminatory practices, whether deliberate or subconscious, in the health care arena have been considered a root cause of health disparities in ethno-cultural, racial groups (Perez, 2003). Specifically, perceptions of health professionals of diverse ethno-cultural, racial, or linguistic groups come into play in the clinical setting affecting diagnosis and treatment (Perez, 2003). Limited English language skills directly impinge on the ability to communicate health problems to health practitioners who, on the other hand, may lack language proficiency in languages spoken by their clients. These types of communication problems have lead to misdiagnosis or unintentionally undermined best treatments.

Different, potentially conflicting, conceptions of health and illness by health professionals and those of diverse groups may lead to serious misunderstandings. These misunderstandings can potentially trigger conflict between what a family considers best health care and the views of health professionals. These disparities are magnified for children and families with disabilities who are also from vulnerable groups such as refugees. Because of all of these factors, diverse groups in the United States, and for example in Canada (Woo, 2000), have specific health care needs associated with their unique experiences.

Moreover, the diversity of the United States, as well as of Canada, is rapidly increasing. Their numbers as part of the national population are also increasing. This means a greater need for health professionals to be able to meet the needs of multicultural groups. According to Congress (see also United States General Accounting Office testimony, July 8, 2003)

> America's racial profile is rapidly changing. Between 1980 and 1990, the rate of increase in the population for white Americans was 6 percent, while the rate of increase for racial and ethnic minorities was much higher: 53 percent for Hispanics, 13.2 percent for African–Americans, and 107.8 percent for Asians.

> By the year 2000, this Nation will have 275,000,000 people, nearly one of every three of whom will be either African–American, Hispanic, Asian–American, or American Indian. (Individuals with Disabilities Education Act Amendments of 1997, p. 4)

Access and quality of care are even more problematic when a child has a disability. A significant reason is related to how the health professional and the family conceptualize a disability. The model embraced by health professionals directly affects interactions with families, more so if the model is not family-centered (see Chapter 2 for a discussion on family-centered care). Another issue is whether the approach embraced by the practitioner regarding disabilities is deficit-based or more strengths-based (Saleebey, 1997). All of these factors are filtered through the cultural lens of both the health professional and the family. Culture in this case is used according to its anthropological concept, specifically in terms of human patterns of behavior or thinking, language, religion, and mores, among others, that shape a person. (Later in this chapter, culture is also discussed in terms of organizational culture, such as the culture of professions, a hospital, a clinic, or a nongovernmental organization involved in providing health care services.)

This chapter explores the role of cultural competence in the health care setting. It describes the significance of cultural responsiveness in serving children with disabilities and their families from diverse backgrounds. Specifically, it explores the following questions: (a) How does cultural competence affect health services delivery when serving children and families with neurodevelopmental disabilities? (b) What factors do health care providers need to consider regarding assessment tools, diagnosis, and interventions when serving culturally diverse children and families with neurodevelopmental disabilities? (c) What constitutes cultural competence in health care delivery to diverse children and families with disabilities? The thesis that emerges is that cultural competence plays a significant role in the work of health practitioners serving children with disabilities and their families, affecting assessment, diagnosis, and interventions or treatment.

The chapter is organized in four parts. First, it discusses traditional concepts of health and wellness as compared to Western or biomedicine, traditional healing practices, and cross-cultural concepts of disability. Second, it addresses cultural and linguistic factors that may affect the appropriateness of assessment tools, assessment, diagnosis, and intervention. It delves into specific ethnocultural and linguistic factors that have historically been used to discriminate diverse groups resulting in an overrepresentation in children with disabilities. Third, it explores those elements that pose challenges in the development and promotion of cultural competence in health care delivery. Finally, it analyzes the salient features of cultural competence in the health care area with a focus on disabilities, their relevance to best practice, and implications for systems change for interdisciplinary teams.

CROSS-CULTURAL CONCEPTS OF HEALTH AND WELLNESS AND HEALTH NEEDS

Even when health professionals have the best interest of a child and his or her family at heart, the culture of the family and that of a health professional may collide. This may be attributed to differences held by each regarding conceptions of health and wellness and more precisely of disabilities. Although some people may not be aware that they are affected by culture, it is a fact that personal and professional demeanor is influenced by cultural background. This intrinsic influence affects the interactions of professionals as well as of families in clinical settings.

What Is Culture, Anyway?

Before proceeding to a more specialized aspect of health and culture, it is important to have a definition of culture. According to Samovar and Porter

> Culture is the deposit of knowledge, experience, meanings, beliefs, values, attitudes, religion, timing, roles, spatial relations, concepts of the universe, and material objects and possessions acquired by a large group of people in the course of generations through individual and groups striving. Culture manifests itself in the patterns of language and in forms of activity and behavior that act as models for both the common adaptive acts and the styles of communication that enable people to live in a society within a given geographic environment at a given state of technical development at a particular moment in time.... Culture is persistent, enduring and omnipresent. (1989, p. 19)

Hence, culture is a framework, a worldview, a cosmology, a way of organizing life experiences for a person or a group transmitted through generations. Culture is not static. It affects every aspect of a person's life, personal and professional. Culture encompasses beliefs, customs, habits, and values, for example, on childrearing, personal relationships, family interactions, or roles ascribed to various members of a group. It also influences perspectives about health and illness, including their origin or treatment. The cultural perspective of a person has a bearing on behaviors and attitudes toward others in such areas as gender and age as well as disability. Sociopolitical and historical factors also shape culture. Thus, for example, some cultures have been segregated or enslaved or experience ongoing discrimination such as many indigenous cultures, whether in the United States, Canada, Australia, New Zealand, or Latin America (Psacaropoulos & Patrinos, 1994; Spring, 1995; United Nations, 1994).

A person's worldview is often anchored on religion or spirituality, whether formally organized or based on magical conceptions of nature. It may also reflect regional or geographical characteristics. In the United States, for example, most people are aware of cultural characteristics prevalent in the South or in the Southwest. Culture is also characterized by language, verbal and nonverbal, dialects, or patterns of speech, which serve as distinct and attractive regional markers. Although students will usually respond with "I don't have an accent," Americans' geographical origin may often be identified based on their accent. Culture is also associated with race and ethnicity. But, culture may encompass racial or ethnic groups. Vasconcelos, an influential Mexican philosopher, considered Latin Americans "la Raza Cósmica" (the Cosmic Race), because Latin America is the only place where all of the races had intermixed—Indian, Afro-descendants, Asians (for example, Chinese), Middle Easterners (Moors from the time of the conquest and other Islamic refugee and immigrants), and European-descendants (Burns, 1994). Finally, the concept of time—circular, linear, future-oriented, or past-oriented—constitutes an important element of a culture that affects academic achievement, leadership, and clinical encounters (Ben-Baruch, 1985, 1999, 2002).

Characteristics of Western and Non-Western Cultures: A Continuum, Not a Dichotomy

Anthropologists have identified some general characteristics that differentiate Western and non-Western cultures. It is important to consider these characteristics as a continuum rather than as a dichotomy because it is impossible to box the broad diversity of people into two categories. Nevertheless, there are broad differences that have been synthesized by O'Hara-Devereaux (1994) in the following six features: (a) universalism–particularism, (b) individualism–communitarism, (c) ascribed–

achieved status, (d) circular–linear concept of time, (e) monochromic–
polychromic (Chronemics), and (e) high context–low context. "Universalism and particularism contrast a preference for drawing general
principles versus a preference for the anecdotal or itemized"
(Guirdham, 1999, p. 57). Cultures that value individualism focus on individual achievement, which is common in Western cultures. Communitarism, on the other hand, is valued by cultures in which the
achievement of the group supersedes that of the individual. Thus, Native American children, who come from cultures that value the achievement of the community, experience difficulty in school settings that
expect them to work for individual advancement, which conflicts with
their cultural experience (Locust, 1989). In Hawaii, for example, literacy
was a problem until schools considered implementing group work and
other culturally responsive teaching practices for Native Hawaiians
(Nieto, 2000). On the other hand, many traditional cultures tend to ad-
here to ascribed status based on class, caste, gender, age, or aristocracy
that can be very problematic. In contrast, countries such as the United
States respect individual achievement. (That said, there are other socioeconomic or historical factors that afford some individuals ascribed status, whether it is wealth or family background, as is the case of the
Kennedy, Bush, Ford, or Rockefeller families in the United States.)

The concept of time that is dominant in a culture can have a significant bearing in clinical settings. For example, families whose conception of time is circular may be less concerned with punctuality as
compared to those who live with a linear concept of time. That is, persons whose concept of time is circular may focus on the social encounter, rather than the precise time at which it may be scheduled to occur.
For them, the past, present, and the future are intricately intertwined.
Ben-Baruch (2002) cited the example of the difficulty health professionals experienced in serving Ethiopian, pregnant mothers with respect to
keeping appointments. The problems were resolved when nurses informed the mothers that they had to come back a day after Chanuka,
which provided a relevant time marker.

Chronemics refers to whether a culture is significantly monochromic
or polychromic (Guirdham, 1999). Persons from Western cultures are
generally monochromic in that they focus on one thing at a time and fin-
ish one task before moving on to the other. In polychromic cultures, persons are characteristically engaged simultaneously in a number of
activities, whether it is carrying out multiple conversations or doing
several things while talking to someone on the phone or in person. In a
hospital setting, this type of behavior can appear chaotic and discon-
certing to a health professional unfamiliar with polychromic cultures,
especially if family members are discussing a major medical decision
regarding a child. It can be particularly so if the family is one in which

individuals other than the parents are the decision makers as it is for the Roma people (Gropper, 1996). Kleinman asserted the following: "... the family is the decision maker" (1988, p. 260). Another complicating factor may arise where a family comes from a high context culture in which affect is accentuated. Although mainstream Americans, especially from the Midwest, tend to be low context, for example, little display of emotions, many diverse groups, such as African Americans, Latino and Hispanics, and Southeast Asians, are high context (O'Hara-Devereaux, 1994). High context cultures are characterized by outward expression of emotions, may need less personal space, and may have more ritualistic greetings. Notwithstanding these broad categorizations, it is important to remember that individual differences are found in every culture.

Culture and the Concept of the Family: Multiple and Diverse

Assumptions may be made that all families are similar in structure despite the dynamic changes in the American family. The North American family has been characteristically classified as nuclear especially because the industrial revolution shaped it to be so. Families, too, may self-identify as nuclear or extended. The nuclear family includes the parents and children only, whereas extended families may incorporate several generations under the same household. The extended family structure, characteristic of diverse groups and Native Peoples in the United States, may be composed of the parents, grandparents, children, uncles, aunts, or cousins.

Why is the concept of the family important in health care settings? Depending on the cultural background of the family, the decision maker(s) may be someone other than the mother or the father. This complicates the health care experience when multiple family members come to a clinical appointment or to a hospital visit. The authority roles in a family may differ from those of the traditional nuclear family. In the Roma culture, the mother-in-law is the decision maker (Gropper, 1996), whereas in the Vietnamese culture, it may be the grandmother or aunt, depending on who stays home to care for the children. For some Muslims, like for the Roma people, the mother-in-law is the decision maker. The Latin American and Hispanic culture varies depending on who makes up the family and who cares for the children. Somali widow mothers became the decision makers, unlike their cultural tradition, although often their oldest child participated in that role because he or she acquired French or English skills much sooner than the mothers (Vargas, 1999a, 1999b). Thus, family-centered care, as described in Chapter 2, may take different shapes, forms, and modalities when working with diverse families. Although cultural sensitivity is one of the features of family-centered care, the practice may still lag the rhetoric.

Major Features of Western (Biomedical) Medicine and Traditional Medicine

If there is any bewilderment over the reason for the need to discuss traditional medicine in the most technologically advanced country in the world, the fact remains that "The number of people without health insurance coverage rose to 41.2 million (14.6 percent of the population) in 2001, up 1.4 million from the previous year, when 14.2 percent of the population lacked coverage" (U.S. Census Bureau, 2001, p. 2). Some estimate the number of uninsured Americans to be as high as 75 million Americans in the last 2 years due to the economic recession. A significant subset of these people may rely on traditional medicine, for different reasons, as the only way to deal with health problems. Some do so because that is the only medicine they know whereas for others it is the treatment they may perceive that they can afford or to which they have access. Others, although they have health insurance, are looking into alternative therapies as complementary to modern medicine. Moreover, ethnocultural groups and indigenous people have relied on traditional medicine for centuries and continue to do so today. It is estimated that about 80% of the world's population rely on traditional medicine[1] (World Health Organization, 2003).

Traditional medicine has been practiced and has contributed to human health for longer than three thousand years. It is considered as a great treasure-house in human history. Traditional medicine refers to ways of promoting, protecting and restoring human health. It existed before the arrival of modern medicine. As the term implies, these are approaches to health belonging to the traditions and culture of each nation, and have been inherited from generation to generation. These traditional approaches, in general, have had to meet the needs of the local communities for many centuries. China and India, for example, have developed very sophisticated systems of acupuncture and Ayurvedic medicine (World Health Organization, 2003, p. 1).

Thus, when serving children with disabilities, families may understand the disability according to their cosmology and traditional medicine concepts. If the health care professional does not acknowledge the symbols or supernatural causes to which families may attribute an illness, disorder, or disability, not only will communication be compromised but also treatment (Barker, 1992). It is important, then, to understand the major differences between traditional medicine and modern or biomedicine as illustrated in Table 3.1.

---

[1]According to Dr. Yuji Kawaguchi, Director of the World Health Organization's Kobe Center, in his opening speech at the International Symposium on Traditional Medicine.

TABLE 3.1

Major Features of Western (Biomedical) Medicine and Traditional Medicine

Traditional Medicine	Western or Biomedicine
Considers the patient as a whole	Considers disease and disability
Minimal cost; easily accessed	High cost; not always accessible
Based on traditions	Based on scientific, empirical data
Frequently combined with magic and religious practices	Ignores magic, religious, or spiritual aspects
Relies on therapeutic alliance with the healer	Relies on therapeutic alliance with the clinician
Personal and community healer	Impersonal, big clinic or hospital, though historically empathy and compassion essential
Uses natural ingredients; inexpensive; easily accessible	Uses pharmacopoeia; can be expensive; by prescription
Symbols are essential	Not based on symbols but on research
Spiritual bases of health and well-being	Physiological or cognitive and affective
Supernatural causes	Natural causes
Circular, not a single cause; not unidirectional	Linear concept of illness based on etiology
Emphasis: interconnectedness (mind, body, and spirit)	Focus on the physical illness, treatment, health prevention, and health promotion as opposed to the whole person
Helpers as experts	Helpers as experts
Patient's faith in God, the Creator, and karmic law is essential	Confidence in physician and medicines
Nonformal, lifelong training	Formal training after college
Taboo foods at certain times	Allergies
Ceremonies and rituals are essential	Ceremonies not part of treatment, but has rituals, for example, history taking
Traditional healer is selected by God, karma, or by the Creator	Self-selected
Healer's faith in God, Creator; karmatic order is essential to heal	Doctor's competence in training and prescription of appropriate drugs

Note. Sources: Vargas, 2001a, 2001b (Prof. Vargas [2001a, 2001b] originally developed this table with elements from Garza, 1998; Kleinman, 1988; and Spigelblatt, n.d.).

79

Specialization has characterized modern medicine to the point that specialists focus on a particular part of the body. Traditional medicine, on the other hand, because it is based on a holistic approach, acknowledges that health is the result of equilibrium among mind, body, and spirit (Locust, 1989). Thus, for a health care practitioner, a child with a disability may be perceived from the angle of a differential diagnosis, whether the illness or disorder is cognitive or physiological in origin, to concentrate on the treatment. However, from a traditional medicine perspective, the mind, body, and spirit connection need to be explored to create balance in that person's life. There is a physiological and cognitive as well as a spiritual explanation for an illness or disability. The cosmology, whether based on God, a Creator, or Karma law, provides an understanding of a disability. A disability may be attributed to a violation of spiritual law or punishment for past grievances. In the Native American and Mexican indigenous people's cosmology, a person with a disability is considered to be a higher spirit who chooses to be born in a body with challenges to teach lessons to others. In this sense, an illness or a disability is perceived as circular, connected to previous lives as well as to future spiritual life. Hence, it may be said that indigenous groups operate from a strengths-based perspective. This is in contrast to modern medicine that may view it as linear and unconnected to previous or future spiritual life, although the field of genetics looks at the genetic makeup of previous and of potential future generations.

Because of such a worldview, the aim of a traditional healer, as Locust (1995) explained, is not to ignore or totally heal the challenge, but to foster balance and adopt an attitude that will help a person be in harmony. It is not about "totally" eliminating the disability or the injury, but about how to live with it. This concept of balance is equally important to other cultures. Traditional Chinese Medicine has the concept of Qi, or the balance of energy in the body, or the law of unity of opposites, Yin and Yang, one of the features of Taoism. Health is equated with balance and harmony (Woo & Li, 2001). Balance is an important element to each of the three spiritual influences in Chinese culture—Confucianism, Taoism, and Buddhism (Woo & Li, 2001).

Traditional healers, be they Chinese medicine doctors, shamans, or witch doctors, are also trusted because their expertise is readily accessible. They are often personal advisors and community leaders whose healing gift is available to those who need it and often at no cost or low cost.

On the other hand, modern medicine is unaffordable to most people especially for those who are uninsured. Biomedicine training is expensive and so are its treatments. Yet, although traditional medicine is not associated with a monetary value in terms of training, traditional healers spend their lifetime in training. In fact, they are recognized at birth and the training may start soon thereafter. The training is rigorous from their perspective because they have to train their mind, body, and spirit. Such training includes knowledge of medicinal herbs, ability to recognize people's needs, as well as specific rituals and ceremonies necessary for healing. These healing practices are based on knowledge acquired through centuries of practice. A common characteristic in both types of medicines is that the physician and the traditional healer are both perceived as experts. Although medical practitioners are bound by professional standards and ethical codes, traditional healers earn their standing on the beliefs that they are selected by God, by Karma, or by the Creator. Both types of healers use rituals, although traditional healers may use elaborate ceremonies. The responsibility of both is demanding. In addition to professional accountability that applies to Western clinicians, traditional healers are also often accountable to the community.

Another similarity traditional medicine and modern medicine share is that both recognize an etiology, diagnosis, and treatment of an illness or disability, although each may attribute a symptom to a different cause. For example, traditional medicine may attribute an illness to eating taboo foods at certain times, as during pregnancy or during a menstrual period. On the other hand, modern medicine may attribute an illness to allergies—to seafood, dairy products, or genetic disorders. These two types of medicine also differ regarding treatment, although ancient cultures, for example the Mayans, practiced surgery.

Although modern medicine is slowly beginning to recognize the importance of respecting patients' faith in symbols or traditional healing practices (Kleinman, 1988), there has been a clear boundary between traditional medicine and modern medicine in hospital settings. Latin American or Afro-Caribbean patients in hospitals may wear religious medals, or keep images of the Virgin of Guadalupe, Crucifix, or statues of Saints at their bedside, or Native Americans arrive for a medical procedure with body painting for spiritual protection (Locust, 2002). Southeast Asians, such as Vietnamese, may have a Buddha or may conduct the Ban skol, the Buddhist ceremony for the loss of the dead. Persons from Middle Eastern cultures use different types of symbols and healing practices including, for instance, incense or myrrh, olive oil, or lemons, or they may have to read the Koran (also referred to as Qur'an or Alcoran). Some medical care practitioners, unfortunately, have scoffed at such practices. Instead, they have insisted that it was their medications and medical procedures that were going to cure the illness and, in some cases, have removed these symbols without the permission of the patients. Patients' spirituality was not only disrespected, but was also violated. Fortunately, the call for cultural competence is beginning to change this.

This discussion of traditional health care is not meant to suggest that it is somehow superior to modern, Western medicine. Modern, evidence-based practice has brought so many important advances to children and families. It is intended to caution clinicians to be aware of and alert to the beliefs and perceptions of those we serve.

Cross-Cultural Concepts of Disability: A Strengths- or Deficit-Based Model

The perceptions of disability cross-culturally are quite mixed. Some view disabilities as a deficit, a defect, something of which to be ashamed, or evidence of God's punishment, as it is for the Vietnamese and for Latin Americans. Other cultures do not even have a word for disability or may refer to a particular disability by its physical characteristic. For instance, Native American cultures, indigenous cultures in Mexico, and other Latin American countries, rather than excluding persons with disabilities, see them as individuals with particular talents according to what they are able to do; in other words, they see the strengths and not the disability (Fletcher & Bos, 1999; Locust, 1996, 1997). People with disabilities, in Western cultures and non-Western cultures, often have been discriminated against due to their disabilities. There is a dark history of imprisonment, chaining, and torturing, although some of these practices continue in some countries. In response to advocates for more humane alternatives, such as Dorothea Lyn Dix in the 19th century, institutionalization became an alternative to previous incarceration practices (Ellery, 2001). Although institutionalization may be considered inhumane by today's standards, the practice continues in many places.

Non-Western cultures may also attribute disabilities to negative experiences, taboos, or forbidden behaviors (deficit-based model). These have to do with violations of strictures during pregnancy or after giving birth. They may also attribute disabilities to physiological reasons that may affect a fetus during pregnancy, for example, if the woman eats the "wrong food." Another reason that may constitute a violation of a pregnancy rule is to be outside during an eclipse without proper protection (Latin America). Other physiological explanations have to do with prenatal or postnatal problems such as movements of wind in the body—that the body is out of balance or in disharmony, that there is excess heat in the body, or a violation of a menstrual taboo. A woman bathing in a river, for example, may trigger a disability in the unborn. A violation of birth rituals may abode an omen to a child. For Latin Americans, a common cause of illness has to do with the *"Caida de mollera"* (fallen fontanel). The case of the Mexican mother of a child with Down's syndrome who assumed his condition was attributed to a fallen fontanel attempted to correct his disability by holding the baby upside down as if such action would correct the fallen fontanel and hence his disability

(Lynch & Hanson, 1992). The mother learned that such an intervention did not work and her child received a referral for special services.

Other explanations of disability include not only violations of birth control and social rules, but also may be ascribed to a contagion. In East Africa, epilepsy is explained on the basis of contact with someone or something considered a taboo. Various cultures around the world have the concept of an "evil eye," which is when someone looks at a pregnant woman or a beautiful child with envy or with evil intent. The result may be a serious illness for the mother or a disability for the baby. Anyone can be vulnerable to the evil eye. Among American Indian and Alaskan Natives, uttering words referring to a disability may provoke giving birth to a child with the disability (Locust, n.d.).

There are also magical or spiritual explanations of disabilities. Ominous sensations or ominous experiences as seeing a spirit, a particular animal, or having an ominous dream may be interpreted as a sign that the baby could be born with a disability or an illness. Although a pregnant mother may have signs of what is to come, there are instances in which she may fall victim of deliberate spells put on her by a bad witch at the request of a person who has ill feelings toward the mother-to-be. The pregnant woman may also be a victim of an unwitting spell. Various cultures attribute disabilities to bad luck or to a baby birth occurring on a negative alignment of the planets, therefore a bad astrology. African and Caribbean cultures may interpret a person with an illness or disability as the result of provoking a spirit or the incarnation of a spirit.

Although many Non-Western causes of illness or disability are in accord with a deficit model, there are a few that reflect a strengths perspective. In *The Spirit Catches You and You Fall Down*, Fadiman (1997) described the interaction among a Hmong child diagnosed with epilepsy, her family, and the American doctors who tried to take care of them. The family viewed the epilepsy only as a gift from the gods and considered that their daughter was especially gifted spiritually. They sought help from Western doctors when their daughter became very ill. However, the Western medical system was overwhelmingly confusing to them. The doctors never thought to ask the family their perspective on what was going on with their daughter. They viewed epilepsy only as a neurological pathology that needed medical intervention. The philosophical differences created a chasm of misunderstandings through which the daughter fell. The anticonvulsant drugs had serious side effects that frightened the parents, causing them to stop giving them to their daughter. Additionally, the directions were in English and very confusing. The story ends in tragedy, for the daughter became comatose and the doctors felt they failed her and her family.

Buddhist cultures may interpret the birth of a child with a disability according to Karma, the law of cause and effect; as paying for past bad deeds or reincarnation into a disabled body to teach others lessons, which may fall under a deficit-based model (Vargas, 2001b). What is critical according to Buddhism is to treat the disabled person well and with respect to avoid accumulating Karma. Everyone has the responsibility to do so, the family as well as the community. Last, a disability may be understood in terms of soul loss. For example, the affliction of a person with a mental disability is attributed to his or her soul leaving the body. In some cases, when this happens, it is believed that another spirit enters the body (Hiegel, 1994).

Although these general characteristics may apply to some members of a group, not everyone from a particular group adheres to those typically associated with them. Thus, it may be that a Latin American or Latino may not believe in the evil eye as it is true that not all Vietnamese practice coining. Recognition of some of the cultural explanations of disabilities may be helpful in understanding families who may hold such views, especially if the explanatory models are deficit-based. Notwithstanding this caution, it may be useful to ask the family members what meaning they attribute to the disability of a child or how they understand the disability in terms of their cultural framework.

CONSIDERATION OF CULTURAL, LINGUISTIC, AND ANCILLARY FACTORS THAT MAY LEAD TO MISDIAGNOSIS

In contemporary North America, factors other than spiritual explanations may result in a misdiagnosis, including differential treatment in diagnosis and treatment (Geiger, 2003). Some of these have had to do specifically with sociohistorical factors discussed earlier, such as segregation, discrimination, pervasive socioeconomic inequalities, and unequal treatment of minority groups and of American Indians and Native Alaskans in the health care field. In some instances, children from minority groups who spoke languages other than English were automatically considered unintelligent, conveying a message to minorities that intelligence was limited to English speakers. Hence, Hispanics, for example, had been historically segregated to special education classes on that basis alone.

In school settings, children often have faced similar challenges resulting in misdiagnosis as attested by the U.S. Congress:

> Studies have documented apparent discrepancies in the levels of referral and placement of limited English proficient children in special education. The Department of Education [of the United States government] has found that services provided to limited English proficient students often do not respond primarily to the pupil's academic needs. These trends pose special challenges for special education in the referral, assessment, and services

for our Nation's students from non-English language background. (Individuals with Disabilities Act Amendments of 1997, 20 USC 1400)

Persistent Challenges With Standardized Assessment and Differential Diagnosis

Because standardized assessment tools have traditionally been normed and referenced on mainstream Euro–American, middle class groups, these instruments have posed problems when applied to children from diverse cultural backgrounds (Artiles & Ortiz, 2002; Figueroa, 2002; Kayser, 1998). Applications of these tools to children from diverse ethnocultural, racial, and linguistic backgrounds certainly have led to misdiagnosis for several reasons. First, the children's cultural background affects how they understand and interpret questions. For instance, children from certain cultural groups tend to be divergent thinkers, thus when answering a question on a multiple choice test, they see more than one possible answer. Although standardized tests may have high reliability and high predictability, minorities may be totally unfamiliar with experiences captured in the items (Artiles & Ortiz, 2002; Figueroa, 2002). Second, tests and assessment tools may be administered by professionals who may be unaware of cultural factors potentially influencing interpretation of questions and responses, including a priori stereotyping (Kayser, 1998). In North America, the lack of bilingual–bicultural personnel has made this even more difficult.

Third, children whose native language is other than English may not have the cognitive, academic language proficiency (CALP) to do as well as native English speakers. These children may present an uneven knowledge of English. That is, they may have, on one hand, vocabulary that is more sophisticated than their age cohort, whereas on another, they may lack common vocabulary (Vargas, 2002).[2] For example, Spanish speakers may be familiar with vocabulary considered common in Spanish but advanced in English. Words such as castigar (to castigate, to punish), suficiente (sufficient, enough), comprender (to comprehend, to understand), or catarro (catarrhal, cold) may be difficult for native English speakers in elementary school but very familiar for Spanish speakers. Thus, testing, even when using bilingual tests, "assumes that lexical and semantic variations across these countries are insignificant in a testing situation in which contextual clues are deliberately diminished, if not excluded" (Figueroa, 2002, p. 54).

---

[2]Personal communication, November 26, 1999, with Afarin Beglari, Cultural Interpreter of the Multicultural Liaison Program, Ottawa, Canada, conducted by Claudia María Vargas (Vargas, 2002).

There is still the need to do assessments through cultural interpreters for languages with no native or bilingual language assessment tools available. These cases present unique challenges because testing through interpreters has been shown to affect validity and reliability (Figueroa, 2002, p. 54; Westermeyer, 1990). It is important to brief with the cultural interpreter to make sure he or she understands the goals of the assessment and nature of the tools (Beglari & Huong Thai, 2000; Kayser, 1998; Vargas, 2000). After completion of the assessment, the evaluator needs to debrief with the cultural interpreter to review any obstacles encountered in the process, whether cultural or linguistic (Kayser, 1998). However, as Vargas (2000) underscored, there is one more critical step, what she called "beyond briefing and debriefing" or the need to follow-up with the family who is often left bewildered with a multitude of names of professionals, unfamiliar treatments, and perplexed over the implications of the diagnosis of their child, not to mention the cultural implications of a disability. As Beglari and Huong Thai (2000) point out, they, as cultural interpreters, continue to work with the families long after the professionals provide a diagnosis and leave. They frequently substitute for the specialized health professional in teaching the parent, for example, specific strategies for working with a child with autism. For families with no English background and totally unfamiliar with the service delivery system, the maze is even more bewildering than for the mainstream group.

Another obstacle has to do specifically with a lack of knowledge of the background of refugee children and children adopted from deprived orphanages. In some countries, these orphanages have become the dumping grounds for children who have been considered disposable for economic reasons (Cooper & Vargas, 2004). Although many refugee and adopted children may adapt without major challenges, except for those associated with cultural adjustment, others may suffer from posttraumatic stress disorder (PTSD), depression, or reactive attachment disorder, as was the experience of Natasha. Specifically, she was challenged with "excessive familiarity with relative strangers" or "frozen watchfulness" (American Psychiatric Association, 2000, p. 130; Kaler & Freeman, 1994). Refugee children who have experienced war violence, directly or as a witness, may be affected by PTSD (as well as reactive attachment disorder), yet there is a dearth of intervention programs, especially for preschool and adolescent children, whose needs may go undiagnosed and unmet (Vargas, 2002). Knowledge of the conditions of their early years of life may shed some light on what challenges they may face in their host country. In this sense, Natasha was fortunate to have a mother who was proactive in seeking information and help for her child, the subject of the next section.

Revisiting the Case Study: When Emotional Deprivation and Posttraumatic Stress Disorder Leads to the Wrong Diagnosis

The VT–ILEHP team decided to do a community assessment to take a fresh look at the challenges Natasha faced, as it does with every family served. To do so, the VT–ILEHP team consulted with the community team and family to explore the questions posed by each. The mother's questions were as follows: (a) Does Natasha have attention-deficit disorder (ADD) or emotional response to earlier experiences? (b) How and when does transition to kindergarten take place? (c) What are some recommendations for intervention and support of Natasha's social functioning? The adoptive mother expressed concern regarding Natasha's speech development, attention span, and attachment concerns. At the time of the adoption, Natasha's speech development was limited to a few or almost no words, although she was 2 years old. Since her arrival to the United States, however, her speech has developed remarkably.

The school staff's questions, among others, were as follows: (a) Does she exhibit characteristics of autism? (b) Does she experience tactile sensitivity and what should be done? (c) What are some recommendations for speech, language, and social development? (d) What should be done about some of the behaviors she displays? The staff conveyed a sense of urgency over her symptoms: lying in a fetal position the floor, staring blankly into space, and echoing back when someone spoke to her. Before attempting to answer some of these questions, it is necessary to define and explain some of these diagnoses.

What Is Reactive Attachment Disorder of Infancy or Early Childhood? The impact of sterile institutionalization was first recognized in response to the stymied development of orphan children institutionalized after World War II. According to the *Diagnostic and Statistical Manual of Mental Disorders* (4th ed., text revision; DSM–IV–TR; American Psychiatric Association, 2000), attachment disorder is attributed to the experience of deprived, barren environments—orphanages for instance, in which children lacked appropriate and consistent caretaking—stymieing emotional, cognitive, and even physical development. "The essential feature of Reactive Attachment Disorder is markedly disturbed and developmentally inappropriate social relatedness in most contexts that begins before age 5 years and is associated with grossly pathological care" (American Psychiatric Association, 2000, p. 127). Furthermore, the DSM–IV–TR states the following caution: "Reactive Attachment Disorder must be differentiated from Autistic Disorder and other Pervasive Developmental Disorders" (American Psychiatric Association, 2000, p. 129).

What is PTSD?   A fairly recent disorder, PTSD was recognized in 1980 in the *Diagnostic and Statistical Manual of Mental Disorders* (4th ed.; DSM–III) in response to the Vietnam veterans' plea to mental health professionals for help with their affliction. In children, the studies lag behind those in adults, though it is a burgeoning field (Perry & Azad, 1999; van der Kolk, 2002). What is PTSD and how does it affect children and adolescents? According to the DSM–IV–TR (American Psychiatric Association, 2000), there are four major factors associated with PTSD: arousal, avoidance, intrusion, and numbing (Sack, Seeley, & Clarke, 1997). Refugee children and adopted children from deprived orphanages may be afflicted by PTSD and attachment disorder (van der Kolk, 2002). Although it is not widely recognized, recent studies indicate that these children may be misdiagnosed with a number of other disorders due to a similarity in symptoms. These misdiagnoses include the following: ADHD, mental delay, autism, bipolar disorder, obsessive compulsive disorder (OCD), schizophrenia, or psychosis (Perry & Azad, 1999). Specifically, refugee children often present attention problems, psychic numbing, or listlessness that may be confused with ADHD or features of autism. They also encounter difficulties with emotional regulation and thus may be misdiagnosed with bipolar disorder. Because PTSD can also produce dissociative features, it has been confused with a diagnosis of schizophrenia.

What Are Relevant Health Issues to Consider in Complex Adoptions? Although the compassion of Americans has been moved regarding appalling conditions in orphanages, there are important factors to consider, especially for children who have been harmed by institutional conditions or have endured abuse. If the children have been victimized, physically, sexually or mentally, their profile will be even more challenging. There may be health issues such as soiling or bed-wetting, sleep difficulties, distractibility, night terrors, unusual startle response, malnutrition, and intestinal infections.

Specific Challenges in Diagnosing a Disability: Potential for Error. Commonly, immigrant and refugee children go through a phase during which they may remain silent. The silence may be attributed to the exhaustion caused by the migration and exile experience (Igoa, 1995). It may also be due to the time during which the children are learning the second language, are having a great deal of input, but may still be unable to articulate responses (Hadley, 1993). Conversely, the silent period may be originating from a developmental psychopathology (Carlson & Sroufe, 1995), environmental deprivation, and subsequent attachment disorder (Beckett et al., 2002; Kaler & Freeman, 1994).

Health professionals may want to rule out whether the child is experiencing typical second language learning issues or whether the child does indeed have a learning disability (Vargas, 2002). A second language assessment of all four skills—listening, speaking, reading, and writing—may be necessary to determine if a child has developed proficient listening and speaking skills but may be struggling with reading and writing skills. An assessment of the child's cognitive-academic language proficiency (CALP) (Cummins, 1986, 1996; Hernández, 1997) may shed light on it. This is particularly significant because a common assumption is that if a child demonstrates proficiency in basic interpersonal communicative skills (BICS), such as conversations with peers or in class, then he or she has acquired the necessary language skills to do well in academic subjects. However, it takes children from 5 to 8 years to acquire CALP, the academic language, often abstract, necessary to do well in academic subjects (Hernández, 1997; Kayser, 1998).

Is it Seizure Disorder or Comorbidity of Attachment Disorder and PTSD? To support Natasha's growth and development, it was critical to do an assessment to determine what was influencing her challenges. Although adopted at a younger age, under 5, the child's development was still at a malleable stage. However, this did not preclude the experience of trauma or deprivation in the orphanage. Natasha had in fact been in two orphanages and was exposed to two different languages, although she had received little stimuli to develop either one. Her adoption, although a positive experience with the prospect of a loving mother and a stable home, represented yet another cultural adjustment. It also brought her face to face with still another language, English. For Natasha, there was evidence of attachment disorder and PTSD. The VT–ILEHP team ruled out a diagnosis of seizure disorder. What the school labeled as seizure was Natasha's frozen watchfulness or listlessness, which may be associated with PTSD as well as with reactive attachment disorder. Some of these behaviors Beckett et al. considered "quasi-autistic behavior[s]" (2002, p. 297).

In her new homeland, Natasha was facing the challenge of acquiring English. This was complicated by the fact that her adoptive mother was multilingual and was raising Natasha to be bilingual, English and French.

Bilingual children face other challenges that may lead to a misdiagnosis. A relevant question to ask for a bilingual child may be, "Is it language interference or learning disabilities?" A bilingual child is naturally acquiring the linguistic system of two languages, unlike a monolingual, native English speaker. Thus, he or she may be trying to understand the linguistic system of the second language and, in the meantime, uses structures, sounds, and a lexicon from one language to compensate for those unknown in the second language. This may affect phonology, syntax, semantics, and pragmatics (Hadley, 1993). Native American children, for example, are often diagnosed as learning or language disabled because their first language may not have sounds of the English language and thus may mispronounce words. Their ability to speak another language, unfortunately, has been perceived as a deficit. However, this could be easily resolved through a deliberate teaching of the unfamiliar sounds through "The Silent Way," or the Orton-Gilligham Multisensory Approach (Sparks, Granschow, Kenneweg, & Miller, 1991), or any other tactics that may help them learn. Once these issues have been considered and problems persist, additional assessment may be necessary to rule out learning disabilities.

Neurodevelopmental Disabilities and Cultural Misunderstandings in the Health Professions

There are challenges that arise related to the expectations of the parents about the outcomes of a treatment in direct contrast to the expectation of the health professionals. The challenges may be based on cultural perceptions or stigma attached to a disability, physical or mental. Because a family member with a disability may bring disgrace to that family in the eyes of his or her community, there may be expectations of treatment that will erase all evidence of past regressions, as it is for the Vietnamese and other Southeast Asian cultures (Singh, 2000; Van Le, 2000). Thus, even when health professionals perform the best surgery or follow the best treatment from a biomedical perspective, cultural factors may affect how the parents or families perceive the outcomes of treatment. This is illustrated in the following example.

Sun Ye was a 3-year-old American-born son of a Vietnamese refugee. He was born with a cleft lip and palate. The family was Buddhist and had a shrine in their living room. Oranges and apples were set on plates in front of the Buddha statue as offerings. Part of their belief system was that troubles in this life were brought on by the misdeeds of the ancestors. Occurrences, such as a child born with a cleft lip, were very public, visual reminders of familial shame. Having had the usual repair done during the first year of life, he was now returning to the local cleft palate team for a final evaluation. The cleft palate team functions as an arena-style interdisciplinary team. Sun Ye's mother, Lee, required an interpreter. Lee had one primary concern. She wanted Sun Ye's hairline scar removed.

Sun Ye was a charming little boy with a ready smile and outgoing personality. He evoked smiles from all the providers at the clinic. They had spent the morning seeing many children with intensive special needs.

Sun Ye was a breath of fresh air to the team. His scar was very light, having no impact on the line of his lips. All the providers were very pleased with Sun Ye's progress and appearance. Lee became more and more upset as her request to have the scar removed was brushed aside. She left the clinic very angry. The providers ended the visit feeling good about their work and largely unaware of the impact of Sun Ye's scar in the life of his family. For Lee, this scar was a visible reminder to her and all in her world that they were being punished for past wrongdoings. She was humiliated.

Paradigm Blindness When Doing a Priori Diagnosis: Is it PTSD or Attachment Disorder, or ASD, or ADHD?   Paradigm blindness is when an individual or group fails to see alternatives because of having embedded beliefs that support a rigid and all-encompassing worldview. For Natasha, there were several issues that may have led to paradigm blindness. Clearly, the child-care staff was at odds with the mother's perception and the evaluation of the consulting team. Embedded beliefs are usually unconscious assumptions about how the world should work (Kalyanpur & Harry, 1999). The child-care providers expressed concern regarding what they considered to be the mother's lack of recognition of the scale of the child's needs—emotional, affective, and cognitive. They interpreted Natasha's gazing into space as seizure activity, although Natasha never appeared to be lost or confused. The mother tried to underscore that, but there was clearly a difference in opinion. Although school team members were clearly bonded to the child, they were critical of the mother. In particular, they felt that the mother did not respond as she should to her daughter's needs. They were critical of this professional mother's busy career and frequent travel, and were adamant that she should stay at home. What the mother saw as the strengths of her daughter, the educational team interpreted as her naïveté toward her daughter. Although the mother had provided the staff with current articles on attachment disorder, the team refused to consider that possible diagnosis and appeared to disregard the relevance of the articles. The school team was insistent on an autism diagnosis instead of an attachment disorder due to the child's persistent behaviors—looking at the ceiling, attachment to inanimate objects, and repeated demands to have certain stories read and continuous requests of "I want a hug."

The interdisciplinary team's intake coordinator interviewed the mother and school case manager regarding the questions they wanted answered. The rift between the family and school became apparent. The school wanted the interdisciplinary team to work through a diagnosis of autism for Natasha. The mother felt strongly that Natasha did not have autism but rather exhibited the classic symptoms of reactive attachment disorders characteristic of children with similar backgrounds as Natasha's. The intake coordinator negotiated with the mother to let the interdisciplinary team consider the autism question. It was reasoned that by doing so, it would resolve the autism diagnosis and provide a format for working through a possible diagnosis of PTSD and reactive attachment disorder. The team worked on these goals and ultimately reached an appropriate differential diagnosis. The result was that the child received the proper diagnosis, the school team was educated, the mother felt like an integral part of the assessment and that her questions were honored, and the relationships among the community providers and the family became more collaborative.

How to Deal With Cultural Bias in Assessment Tools

Before conducting an assessment, there are several questions health professionals may want to consider that address the possible effects of cultural factors. The following ones may be helpful: (a) What is the first language of the child? (b) Where did the child attend school? (c) What is the primary language or what languages are spoken at home? (d) On what population was the assessment tool normed? (e) Are there any assessment instruments normed on specific ethnocultural or racial groups? (f) Are there any assessment tools in the first language of the child? (g) Is there a need for a cultural interpreter for the family? (h) Is the family comfortable with the cultural interpreter selected, or are there potential ethical conflicts in working with a particular interpreter? (See Vargas, 1998, 1999a, 1999b, for a discussion on ethical dilemmas in working with cultural interpreters.) (i) What additional supports will the family need regarding translated relevant materials, referrals to bilingual professionals, continued need for an interpreter, among others? (j) How effective is the current instructional program? (k) Has the child been observed in multiple contexts (Figueroa, 2002)? Although many more questions could be generated, it is relevant to consider each family's unique needs. These questions provide a vehicle.

CULTURAL COMPETENCE CONCERNS SPECIFIC TO NEURODEVELOPMENTAL DISABILITIES

As interactions between health professionals and diverse groups in clinical contexts increase, there is a need to consider what constitutes success regarding treatment or interventions for the health professional as well as for the family. In these circumstances, the expert model may be perceived by traditional families as insufficient or as complicating matters more for the child as well as the family. The next example captures that point.

Organizational Culture in Health Professions: A Mother's Perspective on Medical Success Under the Veil of a Traditional Belief System

When health care providers feel they have delivered a good service and the intended recipient is upset, is in disagreement with interventions, has ethical concerns, and feels unheard, it may be an indication that the care has been incongruent with his or her beliefs (Leininger, 1991). In the story of Sun Ye, the doctors probably felt they delivered excellent care, following all the established procedures for treatment of cleft lip and palate. They felt successful because the culture dictates that a physician provides the best treatment and moves on. Sun Ye's mother, Lee, felt the doctors had lied to her. She reported the surgeon had said she would not be able to see the scar, that it would look great, and that if she were not happy with it, he would fix it. Lee took him literally at his word. She wanted the scar completely removed. The surgeon was surprised that she was concerned because Sun Ye was a beautiful child with a barely perceptible scar. He saw nothing and she saw everything. Lee would not directly confront the surgeon because he represented the authority figure. Culturally for her, this would not be appropriate. She reported her dissatisfaction to the nurse and wanted something done about it.

Precluding Past Discriminatory Practices: Misdiagnosis in Multicultural Groups

The evidence supports the fact that there is overrepresentation of children from diverse backgrounds who are labeled with a disability. In Individuals with Disabilities Education Act Amendments of 1997 (IDEA), Congress recognized the following:

> Greater efforts are needed to prevent the intensification of problems connected with mislabeling and high dropout rates among minority children with disabilities.

> More minority children continue to be served in special education that would be expected from the percentage of minority students in the general school population.

> Poor African–American children are 2.3 times more likely to be identified by their teacher as having mental retardation than their white counterpart.

> Although African–Americans represent 16 percent of elementary and secondary enrollments, they constitute 21 percent of total enrollments in special education.

> The drop-out rate is 68 percent higher for minorities than whites.

More than 50 percent of minority students in large cities drop out of school. (1997, p. 5)

Because of a number of societal inequities, minority children continue to suffer as they are underserved, or poorly served not only by the health system but also by the education system.

Ebonics Dialect or Learning Disabilities?   African American children have too often been misdiagnosed with learning disabilities based on the fact that they may use Ebonics at school and the school may simply be unfamiliar with it, as the next story exemplifies. (For a definition of Ebonics, see the glossary.)

Jimmy Jones was a 7-year-old African American boy with a sparkly personality and mischievous sense of humor. He was living with his maternal aunt and her husband. His birth mother was living on the West coast and heavily involved in drug abuse. His uncle (foster father) was White and the primary contact for the school team. The school speech and language pathologist was seeing Jimmy for a speech and language delay. However, one day the uncle confided in one of the VT–ILEHP team members that Jimmy spoke "White English" at school, but that he usually spoke "Black English" at home. The speech language pathologist trainee from the interdisciplinary team reassessed Jimmy with a tool sensitive to cultural differences, the Test of Language Development. It was discovered that Jimmy did not have an expressive language delay but rather was speaking Ebonics at school. In this situation Jimmy could have been left to deal with the subconscious discrimination of school personnel and its psychological burden for him, internally, and with the burden of a label, externally. Through the intervention of the team, the label was precluded and the appropriate supports were provided to help Jimmy also become fluent in standard English.

Integration of Western (Biomedicine) and Traditional Medicine

A remaining challenge continues to be how to integrate biomedicine with traditional medicine (Duran, Duran, Yellow Horse Brave Heart, & Yellow Horse-Davis, 1998; Locust, 1996, 1997; Mphande & Myers, 1993; Pachter, 1984). Dr. Locust continues to provide an invaluable contribution in this area regarding the experience of American Indians and Native Alaskans. Through lectures and case studies, she continually illustrates examples in which there appeared to be conflict between the two, and how, through her interventions, it was deflected.

Southeast Asians confront conflicts, too. In an interview, the first author (Vargas, 2001b) discussed the experience of a distraught Cambodian mother over the condition of her teenage daughter with Dr. Walpola

Piyananda, a Buddhist monk. As has become prevalent in female Americans obsessed with how slender they must be to be socially accepted and to be attractive, this Cambodian young woman was plagued with anorexia nervosa and bulimia. Her perilous condition had resulted in a hospitalization. Her deteriorated condition meant a long recovery period was necessary, but the physicians were not hopeful. Believing that her daughter was possessed by a "hungry ghost," the mother did not feel that the doctors could help her daughter. She decided to take her daughter and left the hospital.

Instead, the mother took the daughter to the Buddhist temple she frequented. Her daughter was so emaciated that the mother was able to carry her in her arms into the temple and placed her at the feet of the Buddha statue. Bhante (brother) Piyananda rushed to them as the mother cried and pleaded for help saying that her daughter was possessed by a "hungry ghost." Although traditionally, monks do not touch women, the mother laid her daughter's head on Bhante Piyananda's lap while he held her hand and chanted. Both the mother and daughter seemed to respond to the soothing chanting that Bhante Piyananda assured them would eliminate the "hungry ghost." Meanwhile, he asked his assistant monk to puree a fresh apple to feed the youngster. While chanting, he fed her the fresh applesauce a little at a time. To the mother's relief, the daughter was able to hold down the food and fell asleep. Bhante Piyandanda instructed the mother to take her daughter home and to prepare chicken soup. He told the mother that he would go to their home to chant for her daughter and feed her the soup.

Later that evening, he repeated the chanting and asked the mother to grind the chicken meat with the stock and he fed it to the woman's daughter. After a 6-month period, the girl fully recovered with additional spiritual counseling by Dr. Piyandada and psychotherapy by a culturally responsive psychologist. The origin of the anorexia nervosa was that the young woman felt she would be unable to find a boyfriend. According to Bhante Piyananda, this young woman finished school, got a job, and is now happily married. She recovered from the anorexia nervosa.

When Traditional Practices Collide with Biomedicine

There are instances, of course, when some practices in traditional medicine may be in conflict with current biomedical ethical standards as well as with child protection laws (see, for example, Graham, Domoto, Lynch, & Egbert, 2000). These conflicts are not restricted to traditional medicine, as there is evidence of ethical dilemmas in some previous or new medical treatments, such as gene therapy. According to Vargas (1999b), cultural interpreters have played a role in bridging these types of dissonance. The next story (Samantar, 2000) demonstrates that conflict.

A Somali teenager was taken to a traditional healer because she appeared to be suffering from a spirit possession (Sharp, 1994). The treatment consisted in giving the girl a severe beating so as "to beat the devil out of her." The young woman was severely injured and the abrasions were becoming seriously infected. Shukria Samantar, a well-respected cultural interpreter in Ottawa, Canada, heard about the situation through a friend of the family. Although not directly involved, Samantar emphatically conveyed the message that it was critical to take the young girl to the hospital for treatment and that if anything happened to the teenager the parents would be held legally accountable by the authorities. The message got to the family. The parents immediately took the girl to the hospital. The consequence of this experience was that the Somali community got a clear message that this particular traditional healer could not be trusted. The other message was that such practices would carry serious legal consequences. In the meantime, the young girl started receiving treatment for schizophrenia.

The question for health practitioners may remain, how to deal with such complexity? Although some clinical settings may have available cultural interpretation, others may be at a loss. The following section may provide some guidelines because there are no easy recipes to follow.

CULTURAL COMPETENCE IN SERVING CHILDREN WITH DISABILITIES AND THEIR FAMILIES

The cultural tapestry becomes more intricate in serving culturally diverse families with children who may have a disability, as there may be not only the minority status but also the challenges of a disability, as indicated earlier. There are also linguistic and cultural nuances that can transmute the message for both the health professional and for the family. Furthermore, there is the need to bridge the gap associated with lack of access to health care as well as with the quality differential for minorities and Indian Nations people. To meet such challenges, health professionals may need to undergo education to develop or to expand their knowledge and skills in cultural competence as well as to deal with covert and overt clinician and institutional discrimination. For VT–ILEHP, this continues to be an important element, although not one without complexities as the program has moved through various stages in that process.

What Cultural Competence Is Not

It may be useful to address what does not constitute cultural competence. Hadley (1993) associates three commonly mistaken approaches to cultural competence. The first approach she labeled, "the Frankestein approach" (Hadley, 1993, p. 360). It consists in using artifacts from a culture to convey cultural awareness. Everyone is familiar with classrooms decorated with piñatas, a hospital menu that includes tacos, burritos, enchiladas, or convention meals organized according to various ethnic foods. Second, Hadley described the "by-the-way approach" as "Sporadic lectures or bits of behavior selected indiscriminately to emphasize sharp differences" (p. 360). Last, she identified the 4-F approach, as "folk dances, festivals, fairs, and food" (Hadley, 1993, p. 360), the ideal and romantic heritage or experience of a people perceived through music, myths, dance, or holidays.

There are other ways that cultural competence is attempted, although also mistaken. The early part of the 20th century witnessed the use of tests to determine the intellectual superiority of Euro–Americans to other races or ethnicities. As late as the 1970s, scholars were supporting this notion. This is called the "pseudo-scientific racist ideologies" (United Nations, 1995, paragraph 29). The marketing of religious or cultural objects has become a common practice, too, from images of the Buddha to the Virgin of Guadalupe. The history of this country is also full of stereotypic depictions of groups as seen in television, movies, newspapers, and other media, for example, Native Americans as killers, Mexican Americans as lazy, Italians as gangsters, African Americans as welfare recipients, and Asians as overachievers. There are still others who perceive what is termed *high culture* defined as "higher class status derived from knowledge of arts, manners, and literature valued by the dominant society" (Rodriguez, 1995–1996, p. 14) as the only legitimate form of culture. This is a prime example of ascribed status discussed earlier in the chapter.

In an attempt to fit in, some individuals respond to cultural competence by abandoning their own culture and attempting to join another one (Rodriguez, 1995–1996). Others determine that the way to deal with the challenges of becoming culturally competent is by categorizing individuals "into totally discrete groups" while ignoring the intergroup as well as the intra-group diversity (Rodriguez, 1995–1996, p. 14). For instance, Asians are considered to be all the same, yet there are significant differences among Indians, Vietnamese, Chinese, Japanese, and Koreans. The same is true of Latinos and Hispanics whose ancestors were in the Southwest before the Pilgrims arrived in Plymouth; others may come from Mexico, Central America, or South America. Although one may think of American Indians or Native Alaskans and Native Hawaiians as a single group there are dramatic differences among them. In fact, there are over 500 Native American tribes and as many different languages. Last but equally important to consider regarding cultural competence is that "Culture is no excuse for abuse!" (New Zealand Ministry of Child, Youth, and Family, 2001; Violence study could vex Islanders, 1999, p. 7). That is, cultural practices that are harmful, even if widely practiced, cannot be excused on culture alone as the earlier story indicated. One of the tasks of cultural interpreters, according to Vargas (1998, 1999a, 1999b, 2000), has been to educate immigrant and refugee families on health practices that may be in conflict with legal or ethical mandates.

What Is Cultural Competence

Developing cultural competence is complex and not an easy task. Intervening factors include the remnants of past racial and ethnic segregation and discrimination, and clinician and institutional conscious and subconscious bias. In health settings, there is the problem of "the stereotyping called application error, in which epidemiologic information about a population group is inappropriately applied to any member of that group, without consideration of individual characteristics" (Geiger, 2003, p. 442). There are also communication problems, differential conceptions of health, illness, and disability. Hence, there is the social justice element as well as other logistic ones that impact health care (Vargas, 2001a, 2001b). First, cultural competence is *a long-term process*; it is *not* an event (Vargas, 2001a, 2001b). Any serious discussion needs to recognize the *multidimensional* nature of culture in that it affects every aspect of a person (for example, behavior, worldview, way of thinking, and nutrition, as well as societal inequities) (Vargas, 2001a, 2001b). As the case of Sun Ye illustrated, even the best medical intervention can go array if the cultural significance of a scar left from a cleft palate corrective surgery is not addressed. Because of the complexity in cultural meanings, it is important to be willing to *ask* when one does not know or is unsure. Equally important is to recognize that culture does not constitute race alone, but it is much more pervasive, transcending racial categories. This leads to a more complex landscape of what constitutes culture, hence the need to be able to deal with *ambiguity* (Vargas, 2001a, 2001b). In other words, health professionals cannot be expected to be fluent in all the cultures they encounter, thus they inevitably will confront situations in which they may feel puzzled. It then becomes necessary, especially in clinical settings, to *negotiate meanings*, whether it is to negotiate the meaning of an illness, the conception of a disability, or the cultural ramifications of a treatment. This is particularly important before giving a diagnosis and prescribing a treatment. Among the negotiated meanings, clinicians need to ask who makes up the family, and who makes decisions for the family.

Although North American societies are demand-driven, people from diverse cultures may be unaware of services available. Others may feel culturally ashamed to ask for government services. Thus, it may be necessary to *adapt* health care services to meet the needs of the groups that are served, as in the case of environmental health for children in the Central Valley of California or Detroit, MI, where the minority community is engaged as an equal partner in research and implementation of every health intervention (for a discussion of this, see Cooper and Vargas, 2004). Another critical point is to understand the complementarity of traditional medicine and Western medicine and that it is not a zero sum gain, but rather an interaction in which all parties win or that "1 + 1 = 3." Dr. Locust, for instance, works as an integral team member in the Native American Intensive Care Cardiac Unit at the University of Arizona,[3] providing the culturally appropriate and spiritual support for Native American patients. This, of course, does not mean that culture can override ethical and legal imperatives as "culture is no excuse of abuse" (New Zealand Ministry of Child, Youth, and Family, 2001; Violence Study Could Vex Islanders, 1999, p. 7).

As posited in the guidelines of helping professions, cultural competence requires health professionals to be *respectful, empathic, authentic,* and *caring* (May, 1983; Yalom, 1980, 1995), particularly crucial when treating survivors of torture. (For guidance on clinical etiquette when caring for survivors, refer to the therapeutic principles of care developed by the Vancouver Association for Survivors of Torture [Esfandiari & McQueen, 2000], which appear in Appendix 3A.). Lopez and colleagues considered that cultural competence requires "Entertaining and carefully testing cultural hypotheses from multiple sources before accepting cultural explanations" (Lopez et al., 1989, p. 371). And last, it is essential to recognize one's personal culture to recognize that of others. In other words, it is equally important to become aware that we are all "cultural beings" (Rodriguez, 1995–1996, p. 11).

Cultural Competence and Family-Centered Care

In its interdisciplinary model, VT–ILEHP embraces cultural competence and family-centered care as two essential elements. Although Chapter 2 focuses on family-centered care, cultural competence requires a family-centered approach because the concept of family is diverse and rich when approached through the cultural scope (Kleinman, 1988). For clinicians specialized in disabilities, there may be kaleidoscopic meanings to negotiate regarding what constitutes the family of a child, who is or who are the primary caretakers, as well as how the meaning attributed to a disability affects the family within and outside the home. Further, how does the health professional break the news of a

---

[3]Claudia María Vargas interviewed and did rounds with Dr. Locust at the Native American Cardiac Intensive Care Unit, University Medical Center, University of Arizona, February 9, 2001, Tucson, Arizona.

diagnosis of a child to a family if culturally a disability represents a source of shame or spiritual retribution. An essential element of practicing family-centered care is to explore special resources and supports such a family needs, including finding professional cultural interpreters and educational materials to learn about the disability.

Cultural Competence and the Strengths Model

For several centuries, persons from diverse backgrounds have been categorized using a deficit model. Their bilingual and bicultural abilities have been perceived as deficiencies and ones in need of obliteration to be assimilated into the mainstream culture. Interestingly enough, such abilities have been considered assets for persons from Euro–American ancestry. Persons with disabilities have suffered similar misfortunes, especially those with a minority status. However, a strengths-based approach can serve to remedy past inequities, for example, in recognizing the strengths of American Indians and other minorities. For instance, instead of a label as learning disabled, Jimmy received support in expanding his knowledge of standard English without having to give up the use of Ebonics at home. This turns out to be particularly significant in clinical contexts where cultural competence can be translated into a reciprocal process in which both the health care professional and the child/family learn from each other and negotiate meanings (Kagawa-Singer & Chung, 1994). If health professionals are truly to serve all families and all children, and provide equal quality of care, then culturally responsive care is critical, especially in serving children and families with complex health needs.

Organizational Culture and Leadership: Implications for Systems Change

Although ethical standards of health professionals embrace egalitarian principles (Geiger, 2003), cultural competence requires professional and organizational leadership. To demonstrate leadership, practitioners need to look at their professional practices and that of their organizations to assess what requires changing. The organizational culture of the health arena, however, has been driven by the expert model, and one in which the client has been a passive receipt of the diagnosis and treatment directed by the professionals. It has also been an insular culture in terms of introspection, reflection, and change of practices and policies. Reversing such an organizational culture will require genuine commitment to social justice and equal quality of health care for all children. Policies may require changes to reverse inequalities and biases against minority providers as well as minority children and families with special health needs. Organizational culture change also considers the special needs of children and families who may be in need of cultural interpreting services, whether for American Indians or Native Alaskans, Hispanics or Latinos, or Asian Americans.

The current reimbursement structure, unfortunately, does not allow for the extra time needed in providing health care to individuals using cultural and language interpretation. It takes more time to not only make the language translation, but for languages and cultures where there is no direct concept easily translated, then the cultural interpreter needs to bridge the two cultures and explain what each believes and understands. A typical 15-minute office visit for strep throat can easily become 30 minutes. Insurers still do not allow for this time differential.

Best practice from the Western model may conflict with the beliefs held by culturally diverse individuals. There are several models existent to help providers elicit the views of their clients as well as explain their own. Kleinman's (1988; Kleinman, Eisenberg, & Good, 1978) eight questions (see Table 3.2) were developed as an interview for providers to elicit how individuals understand their illness or disability. The interdisciplinary team uses a modified version of this as part of their intake process. Kalyanpur and Harry (1999) developed a process called cultural reciprocity where the provider and client discuss their views of a specific illness or disability, look for their common beliefs, and discuss their divergent ones. Then together they create a plan that is respectful of both. Taking the time at the outset to craft health care plans, interventions, and strategies that are culturally relevant affords the providers and the care recipients the opportunity to be successful (Leininger, 1991). Health care providers need training not only on how to elicit this type of information from families, but also how to explain their own be-

TABLE 3.2

Eight Questions to Elicit Cultural Explanations

1. What do you think has caused the problem?

2. Why do you think it started when it did?

3. What do you think your sickness does to you? How does it work?

4. How severe is your sickness? Will it have a short or long course?

5. What kind of treatment do you think you should receive?

6. What are the most important results you hope to receive from this treatment?

7. What are the chief problems your sickness has caused for you?

8. What do you fear most about your sickness?

Note. Source: Kleinman, Eisenberg, and Good (1978).

liefs about illness and disability, including the possibilities for treat-ment. The training needs to include how to recognize when cultural practices can be integrated into care plans and when they are in conflict with ethical standards and legal mandates. The interdisciplinary team provides ongoing training to its members in the area of cultural compe-tence. Dr. Locust, an American Indian shaman, professor, and author, makes a yearly visit to VT–ILEHP to teach about illness perception among Native people. The Multicultural Liaison Officers from Ottawa, Canada, teach about multicultural perspectives on disabilities and cul-tural interpretation services in diverse clinical settings. All health care providers need an ongoing plan for professional development related to cultural competence.

CONCLUSION

If health professionals serving children with disabilities and their fami-lies truly want to embrace an inclusive, strength-based, family-centered care model, and serve all children and families, they will need to be re-sponsive to diverse groups in the United States. Multicultural groups have traditionally been underserved, served in segregated facilities, or have lacked access to any services. Because these children face the dou-ble burden, the disability and the minority status, they are particularly vulnerable to be underserved or not served at all. Hence, there is a need to develop cultural competence in the health care arena, especially for those serving children who have special health needs.

Developing cultural competence is a long-term process, unsustain-able if dependent on isolated workshops or if only surface features of culture are considered. It needs to be an integral element of the curricu-lum and of every clinical and leadership component of a program, as it has become for VT–ILEHP. To do so, the interdisciplinary team has learned a few lessons. A salient one is to gain an understanding of what constitutes culture, beyond what is simply equated to race or to socio-economic status. Second, learning cross-cultural conceptions of disabil-ity and particularly the implication of this to family-centered care will be necessary. There are two issues associated with cultural competence and family-centered care. One is the fact that there are diverse concep-tions of what constitutes a family. However, there is also the cultural perception of a disability and the negative consequences for families whose culture perceives it as a source of community shame or a punish-ment from God. These two features may have implications on how diag-nosis and treatment is received but also in terms of identifying who is the decision maker in a family. Third, for health practitioners to serve these children and families, they may have to become flexible about how to integrate traditional medicine with biomedicine. Although some practices may be incongruent with professional ethics or child-protections laws, many others can be complementary as well as mutually beneficial. Fourth, clinicians need to become literate in issues associated with cultural biases of assessment, assessment tools, and the need for differential diagnosis. Finally, there is the need for demonstrating leadership in changing the organizational culture—policies, programs, practices, or service-model—in which clinicians work to adopt and foster culturally competent care. Such an organization will need to undergo continuous self-assessment in terms of the changing needs in the communities it serves. Geiger (2003) summarizes it as follows:

> ... the problems and nature of stereotyping and bias need to be taught and discussed repeatedly at every level of the undergraduate and graduate medical [or health field] curriculum, not merely as part of a cultural competency curriculum devoted to the beliefs and behaviors of different groups of patients, but also as effort at self-awareness and recognition of the culture of medicine itself. (p. 443)

In learning these lessons, the interdisciplinary team has come to recognize the essential role of cultural competence in training health care professionals to be leaders in serving children with disabilities and their families who are culturally diverse.

STUDY QUESTIONS

1. How would you go about discerning cultural factors that may impinge on diagnosis when a child's first language is other than English?
2. When serving cross-cultural adopted children, what background issues may need to be explored with the family? How would you go about delving into environmental and cultural influences?
3. In clinical settings, children with special needs may show evidence of traditional medicine interventions. How would you respond as a clinician to a particular treatment and why?
4. As a clinician, you have been called to draft policies regarding serving diverse ethnocultural families. What recommendations would you consider?
5. Regarding an Iranian couple whose view of disability is as a punishment from God, how would you break the news that their baby, who was in the neonatal intensive care unit, shows signs of cerebral palsy? What other perspective would you offer while being culturally sensitive?

GLOSSARY

Chanuka—A popular Jewish holiday celebrating the miracle of light.

Cross-cultural—An exchange between individuals from diverse cultures, a movement across cultures (Visions: BC' Cross Cultural Mental Health, 2000).

Cultural Sensitivity—The awareness of your own cultural influences, the ability to describe them, and the skill to interact successfully with people from diverse backgrounds without imposing your own cultural biases on them (Visions: BC' Cross Cultural Mental Health, 2000).

Culture—The sum total of all learned behaviors and values shared among members of a group and exhibited by individual members of the group. These influences include gender, sexual orientation, religion, ethnicity, race, upbringing, education, geographical origins, and age (Visions: BC' Cross Cultural Mental Health, 2000).

Diversity—An encompassing term used to portray uniqueness of people with components similar to the aforementioned cultural influences (Visions: BC' Cross Cultural Mental Health, 2000).

Ebonics—A word formed from two words: ebony and phonics and refers to the "linguistic code" (Wyatt, 1997, p. 15) spoken by African American speakers of nonstandard American English.

Ethnicity—A societal and political concept used by individuals and groups to describe themselves (Visions: BC' Cross Cultural Mental Health, 2000).

Ethnocultural Group—A group of people who are ethnically and culturally similar.

Explanatory Models of Illness and Disease—The different ways people make sense of and understand illness. There are five components: etiology, onset of symptoms, pathophysiology, course and severity of illness, and treatment (Kleinman, Eisenberg, & Good, 1978).

Inclusive Organizations—Are reflective of the communities they serve, integrate all aspects of diversity in their organizations including policy development, and provide ongoing self-evaluation and professional development in cultural sensitivity.

Multicultural Organizational Change—The process for creating an inclusive organization (Visions: BC' Cross Cultural Mental health, 2000).

Orton-Gillingham Method—An approach to teaching reading that includes the introduction of letter names and sounds and the act of blending sounds to together to form words. The method uses a multisensory sequenced approach that proceeds from the simplest knowledge to more complex in an orderly progression.

Racism—Has several levels: individual, organizational, and ideological. Individual racism are acts that block other individuals based on their race, ethnicity, sexual orientation, culture, or religion; organizational practices and policies are acts that exclude people who are not part of the dominant group; and ideological racism is the belief in the superiority of one group over another (Visions: BC' Cross Cultural Mental Health, 2000).

Rickets—An abnormal formation of bones and cartilage that occurs when there is a deficient amount of Vitamin D in the diet (Thomas, 1993).

Stereotype—A generalized or false image of a group of people applied to an individual member of that group (Visions: BC' Cross Cultural Mental Health, 2000).

Tokenism—When one member of a specific diverse group is included as an answer to the organizational need for becoming inclusive (Visions: BC' Cross Cultural Mental Health, 2000).

Appendix A

VAST[1] Therapeutic Principles of Care

1. Be trustworthy, recognize it takes time to build trust.
2. Stress confidentiality.
3. Avoid assessment and treatment approaches which may re-victimize survivors, such as intrusive probing into past trauma.
4. Ensure that the program participant feels a sense of control over the therapy process.
5. Be sensitive and responsive to the variety and holistic (physical, psychological, spiritual, and social) needs of survivors of torture.
6. Strive to understand the individual in the context of their family and provide care to build or restore healthy family relations.
7. Be alert to triggers in the center's environment, like uniforms or lengthy waiting periods.
8. Seek knowledge about the culture of an individual participant and the human rights conditions and history in their country.
9. Use culturally sensitive and appropriate treatment approaches.
10. Be flexible and willing to be available for survivors.

---

[1]VAST is acronym for Vancouver Association for Survivors of Torture, British Columbia, Canada.

11. Focus on the strengths of the program participant, not solely on their problems.
12. Recognize that interpreters act as cultural interpreters and are a valuable resource as part of the VAST team.
13. Be conscious and responsive to one's own reactions during care, such as countertransference and secondary traumatizations.
14. Maintain an open commitment to human rights.

RESOURCES

The Center for Multicultural and Multilingual Mental Health Services
4750 North Sheridan Road, Suite 300
Chicago, IL 60640
Phone: 773-751-4081
www.mc-mlmhs.org

Association for Multicultural Counseling and Development
5999 Stevenson Avenue
Alexandria, VA 22304
Phone: 703-823-9800 or 800-347-6647
http://www.counseling.org

Center for Multicultural and Multilingual Mental Health Services
4750 North Sheridan Rd. Suite 300
Chicago, IL 60640
Phone: 773-271-1073
Fax: 773-271-7261
http://www.mc-mlmhs.org

Cross Cultural Health Care Program
http://www.xculture.org

DiversityRx
http://www.diversityRx.org

National Center for Cultural Competence
Georgetown University
Child Development Center
3307 M Street, NW, Suite 401
Washington, DC 20007-3935
Phone: 800-788-2066 or 202-687-5387
Fax: 202-687-8899
http://www.gucdc.georgetown.edu/nccc

National Minority AIDS Council
1931 13th Street, NW
Washington, DC 20009-4432
Phone: 202-483-6622
Fax:202-483-1135
http://www.nmac.org

Office of Minority Health Resource Center
U.S. Department of Health and Human Services
P.O. Box 37337
Washington, DC 20013-7337
Phone: 800-444-6472
http://www.omhrc.gov

Search Institute
700 South Third Street, Suite 210
Minneapolis, MN 55415
Phone: 612-376-8955 or 1-800-888-7828
Fax: 512-376-8956
http://www.search-institute.org

Transcultural and Multicultural Health Links
http://www.lib.iun.indiana.edu/trannurs.htm

The Spencer S. Eccles Health Sciences
University of Utah Health Sciences Center
10 N. 1900 E.
Salt Lake City, UT 84112-5890
Phone: 801-581-8771
Fax: 801-581-3632
In partner with the Utah Department of Health's Bureau of Primary
    Care, Rural and Ethnic Health:
http://medstat.med.utah.edu/library/refdesk/24lang.html

University of Washington
Harborview Medical Center
EthnoMed
http://ethnomed.org/ethnomed/index.html

New Mexico Refugee Health Program
New Mexico Department of Health
Tim Rogers, Refugee Health Coordinator
Email: timr@doh.state.nm.us
Phone: (505)-827-2893

P.O. Box 26110
Santa Fe, NM 87502-2110
http://star.nm.org/refugee/about/index.html

British Columbia Ministry of Health Services
Vancouver, B.C., Canada
http://www.healthplanning.gov.bc.ca/hlthfile/bilingua/index.html

Multicultural Health Communication Service
E-mail: mhcs@sesahs.nsw.gov.au
Phone: +61 2 9382 7516
Fax: +61 2 9382 7517
GPO Box 1614
Sydney, NSW 2001, Australia
http://www.cmwf.org/programs/minority/
   youdelman_languageinterp_541.pdf

San Francisco State University
Cross-cultural communication in health care
http://futurehealth.ucsf.edu/cnetwork/resources/curricula/
   diversity.html

Language Interpretation funding:
http://www.cmwf.org/programs/minority/
   youdelman_languageinterp_541.pdf

Medical Home Concept in Various Languages:
The Family Village Project has an Internet guide entitled "Useful Web
   Sites for Parents of Children with Special Health Care Needs." The
   guide features links to language translation sites, one of which allows you to paste a document containing up to 10,000 characters for
   free translation from English to Spanish. The guide is available at
   http://www.familyvillage.wisc.edu/websites.html

REFERENCES

American Psychiatric Association. (2000). *Diagnostic and statistical manual of mental disorders* (4th ed., text revision). Washington, DC: Author.
Artiles, A. J., & Ortiz, A. A. (Eds.). (2002). *English language learners with special education needs: Identification, assessment, and instruction.* McHenry, IL: Delta Systems Co., Inc.
Barker, J. C. (Special Ed.). (1992). Cross-cultural medicine a decade later [Special Issue]. *Western Journal of Medicine, 157.*

Beckett, C, Bredenkamp, D., Castle, J., Groothues, C., O'Connor, T., & Rutter, M. (2002). Behavior patterns associated with institutional deprivation: A study of children adopted from Romania. *Developmental and Behavioral Pediatrics, 23,* 297–303.

Beglari, A., & Huong Thai. (2000). The multicultural liaison officers' perspective in assessing refugee children in the schools. *Refuge, 18,* 46–49.

Ben-Baruch, E. (1985). Conceptions of time: A theoretical framework and some implications for education. In E. Ben-Baruch & D. Newman (Eds.), *Studies in educational administration and policy making* (Vol. 2, pp. 25–34). Beer-Sheva, Israel: Ben Gurion University & Unipress Academic Publications.

Ben-Baruch, E. (1999). Time in education: Developing "time-attitudes" and "patterns of temporal behavior." *Journal of Education and Training, 20,* 74–80.

Ben-Baruch, E. (2002, October). *Cultural conceptions of time.* Lecture delivered at the University of Vermont, Burlington.

Burns, E. B. (1994). *Latin America: A concise interpretative history.* Englewood Cliffs, NJ: Prentice-Hall.

Carlson, E. A., & Sroufe, L. A. (1995). Contribution of attachment theory to developmental psychopathology. In D. Cicchetti & D. Cohen (Eds.), *Developmental psychopathology, Vol 1: Theory and method* (pp. 581–617). New York: Wiley.

Cooper, P. J., & Vargas, C. M. (2004). *Implementing sustainable development: From global policy to local action.* Lanham, MD: Rowman & Littlefield Publishers, Inc.

Cummins, J. (1986). Cognitive/academic language proficiency, linguistic interdependence, the optimum age question and some other matters. *Working Papers on Bilingualism, 19,* 121–129.

Cummins, J. (1996). Empowering minority students: A framework for intervention. *Harvard Educational Review, 56,* 18–36.

Duran, E., Duran B., Yellow Horse Brave Heart, M., & Yellow Horse-Davis, S. (1998). Healing the American Indian soul wound. In Y. Danieli (Ed.), *International handbook of multigenerational legacies of trauma* (pp. 341–354). New York: Plenum.

Ellery, D. (2001). Called to reform: A posthumous interview with Dorothea Dix. *Visions: BC's Mental Health Journal, 12,* 23–24.

Esfandiari, M., & MacQueen, F. (2000). The vitality of interconnectedness: VAST's service delivery programme, first alone, then together. *REFUGE, 18,* 50–55.

Fadiman, A. (1997). *The spirit catches you and you fall down: A Hmong child, her American doctors, and the collision of two cultures.* New York: Farrar, Straus & Giroux.

Figueroa, R. A. (2002). Assessment and identification. In A. J. Artiles & A. A. Ortiz (Eds.), *English language learners with special education needs* (pp. 51–63). McHenry, IL: Delta Systems Co., Inc.

Fletcher, T. V., & Bos, C. S. (1999). *Helping individuals with disabilities and their families: The Mexican and the U.S. perspectives.* Tempe, AZ: Bilingual Review Press.

Garza, M. J. (1998). Healing spirits. *Hispanic,* 30–38.

Geiger, H. J. (2003). Racial and ethnic disparities in diagnosis and treatment: A review of the evidence and a consideration of causes. In B. D. Smedley, A. Y. Stith, & A. R. Nelson (Eds.), *Unequal treatment: Confronting racial and ethnic disparities in health care* (pp. 417–454). Washington, DC: National Academies Press.

Graham, E. A., Domoto, P. K., Lynch, H., & Egbert, M. A. (2000). Dental injuries due to African traditional therapies for diarrhea. *Western Journal of Medicine, 173,* 137.

Gropper, R. C. (1996). *Culture and the clinical encounter: An intercultural sensitizer for the health professions.* Yarmouth, ME: Intercultural Press, Inc.

Guirdham, M. (1999). *Communicating across cultures.* West Lafayette, IN: Ichor Business Books, an imprint of Purdue University Press.

Hadley, A. O. (1993). *Teaching language in context, 2nd Edition.* Boston: Heinle & Heinle Publishers.

Hernández, H. (1997). *Teaching in multilingual classrooms: A teacher's guide to context, process, and content.* Upper Saddle River, NJ: Prentice Hall.

Igoa, C. (1995). *The inner world of the immigrant child.* New York: St. Martin's Press.

Individuals with Disabilities Act Amendments of 1997, 20 USC §1400 P.L. 105–17. Retrieved 4/21/1999 from http://web.lexis-nexis.com/congcom.5=818945fdaf13eoaff18f3dfb.32d334

Kagawa-Singer, M., & Chung, R. C.-Y. (1994). A paradigm for culturally based care in ethnic minority populations. *Journal of Community Psychology, 22,* 192–208.

Kaler, S. R., & Freeman, B. J. (1994). Analysis of environmental deprivation: Cognitive and social development in Romanian orphans. *Journal of Child Psychiatry, 35,* 769–781.

Kalyanpur, M., & Harry, B. (1999). *Culture in special education: Building reciprocal family–professional relationships.* Baltimore: Brookes.

Kayser, H. (1998). *Assessment and intervention resource for Hispanic children.* San Diego, CA: Singular Publishing Group.

Kleinman, A. (1988). *The illness narratives: Suffering, healing and the human condition.* New York: Basic Books.

Kleinman, A., Eisenberg, L., & Good, B. (1978). Culture, illness, and care: Clinical lessons from anthropological and cross-cultural research. *Annals of Internal Medicine, 88,* 251–258.

Lee, C. C., & Armstrong, K. L. (1995). Indigenous models of mental health intervention: Lessons from traditional healers. In J. Ponterotto, J. M. Casas, L. A. Suzuki, & C. M. Alexander (Eds.), *Handbook of multicultural counseling* (pp. 441–455). Thousand Oaks, CA: Sage.

Leininger, M. M. (1991). *Culture care diversity & universality: A theory of nursing.* New York: National League for Nursing.

Locust, C. (n.d.). *American–Indian concepts of health and unwellness.* Unpublished monograph, American–Indian Health Center, University of Arizona, Tucson, AZ.

Locust, C. (1989). Wounding the spirit: Discrimination and traditional American Indian belief systems. *Harvard Educational Review, 58,* 315–333.

Locust, C. (1995). The impact of differing belief systems between Native Americans and their rehabilitation service providers. *Rehabilitation Education, 9,* 205–215.

Locust, C. (1996). Walking in two worlds: Native Americans and the VR system. *American Rehabilitation, 22,* 2–12.

Locust, C. (1997). Counseling strategies with Native American clients. *Directions in Rehabilitation Counseling, 9,* 51–63.

Locust, C. (2002). *American Indian concepts of health and unwellness.* Lecture delivered at the University of Vermont, October 10, 2002, Burlington, VT.

Lopez, S. R., Grover, K. P., Holland, D., Johnson, M. J., Dain, C. D., Kanel, K., et al. (1989). Development of culturally sensitive psychotherapists. *Professional Psychology: Research and Practice, 20,* 369–376.

Lynch, E. W., & Hanson, M. (1992). *Developing cross-cultural competence: A guide for working with young children and their families.* Baltimore: Brookes.

May, R. (1983). *The discovery of being: Writings in existential psychology.* New York: Norton.

Mphande, L., & James-Myers, L. (1993). Traditional African medicine and the optimal theory: Universal insights for health and healing. *Journal of Black Psychology, 19*, 25–47.

New Zealand Ministry of Child, Youth, and Family. (2001). *Let's stop child abuse together: An interagency guide to breaking the cycle.* Christchurch: New Zealand Ministry of Child, Youth, and Family.

Nieto, S. (2000). *Affirming diversity: The sociopolitical context of multicultural education.* New York: Longman.

O'Hara-Devereaux, M. (1994). *Globalwork: Bridging distance, culture, and time.* San Francisco: Jossey-Bass.

Pachter, L. M. (1984). Culture and clinical care. *Journal of the American Medical Association, 271*, 690–694.

Perez, T. E. (2003). The civil rights dimension of racial and ethnic disparities in health status. In B. D. Smedley, A. Y. Stith, & A. R. Nelson (Eds.), *Unequal treatment: Confronting racial and ethnic disparities in health care* (pp. 626–663). Washington, DC: National Academies Press.

Perry, B. D., & Azad, I. (1999). Post-traumatic stress disorder in children and adolescents. *Current Opinions in Pediatrics, 11*, 121–132.

Psacaropoulos, G., & Patrinos, H. A. (1994). *Indigenous people and poverty in Latin America: An empirical analysis.* Washington, DC: World Bank.

Rodriguez, B. (1995–1996). What is cultural competence? Retrieved September 8, 2003, from the Family Resource Coalition's Fall/Winter Report, http://wwwcasanet.org/library/culture/competence-i.htm

Sack, W. H., Seeley, J. R., & Clarke, G. N. (1997). Does PTSD transcend cultural barriers? A study from the Khmer adolescent refugee project. *Journal of the American Academy of Child and Adolescent Psychiatry, 36*, 49–54.

Saleebey, D. (Ed.). (1997). *The strengths perspective in social work practice* (2nd ed.). New York: Longman.

Samantar, S. (2000). *Case 1: Shukria Samantar. Multicultural perspectives on disabilities.* VT–ILEHP Seminar, University of Vermont, Burlington.

Samovar, L. A., & Porter, R. E. (1989). *Intercultural communication* (5th ed). Belmont, CA: Wadsworth.

Sharp, L. A. (1994). Exorcists, psychiatrists, and the problems of possession in Northwest Madagascar. *Social Science Medicine, 38*, 525–542.

Singh, K. (2000). Mental disorder and stigma in the South Asian community. *BC's Mental Health Journal, 9*, 10.

Smedley, B. D., Stith, A. Y., & Nelson, A. R. (Eds.). (2003). *Unequal treatment: Confronting racial and ethnic disparities in health care.* Washington, DC: National Academies Press.

Sparks, R. L., Granschow, L., Kenneweg, S., & Miller, K. (1991). Use of an Orton-Gillingham approach to teach a foreign language to dyslexic/learning-disabled students: Explicit teaching of phonology in a second language. *Annals of Dyslexia, 41*, 96–118.

Spigelblatt, L. (n.d.). Notes from the multicultural parents's meeting at the Children's Treatment Centre. Unpublished raw data.

Spring, J. (1995). *The intersection of cultures: Multicultural education in the United States.* New York: McGraw-Hill.

Thomas, C. L. (Ed.). (1993). *Tabor's cyclopedic medical dictionary.* Philadelphia: F. A. Davis Co.

United Nations. (1994). *Seeds of a new partnership: Indigenous peoples and the United Nations.* New York: Author.

United Nations. (1995). *Elimination of racism and racial discrimination, note by the Secretary General*. Retrieved September 8, 2003, from http://www.unhchr.ch/Huridocda/Huridoca.nsf/0/9e6f1b12d1f055cf8025671c00508c2c?Opendocument

United States General Accounting Office. (2003, July 8). *Health care: Approaches to address racial and ethnic disparities*. Washington, DC: Author.

U.S. Census Bureau. (2001). *Health insurance coverage: 2001*. Retrieved August 27, 2003, from http://www.census.gov/hhes/hlthins/hlthin01/hlth01asc.html

van der Kolk, B. (2002). Assessment and treatment of complex PTSD. In R. Yehuda (Ed.), *Treating trauma survivors with PTSD* (pp. 127–156). Washington, DC: American Psychiatric Publishing, Inc.

Van Le, C. (2000). Stigma and mental illness in the Vietnamese community. *Visions: BC's Mental Health Journal, 9*, 9–10.

Vargas, C. M. (1998). Ethical challenges in refugee research: Troublesome questions, difficult answers. *Refuge, 17*, 35–46.

Vargas, C. M. (1999a). Cultural mediation for refugee children: A comparative derived model. *Journal of Refugee Studies, 12*, 284–306.

Vargas, C. M. (1999b). Cultural interpretation for refugee children: The multicultural liaison program, Ottawa, Canada. *REFUGE, 18*, 32–42.

Vargas, C. M. (Guest Ed.). (2000). Bridging solitudes: Partnership challenges in Canadian refugee delivery. *REFUGE, 18*.

Vargas, C. M. (2001a, October). On a Journey Toward Cultural Understanding. Paper presented at *Vermont Nurses Association*, Smugglers' Notch, VT.

Vargas, C. M. (2001b, November). *Multicultural perspectives on disabilities*. VT–ILEHP Seminar, University of Vermont, Burlington.

Vargas, C. M. (2002). War trauma in children and adolescents: Red flags and interventions for health professionals and educators. Paper presented at Sixth Annual Cross Cultural Mental Health Conference/Refugee Mental Health Symposium, Vancouver, B.C., Canada (October 24).

Violence study could vex Islanders. (1999, January 29). *The Press* (Christchurch, New Zealand), p. 7.

Visions: BC' Mental Health Journal. (2000, Winter). Glossary of key terms. In *Visions: BC' 's Mental Health Journal, 9*, 4.

Westermeyer, J. (1990). Working with an interpreter in psychiatric assessment and treatment. *The Journal of Nervous and Mental Disease, 178*, 745–749.

Woo, S. (2000). Chinese culture and mental health. *Visions: BC's Mental Health Journal, 9*, 11–12.

Woo, S., & Li, R. (2001). Spirituality and mental health in Chinese culture. *Visions: BC's Mental Health Journal, 12*, 23–24.

World Health Organization (WHO). (2003). Traditional medicine: Its contribution to human health development. Dr. Yuki Kawaguchi, Director of WHO Kobe Centre, Opening Speech at International Symposium on Traditional Medicine, Kobe, Japan. Retrieved September 10, 2003, from http://www.who.or.jp/ageing/introduction/background/ds03.html

Wyatt, T. A. (1997). The Oakland Ebonics debate: Implications for speech, language, hearing professionals and scholars. In P. Prelock (Ed.), *Language learning and education*, (pp. 15–18). Washington, DC: ASHA Newsletter.

Yalom, I. (1980). *Existential psychotherapy*. New York: Basic Books.

Yalom, I. D. (1995). *The theory and practice of group psychotherapy* (4th ed.). New York: Basic Books.

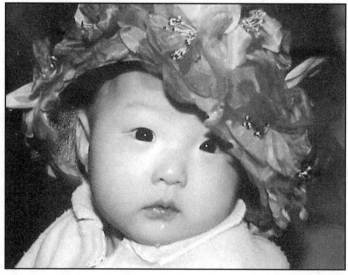

4

Neonatal Intensive Care Unit Follow-Up Clinic: Interdisciplinary Developmental Assessment for At-Risk Infants and Their Families

Deborah A. O'Rourke
Stephen Contompasis
University of Vermont

Malai Holland
Vermont State Department of Health

Questions to Consider

1. What is a neonatal intensive care unit (NICU) and why is developmental screening recommended for low birth weight and other at-risk infants?
2. What is the rationale for an interdisciplinary NICU Follow-Up Clinic?
3. What is the NICU Follow-Up Clinic process?
4. What are the outcomes of the NICU Follow-Up Clinic for infants, their families, and the interdisciplinary team?

KYLIE AND HER FAMILY

Kylie was referred to the neonatal intensive care unit (NICU) Follow-Up Clinic because of both biological and social risks for developmental problems. Kylie is the third child of parents Sally and Don Smith. She was born at 28 weeks gestation weighing 760 grams (1 lb, 11 oz) and delivered by an emergency cesarean section. Kylie is now 9 months old ad-

115

justed age (12 months of age minus the 3 months she was born premature). At birth, her respirations were spontaneous, although an endotracheal tube was placed to administer a single dose of surfactant to improve the function of her immature lungs. Kylie was cared for in the NICU for 3 months and required mechanical ventilation for 7 weeks. She was diagnosed with intrauterine growth retardation, respiratory distress syndrome, a Grade I intraventricular hemorrhage on the right, and chronic lung disease (see Glossary). The results of her vision and hearing screening tests were normal. Following discharge from the NICU, Kylie spent 4 weeks on the pediatric unit before she was discharged home at 4 months of age.

Kylie's family has a number of challenging life circumstances. Mr. and Mrs. Smith are the young parents of three children under 4 years of age, and have no extended family or other reliable support system. They are poor, often unemployed, and food insecure. They live in a very rural part of the state, have an unreliable car, and are often without phone service. The family receives supplemental foods from the Women, Infants, and Children (WIC) program. This includes infant formula for Kylie and milk, beans, cheese, cereal, juice, and peanut butter for the older children.

The Vermont Interdisciplinary Leadership Education for Health Professionals (VT–ILEHP) clinical director talked to Mrs. Smith and the pediatrician about their perceptions of Kylie's health and development before attending NICU clinic. Both reported that Kylie has been quite healthy. She had a few mild upper respiratory tract infections, but her immunizations are up to date and she sleeps, naps, and eats well. Kylie and her family received a few home visits from the Visiting Nurses Association after her discharge from the hospital, but there are currently no in-home or community services available. The Smiths are eager to learn how Kylie is progressing developmentally.

DIMIR AND HIS FAMILY

Dimir is a 9-month-old infant and the second child of parents Sabina and Mirza Mujic. He was born at term following a normal pregnancy and an uneventful vaginal delivery, weighing 3,000 grams (6 lb, 10 oz). Dimir was admitted to the NICU shortly after delivery following the diagnosis of complex congenital heart defects. He remained in the NICU for 5 days for tests and administration of cardiac medications, then spent 3 days on the pediatric floor prior to discharge home at 8 days of age. Dimir's parents were counseled that he would require surgery to repair some of his heart defects within the year, and that his cardiac status and general health would need to be closely monitored. Evaluations of hearing and vision were normal.

Dimir has experienced many health challenges since his discharge home. At 2 months of age, he was hospitalized for pneumonia from a Respiratory Syncytial Virus (RSV) infection (see Glossary). He underwent open-heart surgery at 5 months of age, although he continues to take several cardiac medications. For the past 2 months, he has been experiencing some vomiting on a daily basis and continues to experience poor growth despite a high calorie formula. Mrs. Mujic believes the vomiting is related to Dimir's heart medicines.

Dimir's family immigrated to the United States as refugees in 1995. He lives with his parents and her older sister, Dijana. Albanian is the language spoken at home, thus an interpreter was requested for the clinic visit. Mr. Mujic was an engineer in Bosnia but currently is employed in custodial work during the evenings. Mrs. Mujic was a teacher in Bosnia and is now at home full-time caring for her children. They live in an apartment complex in the city and use public transportation. Many members of their extended family were killed in Bosnia during the war. Although they have no family in the United States, they feel well supported by local Bosnian and Muslim communities. They currently receive visiting nursing services once a week and assistance from the social worker for the Title V Children with Special Health Care Needs cardiac program. Mr. and Mrs. Mujic are concerned about Dimir's nutrition, growth, and developmental progress.

EDWARD AND HIS FAMILY

Edward is 7 months adjusted age (9 months minus the 2 months he was born premature), and the only child of his 17-year-old mother, Sue Clark. Edward came to the clinic with Sue and her parents, Mary and Bill Clark, with whom they reside. Edward was born at 31 weeks gestation and weighed 1,245 g (2 lb, 12 oz). In spite of a relatively uncomplicated NICU and hospital experience, a follow-up head ultrasound revealed a left-sided Grade II intraventricular hemorrhage (see Glossary), as well as cystic changes in the left periventricular region of the brain, an area involved in controlling movements on the right side of the body. Evaluations of hearing and vision were normal.

Sue is currently caring for Edward full-time and receives a great deal of support from her parents. She is eager to complete her high school education, and is communicating with the high school guidance office about potential options. Current services consist only of a WIC food package for Sue because she is breastfeeding. Neither Sue nor Edward's pediatrician expressed specific concerns regarding Edward's growth or development during their conversations with the VT–ILEHP clinical director during the intake process. Sue noted, however, that Edward does not grasp objects often. Her goal for the clinic visit was to learn how Edward is doing developmentally.

INTRODUCTION

This chapter describes an interdisciplinary approach to developmental screening during a NICU Follow-Up Clinic for at risk infants. The interdisciplinary approach and clinic process is illustrated through the stories of three infants and their families who attended the NICU Follow-Up Clinic. Professionals with expertise in different areas of infant growth and development participate in assessment activities. The clinic model and process reflect the pillars of the interdisciplinary leadership program, that is, leadership in maternal and child health, family- centered care, cultural competence, neurodevelopmental disabilities, and interdisciplinary practice, described in Chapter 1.

HIGH-RISK INFANTS: SPECIALIZED CARE AND OUTCOMES

Specialized care for low birth weight (LBW) and premature infants has expanded rapidly in the past few decades and information about the developmental outcomes for these infants continues to emerge. Some infants requiring NICU care are at increased risk for adverse outcomes and careful monitoring of their development is recommended.

Neonatal Intensive Care Services and High-Risk Infants

NICUs provide highly specialized medical care to newborns in an effort to decrease infant mortality and morbidity. In the past 3 decades, there has been a dramatic increase in the number of NICUs in the United States and other developed countries. This began in the 1950s when a small number of centers located in major cities began to provide specialty care for premature infants. The number increased in the 1960s with the formation of regional perinatal units, and by 1985 there were approximately 700 regional units in the United States providing care for premature and ill neonates (Kahn-D'Angelo & Unanue, 2000). The availability of neonatal intensive care services continues to expand, but it is difficult to quantify the current number of units due to variations in definitions of levels of care and criteria that define NICUs.

The increased ability to provide highly specialized neonatal care has resulted in significant improvements in mortality outcomes (Alexander et al., 2003; Lemons et al., 2001; MacDorman, Minino, Strobino, & Guyer, 2002). In the United States, the infant mortality rates decreased from 12 per 1,000 live births in 1980, to 7 per 1,000 live births in 1998 (Guyer et al., 1999). Although declines in infant mortality are well documented, investigations of long-term morbidity are more complicated and information about the incidence of developmental disabilities continues to emerge. The results of long-term follow-up studies reveal that some neonates are at elevated risk for developmental sequelae. Neonatal morbidity is highly associated with birth weight. Infants with the lowest birth weight have the greatest risk for adverse outcomes (Hack et al., 2002; Lemons et al., 2001; Vohr et al., 2000; Wood, Marlow, Costeloe, Gibson, & Wilkinson, 2002).

Low birth weight (LBW) is the term used to describe infants born weighing less than 2,500 g, and *very low birth weight* (VLBW) describes infants born weighing less than 1,500 g (Guyer et al., 1999). The term *extremely low birth weight* (ELBW) characterizes infants weighing less than 1,000 grams (Saigal, Stoskopf, Streiner, & Burrows, 2001). Although most infants are LBW because they were born prematurely (less than 37 weeks gestation), some are small for gestational age due to intrauterine growth retardation. According to the U.S. National Vital Statistics Report for 2000, 7.6% and 1.43% of all births were LBW and VLBW, respectively (Martin, Hamilton, Ventura, Menacker, & Park, 2002). Many LBW infants and all VLBW and ELBW infants require prolonged care in a NICU. Full-term infants with appropriate birth weight may also require the highly technical and sophisticated care of a NICU. This group is smaller in numbers and includes neonates who experienced medical complications at the time of birth, infants with complex congenital and other medical conditions, and infants who are ill. Both groups of NICU graduates are at increased risk for adverse neurodevelopmental outcomes compared to their larger and healthier newborn counterparts.

Developmental Outcomes for High-Risk Infants

A great deal of information is now available about specific morbidities associated with LBW. Often, multiple body systems are affected resulting in any of the following conditions: respiratory distress syndrome, chronic lung disease, retinopathy of prematurity, intraventricular hemorrhage, periventicular leukomalacia, necrotizing enterocolitis, and growth failure (Lemons et al., 2001; see Glossary). Adverse neurodevelopmental outcomes include sensory neural hearing loss, developmental delays, motor and cognitive disabilities, as well as language, learning, and behavioral problems (Bhutta, Cleves, Casey, Cradock, & Annand, 2002; Hack et al., 2002; Vohr et al., 2000; Wood et al., 2002).

The reported incidence and prevalence of developmental delays and disabilities associated with LBW varies across studies and time. In general, most LBW and VLBW infants who experienced minimal medical complications during their NICU stay can expect good developmental outcomes. In contrast, the incidence of adverse developmental outcomes for ELBW is significant. The reported prevalence of major neurodevelopmental disabilities (i.e., cerebral palsy, blindness, and deafness) in ELBW neonates ranges from 28% (Saigal et al., 2001) to 49% (Wood et al., 2002). A recent meta-analysis examined cognitive and behavioral outcomes for LBW and VLBW infants and found a significant impact on cognitive functioning (a 10-point mean difference in IQ from controls), twice the relative risk for Attention Deficit Hyperactivity Disorder (ADHD), and an increased risk for both externalizing (oppositional and conduct disorders) and internalizing (anxiety and depression) behaviors (Bhutta et al., 2002). Longitudinal studies also confirm an increased incidence of learning disabilities, 34% versus 10% for control participants, and an increased need for special education services that reaches the 50% level for school-age children that were ELBW (Saigal et al., 2001).

DEVELOPMENTAL FOLLOW-UP FOR AT-RISK INFANTS

LBW and at-risk infants like Kylie, Dimir, and Edward are at increased risk for developmental delays and disabilities. Careful monitoring of their health and development through ongoing developmental surveillance and developmental screening is essential. An interdisciplinary approach to developmental assessment is advantageous for many reasons.

Developmental Screening and Surveillance

The goal of developmental surveillance and screening is the early identification and diagnosis of developmental delays and disabilities (American Academy of Pediatrics, Committee on Children With Disabilities, 2001; Bennett, 1999). Developmental surveillance is

> a flexible continuing process whereby knowledgeable professionals perform skilled observations of children during the provision of health care. The components include eliciting and attending to parental concerns, obtaining a relevant developmental history, making accurate and informative observations of children, and sharing opinions and concerns with other relevant professionals. (Dworkin, 1993, p. 532)

In contrast, developmental screening is described as a brief assessment, often using standardized developmental measures, to identify children who should receive a more thorough evaluation (American Academy of Pediatrics, Committee on Children With Disabilities, 2001). A developmental delay is defined as "a significant lag in one or more areas of development or a global delay across all areas of development" (Accardo & Capute, 1996, p. 2). A disability is defined as "a physical or mental impairment that substantially limits one or more major life activities" in the Americans With Disabilities Act of 1990, p. 5. According to Part C of the Individuals With Disabilities Education Act (IDEA), infants and toddlers with disabilities are individuals from birth through 2 years of age who:

1. [Are] experiencing developmental delays, as measured by appropriate diagnostic instruments and procedures, in one or more of the following areas:
   i. Cognitive development
   ii. Physical development, including vision and hearing
   iii. Communication development
   iv. Social and emotional development
   v. Adaptive development; or
2. [Have] a diagnosed physical or mental condition that has a high probability of resulting in a developmental delay. (IDEA, 1997, 20 USC § 1432)

Early detection of developmental delays and disabilities is beneficial for infants and their families so that appropriate early intervention services can be implemented as soon as possible (American Academy of Pediatrics, Committee on Children With Disabilities, 2001; Bennett, 1999; Rosenbaum, 1998). Early identification and intervention are indicators of best practices in guidelines published by the American Academy of Pediatrics, Committee on Children With Disabilities (2001), Medicaid Early Periodic Screening, Diagnosis, and Treatment, and the Individuals with Disabilities Education Act of 1997.

The Vermont Developmental Follow-Up Program

The mission of the program is to offer systematic follow-up for Vermont newborns cared for in the NICU, provide timely identification of developmental delays, and initiate appropriate referrals for intervention services and supports for infants and their families. The developmental screening program for high-risk graduates of Vermont's only tertiary level NICU represents a collaborative effort between the Children's Hospital at Fletcher Allen Health Care and the Vermont State Department Division of Children with Special Health Care Needs. This is supported with federal funding from the Maternal Child Health Bureau State Title V Program of the U.S. government (see Chapter 1). The Vermont program uses a three-level system to assess risk for developmental delays and disabilities and to provide follow-up (see Table 4.1). Infants assigned to Level 1 have known neuropathology associated with developmental disability, (e.g., neonatal asphyxia, severe intracranial hemorrhage, periventricular leukomalacia, etc.) and are referred at the time of discharge from the NICU for a comprehensive developmental evaluation and early intervention services provided by the Vermont Title V, Children with Special Health Care Needs (CSHCN) program.

Infants assigned to Level 2 have a moderate to high risk for adverse developmental outcomes, but demonstrate no overt signs at the time of discharge from the NICU. Although most infants assigned to this level experience typical growth and development, some demonstrate early

TABLE 4.1

Vermont Three-Level System of Developmental Follow-Up for Neonatal Intensive Care Unit (NICU) Graduates

Level	Level 1 (Refer to Child Development Clinic)	Level 2 (See in Neonatal Follow-Up Clinic)	Level 3 (Track Via Survey to Primary Health Care Practitioner)
Risk criteria	• Intraventricular hemorrhage, Grade 3 or 4. • Abnormal neurological or neurodevelopmental examination on discharge. • Hydrocephalus requiring management. • Other chronic medical problems at the discretion of the neonatal team. Examples include genetic disorders, cleft palate, and fetal alcohol syndrome.	• Birth weight less than 1,000 g. • Intraventricular hemorrhage, Grade 1 or 2. • Meningitis or sepsis—confirmed bacterial or viral. • Congenital viral infection. • Periventricular leukomalacia. • Apgar score less than 4 at 5 min. • Neonatal seizures treated with anticonvulsants. • Chronic lung condition (requiring oxygen greater than 1 month). • Hyperbilirubinemia requiring exchange transfusion. • Other chronic medical problems at the discretion of the neonatal team; for example, congenital heart defect.	• All children admitted to the NICU not assigned to Level 1 or 2.

signs of delays and disabilities in cognitive, physical, communication, social and emotional, and adaptive areas of development. Consequently, developmental screening is very important, and these infants and their families are encouraged to attend a developmental follow-up clinic at the Children's Hospital or at a regional CSHCN Title V Child Development clinic. Kylie, Dimir, and Edward were all assigned to Level 2 for developmental follow-up and their families were eager to attend the NICU Follow-Up Clinic.

Infants assigned to Level 3 have low risk for developmental problems (e.g., birth weight over 1,000 g, and minimal or no medical complications). However, it is important that their primary health care provider follow them for ongoing developmental surveillance. Community providers are asked to complete and return a developmental survey at 9 months and 2 years to assure close monitoring of these infants, and provide information to the Vermont Follow-Up Program about developmental outcomes. Evaluations of this three-level system are ongoing and preliminary analyses indicate that the program is working well to identify infants with developmental delays and disabilities who are also referred for early intervention services.

Developmental Measures

The task of developmental screening involves assessing emerging functional skills in many areas. There are several developmental categories assessed. One is the area of physical functioning, which includes gross and fine motor skills (movement and manipulation of objects), sensory status (vision and hearing), and general health (growth and sickness) (Rosenbaum, 1998). Second is the category of intellectual development which encompasses play skills and receptive and expressive language skills. Infant temperament, emotional characteristics, and social behavior represent a third developmental category that covers early social interactions, personal preferences, and self-regulatory skills.

Developmental measures may address single or multiple domains or functional areas and vary in format, such as performance-based or interview-based. Performance-based measures rely on the observation of skills demonstrated by the infant during movement, play, and social interactions, or behavioral responses to specific test stimuli or situations. In contrast, interview-based measures ask parents or other caregivers to report on the infant's ability to perform certain tasks and activities.

The detection of developmental delays and disabilities in young infants requires knowledge and an understanding of measurement concepts as well as of early development. The conceptual framework proposed by Kirshner and Guyatt (1985), which is frequently consulted, uses the terms *discriminative, predictive*, or *evaluative* to describe the purpose of health measures. Discriminative measures differentiate between individuals with and without a condition (e.g., normal versus delayed development). Predictive measures are used to predict future functioning based on current performance, and evaluative measures are used to detect changes in function over time. A number of discriminative measures have been designed to screen functional skills in infants and distinguish between typical and atypical development.[1] It is important to utilize screening measures that adequately sample multiple domains of functioning, incorporate different perspectives, and demonstrate strong psychometric properties.

The dynamic and complex nature of early development makes the task of screening for delays and disabilities challenging for several reasons. First, there is variation in typical development associated with individual differences and parenting practices, and these sources of variation must be distinguished from developmental delays and disabilities. Second, the interdisciplinary team needs to consider carefully the environment and context in which developmental screening occurs because a visit to a developmental clinic provides a single snapshot view of an infant's skills. The unfamiliar environment, presence of strangers, and infant state characteristics (e.g., sleepiness, hunger, irritability, etc.), represent some of the variables that may hinder the expression of an infant's true abilities. Third, development is often uneven across different areas of functioning, thus an infant may demonstrate strong language skills and weak motor skills or vice versa. Therefore, the detection of delays requires adequate sampling of skills within and across domains. Finally, it is important to integrate information de-

---

[1]Both standardized and nonstandardized measures are used to identify developmental delays in young children. Standardized measures have been developed for a specific purpose and age cohort, and are administered and scored in accordance with the specific directions and rules published by the test developers (Rosenbaum, 1998). In contrast, nonstandardized measures offer frameworks and guidelines that give direction to the assessment process, but do not have specific rules governing their use. Standardized measures may be norm-referenced (i.e., individual's performance is compared with that of a group) or criterion-referenced (i.e., individual's performance is compared with a criterion). Standardized measures have undergone investigations to determine their psychometric properties, and this information is published and available for review. For discriminative measures, the properties of sensitivity and specificity are particularly important (Rosenbaum, 1998; Streiner & Norman, 1995). Sensitivity refers to the ability of a measure to detect a developmental delay or disability in this situation. Specificity, on the other hand, refers to the ability of the measure to correctly identify the absence of the condition, that is, no delay in development or typical development. Sensitivity and specificity rates of 70% to 80% are adequate, and reduce the risk of false positives and negatives that can result in overidentification and underidentification, respectively.

rived from developmental screening measures with insights gained from observations and interviews with parents and others to determine developmental patterns and preferences over time.

Interdisciplinary Assessment

An interdisciplinary approach to developmental screening utilizes discipline-specific knowledge of typical and atypical development in specific domains as well as expertise in how to assess function within those areas. For example, a physical therapist is in an excellent position to identify and evaluate measures designed to detect delays in gross motor development. A nutritionist brings knowledge of typical and atypical growth, and clinical skills in the measurement and interpretation of growth data. A speech and language pathologist provides expertise in early language development and skills in detecting early signs of the communication difficulties. Thus, an interdisciplinary approach enhances the ability to identify and measure delays, observe and interpret subtle findings within and across domains, make sound clinical judgments, and provide helpful recommendations regarding referrals for further assessments and services.

Interdisciplinary clinicians as a team are well equipped to recognize complex interactions among domains, and describe the impact of delays in one domain on the development of skills and functioning in other areas. For example, a nurse may recognize signs and symptoms of cardiopulmonary compromise, and alert the team to potential implications for communication (e.g., impaired breath support limiting oral expressive skills). At first glance, a clinician might attribute the communication impairment to a neurological cause rather than one that is cardiopulmonary in origin. Clinical judgments and recommendations associated with the interdisciplinary team processes reflect both discipline-specific and collective knowledge, experience, and wisdom. Finally, infants and their families benefit from the opportunity to access the expertise of many individuals and disciplines during a single appointment, thereby decreasing the burden of travel and time associated with multiple medical appointments.

THE NICU FOLLOW-UP CLINIC

The NICU Follow-Up Clinic provides a rich opportunity for faculty and trainees from different disciplines to develop interdisciplinary, culturally competent, family-centered practices while serving a group of infants at risk for developmental delays and disabilities and their families. Interdisciplinary teaming principles and practices outlined in Chapter 1 guide the clinic process. Kylie, Dimir, and Edward's visits to the NICU Follow-Up Clinic are described and illustrate the interdisciplinary screening assessment.

The Interdisciplinary Team and Training

The disciplines represented include faculty and trainees from Nutrition, Pediatrics, Physical Therapy (PT), Occupational Therapy (OT), Speech and Language Pathology (SLP), Audiology, Social Work, Psychology, Education, and Nursing. Trainees benefit from opportunities to learn from the clinical knowledge and expertise associated with each of the disciplines. Their knowledge and understanding of health and development in young infants is greatly expanded. In addition, skills are enhanced in the following areas: (a) interviewing and communicating effectively with families and community providers, (b) observing skills and function across domains of development, (c) administering and interpreting the results of developmental screening measures, (d) interdisciplinary report writing, and (e) engaging infants in developmentally appropriate play. Trainees also learn how to disclose information to parents, whether reassuring or difficult, in an open, honest, respectful, and empathetic manner, consistent with the principles of family-centered care described in Chapter 2.

Developmental Tests and Measures

The interdisciplinary team selected a combination of standardized and nonstandardized measures to screen emerging skills across domains of development (see Table 4.2). Within the broad category of physical functioning, the domains of general health, growth, and nutrition, gross motor function, and sensory status are examined. Play skills, receptive and expressive language skills, and early thinking and reasoning skills are screened in the category of intellectual performance. Finally, although the categories of infant temperament and social behavior receive less attention, in part due to the young age of infants attending the NICU Follow-Up Clinic, some information about these characteristics is obtained during the family interview and through observation.

Screening of physical functioning is conducted through several means. General health information is obtained from the parents during the family interview. Additional information is obtained from the Parents Evaluation of Developmental Status (PEDS) questionnaire, a standardized tool that asks parents 10 questions about their infant's health and development (Glascoe, 1997; Glascoe, Altemeier, & MacLean, 1989). For example, one question asks if parents have any concerns about the way their child moves his arms and legs. A limited physical and neurological examination is performed by the pediatri-

TABLE 4.2

NICU Follow-Up Clinic Measures and Questionnaires

Name of Measure/ Questionnaire	Author or Group—Date	Domain(s) of Development Measured	Type of Measure and Format
Alberta Infant Motor Scale (AIMS)	Piper & Darrah, 1994	Gross motor development	Standardized and norm-referenced; performance-based
Early Language Milestone Scale, 2nd ed. (ELMS–2)	Coplan, Gleason, Ryan, Burke, and Williams,1982	Speech and language development	Standardized and norm-referenced; performance-based
Growth charts	CDC, 2000	Growth (i.e., height, weight and head circumference)	Standardized and norm-referenced; examination
Family interview	VT–ILEHP team, 1997	Health, routines, and temperament	Nonstandardized; interview-based
Hearing checklist	VT–ILEHP team, 1997	Hearing (i.e., respond and localize to sound)	Nonstandardized; performance-based
Neurological and physical exam	Standard practice	Posture, reflexes, muscle tone, and movement	Nonstandardized; examination
Nutrition questionnaire	Baer & Harris, 1997	Eating, digestion, and food tolerance or preferences	Nonstandardized; interview-based
Parents' Evaluation of Developmental Status (PEDS)	Glascoe, Altemeier, and MacLean, 1989	Multiple domains	Standardized; interview-based
Uzgiris-Hunt	Uzgiris and Hunt, 1987	Cognitive development	Non-standardized; performance-based

Note.   CDC = Centers for Disease Control and Prevention. National Center for Health Statistics; VT–ILEHP = Vermont Interdisciplinary Leadership Education for Health Professionals.

cian and focuses on potential signs and symptoms of developmental delays and disabilities or other medical conditions that may be affecting development. Examples of common conditions in at-risk infants are strabismus, abnormalities in muscle tone and posture, middle ear effusion, and wheezing.

Assessment of growth is critical since the growth process is an excellent indicator of overall physical health and poor growth can be a "red flag" that other areas of health or development may be at risk. Parents are also very focused on how their infant is growing, especially after their NICU experience, because growth is often the criteria used to determine discharge home. Growth is assessed through measurement of the infant's length, weight, and head circumference using accurate equipment and measurement techniques. These measurements are then plotted on Centers for Disease Control and Prevention (CDC) growth charts (Center for Disease Control and Prevention, National Center for Health Statistics, 2000), permitting comparisons with infants the same age and sex using percentiles for interpretation of results. For premature infants, the child's adjusted age is used rather than his or her chronological age. In addition, special LBW and VLBW growth charts have been developed and are used clinically, because the literature suggests these infants have a delayed growth pattern. Nutrition is an essential factor in growth and development, and is part of the screening. The nutrition questionnaire identifies parental questions or concerns about how the infant is eating and how to advance foods in his or her diet (Baer & Harris, 1997). This tool is based on a nutrition screening tool (Campbell & Kelsey, 1994), which includes questions about food allergies or intolerance, feeding issues (e.g., poor chewing, swallowing difficulties, choking or gagging), food preferences, and constipation.

Gross motor development is screened using the Alberta Infant Motor Scales (AIMS). The AIMS is a standardized, discriminative measure with strong psychometric properties, including sensitivity and specificity (Darrah & Piper, 1998; Piper & Darrah, 1994). This norm-referenced, observation-based measure assesses the infant's development of motor skills and postural control in the prone, supine, sitting, and standing positions. The motor skills of an individual infant can then be compared with those of infants of the same age from the normative sample and expressed as a percentile.

The domain of sensory functioning includes vision and hearing. Information about the functioning of these systems is obtained in the following ways. First, medical records are reviewed for the results of hearing and vision examinations. Second, parents are asked to identify concerns they may have in these areas. Third, a brief and nonstandardized screening of hearing is performed which examines the infant's ability to localize various sounds, bells, rattles, and so forth, presented in different locations, and obtains information about ear infections and family history of hearing loss. A standardized screening of hearing is always recommended if this had not previously been performed.

Emerging skills in the intellectual performance category are screened using standardized and nonstandardized measures that incorporate interview and performance-based formats. The Early Language Milestone Scale, 2nd ed. (ELMS–2), is a norm-referenced, discriminative measure used to detect delays in receptive and expressive language in infants and young children, and has acceptable validity and reliability (Coplan & Gleason, 1990; Coplan & Gleason, 1993; Coplan, Gleason, Ryan, Burke, & Williams, 1982). The Uzgiris-Hunt scales (U-H) are ordinal, nonquantitative scales that reflect Piaget's theory of cognitive development (Cioni, Paolicelli, Sordi, & Vinter, 1993; Uzgiris & Hunt, 1987). The scales provide a framework to evaluate the sequential unfolding of thinking, reasoning, and play skills demonstrated during the early stages of cognitive development; for example, development of schemes for relating to objects, specifically mouthing, inspecting, banging, stacking, and finding objects. Parents provide invaluable information about their infant's temperament, social, communication, and functional skills during the family interview and through completion of the PEDS response questionnaire (Glascoe, 1997; Glascoe et al., 1989). Finally, all members of the interdisciplinary team observe the infant's interests, skills, and interactions during the assessment activities providing additional information and valuable insights, for example, vocalizations during play, movement, and social interactions.

The NICU Follow-Up Clinic Process

The developmental follow-up clinic consists of three phases: intake, the clinic visit, and report writing and follow-up. During intake, the clinical director conducts telephone interviews with the family to verify their interest in developmental follow-up and availability to attend one of the upcoming clinics. If the family expresses an interest, a short telephone interview takes place in which questions are asked about the infant's health and development and services since discharge from the hospital. For example, Mrs. Smith indicated during intake that Kylie was quite healthy since discharge from the hospital. In contrast, Mr. and Mrs. Mujic expressed concern about Dimir's vomiting and poor growth. Families are asked to identify specific concerns they may wish to have addressed during their visit to the clinic, and the clinic process is reviewed. Specifically, families are informed that the clinic is part of an interdisciplinary training program so many people will be present during the clinic visit. They are also informed that both standardized and nonstandardized measures will be used to screen the infant's skills in different areas of development and the results will be shared at the end of the clinic visit. Follow-up activities, including the interdisciplinary report, are also described. When a family schedules an appointment, a clinical file is then opened and when written permission for release of information is received, medical records are requested. The clinical director contacts the pediatrician's office and other community-based service providers, such as visiting nurses and early interventionists, to inquire about their perceptions of the infant's health, growth, and development, and potential concerns, and to invite them to the clinic visit.

The second phase of the process is the actual clinic visit. The interdisciplinary team meets for approximately 1 hr prior to the first scheduled appointment to plan and prepare for the day's activities. Faculty and trainees learn about the infants and families they will see that day through a review of medical records and summary of telephone interviews with families, primary care providers, and community health professionals. Family and professional concerns are shared with the team along with their goals for the clinic visit. Trainees are assigned specific assessment tasks and roles, for example, conducting the family interview, administering one of the screening measures, or observing the clinic processes. Trainees are paired with a faculty mentor to supervise and assist with each task. Finally, the team takes about 10 min to set up the examination room with developmentally appropriate toys and play materials to encourage performance of physical, cognitive, social, and communications skills.

The clinic appointment for each infant and family is scheduled for approximately 1 hr and 15 min. When the family arrives, the trainee who is assigned the role of assessment coordinator, and the clinical director greet and welcome the family, review the clinic process, and assist in completing insurance and other paperwork if needed. In some circumstances, families may speak English as a second language or have low literacy skills and require assistance to complete various forms. For example, when Dimir's clinic visit was scheduled, arrangements were made for an interpreter and the interdisciplinary team was instructed on strategies to promote effective communication. The family is then introduced to the entire team with an explanation that they will be interacting with only a small number of people at any given point in time. Although some faculty and trainees administer various screening interviews and measures in the clinical examination room, others observe the process through a one-way mirror. Observers record perceptions of the interdisciplinary teaming process, the team's responsiveness to the infant and family, and clarity of communication. They also observe the infant's behaviors during the performance tasks and listen to the family's response to the interview questions posed. For example, given Dimir's medical history, some observers were asked to observe his respiration rate, fatigue with exertion, and level of gross motor activity. During Edward's visit, observers were asked to note whether his body movements were symmetrical and comment on his reach, grasp, and ability to manipulate objects.

In an effort to make the clinic process efficient, several assessment activities occur concurrently. For example, while the assessment coordinator conducts the interview with the family and reviews the PEDS response and nutrition questionnaires, a faculty member and trainee work together to administer the AIMS, the U-H, and ELMS. The physical examination and growth measurements are conducted last because this may be unsettling for some infants. Initially, trainees gain experience in discipline-specific methods of developmental assessment. For example, a physician trains pediatric residents in medical and neurological examination, a physical therapist trains a physical therapist to administer the AIMS, and a speech and language pathologist trains a speech and language pathologist to administer the ELMS–2. There is a progression from discipline-specific to trans-disciplinary training, however, and trainees learn to conduct assessments in other disciplines; for example, the SLP faculty mentors a social work trainee to administer the ELMS–2. After numerous clinics, trainees begin to mentor and support one another to assess development in their discipline-specific area; for example, the SLP trainee assists the PT trainee to administer the ELMS–2. The screening measures are scored immediately after administration and a brief team meeting is convened to discuss assessment results and interpretation of findings. Data from screening measures are integrated with information from observations, interviews, and record reviews and summarized to present to the family along with recommendations about potential referrals for further evaluations, intervention services, and community resources.

The clinic visit concludes with a short (15 min) meeting of the team with the family to share assessment findings and recommendations. This meeting is intentionally structured to be inclusive and responsive to verbal and nonverbal communication of all family members. For example, often a trainee or fellow offers to attend to the needs of the infant and siblings, so parents can focus on the discussion. Particular attention is paid to fathers, grandparents, and other family members who may have questions but are reluctant to raise them in a large group. The assessment coordinator facilitates the discussion and the clinical director takes minutes (see Table 4.3) so the family can take home a written summary of assessment results and recommendations.

Clinic Follow-Up and Report Writing

The third and final phase of the clinic is the follow-up and report writing phase. The day after the clinic visit, the assessment coordinator contacts the family by phone to discuss the visit. If there are remaining questions or concerns, they are raised at that time. The interdisciplinary written report summarizes and integrates the information gathered

TABLE 4.3
NICU Follow-Up Clinic Summary of Visit

Date of Visit

Attendees

Questions and goals for clinic visit

Your child's strengths

Motor development (AIMS)

Speech and language development (ELMS–2)

Thinking and play development (U-H)

Hearing

Growth and nutrition

Recommendations and follow-up plans

Note. AIMS = Alberta Infant Motor Scale; ELMS–2 = Early Language Milestone Scale, 2nd ed.; U-H = Uzgiris-Hunt scales.

through interviews, observations, and from developmental measures. Trainees work with faculty mentors to write up results of screening measures, questionnaires, and interviews. Once completed and verified for accuracy, the results are forwarded to the assessment coordinator who edits and prepares the interdisciplinary report. It is then sent to the family for review and approval. The final report is mailed to the family, primary health care provider, and other professionals or agencies identified on the permission to release information form.

NICU Follow-Up Clinic Visit for Kylie and Her Family

Kylie came to clinic with her parents, Mr. and Mrs. Smith, and her three older siblings. There were no specific concerns raised about Kylie's growth or development in the PEDS response questionnaire, the nutrition questionnaire, or during the family interview. Mr. and Mrs. Smith indicated that they were eager to learn how Kylie was doing compared to other children her age. On physical examination, Kylie appeared very healthy, although she was slightly underweight according to the VLBW growth charts.

The neurological examination was unremarkable with movements, reflexes, and muscle tone symmetrical and normal. Kylie's gross motor skills were normal and consistent with those of 9-month-old infants. She achieved a score of 52 on the AIMS, which corresponds to the 85th percentile for 9-month-old infants. She was able to sit independently, move around on the floor, and pull to a stand using furniture. Speech and language communication behaviors were also found to be within normal limits for 9-month-old infants using the ELMS–2. Kylie cooed, displayed reciprocal vocalization, laughed, and said mama and dada. She alerted and oriented to voice and a bell, and recognized sounds during the hearing screening. Visually, she smiled, recognized her mother, responded to facial expressions, and imitated and initiated gesture games. Her cognitive skills were evaluated using the U-H and her performance was in the normal range for her age.

In summary, Kylie demonstrated age appropriate developmental skills and did not need to return to the NICU clinic for further developmental follow-up. The team cautioned Mr. and Mrs. Smith that the developmental screening tools do not predict later functioning, and many children with VLBW experience academic difficulties in school. Consequently, ongoing developmental surveillance and later monitoring of school readiness are important. They were encouraged to participate in community-based, preschool screening activities supported by the local school and available to all children in their community. Additionally, Kylie was borderline underweight and her growth will need to be monitored closely by her pediatrician. The team inquired about whether social supports and services might be helpful to the Smith family. With their permission, a referral was made to a CSHCN social worker to help contact community agencies and programs that address poverty and food insecurity issues.

NICU Follow-Up Clinic Visit for Dimir and His Family

Examination of growth chart information indicated that Dimir's weight, height, and head circumference measurements were within normal limits in spite of his persistent vomiting. The physical examination revealed an increase in respiratory rate and use of accessory muscles to assist with breathing, a finding consistent with his compromised cardiac status. The neurological examination was normal with the exception of low muscle tone. This is often seen in children with the increased energy requirements associated with congenital heart defects. Dimir's AIMS score corresponded with the 5th percentile, indicating a delay in gross motor development. The amount of movement and exploration of his environment was significantly less than expected for his age. His posture, coordination, and symmetry of movement, however, appeared normal. Although he was unable to sit independently, his balance in this position was emerging, and he demonstrated excellent fine motor and play skills in supported sitting. Delayed motor development is seen in some infants with cardiac conditions when the drive to move and explore is tempered by energy constraints. Dimir's expressive and receptive language skills were observed to be within normal limits for his age using the ELMS–2. He was alert, attentive, and socially engaged with everyone in his environment, especially his parents and his sister. He demonstrated reciprocal vocalizations, displayed monosyllabic babbling (e.g., ba-ba-ba), oriented laterally to a bell, and recognized sounds. His thinking and reasoning skills—visually alert to people and objects, looked for objects that were hidden—were also appropriate for his age according to the U-H evaluation. His vocalizations, however, were low in volume and appeared effortful to maintain.

When the team presented their findings to Mr. and Mrs. Mujic, a number of recommendations were discussed. Although Dimir is growing well, his vomiting is worrisome and merits further attention. The team recommended that the parents contact the pediatrician and cardiologist to gather more information about the cardiac medications and potential side effects. A referral to a nutritionist was made for evaluation and counseling. Dimir's delay in motor development is consistent with cardiorespiratory system compromise, and there are no signs or symptoms of upper motor neuron syndrome or underlying neuropathology suggestive of cerebral palsy. Referrals for home-based early intervention and physical therapy consultation services were proposed and embraced by the family. These services focused on promoting balance for play in sitting and encouraging mobility for independent exploration, while carefully monitoring levels of energy exertion and fatigue that impact vocalization and movement. Dimir's language and cognitive development is right on track for his age. Mr. and Mrs. Mujic expressed their gratitude for the information provided and for the referrals, and expressed their desire to return for a follow-up visit. The team agreed that a follow-up clinic visit was warranted and it was scheduled in 6 months time.

NICU Follow-Up Clinic Visit for Edward and His Family

Edward came to the clinic with his mother, Sue Clark, and his grandparents, Mary and Bill Clark. During the family interview and in the PEDS response questionnaire, there were no specific concerns raised about Edward's growth and development. It was clear from Edward's interactions with his family that he is the center of attention and much loved by his mother and grandparents. They all take great joy in the progress he is making. Edward's grandmother did ask, however, when they should expect him to become a little more independent in mobility and play.

Review of the nutrition questionnaire and growth chart findings showed normal patterns of growth for 7 months of age and no concerns were raised. The physical and neurological examination revealed a number of abnormal findings that included increased muscle tone in all extremities, hyperactive deep tendon reflexes, and persistent primitive reflex patterns (see Glossary). The PT faculty determined that it was not appropriate to administer the AIMS, given the profile of abnormal postures and movements, and instead recorded Edward's motor skills and challenges in narrative format. Abnormal postures were evident in various positions and he demonstrated little spontaneous movement in his arms and legs, although this was more pronounced on the right side. When lying on his back, Edward was able to keep his head in a midline position, but he demonstrated a strong and obligatory Asymmetrical Tonic Neck Reflex when his head was turned to the right. In a supported sitting position, Edward had difficulty keeping his head upright, and he was unable to use his right arm to reach for or manipulate toys, although he was eager to play.

In the area of speech and language development, Edward was an alert, curious, and social infant who wanted to communicate. However, he did not demonstrate age-appropriate skills on the ELMS–2 or U-H. The interdisciplinary team attributed this, in part, to his significant motor impairments. For example, Edward was unable to localize to auditory stimuli due to difficulties with head and trunk control in supported sitting. When he attempted to engage his mother and grandfather visually through mutual gaze, he was unable to sustain eye contact due to postural control problems. On the other hand, Edward demonstrated many strengths and skills. He was calm and very tolerant of being handled and examined by many professionals. Furthermore, the supportive, responsive, and caring interactions between Edward, his mother, and grandparents were evident to all.

A small team met with Edward and the Clark family to share their findings. Edward's strengths and skills were reviewed as well as his significant challenges. Sue and her parents were informed that Edward showed significant motor delays and abnormal neurological findings, consistent with the diagnosis of cerebral palsy. With early identification and intervention, there is much that can be done to promote Edward's development in all areas. Fortunately, many health care organizations, agencies, and professionals are available to help Edward and support his family. Sue indicated that she would like to begin intervention services as soon as possible. A referral was made to the Child Development Clinic at CSHCN for a comprehensive developmental evaluation. Early intervention, physical, and occupational therapy services would be initiated immediately. In addition, Parent-to-Parent of Vermont was contacted to request family support and information.

OUTCOMES OF THE NICU FOLLOW-UP CLINIC

This chapter was introduced with a series of questions posed to help guide the reader through information related to developmental outcomes for LBW and other infants requiring NICU services. Developmental surveillance and screening principles and methods were described, and the practices and procedures of an interdisciplinary NICU Follow-Up Clinic were presented. Three infant and family stories were used to describe an interdisciplinary approach to developmental screening and the outcomes of the NICU Follow-up Clinic. The authors now examine how the clinic processes and practices served the infants, their families, and the interdisciplinary team.

Outcomes for Infants and Their Families

The mission of the Vermont Model for Developmental Follow-Up Program is to offer systematic follow up for Vermont newborns cared for in the NICU, provide timely identification of developmental delays, and initiate appropriate referrals for intervention services and supports for infants and their families. Kylie, Dimir, and Edward required

NICU services and were determined to be at moderate to high risk (Level 2) for adverse developmental outcomes. Kylie and Edward were premature and LBW, whereas Dimir was full-term and normal birth weight, but had complex congenital heart defects. These infants ranged in age from 7 to 9 months at the time of the clinic visit. The developmental screening process utilized during the clinic visits detected a delay in motor development for Dimir, a neurodevelopmental disability for Edward, and typical development for Kylie. Screening of growth and nutrition resulted in the detection of borderline underweight for Kylie, parental concern about vomiting for Dimir, and good patterns of growth and nutrition for Edward. Referrals for community-based early intervention services and supports were initiated for Dimir and Edward. Kylie's family was referred to community-based social service programs to address poverty and food insecurity issues. The mission to provide timely identification of developmental delays and initiate appropriate referrals for intervention supports and services was met in these examples.

Outcomes for the Interdisciplinary Team

The interdisciplinary faculty and trainees staffing the NICU Follow-Up Clinic are guided by the mission to prepare culturally competent, family-centered, and community-based professionals who will be leaders in activities to improve the health of infants, children, and adolescents with or at risk for neurodevelopmental and related disabilities. The family stories offer many examples of how the program attempts to meet this mission through NICU Follow-Up Clinic practices and processes. Some of these examples are highlighted.

The NICU Follow-Up Clinic provides an opportunity for faculty and trainees from many disciplines to work together with infants and their families. In the process, trainees expand their knowledge and skills in the areas of neurodevelopmental disabilities and teaming. Team members help one another identify complex interactions between health and different domains of development and consider the implications for interdisciplinary intervention. For example, the impact of cardiorespiratory compromise on motor development and communication is illustrated in the story of Dimir. Edward's story demonstrates the effect of a motor disability on other domains of development. In summary, as faculty, trainees, community health providers, and families work together in this developmental screening activity, they teach and learn from one another and contribute to an important effort to improve the health of children with neurodevelopmental and related disabilities.

The principles of family-centered care described in Chapter 2 guide the clinic process in several ways. First, the role of parents as the experts knowledgeable in their child's condition is recognized and re-spected throughout the intake and clinic process. Parents are asked about their infant's health, development, and temperament during in-take by telephone, in the clinic during the family interview, and in the PEDS response questionnaire. Parental concerns receive the team's full attention. For example, Dimir's mother was distressed about his vomiting and several referrals were made to address this concern. Dimir's father expressed concern about his son's motor skills, accu-rately identifying a delay in this domain of development. Second, complete and unbiased information is shared with families, even when the news is difficult. Risks of both immediate, and potential, long-term adverse developmental outcomes are acknowledged and communicated to families in an open, honest, and supportive manner. This is illustrated in the stories of Edward, who has a lifelong neuro-developmental disability, and Kylie, who is at elevated risk for later academic and behavioral difficulties. Clinic information is provided to families in ways to promote understanding and accuracy. For exam-ple, a note-taker records the summary discussion between the team and the family, and provides the family with a copy to take home. The assessment coordinator calls the family the day after the clinic visit to debrief and respond to questions and concerns. The interdisciplinary report is first mailed to the family for review and editing before it is forwarded elsewhere. Third, diversity in family structure, ethno-cultural, linguistic, and socioeconomic background, is recognized and respected. This principle is illustrated in the stories of these families. Fourth, family-to-family support and community support and net-working is encouraged through referrals to parent- to-parent organi-zations and early intervention programs. Communication with health care providers and human service agencies and organizations is equally facilitated.

Principles of cultural competence described in Chapter 3 also guide clinic practices and are highlighted in the story of Dimir and his family. Interpreter services were arranged when the clinic visit was scheduled. The faculty mentor guided the trainee through the interview process, ensuring that the questions were directed to both parents and that ade-quate time was allocated for responding. The services of a cultural in-terpreter to facilitate discussions between families and professionals are invaluable (see Chapter 3). A cultural interpreter can provide infor-mation to the team about parenting practices, decision making about care, and insights about attributions regarding the cause and cure of ill-ness and disabilities. Professionals who work with refugee families must be aware of and sensitive to past traumas and current challenges, and knowledgeable about potential formal and informal community supports and resources.

The final interdisciplinary training competency is leadership in Maternal and Child Health Leadership. The NICU Follow-Up Clinic experience provides opportunities for trainees to gain additional knowledge and skills in the area of interdisciplinary teaming and collaboration. Another outcome for trainees is an increased awareness of the links between tertiary care, primary care, and community-based systems of health care, and across government agencies of health, education, and human services. Finally, trainees acquire a greater understanding of health risk determination, that is, LBW morbidity and comorbidity, and how resources and services can be allocated for developmental surveillance and screening.

CONCLUSION

The NICU Follow-Up Clinic addresses the mission of the Vermont Developmental Follow-Up Program by providing systematic follow-up to at risk infants, timely identification of developmental delays, and appropriate referrals for early intervention services and supports. Although most infants assigned to Level 2 of the Vermont Developmental Follow-Up Program display typical development (Kylie), some demonstrate delays in development (Dimir), or early signs of lifelong disabilities (Edward). Families evaluate the NICU Follow-Up Clinic experience positively and often comment on the benefits of an interdisciplinary assessment. The mission of the Vermont Interdisciplinary Training Program is to train family-centered, culturally competent, interdisciplinary leaders in maternal and child health to serve children with, or at risk for, neurodevelopmental disabilities and their families. The Follow-Up Clinic provides a remarkable opportunity for the interdisciplinary training, in which teaching and mentoring occur across disciplines and between faculty, trainees, families, and community providers.

STUDY QUESTIONS

1. How does an interdisciplinary team support the outcomes for low birth weight and at-risk infants?
2. What risk factors in premature and at-risk infants should be considered for developmental follow-up?
3. What are the advantages and disadvantages of a transdisciplinary team approach to the developmental assessment of premature and at-risk infants?
4. What is the role of family-centered care and cultural competence in the developmental follow-up of premature and at-risk infants?

GLOSSARY

Asymmetric Tonic Neck Reflex (ATNR)—A normal reflex pattern of infants present from birth to about 3 to 4 months. It may be a sign of upper motor neuron injury or cerebral palsy if persistent beyond 6 months of age. The ATNR is apparent when rotation of the infant's head to one side is accompanied by extension of the arm and leg on the side the head is turned toward, and flexion of the extremities of the opposite side.

Cerebral Palsy (CP)—Motor impairment secondary to nonprogressive lesions (injury or disruption of the brain) in the developmental period (prenatal to age 5 by some definitions). Diagnosis relies on establishing these three conditions:

1. Motor impairment that is established by the history and physical examination.
2. Etiology (cause) is a static injury or disruption that may be established by history and or brain imaging.
3. Nonprogressive condition—Medical "rule-outs" of progressive or degenerative conditions.

Chronic Lung Disease (CLD)—Term used to describe the pathology found in the lungs of premature infants resulting from the trauma caused by the oxygen and pressure forces from mechanical ventilation.

Deep Tendon Reflexes (DTRs)—The reflex response of muscles when they are rapidly stretched by the examiners hands or reflex hammer. (i.e., striking the patella tendon below the knee which results in reflex contraction of the quadriceps and rapid extension at the knee.) Hyperactive DTRs may be a sign of injury to the upper motor neuron and cerebral palsy. Diminished DTRs may be a sign of low muscle tone or other neuromuscular diseases or disorders.

Endotracheal tube—A flexible tube inserted into the airway to provide mechanical ventilation for low birth weight infants with underdeveloped lungs or other situations of respiratory distress or respiratory failure.

Growth failure—Failure of the child to grow in a typical pattern according to a norm-referenced tool (i.e., National Center for Health Statistics charts).

Intrauterine Growth Retardation (IUGR)—Describes the condition of abnormally slow growth of the fetus in utero. May be due to a variety of conditions such as poor maternal nutrition, impaired functioning of the placenta, or genetic syndromes of the fetus. If later in the pregnancy, may cause loss of subcutaneous fat and low birth weight (asymmetric IUGR). If chronic and earlier in the pregnancy, may cause loss of fat stores, stunted growth in length, and decreased brain and head size (symmetric IUGR) resulting in greater risk for adverse neurodevelopmental outcomes.

Intraventricular Hemorrhage (IVH)—Term used to describe bleeding within the brain of premature infants that occurs in susceptible areas near the lateral ventricles (normal fluid filled spaces) of the brain. Graded in severity from 1 to 4. Grade 3 (bleeding into the ventricles causing obstruction or enlargement of the ventricles) and Grade 4 (evidence of brain tissue injury) are more likely to involve upper motor neurons and result in cerebral palsy.

Muscle tone—The resistance felt by the physical examiner when moving the patient's extremity through its range of motion. Increased tone or "spastic" tone is often a sign of upper motor neuron disruption or cerebral palsy, whereas low tone may be a sign of muscle disease, or other medical conditions affecting the muscle (i.e., malnutrition).

Necrotizing Enterocolitis (NEC)—Inflammation typically of the small intestine of premature infants, that when severe can cause life threatening necrosis (tissue injury) or perforation of the small intestine with resulting infection or inflammation of the abdominal cavity or peritonitis.

Neonatal Asphyxia—Describes the presence of poor oxygenation of newborns (neonates). May be due to poor respiratory effort, underdevelopment of the lungs, compression of the umbilical cord, or a poorly functioning placenta. May result in tissue damage (i.e., brain injury or cerebral palsy or kidney failure).

Periventricular Leukomalacia (PVL)—Destruction of the white matter of the brain in the area near the lateral ventricles of the brain. Presumed to be due to poor blood perfusion in this area of the brain in the medically unstable low birth weight or preterm infant. High likelihood of injury to upper motor neurons traversing this area with adverse neuromotor outcomes, that is, cerebral palsy.

Primitive reflex patterns—Neurologic reflexes normally present in infants. Examples are the startle or Moro reflex, rooting (mouth movements toward light touch on the face), grasping reflexes of the hand or foot, and early stepping responses. If present beyond early infancy, may be a sign of upper motor neuron injury or cerebral palsy.

Respiratory Syncytial Virus (RSV)—A common seasonal upper respiratory tract virus that invades and inflames the lining of the airway (syncytium) and may cause typical cough and cold symptoms in healthy individuals and more serious, or even life threatening illness (bronchiolitis), in low birth weight infants, especially those with chronic lung disease.

Respiratory Distress Syndrome (RDS)—Syndrome of poor lung function in low birth weight premature infants typically caused by immaturity and decreased surfactant production (discussed later).

Retinopathy of Prematurity (ROP)—Abnormal proliferation of the blood vessels of the sensory organ of the eye (retina) common in premature infants, and worsened if treated with high levels of oxygen. Can lead to retinal detachments and vision loss if severe. Can be stabilized by laser surgery.

Sensory neural hearing loss—Caused by damage to the "hair cells" of the auditory nerve or cochlea. Higher risk to low birth weight infants, and may also be caused by ototoxic medicines like gentamicin antibiotics used to treat serious infections of the low birth weight infant.

Surfactant—Naturally occurring "filmy" material which coats the alveoli (minute air sacs) giving them the surface tension to stay inflated under light pressure (works like soap bubbles). When deficient, the lung sacs are collapsed and require pressure (i.e. mechanical ventilation) to remain open and exchange oxygen and carbon dioxide. Artificial surfactants can be administered via the endotracheal tube to treat Respiratory Distress Syndrome in premature infants.

RESOURCES

American Academy of Pediatrics
141 Northwest Point Boulevard
Elk Grove Village, IL 60007-1098
Phone: 847-434-4000
http://www.aap.org

CanChild Centre for Childhood Disability Research
McMaster University
1400 Main St. West, Room 408
Hamilton, Ontario, Canada L8S 1C7
http://www.fhs.mcmaster.ca/canchild

Family Voices
3411 Candelaria NE, Suite M
Albuquerque, NM 87107
Phone: 888-835-5669
http://www.familyvoices.org

March of Dimes Birth Defects Foundation
1275 Mamaroneck Avenue

White Plains, NY 10605
Phone: (914)-428-7100
http://www.modimes.org

National Information Center for Children and Youth with Disabilities
P.O. Box 1492
Washington, DC 20013-1492
Phone: 800-695-0285
http://www.nichcy.org

National Institute of Child Health and Human Development (NICHD)
Building 31, Room 2A32, MSC 2425
31 Center Drive
Bethesda, MD 20892-2425
http://www.nichd.nih.gov

United Cerebral Palsy National
1660 L Street, NW, Suite 700, Washington, DC 20036
Phone: 800-872-5827 or 202-776-0406
http://www.ucpa.org

REFERENCES

Accardo, P., & Capute, A. (1996). A neurodevelopmental perspective on the continuum of developmental disabilities. In A. J. Capute & P. J. Accardo (Eds.), *Developmental disabilities in infancy and childhood,* 2nd ed. (p. 2). Baltimore: Brookes.

Alexander, G., Kogan, M., Bader, D., Carlo, W., Allen, M., & Mor, J. (2003). U.S. birth weight/gestational age-specific neonatal mortality: 1995–1997 rates, Hispanics, and Blacks. *Pediatrics, 111,* e61–e66.

American Academy of Pediatrics, Committee on Children With Disabilities (2001). Developmental surveillance and screening of infants and young children. *Pediatrics, 108,* 192–196.

Americans with Disabilities Act, 42 U.S.C. §12101 (1990).

Baer, M. T., & Harris, A. B. (1997). Pediatric nutrition assessment: Identifying children at risk. *Journal of the American Dieticians Association, 97,* S107–S115.

Bennett, F. (1999). Diagnosing cerebral palsy—the earlier the better. *Contemporary Pediatrics, 16,* 65–73.

Bhutta, A. T., Cleves, M. A., Casey, P. H., Cradock, M. M., & Anand, K. J. (2002). Cognitive and behavioral outcomes of school-aged children who were born preterm: A meta-analysis. *Journal of the American Medical Association, 288,* 728–737.

Campbell, M. K., & Kelsey, K. S. (1994). The PEACH survey: A nutrition screening tool for use in early intervention programs. *Journal of the American Dieticians Association, 94,* 1156–1158.

Centers for Disease Control and Prevention, National Center for Health Statistics. (2000). *CDC growth charts: United States.* Retrieved July 10, 2003, from http://www.cdc.gov/growthcharts

Cioni, G., Paolicelli, P., Sordi, C., & Vinter, A. (1993). Sensorimotor development in cerebral-palsied infants assessed with the Uzgiris-Hunt Scales. *Developmental Medicine and Child Neurology, 35,* 1055–1066.

Coplan, J., & Gleason, J. R. (1990). Quantifying language development from birth to 3 years using the Early Language Milestone Scale. *Pediatrics, 86,* 963–971.

Coplan, J., & Gleason J. R. (1993). Test–retest and inter-observer reliability of the Early Language Milestone Scale, 2nd ed. *Journal of Pediatric Health Care, 7,* 212–219.

Coplan, J., Gleason, J. R., Ryan, R., Burke, M. G., & Williams, M. L. (1982). Validation of an early language milestone scale in a high-risk population. *Pediatrics, 70,* 677–683.

Darrah, J., & Piper, M. C. (1998). Assessment of gross motor skills of at-risk infants: Predictive validity of the Alberta Infant Motor Scales. *Developmental Medicine and Child Neurology, 40,* 485–491.

Dworkin, P. H. (1993). Detection of behavioral, developmental, and psychosocial problems in pediatric primary care practice. *Current Opinion in Pediatrics, 5,* 531–536.

Glascoe, F. P. (1997). Parents' concerns about children's development: Prescreening technique or screening test? *Pediatrics, 99,* 522–528.

Glascoe, F. P., Altemeier, W. K., & MacLean, W. E. (1989). The importance of parents' concerns about their child's development. *American Journal of Diseases of Children, 143,* 855–858.

Guyer, B., Hoyert, D. L., Martin, J. A., Ventura, S. J., MacDorman, M. F., & Strobino, D. M. (1999). Annual summary of vital statistics—1998. *Pediatrics, 104,* 1229–1246.

Hack, M., Flannery, D. J., Schluchter, M., Cartar, L., Borawski, E., & Klein, N. (2002). Outcomes in young adulthood for very-low-birth-weight infants. *New England Journal of Medicine, 346,* 149–157.

Individuals With Disabilities Education Act, 20 U.S.C. §1400 (1997).

Kahn-D'Angelo, L., & Unanue, R. (2000). The special care nursery. In S. K. Campbell, D. W. Vander Linden, & R. J. Palisano (Eds.), *Physical Therapy for Children,* (2nd ed., pp. 840–880). Philadelphia: Saunders.

Kirshner, B., & Guyatt, G. (1985). A methodological framework for assessing health indices. *Journal of Chronic Diseases, 38,* 27–36.

Lemons, J. A., Bauer, C. R., Oh, W., Korones, S. B., Papile, L. A., Stoll, B. J. et al. (2001). Very low birth weight outcomes of the National Institute of Child Health and Human Development Neonatal Research Network, January 1995 through December 1996. NICHD Neonatal Research Network. *Pediatrics, 107,* e1–e8.

MacDorman, M. F., Minino, A. M., Strobino, D. M., & Guyer, B. (2002). Annual summary of vital statistics—2001. *Pediatrics, 110,* 1037–1052.

Martin, J. A., Hamilton, B. E., Ventura, S. J., Menacker, F., & Park, M. M. (2002). Births: Final data for 2000. *National Vital Statistics Report, 50,* 1–101.

Piper, M. C., & Darrah, J. (1994). *Motor assessment in developing infants.* Philadelphia: Saunders.

Rosenbaum, P. (1998). Screening tests and standardized assessments used to identify and characterize developmental delays. *Seminars in Pediatric Neurology, 5 ,*27–32.

Saigal, S., Stoskopf, B. L., Streiner, D. L., & Burrows, E. (2001). Physical growth and current health status of infants who were of extremely low birth weight and controls at adolescence. *Pediatrics, 108,* 407–415.

Streiner, D., & Norman, G. R. (1995). *Health measurement scales: A practical guide to their development and use* (2nd ed.). Oxford, UK: Oxford Medical Publications.

Uzgiris, I. C., & Hunt, J. (1987). *Infant performance and experience: New findings with the ordinal scales.* Urbana: University of Illinois Press.

Vermont Interdisciplinary Leadership Education for Health Professionals (VT–ILEHP) Program. (1997). *Neonatal Intensive Care Unit Follow-Up Clinic, training manual.* Burlington: University of Vermont.

Vohr, B. R., Wright, L. L., Dusick, A. M., Mele, L., Verter, J., Steichen, J. J., et al. (2000). Neurodevelopmental and functional outcomes of extremely low birth weight infants in the National Institute of Child Health and Human Development Neonatal Research Network, 1993–1994. *Pediatrics, 105,* 216–226.

Wood, N. S., Marlow, N., Costeloe, K., Gibson, A. T., & Wilkinson, A. R. (2002). Neurologic and developmental disability after extremely preterm birth. EPICure Study group. *New England Journal of Medicine, 343,* 378–384.

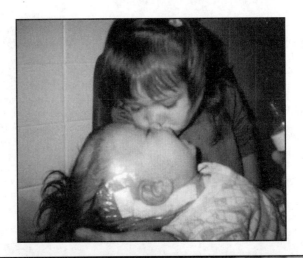

Thank you for all your help!

Love,
Caroline

Community-Based Interdisciplinary Assessment: Considering the Context for a Child With Spina Bifida

Deborah O'Rourke
Ruth Dennis
University of Vermont

Questions to Consider

1. What is the rationale for a community-based interdisciplinary assessment for children with developmental disabilities and special health care needs?
2. What is the process for interdisciplinary, community-based assessment?
3. What are the outcomes of the assessment for the child, family, and community?

DAVID'S STORY: SPINA BIFIDA

David is a 7-year-old boy who lives with his parents and sister in the most rural part of the state. His mother works part time and his father is self-employed. Both parents have extended family that live in the area, but they do not get together often. The maternal grandmother helps out with child care when needed. The family enjoys a number of outdoor activities including camping, fishing, and swimming in the nearby lake in the summer. They enjoy each other's company, and do not have a large circle of friends.

David was born with mylomeningocele, the most severe form of spina bifida (divided or cleft spine), in which part of the spinal cord and other tissues protrude through the malformed spinal vertebrae and form a sac on the back. Shortly after birth, David underwent surgery to close this lesion in his lower back. He was also diagnosed at that time with hydrocephalus and Arnold-Chiari malformation, two associated malformations in the brain, and he required a ventriculo-peritoneal shunt to manage the fluid buildup on the brain associated with hydrocephalus. David has multisystem impairments and health problems including a loss of sensation and paralysis in his legs, impaired bowel and bladder function, musculoskeletal deformities, and a latex allergy. David can walk short distances using long leg braces and crutches, and has a manual wheelchair that he can self-propel.

David's family lives in a small rented house that is not wheelchair accessible. Their home is about four miles outside the village where the school is located, on a rural paved road. The family has one car. Issues of poverty and underemployment are ongoing challenges for his parents. Other health problems in the family include his sister's asthma and his father's arthritis.

David began receiving home-based early intervention services shortly after birth. At 3 years of age, he attended a special education program integrated in a local preschool. When his family moved to their current home, he began kindergarten with an Individualized Education Plan (IEP). He is now in the first grade at the same kindergarten through sixth-grade school of 250 children; his sister is in the third grade. David is included in a regular class with individual support and assistance from a paraprofessional. He is the only student with spina bifida in his school. His school team members include his first-grade teacher, special education case manager, paraprofessional, school nurse, guidance counselor, principal, consulting physical therapist (PT), physical therapy assistant (PTA), and occupational therapist (OT).

David has received primary medical care from the same pediatrician since he was 2 years old. Specialty services are provided through the State Health Department Title V Children with Special Health Needs (CSHN) clinics, and include Spina Bifida, Wheelchair and Seating, Child Development, and Orthopedic clinics. Medical specialists both in and out of state include a pediatric neurosurgeon, general surgeon, pediatric neurologist, orthopedist, developmental pediatrician, urologist, and nephrologist. David has had 24 surgeries since birth, which have included neurosurgery, urological, and orthopedic surgeries. He has received OT, PT, and nursing services through a local home health agency.

David's special education case manager referred him for an interdisciplinary community-based assessment. David's parents agreed to participate in the assessment. Both the family and school personnel hoped to identify strategies to promote health, academic success at school, and independence.

INTRODUCTION

This chapter describes the community-based interdisciplinary assessment model. Examples of the steps included in the model are drawn from David's story, presented earlier. The development of the model was guided by emerging best practices in education and health care and attends to the International Classification of Functioning, Disability, and Health (ICF) framework (World Health Organization, 2001). The ICF classifies health and health-related components using the categories of body structure and function, and activities and participation. Contextual factors such as environmental and personal factors also influence health, disability, and functioning and are included in the ICF model. This interdisciplinary assessment model is under constant refinement as the faculty and fellows strive to implement the pillars of the training program discussed in Chapter 1.

In the United States, the Maternal and Child Health Bureau (MCHB) and the American Academy of Pediatrics (AAP) define children with special health care needs as "those who have or are at increased risk for chronic physical, developmental, behavioral, or emotional conditions and who require health and related services of the type or amount beyond that required by children in general" (McPherson et al., 1998, p. 138). According to this definition, the estimated prevalence of American children with special health care needs is 18%; 7% experience limitations in social roles such as school or play and 0.2% experience significant limitations in Activities of Daily Living (ADLs), such as dressing, bathing, and eating (Newacheck et al., 1998). David is representative of a small subset of children with special health care needs because he experiences limitations in social roles and ADLs as a result of his health condition.

Another term that may be used to describe David's condition is developmental or neurodevelopmental disability. "Developmental disabilities include such conditions as mental retardation, behavioral disorders, and cerebral palsy that result from abnormal development or injury to the brain and central nervous system during infancy and early childhood" (Institute of Medicine, 2001, p. 4). This group of children represents a subset of children with special health care needs and the estimated prevalence in the United States is 4% of the total population (Institute of Medicine, 1991). Eighty percent of the world's children live in developing countries where the prevalence of developmental disabilities is unknown but believed to be much higher due to increased exposure to many causative agents, for example, infections, poor nutrition, trauma, poverty, lack of clean water, and so forth, and reduced access to or no medical care (Institute of Medicine, 2001; World Health Organization, 2001). Although developmental disabilities vary in their severity and resulting functional limitations, the early onset and lifelong nature of these conditions have an enormous impact on children, their families, and communities (Institute of Medicine, 1991). In the United States and worldwide, the families of children with special health care needs and developmental disabilities experience disproportionate economic and social disadvantages and health care disparities (Institute of Medicine, 2001; Newacheck et al., 1998; Satcher, 2001; World Health Organization, 2001). There are national and international efforts to develop models of care to better serve these children and their families in their communities (American Academy of Pediatrics, 1999; American Academy of Pediatrics, 2000; American Academy of Pediatrics, 2001; Institute of Medicine, 2001).

Children with developmental disabilities often require specialized medical care and educational services that are provided by many professionals, service systems, and organizations. One of the great challenges confronting families and providers is coordination and integration of care (American Academy of Pediatrics, 1999). For example, children are often referred to numerous specialists and clinics for assessments. Recommendations arising from the assessments may translate into referrals to other specialists for additional information, thus generating a series of demands on the child and family that can seem scattered, overwhelming, and potentially endless. In addition, single discipline assessments may generate disjointed, confusing information that can raise more questions than were originally asked, and may focus on issues that are not priorities for the child and family. As a result, the family and local service providers are often faced with overlapping or contradicting recommendations on the one hand, and gaps in information that they specifically need on the other (Giangreco, 1996).

Although there is a value in gaining the perspectives of many specialists, the burden of sorting, prioritizing, and coordinating the information generated through discipline specific assessments typically falls on the family and community providers. They may have difficulty using the assessment results to plan services and programs in their communities that meet the child and family's current needs. The community-based interdisciplinary assessment model described in this chapter was developed to address many of these concerns. We discuss each of the questions posed at the beginning of the chapter beginning with a rationale for the interdisciplinary assessment model. Remaining sections incorporate David's story to illustrate the context, process, and outcomes of the model.

RATIONALE FOR AN INTERDISCIPLINARY, COMMUNITY-BASED ASSESSMENT

Children with special health care needs and developmental disabilities live with the long-term implications of chronic and complex conditions.

In contrast to the experience of children suffering from acute illnesses, they are likely to need an array of specialized medical interventions, individualized educational approaches, and community supports to maintain their health, benefit from education, and participate in community life. The families experience their child's disability in unique ways. As with all families, they know both joys and challenges that change over time. Each family member has strengths and needs related to his or her ability to care for the child with a developmental disability (Bishop, Woll, & Arango, 1993). They often rely on support from each other and input from professionals across various disciplines to address their needs for information, intervention, and services. No one professional can realistically provide the range of ongoing specialized services or plan for the individualized supports needed by the child and his or her family. Professionals from a number of disciplines must find ways of working as a team to share their knowledge and expertise with families and each other (Bishop, Skidmore Taylor, & Arango, 1997). In our experience, we have found that an interdisciplinary approach and community focus best meet the needs of the child and family.

Why Interdisciplinary?

Merely having a group of professionals in the same place at the same time does not ensure that they have the skills and strategies required to work as a team. Effective teams include parents as equal partners. They develop and use collaborative team processes to work effectively, efficiently, and respectfully with each other. In this approach, it is important that team members listen and learn from others, recognizing that there is much to be gained from the unique perspectives of all (Thousand & Villa, 1992). The importance of team process cannot be overstated. Although an interdisciplinary assessment approach provides a mechanism for involving professionals from a number of disciplines, collaborative processes and strategies ensure that the family and professionals share a common focus. There is a rich literature related to collaborative teamwork, and important elements of the collaborative process are described in Chapter 1.

When a collaborative team adopts a family-centered approach (see Chapter 2), the shared focus of an interdisciplinary assessment reflects the concerns and priorities of the family. By working collaboratively, the team can address these priorities more effectively than individual members working in isolation. Through the collaborative team process, individual members build their capacity to support the child and family, share resources, and establish networks across disciplines and programs. Collaborative teamwork does not stop there, however. It also involves a commitment to revisiting and refining processes over time. Team members recognize the importance of reflecting on their work together, individually and as a group, so there is ongoing attention to building the important skills of trust, communication, shared resources, and personal and team accountability (Johnson & Johnson, 1991). Collaborative team processes optimize the time and effort of all team members so that important information is obtained and shared, and relationships among team members are strengthened.

Why Community-Based?

Communities support children, families, and professionals in their efforts to be successful (Dunst & Trivette, 1990). Community is more than a physical place. It is a social phenomenon, a sense of belonging, and a human context that provides meaning to everyday experience. Because children with complex health issues live with their families, go to school, receive health care, and are members of unique communities, assessments implemented in the family's community contribute to a holistic and individualized view of the child and family's strengths and challenges. They also provide a concrete context for service and program recommendations made by the team, drawing from a range of formal and informal supports available in the community. Interdisciplinary team members who travel to the family's community see the child in a light quite different from a traditional clinic setting. They are able to see where the child and family live, where the child goes to school, and where he or she receives services. They can talk to people who interact with the child on a regular basis and who have known him or her over time. The community-based assessment model described in this chapter intentionally explores the important contexts of the home, health care, educational, and child-care settings. Depending on the assessment questions, siblings, friends, local therapists, baby sitters, teachers, paraprofessionals, pediatricians, grandparents, school principals, bus drivers, and so forth, might all contribute valuable information in the assessment process. This input is typically missed in a clinic-based assessment.

PROCESS FOR INTERDISCIPLINARY, COMMUNITY-BASED ASSESSMENT

The interdisciplinary assessment model is a key training component of the Maternal and Child Health Leadership Education in Neurodevelopmental Disabilities (MCH LEND) program for advanced level practitioners described in Chapter 1. The model involves a number of steps: (a) referral, (b) intake in the community, (c) a preassessment planning meeting, (d) a community assessment visit, (e) a postassessment planning meeting, (f) a community follow-up meeting, (g) a community assessment report with agreed-on action plans, and (h) community assessment follow-up. The community assessment process takes about 3 to 4 months to complete. At the conclusion of the assessment, the team is provided with resources individualized for the child's family and local team members. To ensure that all persons involved understand the process, a Community Assessment Checklist is shared with families and providers so they can track important steps, dates, and locations for the assessment activities (see Table 5.1). Each step of the assessment process is explained in the following paragraphs.

Referral

Children referred for a community-based interdisciplinary assessment have complex health and service needs. A family member, primary health care provider, educator, or other community service provider can make referrals for the interdisciplinary assessment. Referrals are made directly to the program's clinical director. After contacting family members for their permission, the clinical director reviews the assessment processes with the family and key community service providers (usually the educational case manager and pediatrician) to determine if an interdisciplinary assessment through the Vermont Interdisciplinary Leadership Education for Health Professionals (VT–ILEHP) Program is a good match to address the needs of the child, family, and local providers. The clinical director explains that faculty and trainees from 11 related disciplines compose the interdisciplinary team, as described in Chapter 1. He or she further explains that the interdisciplinary team works with the family and local service providers to plan and implement a collaboratively developed assessment, and that all trainees and fellows work closely with their faculty mentors and with the clinical director during the assessment processes. One trainee or fellow is assigned as the assessment coordinator and maintains close contact with the family and community team throughout the process.

When the family, community service providers, and the interdisciplinary assessment team agree that the referral is appropriate, potential dates of meetings and the community assessment date are explored and tentatively scheduled. A clinical file is created that contains a signed release of information, permission to videotape, records of communications with community team members and family, and other pertinent information gathered during the assessment process. With parent approval, participation from various community service providers is encouraged in the preassessment and postassessment planning meetings. After the clinical director obtains a release of information from the family, requests for relevant reports and documents are made and information is forwarded to the clinical director for use by the interdisciplinary

TABLE 5.1
VT–ILEHP Community Assessment Checklist for Families and Providers

Assessment Coordinator: _____

Child/Family: _____

1. Intake:
   ___ Intake interview scheduled with Clinical Director, family, and team. Be sure accurate releases are on file during the interview with the family.

2. Preassessment Planning Meeting Date _____
   ___ Family, community team, and Primary Health Care Provider (PHCP) are invited to this meeting and have received parking passes and directions.
   ___ Community visit date for assessment is confirmed.
   ___ Assessment activities are planned and responsibilities assigned.

3. Community Assessment Visit Date _____
   ___ Assessment Coordinator ensures that the community team and family knows who is coming, and that all details are set.

4. Follow-Up Call
   ___ Assessment Coordinator makes follow-up phone calls to the family and case manager within 1 week of the assessment.

5. Postassessment Planning Meeting Date _____
   ___ Assessment Coordinator in collaboration with his or her faculty mentor presents the assessment information.
   ___ As a result of this meeting, a working draft of the report is written and given first to the family and then the case manager and PHCP for editing prior to the community follow-up meeting.
   ___ Assessment Coordinator contacts these individuals and makes any necessary changes within 2 weeks of their having received the working draft.

6. Community Follow-Up Meeting
   ___ Assessment Coordinator contacts the family, case manager, and PHCP to schedule a community follow-up meeting.
   ___ Assessment Coordinator ensures that the family, case manager, and PHCP have received the edited report at least 1 week prior to this meeting.
   ___ Additional edits and updates from the community team are received.
   ___ Action plans for each recommendation are created.

7. Community Assessment Report
   ___ A final report is generated including all edits, updates, and action plans.
   ___ The final report is mailed to the family, PHCP, school team, CSHN, and any others the family requests, within 2 weeks of the follow-up community meeting.

8. Community Assessment Follow-Up
   ___ Assessment Coordinator works with the family and team to implement recommendations made from the assessment and action plans developed at the community follow-up meeting.

Note. VT–ILEHP = Vermont Interdisciplinary Leadership Education for Health Professionals; CSHN = Children With Special Health Care Needs.

assessment team. These reports typically include health records, specialist reports, educational plans (i.e., Individualized Family Service Plan or Individualized Education Plan), therapy notes, and results of previous evaluations and testing.

Intake in the Community

The next step in the interdisciplinary assessment process is to gather information through intake interviews with the family, pediatrician, and school or community program personnel. There are a number of important contexts that impact the child with special health needs and have the potential to support and enhance his or her health, functioning, and participation. These contexts include the family, the school, and service systems, as well as informal groups and activities in the community. Each child and family has a unique context and story as was described earlier in David's story. It is in these contexts that the intake and assessment process is initiated.

Two members of the interdisciplinary team, the team member serving as assessment coordinator and the clinical director, travel to the child's community and home to conduct individual interviews using a standardized protocol. Versions of the interview protocol are adapted for the family, primary health care provider, and educational or program case manager. The interview includes open-ended questions to gather specific family and community information (see Table 5.2 for the primary health care provider interview questions).

Information from the family is used to develop a genogram and ecomap. A genogram (Goldrick & Gerson, 1985) is a tool used to record information about family members and their relationships over at least three generations (see Fig. 5.1). The genogram provides an efficient summary of family members and patterns and events that have recurring significance in a family's life. An ecomap (Hartman & Laird, 1983) provides a picture of the family in the context of their community, including situations and relationships that impact the family (see Fig. 5.2). The interdisciplinary team uses the ecomap to identify family and community resources as well as to examine conflicts between families and current or available resources.

The intake interviews provide families and community service providers with an opportunity to share their perceptions of the child's strengths and challenges across settings and to tell important stories. Intake in the community also allows the interdisciplinary team to see the community environments where the child lives, spends his or her time, and receives services, and to listen to the stories being told. The interviews conclude with the identification of three to five priority ques-

TABLE 5.2

*VT–ILEHP Community Assessment Intake Worksheet: Primary Health Care
Provider Interview*

Intake completed by: _____

Interviewee: _____

Date: _____

1. How would you describe this child?

2. What are his or her strengths?

3. What, if any, diagnosis does he or she have? What are his or her challenges?

4. What are his or her health concerns (include medications, hearing, and vision testing)?

5. What are your strengths and challenges in providing health care to this child?

6. Who or what individuals or agencies are currently involved and what is their role (include medical specialists)?

7. Is there a case manager and team currently in place?

8. Do you feel as if you are a part of the team?

9. Do you attend community team meetings?

10. Expand on this (practice barriers or supports).

11. When is the best time for you to attend community meetings?

12. How much notice do you need?

13. What is the best way to reach you?

14. What are the three most important questions you would like the VT–ILEHP team to consider during this community assessment?

Note. VT–ILEHP = Vermont Interdisciplinary Leadership Education for Health Professionals.

tions from the family, educational or program personnel, and the primary health care provider. These questions serve as the focus for the interdisciplinary assessment.

The assessment coordinator is then responsible for synthesizing the intake information, reviewing records and reports that have been sent, preparing a genogram and ecomap, and reviewing the assessment questions with the clinical director and the family before presenting the information at the preassessment planning meeting. The assessment co-

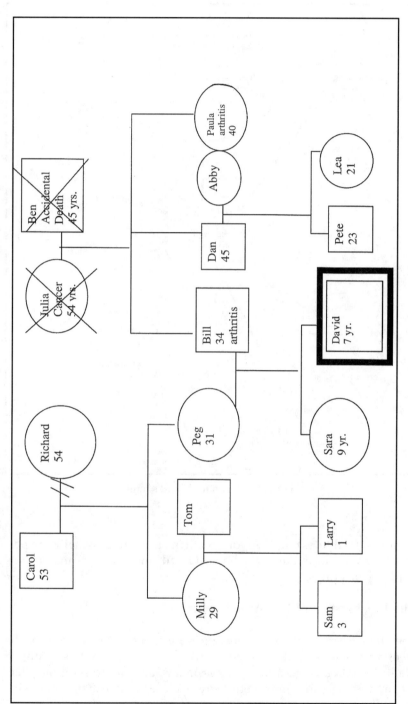

FIG. 5.1. Genogram of David's family.

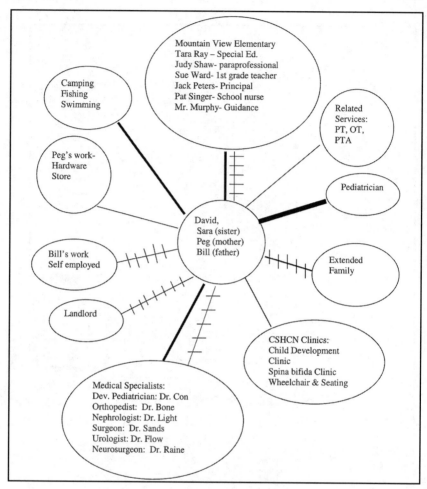

FIG. 5.2.   Ecomap for David's family.

ordinator facilitates family involvement in all meetings, whether in person, over speakerphone or via video, if family members are unable to attend any meetings.

The Preassessment Planning Meeting

The preassessment planning meeting is the next step in the process. The meeting provides a unique opportunity for a large and diverse group of family members, community professionals, and interdisciplinary faculty and trainees to come together in one place to share their knowledge of the child. The purpose of this meeting is to present information gathered during intake and to plan ecological assessment strategies that address the priority questions raised by family, primary health care provider, school, and community service providers. The strategies that may be used to gather assessment information include record review, interviews with key personnel, observations, and administration of appropriate tests and measures. Children like David have lengthy medical and educational records that contain important information for the team and the assessment process. These records include medical reports, test results, educational plans, progress notes, and consultation reports. Interviews are scheduled, either in person or by telephone, with family members, health care providers, and school personnel to learn more about the child and his or her health and functioning across settings. Observation is another assessment strategy. A great deal is learned about the child and his or her activities and participation through observations in different environments throughout the day. Interdisciplinary assessment team members are encouraged to use frameworks, formal tests and measures, and informal tools they have learned through their coursework as strategies to explore questions across environments in areas such as health (e.g., nutrition checklist), communication (e.g., observation framework for communicative intent), social interaction (e.g., observation of initiations with peers and adults), play (e.g., Transdisciplinary Play-Based Assessment; Linder, 1993), sensorimotor abilities (e.g., Sensory Profile; Dunn, 1999), and attention (e.g., Conners' Rating Scales; Conners, 1989). Although each professional brings the perspective and skills of his or her specific discipline to the planning meeting, the assessment strategies that are adopted by the team usually require that individual team members share knowledge, roles, and tools across disciplines and that they tailor their assessment activities to address the target questions.

The preassessment planning meeting is typically scheduled for 1 to 2 weeks after intake and occurs at the university. All interdisciplinary faculty and trainees attend the 2-hour meeting. Family members and the child's community service providers are urged to attend as well, so there may be 20 to 25 individuals at the meeting. The assessment coordinator makes arrangements for the family and community providers to attend, supplying directions, parking, and other logistical information. The assessment coordinator also works with his or her faculty mentor and the clinical director to prepare a written intake summary and to develop an agenda for the meeting.

Intake Summary. The three- to six-page intake summary includes information from intake interviews with the family, community service providers and the pediatrician, information from educational and medical records currently available, and a synopsis of a child's educational programs and the goals guiding them. The intake summary lists the child's strengths and challenges (e.g., the child is compassionate and creative but has difficulty with peer interactions), includes diagrams of the ecomap and genogram, and presents the key questions of the family, primary health care provider, and community service providers that were generated during intake. The assessment coordinator categorizes these questions when there are several questions related to the same general topic. For example, in the category of "health," questions might include the following: (a) Is David's catheterization being carried out appropriately in the school setting? (b) When will David be able to self-catheterize? In the category of "communication," questions might include: (a) Does David understand what is being said to him by his teacher and peers? (b) Does he have sufficient opportunities to communicate his needs? The intake summary concludes with information from the school or community program regarding the student's daily schedule, team member names, and directions to the school and community locations that will be necessary for scheduling the assessment day activities.

The Agenda.   The assessment coordinator prepares an agenda for the 2-hr preassessment planning meeting which has three major components: (a) introductory activities (review process and assessment steps, goal of meeting, and role assignment), which typically take about 30 min, (b) divergent and convergent creative problem-solving strategies (brainstorming for many ideas and prioritization of the most promising ideas), which may take 70 to 80 min, and (c) team processing and wellness activities, which take about 5 to 10 min. A sample agenda is included in Table 5.3.

The assessment coordinator serves as the facilitator of the preassessment planning meeting. As facilitator, the assessment coordinator leads the discussion, ensures the agenda is being followed, and involves all participants in the discussion. The facilitator also reviews the norms of the team. Examples of meeting norms that have been developed by the interdisciplinary assessment team are included in Table 5.4.

There are several other roles critical to the efficiency and effectiveness of the planning meeting. Two team members are assigned as recorders to take notes either on chart paper or the computer). A timekeeper is identified to help set time limits for the agenda items, to keep track of time for each item, and to help the team negotiate times for priority items. The role of equalizer is used to ensure equal air-time for all participants. A jargon buster is assigned to listen for unfamiliar terminology and to ask for clarification for the group as needed. The role of processor is used to evaluate the meeting process and reflect on discussions that went well or were challenging. Finally, a wellness provider is selected to offer a poem, reading, or reflection that ends the meeting on a high note.

TABLE 5.3

Sample Preassessment Planning Meeting Agenda

Introductory activities—30 min.

Introductions (10 min)
- Individual introductions (name, role).
- Review of the Interdisciplinary Community Assessment steps and dates.
- Description of the specific step and goal for this meeting.
- Team role assignments.
- Review of meeting norms, including the expectation of confidentiality.

Sharing Intake Information (10 min).
- Pictures and videos.
- Review—Child's strengths and challenges, family ecomap and genogram posted on large flip chart pages on wall.

Intake summary distributed and read by team (10 min).

Divergent and convergent creative problem-solving strategies (brainstorming for many ideas and prioritizing most promising ideas; 70–80 min).
- Review priority questions categorized by topic on large sheets of paper taped to the wall (2 min).
- Determine order that categories are to be addressed and time allotted to each category (3 min).
- Divergent brainstorming and convergent strategies for each category (about 20 min per category, but may vary).

Team processing and wellness activities (5–10 min).

During the divergent and convergent creative problem-solving portion of the meeting, team members use a specific approach, based on the Parnes Creative Problem-Solving Process (Parnes, 1992), to develop a plan for the assessment. They begin by identifying possible strategies to gather assessment information through brainstorming. These strategies were described earlier, and include the use of interview questions, observations, tools or record review activities. The facilitator reminds the group that the purpose of brainstorming is to generate as many ideas as possible, and to withhold judgment and side conversations about unrelated issues. Although it may be tempting, this is not a time to answer specific questions, or to generate new questions for discussion. As the facilitator, the assessment coordinator fields ideas from the interdisciplinary group, family, and community members. Participants are asked to present their ideas succinctly, and indicate specific strategies for getting answers to those questions posed by the family, case manager, and primary health care provider. For example, participants

TABLE 5.4

ILEHP Meeting Norms (Developed September 2000)

1. Use first names in all discussions (check with parents).

2. Explain the ILEHP assessment or assessment follow-up process for new people attending.

3. Show respect during all meeting discussions (e.g., know when to be quiet, be patient, take turns).

4. Take personal responsibility for checking in on comfort level of participants, be respectful of other team members, and speak out as necessary.

5. Keep an empty chair present to represent families if no families are present to remind us to be aware of them in all our discussions.

6. Be compassionate and honest in your self-reflection.

7. Use person first language.

8. Begin all meetings with introductions and wear name tags.

9. Insure confidentiality of child and family information shared in the meeting, return written materials after the meeting, and maintain written records in secure files.

Note. ILEHP = Interdisciplinary Leadership Education for Health Professionals.

might want information about the child's communication with peers which could be gathered through interviews, observations, or the use of a specific tool. By presenting their ideas in this way, the facilitator and recorders are better able to synthesize key points of discussion and optimize the meeting time. Two recorders are working together to ensure that all ideas are captured in writing. One records on large paper in the front of the group so that all can view and build on others' ideas. The second recorder works on a computer and codes and records the same ideas to maintain a hard copy.

When a 5-min warning is given before end of the time allotted for each segment, team members begin the convergent step in the creative problem-solving process. They review the assessment activities that have been suggested and clarify those which are most practical and promising for addressing the assessment questions. The assessment coordinator uses the results of both the divergent and convergent ideas to develop a plan for the community assessment day. Each category of questions is addressed in this way.

Time management during this stage of the meeting is important. If it becomes apparent that there is a need to spend more time in one category, the team may agree to borrow time from another area. The team always negotiates time extensions so that all topic areas can be discussed. Ten min are reserved at the end of the meeting agenda for processing and wellness. During this portion of the meeting, the group has an opportunity to reflect on how they achieved their goals, addressed the norms, and maintained constructive relationships. Usually, wellness is a story related to the child, or may be a snack or a poem. The intent is to leave the meeting on an optimistic and enthusiastic note.

Not all of the interdisciplinary team members will travel to the community for the assessment. A smaller group of about nine (four faculty members and five trainees), who will be going to the community on the assessment day, meet briefly after the large group meeting. They plan logistics such as transportation, times, and materials needed.

For David's assessment, the physical therapy fellow served as the assessment coordinator. During intake, she and the clinical director traveled to the town where David lived to meet with his parents in their home and with his educational case manager at his school. His pediatrician was visited in a nearby town where he had his office. The information gathered at intake was used to prepare an intake summary, which was shared with the interdisciplinary team and community professionals at the preassessment planning meeting.

David's parents, his pediatrician, his special education case manager, and his first-grade teacher attended the preassessment planning meeting at the university with the interdisciplinary assessment team. The agenda for the planning meeting included the standard introductory activities. The assessment coordinator showed a short videotape of David at his school and described his strengths and challenges, which were posted on large paper in the front of the room. David was described as being strong-willed and determined, mischievous, fun loving, and caring. Social skills were also identified as an area of strength. His challenges were perceived to include his many medical and health needs, and difficulties in some areas of cognitive functioning.

Information about David's family relationships (genogram—see Fig. 5.1) and his families' relationships in the community (ecomap—see Fig. 5.2) were also posted on large pages and reviewed by the assessment coordinator.

From the genogram displayed in Fig. 5.1, the team could see that David is one of two children living at home with his parents, and that both parents have small families. No other family members have spina bifida. Both paternal grandparents are deceased, but David's maternal grandmother and grandfather are healthy. There is a family history of arthritis on his father's side of the family.

The ecomap, as seen in Fig. 5.2, illustrated that the relationship with most of the extended family is not strong and, in fact, could be stressful at times. There was a strong relationship with the pediatrician and with the maternal grandmother. There were many other specialists involved with David and his family; some relationships were strong, others were stressed by communication and access problems. The home health nurse was also perceived as a supportive person in the family' life. There was a neutral relationship with the mother's employer; the father's self-employment was at times stressful. The relationship with the landlord was stressful because he frequently failed to respond to requests for repairs and accommodations. There was a strong relationship with the special education teacher and the regular first-grade teacher. There was a stressful relationship with the school nurse, the paraprofessional, and, at times, the principal. OT and PT were provided through the school.

The written intake summary prepared by the assessment coordinator was then distributed to all participants. It contained the information that had just been described orally. It also included information from a review of records that had been shared with the team describing developmental history, health and medical issues and interventions, surgeries, and educational history. This information was organized in a timeline format so that readers could visualize the important events in David's history. The intake report included a summary of David's most recent IEP, which indicated that his educational goals were in the areas of reading, gross motor and fine motor functioning. He was included in his regular first-grade class and received full-time paraprofessional support, physical therapy one to two times per month, and special educator support in reading four times a week in the resource room. Accommodations to his school program included a wheelchair accessible bus and classroom, and adaptations for independent mobility in his wheelchair. At school, he used a wheelchair, long leg braces, a walker, loftstrand crutches, and a therapy ball. Staff required training from the PT in transfers and mobility. Although it was not mentioned in the IEP, David required catheterization one time during the school day that was performed by the school nurse.

The group spent about 15 min reviewing the written intake summary, which included the questions posed by David's family and community service providers during intake.

Prioritized questions from David's family were as follows:

• Why is David having perception problems, and how does this affect his ability to learn?
• What can we do to help him learn, especially in the area of memory?
• When will David be ready to start self-catheterization?
• How can we support his independence?

David's school team's questions were as follows:

- Is there information about spina bifida to help with David's programming and physical and health-related care at school?
- What are the best teaching methods and strategies to help David learn and be successful?
- What is the appropriate level of academic challenge for David?
- What is the best way to share information about spina bifida with school staff to promote consistency in program planning?

David's pediatrician's questions were as follows:

- What can be done to promote greater coordination of care across settings, especially related to urinary tract issues?
- How can everyone involved in David's life arrive at a mutual understanding of his needs, challenges, and strengths?
- How can we help David learn about his condition and resulting health challenges and develop the self-care skills over time?

In the intake summary, the assessment coordinator grouped these questions into three topical categories, so that similar questions could be dealt with at the same time. These categories were as follows: (a) coordination of health and medical care, (b) school programming, and (c) self-care and life skills. She prepared large flip chart pages for each category of questions and posted them in the front of the room. She asked family members which category they would like to begin with to brainstorm possible assessment strategies. David's parents indicated that they would like to begin with the coordination of health and medical care category. Although all three categories were addressed in David's preassessment planning meeting, for the sake of brevity, we share the ideas generated through the creative problem-solving process in the initial category, coordination of health and medical care. The ideas generated for interview questions, record reviews, tools or measures, and specific observations that should be made across settings included the following:

Interview questions to be asked of the parents, school personnel, and community providers follow:

1. What information do you need to gain a better understanding of David and his health conditions?
2. Are you aware that David has hydrocephalus that is managed with a ventriculo-peritoneal shunt? Do you have the information you need regarding precautions, signs, and symptoms of shunt malfunction and implications?
3. What is your understanding of David's bladder function and recurrent urinary tract infections?

4. How often is David catheterized at home and at school? What techniques do you use to catheterize David? Is a protocol used for catheterization? When will David be able to self-catheterize?

5. When do you use David's braces, wheelchair, and other assistive devices? What are the challenges associated with using his special equipment?

6. What is the current method of information you use to share information with others, such as his physician, specialists, school personnel, family, and therapists? How is written information from specialty clinics shared with appropriate team members across settings?

7. Do you feel you have the support needed to interpret medical information provided to you? Who communicates with school personnel about David's health status and needs? What are the barriers to coordination of health care and services?

8. What does David know and understand about spina bifida?

Records to be reviewed follow:

- David's medical record at the pediatrician's office.
- School schedule and program.
- Hearing and vision evaluations.
- OT and PT evaluations and progress reports.
- Neuropsychological report.
- Reports from school.
- Clinic information from Children with Special Health Needs (CSHN) and all specialty medical clinics.
- Speech language pathology assessment.
- School health records.
- School attendance record.

Specific measures or tools to be used follow:

- PEDI—Pediatric Evaluation of Disability Assessment.
- SFA—School Function Assessment.
- Semistructured interview to assess David's understanding of his condition.

Observations across setting follow:

- Catheterization procedures.
- Mobility and transfers.
- Endurance and fatigue.
- Accommodations in the classroom.

- Accessibility issues and architectural barriers.
- Safety and injury prevention.
- Use of adaptive equipment.
- Posture and positioning for function.

Community Assessment Visit

The assessment day in the community typically occurs 1 to 2 weeks after the preassessment planning meeting. The interdisciplinary assessment team travels in one or two cars or a van so that discussion in preparation for the assessment day can occur among faculty and trainees. Often the travel is 1 to 2 hr in length on country roads to remote settings. The assessment coordinator plans the day and shares information with each participating interdisciplinary assessment team member prior to the community visit. There are usually seven to nine interdisciplinary team members who travel to the community on the day of assessment. They typically observe or interview 7 to 12 people in the community, including the child and his or her family. The assessment coordinator works with both the host school or community program and the family to schedule interviews, observations, and other assessment activities, and to secure a space for the team to work that minimizes disruption for the child, family, and school personnel. He or she prepares a master schedule that includes the schedule for activities in the school or community settings and at home, indicates the persons responsible, and materials that will be needed. He or she assigns each trainee to work with a faculty member for administration of tools, observations, and interviews, although the faculty member is often from a different discipline. The assessment coordinator also prepares an individual folder for each team member that indicates his or her specific responsibilities and schedule. Interviews that have been designed for each respondent are included in the assessment team member's folder, as well as protocols for tools or measures they will be using. Any training needed by an assessment team member to use tools appropriately is arranged in advance.

On the day of the assessment, the assessment coordinator insures that all community protocols for visitors to schools, day care, or a medical office are observed and that introductions are made to appropriate school and community personnel and family members. He or she deals with all unanticipated events and insures smooth communication among the interdisciplinary team, the family, and community service providers. Meetings with the family in the home and observations of the child at home are scheduled at the family's convenience, usually after school. A smaller subgroup of the interdisciplinary team goes to the home. Two individuals usually interview the family about additional questions that were raised in the preassessment planning meeting and two others engage the child in play or conversation, or observe the child engaging with his or her siblings. Assessment activities may also be scheduled at the pediatrician's office, child-care settings, or other community sites. Some interviews are conducted over the phone, at a later date, if people are unavailable on the day of community assessment. The team typically spends about 6 hr on site in the community. Additional time may be required for travel.

Toward the end of the assessment day, the interdisciplinary team meets to process the community assessment. In Vermont, where the team may need to travel for several hours, processing often occurs in the car. A team self-evaluation tool is used to evaluate and discuss the team's performance during the community visit related to preparation, collaboration, sensitivity to local norms, and ability to complete tasks. During processing, assessment findings can be discussed, noting key observations that address the questions across settings, and identifying differences in interpretation of observations based on discipline specific and other perspectives. The team also determines if there are outstanding tasks and information to be gathered. The assessment coordinator uses this time to clarify responsibilities and deadlines for submission of written assessment information. Write-ups of all interviews must be reviewed by the faculty partner and then by the interviewees themselves to check for accuracy before forwarding them to the assessment coordinator.

Interdisciplinary team members met the morning of David's assessment at his school. The educational case manager had reserved a conference room in the school for the team to use as a base of operation for the school day. The schedule of assessment activities and individual assignments had been shared with interdisciplinary team members prior to the assessment day. Observations of David's typical routines were planned in a number of settings, including on the school bus, in school hallways, classroom, playground, gym, lunchroom, library, bathroom, and music room. No more than two team members observed at one time to minimize the distraction to David and his classmates. For example, the PT and the social worker observed David's positioning on the school bus, his ability to maneuver his wheelchair through the snow, open the door, and manage his clothing and school materials in the classroom. His typical afterschool activities were observed at home with his parents and older sister. Specific measures that were used included the PEDI interview with his parents and the SFA interviews with school personnel.

Interviews were constructed for specific individuals. Some interviews posed the same questions to different people, and others were individualized for the respondent. For example, one set of interview questions was used with all school staff to determine their level of understanding related to coordination of health and medical care. These interview questions explored their knowledge of health consequences of spina bifida and potential impact on David's school performance. For example, school personnel were asked if they knew that David had a shunt and if they were aware of signs and symptoms of shunt malfunction. Another interview was designed specifically for David to determine his understanding of his own condition. For example, David was asked to name the condition he had and what it meant for him. The family, school nurse, paraprofessional, and pediatrician were asked questions related to catheterization protocols and procedures. In all, 13 interviews were conducted and involved the parents, David, his sister, his pediatrician, PT, special education case manager, classroom teacher, school nurse, principal, guidance counselor, bus driver, gym teacher, and paraprofessional. When team members were not assigned for an observation or interview, they used their time to complete record review tasks.

The interdisciplinary assessment team members engaged in team processing for about 30 min at the end of the school day. Some team members had been able to complete their assessment tasks and had their results checked by their faculty partner. Most others had tasks that remained to be completed, such as scoring of tests and measures, preparing written summaries of observations and interviews, and checking interview summaries with faculty partners and interviewees. There were still several interviews that needed to be completed by telephone with therapists and physicians who were not present in the community that day. The deadline for having all information to the assessment coordinator was negotiated by the team and was set for 2 weeks. Following the processing activity at the school, the team separated to continue assessment activities in other settings. Three team members met with David and his family in his home after school. David's family lived in a mobile home with their cat and two dogs. David's room had a bed, dresser, clothes, cardboard boxes filled with toys and books, and stuffed animals on the floor. Two others went to the pediatrician's office in a neighboring town to review medical records and conduct an interview.

Postassessment Planning Meeting

During the postassessment planning meeting, information gathered through assessment activities is reviewed and recommendations are developed to address the key questions posed by the family, primary health care provider, and community service providers. The meeting is planned for 2 hr and utilizes collaborative teaming processes and creative problem-solving strategies as introduced during the planning meeting. The meeting is held at the university and is attended by the same persons who participated in the preassessment planning meeting, that is, all interdisciplinary faculty and trainees, family members, and community service providers who the family wants to attend. The outcome of the meeting is to identify a set of three to five priority recommendations to address each of the questions and categories.

Before the meeting, the assessment coordinator prepares a working draft of the assessment findings that synthesizes information from observations, interviews, record review, and tests and measures. This document may take a variety of forms and may include tables, charts, timelines, or narratives.

The assessment coordinator also prepares an agenda for the postassessment planning meeting. Once again the typical agenda includes introductory activities, divergent and convergent creative problem solving, team processing, and wellness. As with the preassessment planning meeting, introductory activities require about 30 min and include a review of the interdisciplinary assessment steps and an explanation of the postassessment planning meeting and the intended outcomes. The facilitator reviews background information regarding the child and family and meeting norms. Roles are assigned and, once again, two people serve as recorders. Participants are then asked to review the working draft of assessment findings.

The next 70 to 80 min of the meeting are dedicated to divergent and convergent creative problem-solving strategies to generate potential recommendations. There may be some discussion or clarification of assessment findings at this point. Each category of questions is dealt with during this portion of the meeting. Team members are first encouraged to generate many possible recommendations during the brainstorming segment, followed by 5 min of ideas for converging recommendations. During the convergent step, team members synthesize, combine, or reframe ideas raised during brainstorming so that three to five priority recommendations are identified for each category. The meeting ends with processing and wellness activities. Those who will be attending the community meeting, including the assessment coordinator, faculty mentor, the interdisciplinary training director, and program director, meet briefly with parents and community providers to confirm the date, time, and location of the Community Follow-Up Meeting.

David's parents, his educational case manager, his teacher, school nurse, and pediatrician attended his postassessment planning meeting with the interdisciplinary team. Together they identified priority recommendations that addressed the three categories of assessment questions that were the focus of David's assessment. More than four recommendations were identified in the coordination of health and medical care category because participants at the meeting felt this category reflected pressing needs for David, his family, and community providers. Recommendations were made in all three categories. Recommendations for the coordination of health and medical care included the following:

1. Provide an in-service program on the topic of spina bifida for school personnel who currently work with David and are likely to work with him next year.
2. Review the current written health plan for the school and revise, if necessary, to include recognition and management of emergency and non-emergency situations associated with spina bifida (i.e., shunt malfunction, latex allergy reaction, skin problems, etc.).
3. Develop a written protocol describing exactly how catheterization should be performed (i.e., frequency, method, medical supplies needed, position, etc.) across settings.
4. Develop an annual appointment calendar and master list with telephone and fax numbers and e-mail addresses of health care providers and organizations currently involved in David's care to promote ease of communication between family members, pediatrician, and specialists, and a written protocol of who should be contacted in the event of specific health situations.
5. Schedule regular team meetings with the core team (i.e., family, pediatrician, and school personnel) to solve problems that arise and monitor progress.

Recommendations for school programming included the following:

1. Review daily school schedule to minimize disruption of academic programming with health care routines.
2. Facilitate a meeting of related service providers (OT, PT, Speech Language Pathologist) to determine how each can and will support David's IEP goals and promote access to his educational program in inclusive settings.
3. Plan a meeting with the neuropsychologist and school personnel to interpret the previous evaluation and provide potential strategies and accommodations to enhance academic performance in reading and spelling.

Recommendations for self-care and life skills included the following:

1. Review results of the SFA with school personnel and determine ways to increase David's level of independence and participation at school.
2. Develop a care book for David to explain his condition and needed medical care to help promote understanding and self-care.

3. Obtain resources related to promotion of self-care and life skills in children with spina bifida.

Community Follow-Up Meeting

The purpose of the community follow-up meeting is to share assessment results, review recommendations, and develop collaborative action plans to implement the recommendations. Local community service providers, the family, and the child, if appropriate, attend the meeting. Four members of the interdisciplinary assessment team typically attend, so that meetings often include 10 to 20 people. The location of the meeting is determined by the family and often occurs at the school, community health center, or program site. The outcome of the meeting is to develop action plans that can be supported by local team members and to identify information resources that would be helpful to the local team members as well as to the family.

There is a great deal of interdisciplinary team preparation for the community follow-up meeting. The assessment coordinator, with support from other interdisciplinary team members, prepares a working draft of the community assessment report and begins to compile a resource notebook for the family and community service providers.

The draft of the community assessment report is prepared, using a standard template that includes identifying information related to the child, family, and referral source, the date of the community assessment, and a listing of interdisciplinary team members. Other sections of the report include referral questions raised during intake, background information, and a summary of assessment findings and recommendations for each category of questions. The report is typically 8 to 10 pages. The interviews, written reports of observations, scored tests and measures, and summaries of record reviews are attached to the report in an appendix. The faculty mentor, clinical director, training director, and program director read and edit the report drafted by the assessment coordinator. The draft is then shared first with the family. If requested, members of the interdisciplinary team can arrange to deliver the report to the family and review it with them face to face. Changes and suggestions identified by the family are addressed prior to forwarding the draft report to the pediatrician and key community service providers. The intent of sending the working draft of the report before the community follow-up meeting is to give family members and community service providers an opportunity to reflect on the report and be prepared to focus on recommendations and action planning at the community follow-up meeting. The report is also placed in the file at the interdisciplinary team office so that all interdisciplinary faculty and trainees can review it and suggest materials for the resource notebook.

The assessment coordinator begins to prepare a resource notebook prior to the community follow-up meeting that contains information to support recommendations of the interdisciplinary team. Resource notebooks may contain evidence-based practice research articles, brochures and flyers of available resources, published evaluation and intervention protocols, equipment catalogs, and Web sites of national and international organizations. The intent of the resource notebook is to individualize information for the child, his or her family, and team that provides information and other resources that may be helpful now and in the future.

The assessment coordinator facilitates the community follow-up meeting. The meeting begins with the standard introductory agenda items, including introductions, role assignment, review of the process and the intended outcomes, as well as a review of meeting norms. The facilitator then asks for updates related to the assessment information, and requests that any changes to the working draft be written on the hard copy and submitted at the end of the meeting. Updates, comments, and edits are reviewed prior to the preparation of the final version of the report.

The majority of the meeting time is devoted to reviewing recommendations and developing specific action plans that are acceptable to the team. As part of the action planning process, specific steps of the plan and the persons who will be responsible for implementing the plan are identified. Timelines are also established. Members of the interdisciplinary team may be involved in action plans to accomplish specific tasks or provide information and resources in an effort to distribute the workload and ensure feasibility of the plan. The meeting concludes with processing and wellness activities.

After the community meeting, the assessment coordinator incorporates relevant edits, feedback, and agreed-on action plans into the final draft of the community assessment report. He or she also completes the resource notebook with materials needed to support specific action plans. The assessment coordinator ensures that the family, the primary health care provider, and community providers receive final copies of the community assessment report and the resource notebook.

David's community assessment report was prepared in draft form and reviewed by his family prior to its distribution to the pediatrician and school team. It included the key recommendations developed at the post-assessment meeting, as described earlier. The community follow-up meeting was held in his school library. David's parents, pediatrician, school case manager, first-grade teacher, principal, instructional assistant, school nurse, consulting PT, bus driver, a nurse from CSHN clinics, as well as four interdisciplinary team members, attended. Updates were shared with the team. A recent visit with the orthopedic clinic team indi-

cated that hip and knee flexion contractures had worsened and that surgery was recommended for hamstring lengthening over the summer.
Family friends had built a ramp leading to the front door of David's
house so that he could bring his wheelchair into his home. David's father
had begun working at a new job that would provide full-time employment for at least the next 6 months.

At David's community follow-up meeting, action plans were made
based on recommendations in all three question categories. As an example, the action plans made in the category of coordination of health and
medical care included the following:

The 4 specific recommendations to improve the coordination of
health and medical care are listed below. Each recommendation was accompanied by at least 1 action plan and the persons responsible for implementing the plan are identified.

1. Provide an in-service program on the topic of spina bifida for
school personnel who currently work with David and are likely to
work with him next year. ACTION PLAN: The interdisciplinary
team will organize an in-service on spina bifida for school personnel and assemble print materials and other resources (e.g., Web
sites, videos, etc.) that are relevant to David and his functioning at
school. The in-service will be videotaped so it can be used in the future. PERSONS RESPONSIBLE: Pediatrician and assessment coordinator. Timeline: Scheduled in 1 month at a time convenient for
school personnel.

2. Review current written health plan for school and revise, if
necessary, to include recognition and management of emergency
and nonemergency situations associated with spina bifida including shunt malfunction, latex allergy reaction, skin problems, and
so forth. ACTION PLAN: Meet to revise, and individualize David's current school health plan to address potential health problems that require immediate attention, including latex reactions,
shunt malfunction, skin breakdown, joint problems, and urinary
tract infections. PERSONS RESPONSIBLE: Assessment coordinator, pediatrician, parents, school nurse, special case manager, and
PT faculty mentor. Timeline: First meeting within 1 month, plan to
be completed in 3 months.

3. Develop a written protocol describing exactly how catheterization should be performed (i.e., frequency, method, medical supplies needed, position, etc.) across settings. ACTION PLAN:
Develop a protocol for catheterization and self-catheterization
training. PERSONS RESPONSIBLE: Assessment Coordinator, pediatrician, paraprofessional, CHSN nurse, pediatrician in consulta-

tion with nephrologist, urologist, parents, and David. Timeline: 6 weeks, and would be included in individualized plan above.

4. Create a mechanism for greater clarity in communication between family, pediatrician, school personnel, community providers, and specialists by preparing and sharing contact information and yearly appointment schedule (include telephone and fax numbers and e-mail addresses of health care providers, their roles, and all organizations and agencies currently involved in David's care), and developing a written protocol of who should be contacted in the event of specific health situations. Schedule regular team meetings with core team (i.e., family, pediatrician, and school personnel) to problem solve issues. ACTION PLAN A: Develop and share contact information, yearly appointment schedule, and develop a written protocol detailing who and when people on the list should be contacted for specific health problems or concerns. PERSONS RESPONSIBLE: Assessment coordinator, pediatrician, and parents. Timeline: By beginning of school year in approximately 4 months. ACTION PLAN B: Schedule regular team meetings at school with core team (i.e., family, pediatrician, and school personnel) to problem solve issues that arise and monitor progress. PERSONS RESPONSIBLE: School case manager and family.

Following David's community follow-up meeting, the assessment coordinator revised the draft report to incorporate the agreed-on action plans. The final version of the report and copies of the resource notebook were sent or delivered to his family, pediatrician, and school team. The resource notebook included publications from the Spina Bifida Association of America addressing topics such as medical and health care, hydrocephalus, shunt functioning, bowel and bladder care, catheterization procedures, urinary tract infections, bracing and mobility, and communication that were relevant for children with spina bifida. Research articles focusing on health, development, and secondary conditions associated with spina bifida were also included. National and international Web sites were researched and shared, indicating the types of information and support they might provide for David, the family, and local team members. Contact information for the local and statewide health and family support services, and Parent-to-Parent of Vermont, was also provided. Two books were purchased for the team, one written for parents and another for children with spina bifida, *Children with Spina Bifida: A Parent's Guide* (Lutkenhoff, 1999), and *SPINabilities: A Young Person's Guide to Spina Bifida* (Lutkenhoff & Oppenheimer, 1997).

The specific outcomes of David's interdisciplinary community assessment were reflected in the action plans agreed on and operationalized by his local team, with support from interdisciplinary team members. Other important outcomes for David, his family, and local service providers became apparent over time. Some of these included positive changes in his health, independence, communication, and understanding of his own condition. David learned to self-catheterize 6 months following the community assessment, and incidents of urinary tract infections decreased. He was supported to develop greater independence in mobility in the school environment through removal of architectural barriers. He gained increased access to school facilities and materials as a result of specific skill training in wheelchair management and transfers, and through environmental modification of his workspaces. His learning and expressive communication and ability to participate in classroom instruction improved through use of a computer at school and accommodations to his reading program. David developed a better understanding of his condition and diagnosis through literature and video resources appropriate for young children. He also met other children with disabilities through the Internet and through activities planned by his parents through the Parent-to-Parent of Vermont Program in a nearby town.

There were positive outcomes for David's family and his local team members as well. His parents received support from another family of a child with spina bifida through a Parent-to-Parent match. They also developed online relationships with several other families through a national Web-based chat room. The school team began to meet regularly with the parents and pediatrician to solve issues at home and school, and to monitor progress and plan programs to support both David and his sister. Medical information was interpreted by his pediatrician and school nurse, and made accessible for the school team. The community service providers increased their awareness of, and appreciation for, the expertise and knowledge of David's parents in caring for his complex needs. School and community providers gained a better understanding of the lifelong health issues confronting David and his family. Although there was nothing that could simplify the number of people involved in their lives, David's parents were better supported in their efforts to coordinate and manage the array of services needed to care for David at home and in his community.

OUTCOMES OF THE INTERDISCIPLINARY ASSESSMENT

The promotion and enhancement of the health and well-being of children with developmental disabilities and special health care needs is the primary goal and intended outcome of an interdisciplinary community-based assessment. There are many potential barriers and challenges to providing comprehensive assessments for children with complex health and educational needs. One of these challenges is the need for information from many professionals from various disciplines, who may work in different organizations and locations. These professionals may not be familiar with the child and family's community or their living situation. Despite best intentions, timely and clear communication among various specialists and community service providers is often the exception rather than the norm for families, who are then left with the responsibility of translating the information to their local community service providers. As a result, both families and local community providers are often provided incomplete, outdated, or contradicting information and recommendations. In contrast, the interdisciplinary community-based assessment approach ensures that information is shared among all team members and that the outcomes of the assessment are relevant to the family and local service providers. In this model, the family, primary health care provider, and community professionals drive the assessment by the interdisciplinary team. They determine the priority questions to be addressed and collaborate in developing recommendations and action plans so that information from specialists is translated into relevant outcomes for the child and family.

Outcomes for Children and Their Families

Interdisciplinary professionals need to work as partners with the family to provide optimal outcomes for the child. When an interdisciplinary assessment team embraces the principles of a family professional partnership, family members are included in all team processes and have the leading role in identifying the questions to be addressed in the assessment. Assessment information is shared in full with the family, and they collaborate in the development of recommendations and action plans for their child. A family-centered assessment approach acknowledges that family members are the experts on their own child and family. In many cases, families have also developed extensive knowledge of their child's disability and its natural history, associated problems, and appropriate treatments. A family-centered approach ensures that the outcomes of the interdisciplinary community-based assessment are respectful, strengths-based, individualized, and feasible for the child, family, and community.

Outcomes for Interdisciplinary Team Members

To work as partners, interdisciplinary professionals and family members need to adopt a collaborative framework, practice together, and reflect on their collaborative teaming skills, and refine their teaming strategies over time. Collaborative teaming requires that the appropriate team members are involved, that building and maintaining relationships among team members is a priority, and that the work of the team is accomplished in a timely and efficient manner. Individuals are encouraged to share knowledge and resources and to be personally accountable to each other for following through on their commitments. An important outcome of the interdisciplinary community-based assessment is an increased awareness of the roles and contributions of all team members. The exchange of knowledge and experience among all team members provides an opportunity for professional growth and development, and results in a more holistic, ecologically relevant approach to assessment.

The interdisciplinary team gains an awareness of resources and realistic constraints that exist in the community by involving local service providers and others who regularly interact with the child and family in the assessment process. Local providers contribute valuable information about important factors such as the availability of transportation, skilled personnel, and the social, political, and cultural norms of the community where the family lives. Community providers, friends, extended family, and others who may be involved in the assessment process often have information to share about formal and informal supports available to the family such as local church groups, recreational opportunities, programs across and within local agencies, child care, or after-school programs. All of this information will impact the specific action plans that are the outcome of the assessment process. Assessments that incorporate this information are more likely to result in a shared ownership of recommendations and promote consensus regarding action plans, which will move the assessment process forward. This is in contrast to more traditional clinic-based assessments where many recommendations are often generated, but few are implemented because they may not fit the context of the child, family, and community.

Training Outcomes

As a component of a MCH LEND training program, the assessment model prepares trainees and fellows to implement best practices in providing services to children with developmental disabilities and special health care needs and their families. This is an important long-term outcome that focuses on building the capacity of the service system. Trainees and fellows from a number of disciplines are mentored by an interdisciplinary faculty in the practice of collaborative teaming and in the tenets of culturally sensitive and family-centered care. They both increase skill in their own discipline and acquire new perspectives and knowledge from others. An outcome of this training component is to create leaders with a vision of how assessments can be responsive to children, families, and communities and result in meaningful interventions that improve the health of children. Trainees acquire greater knowledge of developmental disabilities, an increased awareness of the impact of the child's disability across settings, respect for the family's knowledge, skills and challenges, understanding of constraints and opportunities that exist in communities, and an appreciation of the value of sharing knowledge and support for each other through relationships that bridge professional disciplines, agencies, and programs.

CONCLUSION

Although there will always remain a need for the knowledge and skills of many professionals in the lives of children with developmental disabilities and special health care needs, a collaboratively planned, interdisciplinary, community-based assessment can enhance the continuity and coordination of care for children and their families. Our assessment model is congruent with the World Health Organization's ICF framework. The child's health is carefully evaluated using the ICF categories of body structure and function, and his or her activities and participation. In addition, the assessment model is attentive to the ICF contextual factors, that is, environmental and personal factors. The inclusive nature of the assessment process, and the resulting scope and depth of information gathered, provides a holistic view of the child, the family, and the community. The observed outcome is the improved health and functioning of the children with special health care needs and their families in their communities.

STUDY QUESTIONS

1. What is the role of families in the assessment of their children with special health care needs?
2. How do consulting interdisciplinary teams support and not supplant service systems already in place struggling to address the needs of children with special health care needs?
3. What are some of the health and contextual factors interdisciplinary teams need to consider in their assessment of children with special health care needs?

GLOSSARY

Arnold Chiari malformation—A condition in which the inferior poles of the cerebellar hemispheres and the medulla protrude into the spinal cord, causing hydrocephalus; usually accompanies spina bifida and meningomyelocele.

Catheterization—A process of inserting a tube into the body to introduce or remove fluid.

Ecomap—A paper-and-pencil simulation that depicts a family in the context of their community, identifying available resources and relationships among services currently being accessed.

Genogram—A representation of a family tree that provides information about a family's history for at least three generations.

Hydrocephalus—An abnormal amount of fluid within the brain which makes the head enlarge.

Meningomyelocele—A swelling of the spinal cord and membranes through a defect in the spinal cord.

Nephrologist—A physician who specializes in the condition and diseases of the kidney.

Shunt—A device used to provide an alternative path for fluid to drain from the brain.

Spina Bifida—A congenital defect of the spine in which a portion of the spinal cord and its membranes are exposed through a hole in the backbone.

Urologist—A physician who specializes in the condition and diseases of the urinary system.

RESOURCES

Family Voices
3411 Candelaria NE, Suite M
Albuquerque, NM 87107
Phone: 888-835-5669
http://www.familyvoices.org

International Federation for Hydrocephalus and Spina Bifida
Cellebroerstraat 16
B-1000 Brussels, Belgium
Phone: +32 (0)2 502 0413
http://www.ifglobal.org

March of Dimes Birth Defects Foundation
1275 Mamaroneck Avenue
White Plains, NY 10605
Phone: 914-428-7100
http://www.modimes.org

National Easter Seal Society
70 E. Lake Street
Chicago, IL 60601
Phone: 312-726-6200 or 800-221-6827
http://wa.easter-seals.org

National Information Center for Children and Youth with Disabilities
P.O. Box 1492
Washington, DC 20013-1492
Phone: 800-695-0285
http://www.nichcy.org

National Organization for Rare Disorders
55 Kenosia Avenue, P.O. Box 1968
Danbury, CT 06813-1968
Phone: 800-999-6673
http://www.rarediseases.org

Spina Bifida Association of America
4590 MacArthur Boulevard, Suite 250
Washington DC, 20007
Phone: 202-944-3285or 800-621-3141
http://www.sbaa.org/index.shtml

REFERENCES

American Academy of Pediatrics, Committee on Children With Disabilities. (1999). Care coordination: Integrating health and related systems of care for children with special health care needs. *Pediatrics, 104*, 978–981.

American Academy of Pediatrics, Committee on Children With Disabilities. (2000). Provision of educationally-related services for children and adolescents with chronic diseases and disabling conditions. *Pediatrics, 105*, 448–451.

American Academy of Pediatrics, Committee on Children With Disabilities. (2001). Role of the pediatrician in family-centered early intervention services. *Pediatrics, 107*, 1155–1157.

Bishop, K. K., Skidmore Taylor, M., & Arango, P. (1997). *Partnerships at work. Lessons learned from programs and practices of families, professionals and communities.* Burlington: University of Vermont, Department of Social Work.

Bishop, K. K., Woll, J., & Arango, P. (1993). *Family/professional collaboration for children with special health care needs and their families.* Burlington: University of Vermont, Department of Social Work.

Conners. (1989). *Conners' rating scales.* North Tonawanda, NY: Multi-Health Systems.

Dunn, W. (1999). *Sensory profile: Users manual.* San Antonio: TX: Psychological Corporation.

Dunst, C., & Trivette, C. (1990). Assessment of social support in early intervention programs. In S. Meisels & J. Shonkoff (Eds.), *Handbook of early childhood intervention* (pp. 326–349). New York: Cambridge University Press.

Giangreco, M. F. (1996). Assessment of social support in early intervention programs. In S. Meisels & J. Schonkoff (Eds.), *Handbook of early childhood intervention* (pp. 326–349). New York: Cambridge University Press.

Goldrick, M., & Gerson, B. (1985). *Genograms in family assessment.* New York: Norton.

Hartman, A., & Laird, J. (1983). *Family-Centered social work practice.* New York: Free Press.

Institute of Medicine, Committee on a National Agenda for the Prevention of Disabilities. (1991). Executive Summary. In A. M. Pope & A. R. Tarlov (Eds.), *Disability in America: Toward a national agenda for prevention* (pp. 1–15). Washington, DC: National Academy Press.

Institute of Medicine, Committee on Nervous System Disorders in Developing Countries. (2001). *Neurological, psychiatric and developmental disorders: Meeting the challenge in developing counties* (pp. 113–176). Washington, DC: National Academy Press.

Johnson, D. W., & Johnson, F. (1991). *Joining together: Group theory and group skills* (4th ed.). Englewood Cliffs, NJ: Prentice Hall.

Linder, T. W. (1993). *Transdisciplinary play-based assessment: A functional approach to working with young children* (Rev. ed.). Baltimore: Brookes.

Lutkenhoff, M. (1999). *Children with spina bifida: A parent's guide.* Bethesda, MD: Woodbine House.

Lutkenhoff, M., & Oppenheimer, S. G. (Eds.). (1997). *SPINabilities: A young person's guide to spina bifida.* Bethesda, MD: Woodbine House.

McPherson, M., Arango, P., Fox, H., Lauver, C., McManus, M., Newacheck, P. W. et al. (1998). A new definition of children with special health needs. *Pediatrics, 102,* 137–139.

Newacheck, P. W., Strickland, B., Shonkoff, J. P., Perrin, J. M., McPherson, M., McManus, M. et al. (1998). An epidemiologic profile of children with special health care needs. *Pediatrics, 102,* 117–123.

Parnes, S. J. (Ed.). (1992). *Sourcebook for creative problem solving: A fifty-year digest of proven innovation processes.* New York: Creative Education Foundation Press.

Satcher, D. (U.S. Surgeon General). (2001, March). *Special hearing on promoting health for people with mental retardation.* U.S. Senate Committee on Appropriations, Anchorage, AK.

Thousand, J. S., & Villa, R. A. (1992). Collaborative teams: A powerful tool in school restructuring. In R. A. Villa, J. S. Thousand, W. Stainback, & S. Stainback (Eds.), *Restructuring for caring and effective education: An administrative guide to creating heterogeneous schools* (pp. 73–108). Baltimore: Brookes.

World Health Organization. (2001). *International classification of functioning, disability, and health.* Geneva, Switzerland: World Health Organization.

6

Care Coordination in Challenging Contexts: Attention Deficit Disorder, Language Learning Disabilities, and Hearing Impairment

Martha P. Dewees
Jean E. Beatson
University of Vermont

Priscilla Douglas
Fletcher Allen Health Care

Questions to Consider

Consider, as a member of an interdisciplinary team, the following questions as you learn about care coordination for children and families with complex needs in challenging contexts:

1. In what ways does care coordination provide a bridge for children and families with multiple health needs in challenging contexts?
2. How can interdisciplinary teams address societal issues of poverty, exclusion, and disempowerment?
3. How can interdisciplinary providers implement family-centered care when families are split apart?
4. How can service systems be changed in ways that support children, families, and practitioners?

CAROLINA'S STORY: ATTENTION DEFICIT
AND LANGUAGE LEARNING DISABILITY

Carolina was an 8-year-old girl who lived with a foster family in a small town about 20 miles from her birth mother. The foster family was ready to move into adoption proceedings once parental rights were terminated as expected. The foster family was middle class, loved Carolina, and was also committed to helping her maintain a solid relationship with her birth mother, Jane. Jane's older son, John, had also been removed from her care by the state, and had already been adopted by this same foster family.

Jane was a single parent with cognitive developmental delays. Chronic poverty further challenged Jane and Carolina; they had no telephone and no car. Jane's extended family had little to offer her in the way of either material or emotional support. Jane has an abiding love for her children and is deeply grieving the loss of her family.

Carolina is a playful, fun-loving child with a great sense of humor. She is very social and curious. Her challenges include Attention Deficit Hyperactivity Disorder (ADHD) treated with Ritalin, receptive and expressive language delays, hypernasality, articulation problems, chronic otitis media with fluctuating conductive hearing loss, and a surgically repaired submucous cleft palate. There are also concerns about listening and auditory processing. School personnel note her behavior problems as aggression toward her peers and characterize them as kicking, hitting, biting, and general opposition to the requests of her mother and some other adults. On one occasion, school staff thought she was making sexually suggestive gestures in the girls' bathroom. She was on an Individualized Education Plan (IEP) receiving special education services at school.

Carolina's early health history was rife with concerns. She had mild developmental delays and repeated ear infections. She had a hernia operation at six months and a fractured femur of questionable origin at 1 year. In kindergarten, Carolina failed her school hearing screen and her teacher noted "poor listening skills" and distractibility, along with behavioral problems with other children. She continued to fail school hearing screens, but there was no evidence of medical follow-up as the school nurse recommended. Carolina was retained in kindergarten that year.

By second grade, Carolina had a full psychological evaluation, showing "intellectual function estimated to be in the 'low average' range." Testing showed low receptive and expressive language scores, auditory processing weaknesses, and reading skills that were 2 years behind. A psychological evaluation identified ADHD, and Carolina was started on Ritalin. Teacher observations included concerns about distractibility, impulsivity, inability to follow oral directions, disruptive behavior, and difficult-to-understand speech.

Jane had been concerned about the nasality of Carolina's speech since she began to talk, but health care providers had dismissed her concerns. An examination done by the speech–language pathologist from the interdisciplinary team revealed a previously undiagnosed submucous cleft palate. The combination of chronic otitis media with resultant fluctuating hearing loss and the undiagnosed cleft palate had a serious impact on Carolina's learning. Her inattentiveness was exacerbated by an inability to hear well. Her expressive language problems and nasality made her speech difficult to understand.

Carolina's family practice physician referred her to the interdisciplinary team for care coordination. Her doctor was frustrated by Carolina's inconsistent health care, Jane's noncompliance with medical regimes, time-consuming and difficult communication with the school team, and the overwhelming presentation of family problems at the doctor's visits that Jane managed to make. The doctor hoped that care coordination provided by the interdisciplinary team would resolve these challenges.

INTRODUCTION

This chapter sets out to explore the model for care coordination that the interdisciplinary team uses when serving children and families with complex needs. The chapter discusses the purpose of care coordination and the role of team members through family stories. It views care coordination from the perspective of children, families, and community teams as well as from the perspective of training health professionals in an interdisciplinary model.

The chapter is divided into four parts. Part I describes care coordination. Part II tells Carolina's story and is followed by care coordination for Carolina in Part III. Part IV explores the lessons the interdisciplinary team learned.

CARE COORDINATION:
WHAT IS IT AND HOW DOES IT WORK?

The following section describes the nature of care coordination in the context of the interdisciplinary team. It addresses the specific principles incorporated in the care coordinator's approach with the family and community teams and spells out how they are implemented.

What Is Care Coordination?

The ultimate purpose of care coordination is to improve the health of children with special needs through family-centered, culturally competent care that is responsive to the real and pressing needs children and families face. It is a process in which families prioritize their concerns regarding their child with special needs. From this process the interdisciplinary team sets goals in collaboration with the community team. The interdisciplinary team assigns a care coordinator to work closely with the family and the community team to ensure action plans are made and implemented to attain identified goals.

Although the Individuals with Disabilities Education Act (IDEA) does not mandate care coordination, best practice requires family-centered and culturally competent approaches (Smith & Prelock, 2002). School teams that adopt this type of family-centered service model in caring for children with chronic health needs are finding that their knowledge of the relation between health status and learning increases (Thies & McAllister, 2001).

From the start, the Vermont Interdisciplinary Leadership Education for Health Professionals (VT–ILEHP) program trains care coordinators in the guiding principles of family-centered care, cultural competence, strengths-based practice, neurodevelopmental disabilities, and collaborative teaming. (Chapters 2 and 3, respectively, describe family-centered care and cultural competence comprehensively.)

Strengths-based practice assumes that all children and families have inherent strengths. In addition to anything a child, parent, or family is adept at doing, other strengths include love, hopes, and dreams for a child. Benard (2002) summarized a series of core premises of a strengths and resilience approach to youth. Among these is an affirmation of the innate resilience of all people. Other beliefs assert that caring adults can make a significant difference in the lives of youth through interventions that demonstrate respect for their gifts and talents. In addition, she recommended that providers listen to and acknowledge the pain that at-risk youth may experience. She believes providers should ask youth about their interests, dreams, survival, and positive times, as well as link them to resources and opportunities. This approach assumes that inherent individual strengths will assist youth in overcoming their challenges. It is important, therefore, for the care coordinator to look for these strengths and reflect on them when meeting families.

In addition to using family-centered, strengths-based, and culturally competent approaches, care coordinators need to acquire other skills (Smith & Prelock, 2002). Knowledge and coordination of resources is important in linking children and families to available supports. Understanding the context in which a child and family live lends an understanding of the supports they are likely to need. Collaborative teaming skills facilitate the team's focus on a child and family and ensure that the action plans move forward. Care coordinators can come from any health profession and it is important that they are competent in their respective disciplines. Care coordinators do not have to have all the answers, but they must know how to get the information and be meticulous in their follow-through with families, whether it is placing a call to a specialist or getting articles or resources to the family (Beatson, 1999, unpublished manuscript).

How Is Care Coordination Implemented?

The care coordinator meets with the family members and listens to their story. As it unfolds, the care coordinator looks for strengths and listens for challenges or unmet needs. The care coordinator reflects back to the family what he or she sees and hears. Through this process, the participants refine and prioritize potential goals.

Next, the care coordinator meets the community team by asking to attend one of their meetings. After introductions are made, the care coordinator explains the care coordination model. Together the interdisciplinary team, the community team, and the family discuss the family-prioritized goals and make action plans. It is essential for the community team members to feel their work is being enhanced and not increased (Thies & McAllister, 2001).

Remembering that the overall purpose is to improve the health of children with special needs, the VT–ILEHP interdisciplinary team members pay attention to the specific disabilities and health needs of the child. These include reviewing completed assessments and developing care plans and accommodations. Although the child with special health needs is central to care coordination, the family and community teams create the context for the work.

CARE COORDINATION FOR CAROLINA: AN IN-DEPTH LOOK AT THE ISSUES

This section focuses on the unique and challenging contexts that were salient in Carolina's situation. The authors present these contexts through the frameworks that underlie the interdisciplinary team's care coordination model. These are family-centered care, strengths-based community practice, cultural competence, and neurodevelopmental disabilities.

Family-Centered Care

The establishment and maintenance of family-centered care emerged as a significant challenge for all members of the interdisciplinary team. Some aspects proved more difficult than others. The need to build a relationship, initially, at least, by listening to the family's story (Smith & Prelock, 2002) and attending to and understanding their experience (Beatson & Prelock, 2002) became a primary concern to the interdisciplinary team. The care coordinator met with Carolina's mother, Jane, and with her foster family. By her own account, Jane reflected that the care coordinator's hearing her story without offering criticism or corrective advice validated the legitimacy of her position. Although the story was often not easy to hear and presented some concerns for the safety of Carolina, this commitment to listen to the family's perspective is a core value of the interdisciplinary team. In listening to Jane talk, the care coordinator recognized that her strengths included her long-term knowledge of Carolina's medical background, health history, and Carolina's overall needs. Jane also had a deep love for Carolina and dreamt of reuniting her family. The foster family's strengths included their love for Carolina, their openness toward Jane, and their commitment to include her in Carolina's life.

Ethnographic research methods (see Cook, 2000) involving "not knowing" standpoints guided the team to see Jane as the expert in her experience. These methods also assisted the interdisciplinary team in understanding the meaning she made of Carolina's situation. Carolina's care coordinator was well versed in narrative methods of interviewing and committed to the ethnographic position of naturalistic discovery, rather than prescription (Leigh, 1998), in the initial phases of the work. Not surprisingly, this early effort went quite smoothly as reflected in Jane's verbally positive responses regarding that dimension of the work.

When the care coordinator attended Carolina's community team meeting, Jane was not there and it was evident that there was little effort to support her inclusion in educational or developmental processes such as IEP meetings. She was either invited at the last minute when it would be impossible to arrange transportation, invited but told she could not bring her boyfriend (who provided her transportation), or not told at all. It became clear the school was experiencing difficulties in understanding the legalities regarding foster care, parental rights, and with whom they were supposed to be communicating. The school team members assumed that they needed to communicate only with the foster family, but because the state had not terminated Jane's parental rights, school personnel should have communicated with both Jane and the foster family.

Although Jane's exclusion was an egregious breach of her rights, it was also harmful for Carolina, because Jane remained the single most knowledgeable person about Carolina's medical and educational history. Jane was not seen as a valuable or even legitimate participant in those processes. The disdain that some of the school staff held for her, illustrated by their off-hand, disparaging comments regarding her participation, made respectful advocacy a significant purpose for the interdisciplinary team. Gathering and presenting legal information regarding foster care and parental rights became another care coordination goal. After this was accomplished, the interdisciplinary team developed a plan to improve communication among Jane, the foster family, and the school team. The support of the foster parents was essential in helping the school team accept the idea that Jane was still instrumental in the care of Carolina.

Another challenge to family-centered work arose because Jane has a developmental disability and was parenting without the support of a partner. The assumption of capability, the right to control one's life, and the ongoing commitment to the family's own choices can tax the responsible provider's sensibilities and ethical commitments. The interdisciplinary team's efforts to see Jane in terms consistent with a strengths-oriented, family-centered approach (Shelton & Stepanek, 1995) were legion. This approach posed a continuous challenge, particularly as it was juxtaposed to Carolina's welfare and safety. Gilson, Bricourt, and Baskind (1998) reminded us that many people with disabilities assert that they have been treated by professionals "as though they had categorically fewer aspirations, abilities, and perhaps even fundamental rights than did non-disabled people" (p. 188). The interdisciplinary team struggled against these attitudes throughout Carolina's care coordination.

Genograms and Ecomaps.   Another task of the care coordinator was to engage in family mapping exercises (McGoldrick, Gerson, & Shellenberger, 1999) consisting of a genogram and ecomap (Compton & Galaway, 1999) to gain a visual understanding of the complexities of relationships (see Chapter 4). For Carolina's care coordinator, drawing the family tree and community supports was very challenging. Jane was the birth mother and still retained parental rights, yet Carolina lived with foster parents in another town (ironically, Jane's hometown) who had made known they would like to adopt her. The question of "who is the family here" provided a poignant reminder of the ambiguity in the situation, the emotional tug of war inherent in such a constellation, and the power aspects of "child removal." The care coordinator's initial mapping efforts immediately highlighted the tensions in the situation that remained prominent throughout the interdisciplinary team's work with this family. The worker from the child welfare department invited Carolina to discuss her place in the genogram as well (Altshuler, 1999). This process validated Carolina's confusion regarding her "place" and also provided a forum for her to talk about her emotions and hopes for the future.

The ecomap also generated tension because it illustrated the question about the appropriate placement of the interdisciplinary team and ultimately its role. The care coordinator placed the interdisciplinary team midway between Jane and the foster family (seeing Carolina as the central "client"), but this raised a philosophical tension between child-centered and family-centered care. A reminder of the interdisciplinary team's firm commitment to the child's welfare helped to resolve this tension. One member described reviewing the United Nations "Rights of the Child" (United Nations, 2002) and recommitted to supporting the principles that would give Carolina the best chance to fulfill the basic human needs explicated in the Declaration of Universal Human Rights. Ultimately, and sadly, there seemed little way to resolve this apart from Carolina's removal from Jane's care. This was one of the central struggles among interdisciplinary team members and they still remember it as poignant.

The concern for the interdisciplinary team's position on the ecomap also suggested differential placement of individuals on that team. Professional role is highly important to all disciplines in the helping fields, but the boundaries and definitions are not standard, particularly around the line between friend and client. Professionals may see these parameters as private choices as long as they are explicit about which "hat" they wear in which context. In Jane's situation, this became a contested issue. In a study conducted in Vermont, parents described the "ideal care coordinator" as a good friend (Beatson, 1999, unpublished manuscript). Yet, some interdisciplinary team members were not comfortable with their colleagues' assumption of the "friend" role. Lawlor and Mattingly (1998) also found, in their research with families and teams, that relationships evolved into friendships. Some mitigation of this issue occurred in Carolina's situation when the interdisciplinary team clarified which activities were "professional" and which were "personal." Some of the other professionals involved (notably child welfare officials) found, however, the "hat" switching" to be problematic.

Working Principles for Care Coordination.   Family-centered care's commitment to support and honor the family's rights, dreams, hopefulness, and love of their child collided almost immediately with the specialized "best practices" strategies of the child welfare and mental health providers (Lawlor & Mattingly, 1998). Jane never internalized the dominant culture's values by "complying" with recommendations and various dicta regarding what constitutes adequate care for a child. Further, child welfare staff scrutinized the degree and nature of her "attachment" to her children and evaluated it as lacking (see DeMaria, Weeks, & Hof, 1999, for attachment genogram considerations).

Because Carolina was in foster care, her welfare was contingent on the efforts of the foster family to follow through on medical and educational recommendations. This put the care coordinator in the position of supporting both birth mother and foster parents, which Jane occasionally found confusing. The foster parents had been open, exceedingly cooperative, and remarkably insightful as to the emotional and psychological stresses on both Jane and Carolina. They also had a clear and abiding investment in Carolina's future as a member of their family. As Carolina became more integrated into the foster family, she incorporated their mannerisms, expectations, and rituals, including becoming a mannerly child with all of the associated behavioral implications (e.g., saying "please" and "thank you," eating "fruits and vegetables"). This seemed to threaten Jane's own sense of identity as she witnessed her daughter's transformation. Jane's response, changeable as it was, sometimes included full-blown anger as well as an irritable reaction to some of the requests made of her. The interdisciplinary team's role then became to encourage Jane's cooperation with the foster parents, both for Carolina's overall adjustment, and also to enhance the likelihood that Jane could retain voluntary access, courtesy of the foster parents, to Carolina, in the event that they adopted her.

Carolina, too, needed support as she struggled with finding her place in this new family, while visiting her mother regularly. She was confused when Jane told Carolina that she would eventually be coming back home. Carolina's foster parents were open to talking about this issue with her. Carolina also had regular psychotherapy in the community where these tensions were discussed.

The interdisciplinary team continued to work with the family until quite close to Jane's court date for termination of parental rights. Some interdisciplinary team members volunteered to testify in court about Jane's love for her children. Once the court terminated parental rights, the interdisciplinary team members assumed another critical role in their support of Jane in her grieving process and in their effort to facilitate her constructive, ongoing contacts with Carolina and the foster family.

Parents With Disabilities.   Jane is a woman with cognitive limitations and a family history of poverty and marginalization. A self-described "slow-learner," she left school at an early age after giving birth to a son, some 7 years older than Carolina. The family kept the paternity of her son secret for some years as the father was married to another relative. For a few years she had physical and emotional support from siblings but as they grew into adulthood, this waned. She moved to a larger city and began to establish many more social relationships among peers.

Service providers characterized Jane as making non-child-centered decisions that were harmful to, or at least negligent of, her children's interests. Her situation seemed to support the overrepresentation of parents with disabilities in child maltreatment or neglect (Bhagwanji, Bennet, Stillwell, & Allison, 1998). She repeatedly indicated that she thought she was a good parent and that there was nothing wrong with the way she dealt with her children. At the same time, when she was more introspective, she recognized the stigma and isolation of being "delayed" and described with some bitterness the discrimination she experienced (see Mackelprang & Salsgiver, 1999). She particularly bristled at the multiple "expert" opinions she started to receive from "authorities" as her children grew. She felt assiduously undermined, closed out, and devalued, although she knew she had a wealth of knowledge (Kalyanpur & Harry, 1999) regarding Carolina. For example, she had reported Carolina's hypernasality over and over again and no one listened. Occasionally, at her low points, she momentarily saw herself as inadequate in a way consistent with "internalized oppression" (Pheterson, 1990, p. 34), a phenomenon in which an individual accepts as accurate the external, oppressive judgments of others. Ironically, her cognitive disability prevented her from sustaining insight that could lead to meaningful growth and change.

Child welfare workers have sometimes a painful, dual role in strengthening families and protecting children through removal when necessary. The question of when the strengthening efforts succumb to the focus on child removal constitutes an extremely problematic choice-point with ominous repercussions that child welfare workers recognize. They offered Jane many services and supports that she could not or would not accept. Child welfare workers acting alone are not in the position to mediate the lack of natural social supports (see Feldman, 1994), poverty, unemployment, isolation from extended family, or poor parenting models that seem often to accompany disability. The frustration that emerged as Jane refused supporting services predictably led to a focus on her inability or unwillingness to parent. The challenges of providing supports (Mary, 1998) to Jane and of encouraging a safety focus that she could accept proved insurmountable within the time frame given to her. As Carolina was in a foster home, Jane felt that accepting services she did not really want was futile.

Strengths-Based Community Practice

The circumstances of Carolina's foster placement required a change in school district as well as the individual school. The interdisciplinary team had seen Carolina a year prior to this move and made a series of recommendations from the community assessment conducted at her

former school. When she changed schools, few of the recommendations followed her in a timely manner, for several reasons. Because
Carolina was then in the custody of the state, she had little in the way
of effective advocacy for the services she needed, although Jane retained full parental rights. The child welfare worker tried to secure
Jane's cooperation in sending records; however, their relationship was
compromised because Jane saw her as responsible for taking away
Carolina. As a result, Jane was sometimes uncooperative. This trig-
gered a relatively prolonged period of inadequate services in addition
to the usual disruptions when children move. Because a trusting relationship existed between Jane, the care coordinator, and some of the
faculty, the interdisciplinary team was instrumental in assuring implementation of the recommendations made by the previous school,
such as monthly hearing tests by the school nurse, advantageous seating in the classroom, and an in-service of school personnel regarding
fluctuating hearing loss.

Carolina's experience in school was strained, at least at first. She
brought with her many of the same behaviors, generated of poverty,
which she shared with her mother. School staff did not see these as legitimate sequelae of being poor as much as character flaws, and accordingly, they did not consider them acceptable. In addition, she brought
some of the adaptive behaviors of an emotionally needy child. Most of
the new school personnel struggled with trying to shape more acceptable and conducive-to-learning behavior on Carolina's part without
jeopardizing her natural social strengths and abilities to relate (see
Huntley, 1999). This was a touch-and-go process for a while, but
Carolina had the capacity to evoke a loyal, warm emotional response,
and over time she won over most of the school staff. For example,
Carolina was very enthusiastic about her reading time with a particular
teacher and she would often crawl into the teacher's lap to get a hug at
the beginning of her session.

The school team's reluctance toward including Jane presented the
interdisciplinary team with another challenge regarding
strengths-based practice. This involved maintaining a stance of view-
ing other professionals from a perspective of strengths when some of
their attitudes and behaviors seemed negative. This struggle, however, provided an opportunity for subsequent reflection and interdisciplinary team processing. For example, the interdisciplinary team
was upset about the school case manager's explicit negativity toward
Jane. The care coordinator reminded the interdisciplinary team about
its commitment to strengths-based practice and led the team through a
process of identifying the school case manager's strengths. This created a shift in attitude which helped bridge the strain between Jane
and the case manager.

Cultural Competence

Closely intertwined with the strengths-based approach, culturally sensitive practice presents a compelling challenge as well. In the case of Carolina, the cultural variables were in some ways subtle. Jane and her family derive from similar racial and ethnic stock as many of the interdisciplinary team members. She was not a member of a minority in the anthropological sense. Her background as a woman from a primarily rural area in which poverty abounds provided her with the coping strategies of her peers. Socioeconomic class may be a more apt category relating to the differences between Jane and contemporary "mainstream" society. Her cognitive challenges suggest another subgrouping of individuals with developmental disabilities. For example, some of her friends shared a common history as formerly institutionalized persons with developmental disabilities. This seemed to connect them both socially and emotionally.

The care coordinator, filling her "obligation" (Gil, 1984, p. 20) to develop an understanding of Jane's experience, worked hard to validate what she brought to the interdisciplinary team. She respected that as a young, female, privileged, middle class graduate student she had very little experience with anything like what Jane experienced as a single mother with a disability, trying to raise a child with disabilities. She strove to understand Jane's behavior, not as demonstrating her "dysfunction" but as representing a difference (Leigh, 1998).

For example, Jane shared many typical mainstream values, but not all. She saw many professionals as "La-dee-dah" and said they were "uptight" about sex. She described a more open and loose sense of personal and sexual privacy than most members of our society uphold (this issue was extremely important in Carolina's removal). "Work" carried an onerous flavor, and although it was sought for financial reward, it reflected little of the satisfaction many members of the middle and upper class find in it. "Time" was much more fluid as it is sometimes found to be in some non-Western cultures. Occasionally Jane enthusiastically took up "class and status" as power issues that she described in terms of what some people could do and others could not. Finally, the care coordinator also explored the intricacies of foster care (see Rounds, Weil, & Bishop, 1994), including Jane's understanding of various court proceedings, the impact that poverty had on her, and the meaning she gave to the strengths and strategies her own culture had given her with regard to raising children (Saleebey, 2002).

Understanding the differences in meaning that Jane gave to several mainstream value orientations (such as protecting children from sexual predators and maintaining adult privacy in sexual relations) assisted the care coordinator and her mentor in engaging with her, but ultimately did not provide a resolution. Jane's record was replete with accounts by varying professionals of their efforts to educate her around the physical and psychological safety of her children. She simply could not integrate those values in any meaningful way. Her personal needs for friendship and love at times superseded her children's needs. She could not always follow through on important appointments, sometimes because she had no transportation or money, and sometimes because she could not see the relative importance. Various service providers threatened, cajoled, and otherwise tried to convince her she could learn to abide by some simple rules of child-care conduct (e.g., providing supervision, following through on medical needs, finding legitimate caretakers, and refusing to allow child molesters into her house) that would help her keep her children. In the end, Jane could not attain a level of understanding that was deep enough to influence her behavior and allow her to retain custody of her child.

Neurodevelopmental Disabilities

Jane's compromised ability to care for her children as well as the structural, socioeconomic barriers of her situation, contributed to the fragmentation of Carolina's health care. Facing biased responses based on her inability to comply with treatment recommendations and scheduled appointments, Jane experienced a negative relationship with a potential medical home. This lack of stable care (see Chapter 2) resulted in a series of health problems for Carolina as her care shifted to another community. Ironically, just as Jane was unable to follow through on medical recommendations, the information she did have about Carolina's development and status went unacknowledged.

Although Carolina had been identified as a child with chronic otitis media, otitis media with effusion, and fluctuating conductive hearing loss, she had not received consistent medical follow-up for ear infections, and Jane had not consulted an otolaryngologist on her behalf. Carolina had also never received a full audiological evaluation to assess hearing sensitivity, middle ear function, and speech recognition ability. Had Carolina seen an otolaryngologist early on, she might have received ventilation tubes or other medical management procedures that could have improved her hearing and reduced the frequency of her ear infections. With better documentation of her hearing loss, she might have received additional accommodations and services in her school. Earlier recognition of the physical reasons for hypernasality and poor intelligibility would have better guided her speech therapy as well. Such recognition might also have strengthened the need for follow-up for her ear infections through the knowledge that the presence of cleft palate is strongly associated with middle ear problems.

Chronic otitis media with fluctuating hearing loss, which Carolina suffered, has been associated with listening difficulties, inattentive behavior (particularly in background noise), auditory processing deficits, speech and language delays, and subsequent academic difficulties (Alpiner & McCarthy, 2000; Roberts & Hunter, 2003). Research suggests that many variables are involved, including the notion that the home environment may be more predictive of early math and expressive language skills through second grade than otitis media with effusion and hearing loss (Roberts, Burchinal, & Zeisel, 2002). Factors such as the style and amount of talk and conversation in the home, reading to a child which includes discussing meaning and inferences, and the overall organization, responsiveness, and support of the home environment, can predict early language development. Given Jane's own developmental delays, it is probable that Carolina did not have consistent and rich auditory stimulation or language modeling at home, factors which may have contributed to delays in speech and language, and limited listening skill development.

Based on the interdisciplinary team's speech–language pathologist's findings, the team made a referral to an ear, nose, and throat specialist who confirmed a submucous cleft palate, performed surgery to correct it, and placed ventilation tubes in both ears. Immediately following the surgery, Carolina's speech sounded clearer and less nasal, but apparently the postsurgery swelling only temporarily facilitated closure of the surgical repair. Within 6 weeks, the hypernasality was again apparent, although everyone agreed it was better than before the surgery. Her physician referred her to a speech–language pathologist, at the local university, who specialized in cleft palate. However, her attendance at therapy sessions was inconsistent due to Carolina's frequent illnesses and transportation difficulties. Follow-up audiological evaluation revealed that her hearing was much better with the ventilation tubes in place. Unfortunately, the tubes fell out within 6 months and the chronic ear infections and effusion resumed. The interdisciplinary team recommended that the school nurse carry out monthly hearing checks to better document Carolina's hearing levels and support the need for ongoing services and accommodations. These services and accommodations also included advantageous seating in the classroom as well as installation of a frequency modulated (FM) auditory enhancement system. Using this system, the teacher wears a microphone and transmitter that sends her voice to several speakers placed around the perimeter of the room. A deaf and hard of hearing consultant conducted an in-service program for school personnel regarding the detrimental effects of fluctuating hearing loss, use of the FM system, and teaching strategies to optimize auditory learning. Improved home–school communication and assistance to Jane with transportation resulted in more consistent medical follow-up.

Carolina's situation provided a rich educational experience not only for trainees and fellows interested in leadership in health professions, but for the entire interdisciplinary team. Throughout care coordination, the interdisciplinary team struggled with the unique challenges that Carolina and Jane faced every day. The next section describes the lessons we learned through our work and relationships with this family and those who served them.

LESSONS LEARNED

The breadth and depth of the lessons that the interdisciplinary team learned ranged from the role of the interdisciplinary team to national policy. These lessons, described later, related to the following: (a) training parameters, (b) understanding families with complex needs, (c) effects of poverty, (d) impact of termination of parental rights, (e) ethical dilemmas, (f) outcomes, and (g) policy implications.

Training Parameters

The two major training parameters were the evolution of care coordination and the role of a comprehensive assessment as a beginning point for care coordination. This section addresses each of them.

Evolution of Care Coordination.   In the early years of the training grant, the interdisciplinary team envisioned a model of care coordination that would place the families' needs at the center of the work. The vision included a seamless model of care for families interfacing with multiple agencies and systems, including mental health and developmental disabilities, education, early intervention, Medicaid, and health care. Schools and physicians referred children with special health care needs and their families, many of whom were living in very challenging situations, such as was Carolina and her family, to the interdisciplinary team for care coordination. It became evident that trainees and fellows were not in a position to provide this vision of care coordination because they had no real authority to do this work. The community case managers had mandated work to do and could not relinquish their roles to a student with a vision. Thus, school case managers rightly viewed the care coordinator as an add-on to the child's community team, and often as an extra set of hands or advocate for the family.

The most frequently asked question of the trainees and fellows by the community teams regarded their role on that team. The trainees and fellows came to the interdisciplinary team and asked the faculty the very same question: "What is my role, what am I supposed to be doing?" This question led the faculty to make some significant changes in the care coordination model.

First, we decided that care coordination would be provided only following a community-based assessment by the interdisciplinary team. The interdisciplinary team learned over time that it had to become much more collaborative with the existing teams and work very hard to understand the systems level of issues. The role of the care coordinator was to collaborate with the community team in implementation of the recommendations generated in the interdisciplinary team's assessment report. The second major change was that the interdisciplinary team would offer care coordination as community assessment follow-up through the end of the academic year in which it completed the assessment. We would extend care coordination for a second year on a selective basis and the focus would remain on recommendation implementation. Because of these changes, the community teams, the trainees and fellows, and the faculty finally came to understand the role of the care coordinator.

The interdisciplinary team remained committed to the vision of the family at the center of care coordination. The family was instrumental in identifying problems that needed to be addressed through the interdisciplinary assessment and assisted in generating recommendations for the interdisciplinary report. Although we narrowed the scope for purposes of more appropriate training, the interdisciplinary team has remained deeply committed to family-centered care in challenging contexts and has worked hard to develop respectful relationships with families and children with special health needs.

The Role of a Comprehensive Assessment. For several reasons, the interdisciplinary team considers community-based, family-centered assessment for children with special health needs as a critical beginning point for their work with children, their families, and the teams that serve them. (For a complete discussion on the assessment process, see Chapter 4.) First, it allows us to approach everyone with a holistic, strengths-based view, thereby setting a positive tone. We address the families and teams' most pressing questions and concerns, pulling together multiple sources of information. Because we are part of a university setting, we have access to a wide range of current best practice initiatives and research that we can bring to bear on the daily challenges faced by community teams. Working within our own process in service to children, families, and teams affords us the legitimacy of presence at the table. We strive to do this in such a manner that everyone grows and learns. We have found that teams serving children and families with complex needs seek the help of our interdisciplinary team for all of the aforementioned reasons.

Families With Multiple and Complex Needs

Carolina and her mother faced several formidable obstacles for which the community offered multiple interventions, including foster care for both Jane and Carolina. Because of her personal characteristics and developmental disability, Jane was not able to accept the services that might ultimately have allowed her to keep custody of Carolina, which was her most heartfelt wish. Jane felt discriminated against and intruded on by some service providers in spite of, and because of, the number and invasiveness of the "wrap-around" services they offered. Her refusal of these offers in turn made it more difficult for many providers to maintain their family-centered and strengths-based perspectives. Although Jane responded positively to the interdisciplinary team, the team was not able to facilitate the behavioral changes in Jane regarding Carolina's care that might have effected a happier ending. It seemed evident that human service professionals need to find a way to respond differently to those who challenge their ideas about effectiveness. At the same time, it became clear as a training issue that the challenges facing Jane went far beyond the scope of care coordination.

Poverty and Its Effects

The poverty that Jane and Carolina faced seemed to reach out into all corners of their lives. It had a major impact on the perception of Jane as an unfit parent, as she persistently could not follow through on Carolina's medical needs or provide adequate financial care for her children. Her constant quest for work to meet income expectations shaped her behaviors and influenced Carolina's socialization. Ultimately, the team recognized that it could not ameliorate the impact of Jane's poverty.

Impact of Termination of Parental Rights

The anticipation of termination of parental rights in Carolina's story had a dramatic impact on all the parties involved months before the event actually took place. A description of these impacts follows.

Jane.   As a mother, Jane had experienced the rigorous vigilance of child welfare, school, and the community with a bitter sense of being spied on constantly. She frequently complained of never being "good enough" while, in her view, others were allowed to steal her child. She felt confused one minute, sad the next, and outraged the next. She experienced a lengthy, ongoing struggle to make sense of this situation.

Carolina.   Carolina's new house seemed to her to be "in the country." It smelled good. No trash or garbage cluttered the entrance; no bot-
tles or smoke greeted her at the doorway. It was not at all like home. Her
new "parents" were easygoing with her but also had clear expectations.
They seemed to like her, but there were rules. She had to say "please"
and "thank you" and had to participate in a regular dinner at a regular
time. She heard the following: "sit down at the table," "eat your vegetables," "take a bath," and "do your homework." She tried to do what she
was told and felt good when she got attention and approval. For example, she exclaimed to her care coordinator that she ate "EVERYTHING"
now. But who was really her mother? For quite awhile, she just wanted
to go home.

Foster Parents.   Carolina's foster parents made extraordinary efforts to keep communication and contact open between Carolina and
Jane. They told Carolina they knew they were not her parents and that
they understood it was hard for both her and her mother. The emotional
energy they invested in maintaining the open boundaries required in
raising someone else's child while maintaining their own sense of family with their other children was considerable. It was clearly a challenge
they embraced with impressive success.

The Interdisciplinary Team and Other Professionals.   Jane was not
alone in her sorrow and frustration. Her anguish was palpable and it influenced everyone who worked with her. A pervading sense of loss and
regret permeated her instinctive mother's defenses and invaded the
sensibilities of the child welfare worker, the foster parents, the school
personnel, and the interdisciplinary team. The interdisciplinary team
was torn in its efforts to support Carolina while she went through the
foster care process and prepared for termination of her mother's parental rights. It struggled with its role in supporting both Jane, as birth
mother, and the foster parents. Ultimately, we learned that it is possible
to do both and impossible to avoid the attendant grief.

Ethical Dilemmas

The work with Jane's family generated some ethical dilemmas within the
interdisciplinary team. The first involved the potentially conflicting positions inherent in maintaining a commitment to family-centered care.
Defining how the family is constituted and working through the conun-
drum between what appears best for a child and what is in the realm of
parental goals and rights provided one of the more difficult ethical conflicts. Because of Jane's inability to keep Carolina in a safe environment

and the interdisciplinary team's commitment to children's rights, it was particularly difficult to advocate for and support her continued, imminently dangerous efforts at parenting. On the other hand, because Jane so earnestly loved her daughter and demonstrated such devastation at her loss, it was likewise difficult to advocate for Carolina's removal.

It was also challenging for the care coordinator to find ways to support all parties to the family dynamics. For example, she struggled with how to support Jane while reconciling what seemed an inevitable path of termination of parental rights. Ultimately, the effort went into acknowledging and validating Jane's grief while assisting her to connect with the foster parents in a positive way so that she could continue to be a presence in Carolina's life.

Carolina, too, required and will continue to require, ongoing, caring assistance in dealing with the loss of her mother. As supportive and committed as her adoptive parents were, she experienced the same kind of loss as did Jane, and will need to continue to negotiate her new relationship within the context of an adoptive family. The interdisciplinary team supported the understanding and the efforts of the adoptive family as they underwent this transition.

Early in the process, Jane saw the interdisciplinary team's support of the foster parents as disloyalty to her. This scenario demanded the care coordinator's ongoing creativity and patience. The interdisciplinary team generally encouraged the foster parents in their recognition of the issues in Carolina's transition from one home life to another. The interdisciplinary team was able to work with them in facilitating Carolina's adjustment to a new school and continuation of the medical and psychological services she needed to successfully make the transition. Jane eventually grew to recognize as supportive the various efforts of individual interdisciplinary team members.

Outcomes

With a mix of perceived successes and challenges in this case, the interdisciplinary team clearly accomplished a number of outcomes consistent with the goals and mission of the program and, more important, critical to Carolina's future. These included the following:

- The establishment of an effective team in the new school and coordinated services.
- Regularly scheduled direct services provided by a speech–language pathologist, social worker, and guidance counselor.
- Identification and subsequent surgical repair of submucous cleft palate with resultant improved focus in speech therapy and improved intelligibility.

- More consistent medical and audiological follow-up including placement of ventilation tubes.
- Closer monitoring of Carolina's hearing at school with better recognition of the impact of her fluctuating hearing loss on listening and attending behaviors.
- Implementation of services and strategies to improve Carolina's listening skills and the acoustical environment.
- The establishment of a strong connection with a medical home.
- Maintenance of ongoing semiweekly psychotherapy in the community.
- Significant support for Jane regarding issues of loss inherent in the termination of her parental rights; renegotiation of Jane's participation in local mental health care in a way she could accept.
- Facilitation of Jane's continuing connection to Carolina's life through active work with the foster family to reinforce the importance of her role as birth mother.
- The humbling of an interdisciplinary team which recognized its shortcomings in meeting its own goals for competence, recognized its limitations in averting the separation of a family, and now has a better understanding of the team's role in care coordination and the conflicts inherent in challenging contexts.

The interdisciplinary team learned that the tension generated by conflicting discipline-specific perspectives (e.g., social work versus speech–language pathology versus pediatrics) served as a catalyst for clarification of what could and could not be done for Carolina and Jane. We also learned that the struggle was creative to true interdisciplinary practice. Out of respect for the value of this creative struggle, we now have processing meetings in which the interdisciplinary team can explore and integrate complex issues. These meetings have two purposes: to reflect on our own behaviors as interdisciplinary team members and to serve as a confidential venue to talk about difficult issues and conflicts within our work. We learned to keep our hearts open and to move through the process.

Policy Implications

Carolina's story exposed trainees and fellows to the implications of a number of important policy issues on multiple levels. National, state, and local policies concerned with mental health, child welfare, and poverty played a large role in Jane's complex efforts to survive with her family intact. Many services derived from mental health, child welfare, and social welfare policies were available to Jane. Such services are designed to support people with disabilities, sustain stable families, and provide adequate income for those without other resources. Because she could not accept their intrusion into her life, Jane did not participate in many of them. The disconnects between the intent of such policies and services and the realities of Jane's life were easy to see. That is, the very nature of Jane's cognitive and emotional disabilities (along with her fierce independence) prevented her from availing herself of the supports and services that would have enabled her to keep her child. Clearly, changing or amending them to be more responsive to the "Janes" of this country would require a sophisticated and gargantuan effort.

In the area of individual rights, policies surrounding the various rights of children and parents with developmental disabilities are sometimes in direct conflict. Keeping children safe and keeping families together is not always possible. Recognition of this and dialogue around its resolution seems necessary. Although some of this debate is purely ideological, its repercussions come into very concrete conflict in certain social locations.

On a more local level, policies defining the supportive role of child welfare seemed lacking vis-à-vis its role of protection. The literature suggests a need for greater emphasis on the welfare orientation to balance the current dominance of protection-oriented risk-management approaches (Anglin, 2002). The research identifies professional and organizational constraints on workers' inclination to prioritize welfare functions over risk management (Spratt, 2001), and Gray (2002) called for earlier intervention through "befriending" activities that enable more effective, timely, and genuine support in the home. Renewed logistical strategies could also facilitate a child's adjustment to state's custody more effectively even when the child moves to a different catchment area. School teams working with children in state's custody need to have clear policies and procedures for understanding parental rights and ensuring these are upheld. Although the protective role of child welfare was important to Carolina's well-being, some of the shifts cited earlier might have made a difference.

CONCLUSION

Carolina's story provided the interdisciplinary team with a complex and engaging arena for work and training. The major and challenging foci for interdisciplinary work with this particular family were managing the tensions among family-centered care, maintaining a strengths perspective, and respecting the rights of the child. All of these core training dimensions manifested themselves in complex ways. They called on interdisciplinary team members to examine, in some depth, their own biases and coping strategies, which was singularly valuable for trainees and fellows. In addition, they called on interdisciplinary team members to enter into a dialog with each other, as well as other community players, about appropriate arenas for participation.

One of the unexpected outcomes of this work occurred in the recognition of more workable parameters of the team's efforts. We learned where the interdisciplinary team could and could not be effective, both as a training vehicle and as a community capacity building program. This, in turn, resulted in a major contribution to the VT–ILEHP interdisciplinary team's ongoing self-definition, goals, and further efforts to promote responsible, effective leadership training for health care professionals in an interdisciplinary context.

STUDY QUESTIONS

1. What are the some of the challenges in implementing care coordination for children with complex health needs and their families?
2. How effective is your team in recognizing and considering issues of poverty in the assessment and intervention planning of children with complex health needs and their families?
3. What is the role and responsibility of an interdisciplinary team when serving children with special health care needs who have shared custody or foster home placement?
4. How well prepared is your team to respond to parents with developmental disabilities who have children with special health care needs?

GLOSSARY

Auditory processing—How the brain processes auditory information received from the ears, enabling the individual to learn effectively through listening and understanding.

Conductive hearing loss—Hearing loss associated with difficulty conducting sound and vibration from the outer ear to the inner ear; in children this is most commonly caused by a condition such as otitis media.

Fluctuating hearing loss—Hearing loss that changes over time, usually associated with changes in middle ear pressure and fluid in the middle ear.

Frequency modulated (FM) systems—These are devices which use frequency modulated (FM) wireless radio waves to take sound from a source such as a teacher's voice, and send it to a receiver used by a person with hearing loss or listening and attention difficulties. The receiver can be a child's hearing aid, headphones, speakers arranged around the perimeter of a classroom, or a small speaker which is placed on the child's desk or work area. These systems can greatly improve reception problems due to noise, distance, or reverberation.

Hypernasality—The quality of the voice which occurs when the soft palate fails to keep sound from entering the nasal cavities.

Otitis media—Infection or inflammation of the middle ear space (between the eardrum and the inner ear). Otitis media is usually further specified as the following:

- *Acute otitis media*—Infected fluid behind the eardrum, usually with a rapid onset of fever and pain.
- *Chronic otitis media*—Infected fluid behind the eardrum, persisting despite treatment with antibiotics, and sometimes associated with drainage from a perforation of the eardrum.
- *Otitis media with effusion (OME)*—Fluid behind the eardrum which is not infected.
- *Chronic OME*—Fluid persisting in the middle ear for longer than 6 to 8 weeks.

Otolaryngologist—A physician who specializes in ear, nose, and throat problems.

Submucous cleft palate—A condition where the soft palate may appear to be normal because the mucous membrane is intact, but the muscular tissue underneath may be abnormal or inadequate, allowing air to enter the nasal cavities during speech.

Ventilation tubes—In cases of chronic otitis media or chronic otitis media with effusion, the otolaryngologist may surgically insert a small plastic tube into the eardrum, allowing the middle ear to drain and ventilate.

RESOURCES
WEB SITES

Children, Families, and Disabilities

www.caseyfamilyservices.org—Nonprofit child welfare organization providing a broad range of services to meet the needs of vulnerable children and families. Focus is on public policy, human service reform, and program development, as well as resource connections.

www.childrenwithdisabilities.ncjrs.org—National site with link to the federal government's Web site (http://firstgov.gov/) which identifies federal, national, state, and local resources with links to Medline, the U.S. Department of Housing and Urban Development, and other similar resources.

www.disabledparents.net—"One-stop" site for parents with disabilities; features personal narratives, practical information (such as accessible recreation sites and toys depicting people with disabilities), and links to empowerment network.

www.thearc.org—National organization of and for people with mental retardation and related developmental disabilities. Focuses on the promotion of supports and services while pursuing legislative goals and publishing position statements on advocacy, criminal justice, guardianship, civil and human rights, and so forth.

www.unicef.org.crc.fulltext.htm—This site provides the full text of the United Nations Convention on the Rights of the Child.

Hearing Loss and Cleft Palate

www.asha.org—The American Speech Language Hearing Association provides information to help understand communication and communication disorders.

www.asha.org/hearing/disorders—Includes information on the causes and effects of hearing loss in children and provides other resources.

www.cleftline.org/publications/submucous.htm—The Cleft Palate Foundation is a nonprofit organization dedicated to optimizing the quality of life for individuals affected by facial birth disorders. This site explains submucous cleft palate.

ORGANIZATIONS

Casey Family Services (discussed earlier). Serves the New England and Baltimore areas. For specific addresses, see info@caseyfamilyservices.org

The Arc of the United States
Headquarters
1010 Wayne Avenue, Suite 650
Silver Spring, MD 20910
301-565-3842
301-565-3843 (Fax)
301-565-5342 (Fax)

Public Policy
1331 H Street, NW, Suite 301
Washington, DC 20005
202-783-2229
202-783-8250 (Fax)

Sibling Support Project
6512 23rd Avenue, NW, Suite 213
Seattle, WA 98117
206-297-6368

REFERENCES

Alpiner, J. G., & McCarthy, P. A. (2000). *Rehabilitative audiology: Children and adults* (3rd ed.). Philadelphia: Lippincott Williams & Wilkins.

Altshuler, S. J. (1999). Constructing genograms with children in care: Implication for casework practice. *Child Welfare, LXXXVIII*, 6.

Anglin, J. P. (2002). Risk, well being, and paramountcy in child protection: The need for transformation. *Child and Youth Care Forum, 31*, 233–255.

Beatson, J. E. (1999). *In their own words: What families tell us about the ideal care coordinator.* Unpublished manuscript.

Beatson, J. E., & Prelock, P. A. (2002). The Vermont Rural Autism Project: Sharing experiences, shifting attitudes. *Focus on Autism and Other Developmental Disorders, 17*, 48–54.

Benard, B. (2002). Turnaround people and places. In D. Saleebey (Ed.), *The strengths perspective in social work practice* (3rd ed.; pp. 213–227). Boston: Allyn & Bacon.

Bhagwanji, Y., Bennet, D., Stillwell, M., & Allison, A. (1998). *Relationships with parents with disabilities: Perceptions and training needs of Head Start Staff.* Urbana: University of Illinois Press.

Compton, B. R., & Galaway, B. (1999). *Social work processes* (6th ed.). Pacific Grove, CA: Brooks/Cole.

Cook, D. S. (2000). The role of social work with families that have young children with developmental disabilities. In M. Guralnick (Ed.), *Interdisciplinary assessment of young children with developmental disabilities* (pp. 201–218). Baltimore: Brookes.

DeMaria, R., Weeks, G., & Hof, L. (1999). *Focused genograms.* Philadelphia: Brunner/Mazel.

Feldman, M. A. (1994). Parenting education for parents with intellectual disabilities: A review of outcome studies. *Research in Developmental Disabilities, 15*, 299–332.

Gil, R. M. (1984). The ethnic patient: Implications for medical social work practice. In *Cross-cultural issues: Impact on social work practice in health care: Conference proceedings* (pp. 19–32). New York: Columbia University Press.

Gilson, S. F., Bricourt, J. C., & Baskind, F. R. (1998). Listening to the voices of individuals with disabilities. *Families in Society, 70*, 188–196.

Gray, B. (2002). Emotional labour and befriending in family support and child protection in Tower Hamlets. *Child and Family Social Work, 71*, 13–22.

Huntley, J. (1999). A narrative approach to working with students who have 'learning difficulties.' In A. Morgan (Ed.), *Once upon a time ... Narrative therapy with children and their families* (pp. 35–51). Adelaide, South Australia: Dulwich Centre Publications.

Kalyanpur, M., & Harry, B. (1999). *Culture in special education* (pp. 15–45). Baltimore: Brookes.

Lawlor, M. C., & Mattingly, C. F. (1998). The complexities embedded in family-centered care. *The American Journal of Occupational Therapy, 52*, 259–267.

Leigh, J. W. (1998). *Communicating for cultural competence.* Boston: Allyn & Bacon.

McGoldrick, M., Gerson, R., & Shellenberger, S. (1999). *Genograms: Assessment and intervention* (2nd ed.). New York: Norton.

Mackelprang, R., & Salsgiver, R. (1999). *Disability: A diversity model approach in human service practice.* Pacific Grove, CA: Brooks/Cole.

Mary, N. (1998) Social work and the support model of services for people with developmental disabilities. *Journal of Social Work Education, 34,* 247–260.

Pheterson, G. (1990). Alliances between women: Overcoming internalized oppression and internalized domination. In L. Albrecht & R. Brewers (Eds.), *Bridges of power: Women's multicultural alliances* (pp. 34–48). Philadelphia: New Society Publishers.

Roberts, J. E., Burchinal, M. R., & Zeisel, S. A. (2002). Otitis media in early childhood in relation to children's school-age language and academic skills. *Pediatrics, 110,* 696–706.

Roberts, J. E., & Hunter, L. (2003). Otitis media and children's language and learning. *American Speech Language Hearing Association Leader, 18,* 6–19.

Rounds, K. A., Weil, M., & Bishop, K. K. (1994). Practice with culturally diverse families of young children with disabilities. *Families in Society, 38,* 3–13.

Saleebey, D. (Ed.). (2002). *The strengths perspective in social work practice* (3rd ed.). Boston: Allyn & Bacon.

Shelton, T. L., & Stepanek, J. S. (1995). Excerpts from family-centered care for children needing specialized health and developmental services. *Pediatric Nursing, 21,* 362–364.

Smith, V. K., & Prelock, P. A. (2002). A case management model for school-age children with multiple needs. *Language, Speech, and Hearing Services in Schools, 33,* 124–129.

Spratt, T. (2001). The influence of child protection orientation on child welfare practice. *The British Journal of Social Work, 31,* 933–954.

Thies, K. M., & McAllister, J. W. (2001). The health and education leadership project: A school initiative for children and adolescents with chronic health conditions. *Journal of School Health, 71,* 167–172.

United Nations. (2002, January 24). *The convention on the rights of the child.* Retrieved January 24, 2002 from http://www.unicef.org.crc.fulltext.htm

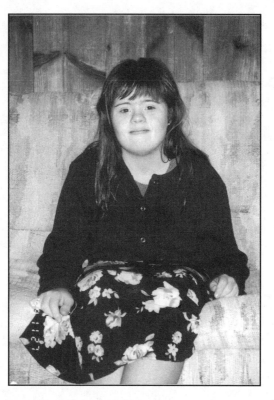

On the Cutting Edge of Ethical Dilemmas: Reconciling an Adolescent's Transition to Adulthood

Stephen Contompasis
Sara Burchard
University of Vermont

Questions to Consider

1. What are the current laws in your home state or country with regard to guardianship?
2. What are your state or national laws with respect to marriage and sterilization in individuals with developmental disabilities?
3. What service systems, if any, are typically involved in supporting youth with disabilities in transition, and from where do their mandates originate?
4. What systematic approaches (i.e. protocols, charts, practice guides) are available to assist youth, families and their teams in transition?
5. What role might young adults with disabilities play on teams and how can this process be facilitated?

JACQUES'S STORY

Jacques Boucher is a 19-year-old youth living with his stepfather, mother, and younger sister, age 3, on his stepfather's farm in the far northeast region of Vermont. The North East Kingdom (as it is referred to in Vermont) is a large, undeveloped area of Vermont with forests, small villages, a few small towns, most under 2,500 inhabitants, and dairy farms. There is chronically high unemployment in the area and a greater degree of poverty than in other areas of the state. There is no industry, and farming, small businesses, and some recreational businesses are the economic mainstay of the region.

The natural beauty of the area is impressive, with tall mountains rearing above rolling hills, evergreen forests, small lakes and streams, scattered farms and residences. The bucolic nature and beauty of the area belie the chronic poverty lying beneath the surface. The fast pace, suburban sprawl, huge shopping centers, and malls that have changed the face of America have not affected this area. Here, there is also a strong sense of community. Families have known each other for generations. The fly-fishing is considered by some to be the best in the Northeast United States, and the large lake between Vermont and Canada offers wonderful winter ice skating races, ice fishing, summer boating, fishing, and swimming activities. Due to its distance from population centers, this area is not heavily trafficked by tourists. Lying on the doorstep of Quebec, there is a strong French Canadian culture in this area and frequent interaction across the national boundary. Some families, including Jacques's, speak French at home, and raise their children bilingually. Because they live close to the border, some families frequently cross to visit family, shop, or hunt, and some may even work or go to school in Canada.

Jacques was born in the North East Kingdom and began having seizures in his first month of life. Developmental delays were noted by his first birthday. His mother was from a family with a long tradition of farming. His early life was marred by parental conflict and documented abuse from his biological father. After his mother's divorce and remarriage when Jacques was about 4 years old, his life stabilized. Jacques's mother remarried another Kingdom native, a farmer named Renée. Jacques has lived continuously on a small dairy farm with his reconstituted family since then, attending a small, rural elementary school through the eighth grade, and then a rural, union high school from grades 9 through 12. Jacques remains in school beyond Grade 12 under special education law that allows education services until the child's 22nd birthday, if still eligible and in need of services.

Vermont began an aggressive program of mainstreaming and inclusion of students with developmental challenges in the early 1980s. Rural schools ranging from 50 to 80 students, such as Jacques's, never had special classes as such, due to the low population density of the schools. Therefore, Jacques was in regular education classes the majority of his school day throughout elementary and high school years and received support from instructional assistants. He received individual instruction, "pull-out services," and other accommodations. The most significant accommodation was the provision of facilitated communication (described later in more detail), for which training began in the fourth grade. By this time, Jacques had received the diagnosis of autism. He had not developed oral communication, although he could, and does, shake his head "yes" and "no," utter a few repetitive, echolalic phrases, and can now point to written cards with "yes" and "no" when asked to make a choice between two items. Through a Canon Communicator he is able to type with and without assistance in very short phrases. (A Canon Communicator is a small, hand-held typing device that prints on a paper tape like an adding machine.) More recently, Jacques has been assisted in learning to type on a computer, although that has not been entirely successful, as he often resists using a computer.

Facilitated communication (FC) was deemed a great success with Jacques. By seventh grade, he was able to facilitate with a number of people: his mother, his instructional assistant, his teacher, and a counselor at school. With this means of communication, Jacques's performance at school improved dramatically, and he was considered to be especially good at math. FC, however, is among several therapies that have no well-documented, empirically based verification of effectiveness (American Academy of Child and Adolescent Psychiatry, 1993; American Association on Mental Retardation, 1994; New York Department of Health, 1999). In fact, strong evidence has been presented to the contrary (Green & Shane, 1994; Hudson, Melita, & Arnold, 1993), but in the case of Jacques, it was accepted as reliable by school personnel and family members.

At the time the interdisciplinary team was called in to do a comprehensive assessment, Jacques was taking classes with eleventh-grade students. This included such course work as regular high school algebra, English, and social studies courses. With the help of a full-time instructional assistant and using FC, he was able to do some, but not all, of the academic work.

Jacques was referred to the interdisciplinary team by his community team at the beginning of the school year. The team included his mother and stepfather, both of whom were active members, the special education case manager, his instructional assistant, and a case manager from the local developmental services agency. The latter member was included in preparation for planning transition to adult community-based services. These services are designed to support adults with disabilities and are offered through the local community mental health and disability agencies in Vermont.

The referral questions for the interdisciplinary team revolved around transition issues; in essence, preparing Jacques for life after high school. There were, however, very different views among Jacques's community team members about what direction transition should take. His teachers felt that Jacques should continue his education by attending a college. Parents, based on FCs they had been receiving over some time from Jacques, were intent on exploring community-supported living and supported employment. There were, however, quite diametrically opposite views of what Jacques wanted, based on his FCs with different parties. At home, through FC, Jacques had for some time been communicating that he did not like school, that he was stressed out at school, and that instructors were "short" with him, at times lost patience and abandoned him in a small, enclosed classroom alone, and that he wanted to leave school. His parents were interested in exploring the option to leave school.

At school, however, Jacques was communicating through FC to his case manager and aide that he was very unhappy at home. He resented his stepfather who pushed him to perform some personal and household daily living activities and homework, and even indicated that he was being abused. These accusations had resulted in an investigation by the local child welfare agency (according to Vermont statute, school personnel are mandated reporters). Although the abuse allegations were not substantiated, they resulted in some hard feelings and distrust between the family and school personnel on Jacques's community team.

At intake by the interdisciplinary team, the family, school team, and health provider independently identified referral questions for the first assessment planning meeting. Jacques's family identified three needs: making a transition plan for Jacques, helping Jacques to get connected with the autism community for socialization, and a number of health management issues including how to control Jacques's weight, provide sufficient exercise, answer questions about the long-term effects of his seizure medications, and assessing his risk for developing diabetes. Jacques's physician identified weight loss and physical fitness as a focus for the assessment as well as determining what other services might be available to meet Jacques's needs.

The school team identified five areas for assessment. The first three were similar to what Jacques's parents identified: transition planning, networking with the autism community, and health concerns. In addition, the team requested assessment for sensory needs, and how to help Jacques become an oral communicator, which Jacques identified through FC as a strong personal goal. The school's specific questions concerning transition planning were as follows: how to help Jacques establish and maintain friendships and develop life and job skills, how to teach sex education and appropriate sexuality, and whether the school program should be focused on academic or adaptive skills.

INTRODUCTION

As children grow and develop over the years they transition through many stages of personal growth. It is expected that as children transition through adolescence and into adulthood that they will master a number of skills and take on increasing personal responsibility, develop as individuals with their own identity, and begin a process leading toward eventual separation from the child/parent dyad to the adult–child/parent dyad. This chapter explores the complexity in dealing with transition from childhood to adulthood for children with disabilities, especially when the youngster's goals for the future collide with those of the guardian(s) and the school or community team. It also illustrates how the complexity increases when the young adult communicates through a controversial alternative augmentative communication system (AAC).

The chapter explores specific ethical dilemmas that emerge as in the case of Jacques: (a) authenticity of communication through AAC; (b) conflict about adulthood goals (including guardianship) between the youngster, the school team, and the parent(s); (c) the interdisciplinary team's responsibility to the young adult, to the community team, and to the parents; (d) dissonance in the perception of the role of the interdisciplinary team by the school or community team, the parents, and the responsibility of the interdisciplinary team to the youngster; and (e) communication with parents with complex needs. In analyzing these dilemmas, the chapter considers how the culture of the family mediates the expectations for the youngster, for example, interdependence versus independence, gender ascribed roles, rural versus urban, socioeconomic status, and any other cultural factor. Finally, the chapter discusses implications for systems change, and suggests specific policy alternatives regarding transition to adulthood for youngsters with disabilities who may consider independent living.

TRANSITION PLANNING FOR A COMPLEX FAMILY AND SITUATION

Transition planning for young adults is likely to involve many agencies, services, and disciplines. It may also require thoughtful planning across multiple contexts such as the home, school, community, health care systems, and the workplace. The role of each of these contexts is discussed later. Ideally, an integrated approach across these systems and contexts will benefit the young adult in transition and his or her family.

Special Education Planning and Requirements for Transition

Although special education has provided access to education for children with disabilities, it has not fully ensured that all children with disabilities are prepared for employment and independent living. In November 2000, the National Council on Disability and the Social Security Administration reported that only 27% of students receiving special education earned a high school diploma and only 59% were competitively employed 3 to 5 years postgraduation (National Council on Disability, 2001).

To address these shortfalls, the Individuals with Disabilities Education Act (IDEA), reauthorized in 1997, added requirements for transition planning toward greater independence on graduation. The IDEA describes transition as a coordinated set of activities for a student, designed with an outcome-oriented process, which promotes movement from school to postschool activities, such as postsecondary education, vocational training, integrated employment (such as supported employment), continuing and adult education, adult services, independent living, or community participation (Individuals with Disabilities Education Act, 1997). Transition activities must be included in the student's Individual Education Plan (IEP) by age 16 and when appropriate may begin at age 14 or younger. Transition activities are required to take into account the student's preferences and interests. Other considerations may include exposure to community experiences and the development of employment and adult living skills. Interagency agreements are documented in the plan if other community supports are needed.

Developmental Services, the Developmental Disabilities Assistance and Bill of Rights Act of 2000, and the Olmstead Decision

The Developmental Services and the Developmental Disabilities Assistance and Bill of Rights Act of 2000 (DD Act) was enacted to ensure that people with developmental disabilities and their families receive the services and supports they need and participate in the planning and designing of those services. Direct services, however, are neither funded nor mandated by this act and states have discretion regarding the services provided. The Administration on Developmental Disabilities (ADD) is the United States Government organization responsible for implementing the DD Act. The staff and programs of ADD are part of the Administration for Children and Families of the U.S. Department of Health and Human Services. The DD Act established eight areas of emphasis for ADD programs: (a) employment, (b) education and early intervention, (c) child care, (d) health, (e) housing, (f) transportation, (g) recreation, and (h) other formal and informal community supports that affect quality of life. Under the DD Act, each state has a developmental disabilities council and a protection and advocacy (P&A) system to empower, protect, and advocate on behalf of persons with developmental disabilities.

Jacques was served by the Vermont Department of Developmental and Mental Health Services, which is the agency responsible for the provision of services to children and adults who have developmental disabilities. As in most states, funding for this agency and its services comes predominately from state appropriations that are then matched with federal Medicaid dollars to provide specific services. Services are not mandated, and funding is limited by priorities set to serve individuals in greatest need. Recent estimates suggest that up to 75% of adults with disabilities are not served (Vermont Department of Developmental and Mental Health Services, 2002a, 2002b). Many of these persons live at home with their families and may benefit from "natural supports" in their community, yet they may also have unrecognized needs. They may "enter" the system at a later time as a result of family crisis such as illness or death of a parent or guardian.

Although there is no federal law mandating community-based services in general for adults with disabilities, in 1999 the U.S. Supreme Court, in *Olmstead v. L. C.* (1999), the "Olmstead decision," construed Title II of the Americans with Disabilities Act to require states to place qualified individuals with mental disabilities in community settings, rather than in institutions. This is based on the determination of treatment by professionals that such placements are appropriate, that the affected persons do not oppose such placements, and that the state can reasonably accommodate the placements, taking into account the resources available to the state and the needs of others with disabilities.

Health and Safety for Young Adults in Transition

Children with complex neurodevelopmental disabilities and their families may encounter difficulty in the transition from pediatric health care providers to adult health care providers (Blum et al., 1993). It is not uncommon for these young adults and their families to feel comfortable with their pediatrician and to rely on that pediatrician well beyond the age for typical transition (age 21) to adult health care providers. On the other hand, some pediatricians may also express an unwillingness to transition these young adults from their practice out of genuine concern that adult health care practitioners in their area may lack the specific skills and training to carry out health services for individuals with developmental disabilities. For instance, pediatricians who deal with young children are comfortable with evaluating individuals who require the assistance of others (i.e., parents) to present their concerns and history of an illness. Pediatricians may also be more comfortable observing physical signs of illness or pain in the nonverbal child or individual with disability. Over the years, pediatricians and family members come to "know and sense" when something is "not right" for the nonverbal child or young adult.

Formal training in the interview and examination of patients with developmental disabilities may not be included in family practice or internal medicine training programs (Magrab & Millar, 1989). A young adult may be provided excellent health care for a number of years into adulthood by his or her pediatrician, however, pediatricians may not be as well trained or develop or maintain necessary skills for treating conditions of an aging population (American Academy of Pediatrics, 2002).

The American Academy of Pediatrics (American Academy of Pediatrics, 2002) recognizes the importance of uninterrupted health care services for adolescents with special health care needs, many of whom have developmental disabilities moving into adulthood. A policy statement on health care transition for young adults with special health care needs was adopted in December of 2002 in consensus with the American Academy of Family Physicians and American College of Physicians-American Society of Internal Medicine (American Academy of Pediatrics, 2002). The American Academy of Pediatrics policy statement cites as its goal that by the year 2010 all physicians providing primary and specialty care to young people with special health care needs will understand the reasons for transition from child-oriented to adult-oriented health care. These physicians are expected to have the knowledge and skills to facilitate the process, and know if, how, and when the transfer of care is indicated. Specific areas to consider include the following: uninterrupted and smooth transition to comprehensive care, training and certification of all involved in this transition of care, and portability and accessibility of medical records in the transition. Another important goal cited is the use of a written transition plan by age 14, and affordable and continuous health care insurance for the youth in transition (American Academy of Pediatrics, 2002).

Promoting Sexuality Education and Safety for Children and Young Adults With Disabilities

Sexual health and safety are two other important health considerations for youth in transition. Adolescents with disabilities have the same rate of sexual activity as adolescents without disabilities (Suris, Resnick, Cassuto, & Blum,1996). However, children in special education may not receive or benefit from the same degree of sexuality education as their peers without disabilities, although they may be at greater risk for sexual abuse (American Academy of Pediatrics, 1996).

Jacques's family did not identify his sexuality as a key area for transition to adulthood but expressed a concern that the developmental service worker assigned to Jacques was possibly a homosexual. Their concern was not founded on any allegations of unprofessional behavior. Jacques's autism, communication, and developmental challenges required adaptations to make sexuality training a part of the transition to adulthood. Jacques had minimal educational or other life opportunities to discuss or understand his own sexuality and the appropriate expression of his sexuality with others. Jacques did not attend school or community social functions as a young child or youth that would help him to learn the social conventions of friendship, companionship, and dating. Individuals working to support persons with disabilities are realizing that sexuality and its expression are as much a part of the activities of daily living as is grooming, dressing, or any other self care. Although it is a neglected area, sexuality education should begin early and be tailored to the child's developmental needs. Persons serving young adults with disabilities in transition would be remiss not to assess students' current level of understanding of themselves as sexual beings as well as by not planning for their safety regarding sexuality issues.

INDEPENDENT LIVING AND GUARDIANSHIP ISSUES FOR THE YOUNG ADULT IN TRANSITION

When planning transition for young adults with disabilities, a common concern to many families is the issue of guardianship. For most of the last century, if not longer, individuals with intellectual challenges were thought to be unable to make decisions for themselves or to be able to live independently or semi-independently in the community. At one time, all states had laws that required sterilization of persons with disabilities, often children, as an outcome of the Eugenics movement of the early 20th century, during which fears of overpopulating with persons of low intellectual ability were rampant (Shearer, 1976). Laws precluding persons with mental retardation or other intellectual challenges from owning property, voting, or getting married were prevalent throughout the United States. Until after the middle of the last century, persons identified as mentally retarded had no civil rights in this or in many other countries (Kugel & Shearer, 1976; National Institute on Mental Retardation, 1981). However, it should be noted that many people who could have been identified as "mentally retarded" never came to anyone's attention and lived their lives in the community exercising their rights (Edgerton, 1969; Edgerton & Bercovici, 1976). Any identified persons that were not housed and cared for by their families who came to public notice were placed in large institutions throughout the country (Shearer, 1976).

This situation began to change in the 1960s and 1970s. Influenced by the civil rights movement (see Chapter 10), parents organized to advocate for their children who were disenfranchised. A particularly active group was the Association of Retarded Children, now known only as ARC. By then, better information about the capabilities of people with intellectual challenges was available. There were exposés of the horrific nature and experience of institutionalization (Blatt & Kaplan, 1974; Shearer, 1976). The dehumanizing treatment of persons with disabilities by the Nazis was also well known. With the support of national leaders who had family members with mental retardation, such as John F. Kennedy and Hubert Humphrey, efforts to establish the civil rights of people who may be considered intellectually challenged were initiated (National Institute on Mental Retardation, 1981). Sterilization laws began to disappear, marriage laws began to be challenged, and the right to live in the community became supported in law and in court, although many people throughout this country still remain in institutions due to lack of fiscal resources to provide and support community placements (Braddock, 2002; Lakin, Braddock, & Smith, 1994). In 1972, the right to a free and appropriate education in the least restrictive environment was established for children with disabilities through enactment of the Education for All Handicapped Children Act of 1975. These changes came about during the last 30 years. Their implementation has been quite uneven across the states, due in part to flexibility allowed in states' interpretation of subjective concepts like "appropriate" or "least restrictive" as it applies to inclusion of children with disabilities with their nondisabled peers. Currently, an adult's right to self-determination, unrestricted living, working, and relationships in a community setting, is protected unless it can be determined in a court of law with appropriate legal representation for the individual with a disability, that the individual has committed a crime or there is evidence that he or she is unable to exercise his or her rights without self-endangerment or endangerment to others (Developmental Services and the Developmental Disabilities Assistance and Bill of Rights Act of 2000).

This assertion of the rights of all adult citizens has brought many changes to guardianship laws (Dinerstein, Herr, & O'Sullivan, 1999; Kindred, Cohen, Penrod, & Shaffer, 1976). Guardianship laws have always been the basis for one person to legally exercise the rights of another who is deemed incapable of exercising his or her own rights. Now, however, that determination is not made solely on the basis of an IQ score or diagnostic label, as was historically the case (American Association on Mental Retardation, 2002). All persons are deemed capable before the law until it can be demonstrated before a court that the person requires some supervision. In addition, that supervision is no longer a blanket supervision (Dinerstein et al., 1999). Only those critical aspects of decision making that are shown to be at issue are subject to guardianship control. Among those specific decision areas are the following: general supervision, finding housing, employment, habilitation, education; buying and selling property; making contracts, controlling personal monies, making legal decisions (to sue or defend against legal action); and making medical decisions. In theory, a court would find for a limited guardianship, that is guardianship over only the decisions that are needed, for example, medical decisions. Persons with cognitive challenges are considered autonomous and independent unless it is demonstrated in a court of law that some aspect of decision making should be delegated to another adult (guardian). Even then, guardianship may be seen as provisional and temporary, and procedures for review are in place, although few states may initiate them (American Association on Mental Retardation, 2002b). Even with guardianship in place, the guardian should obtain "assent," if not consent, from the individual, and the guardian's decision should not be based on "best interest" of the individual, but rather on a determination of what the individual would say if he or she were able to make that decision (American Association on Mental Retardation, 2002d).

A judgment on whether to limit an individual's self determination requires a thorough assessment of decision making and adaptive abilities in the areas of question by an independent professional assessor, often a psychologist or psychiatrist (Protective Services for Mentally Retarded Persons, 1977). This assessment includes determining whether there is social support for advising and assisting that person short of guardianship. The challenged person's views and opinions are also assessed, and that person has legal counsel to represent him or her in any legal proceeding to limit his or her rights. (American Association on Mental Retardation, 2002c; 18 V.S.A. §§ 9301 et seq.).

In Jacques's case, at the recommendation of the interdisciplinary team, his mother began a process in which she obtained legal guardianship for making decisions specified in Vermont law, choosing residence, employment, medical decisions, contracts, and handling money (18 V.S.A. §§ 9301 et seq.). At the same time, both his mother and the school personnel who had worked with Jacques for many years, maintained that he was capable of communicating and making his preferences known through FC and that he was, in fact, quite intellectually capable. This poses an ethical dilemma, for in this case, the school was advocating firmly, even speaking of legal action, to maintain Jacques in school. At the same time, Jacques's parents were actively working, outside the community team and the transition planning process, to find a supported community placement for Jacques in a nearby village. Jacques, meanwhile, communicating by FC, was telling his parents that he no longer wanted to live at home and did not want to continue in school. He was also showing, by his behavior, that he really enjoyed and looked forward to spending days at his respite provider's home, and through FC with the provider, that he wanted to move in and live with him. However, family members had concerns about that arrangement, feeling that Jacques could be at risk based on the assumption that the respite provider was a homosexual.

In this situation, the interdisciplinary team asked the questions: whose voice is heard? What happens when Jacques's voice differs from that of his family or the school or both? And what is Jacques's voice?

NATURAL SUPPORTS AND RURAL ISSUES FOR YOUNG ADULTS IN TRANSITION

Vermont began developing an array of supports for adults with developmental challenges during the demand for deinstitutionalization and normalization occurring in the 1970s and 1980s. Group homes, supervised apartments, developmental "foster" homes, and an array of community employment options, competitive work and supported work—independent employment, supervised employment, supported employment, volunteer "job" opportunities—became available to persons with disabilities. However, the realities of the numbers of people needing these supports and financial limitations has led to efforts to develop and rely on "natural supports." Natural supports, such as neighbors and friends, are often the sources for housing and job opportunities on which most people rely, rather than professional, paid supports. Natural supports are more in keeping with the philosophy of "like other people," community inclusion, and normalization (National Institute on Mental Retardation, 1981; Wolfensberger, 1991). Pragmatically, family and individual support needs are greater than either human or financial resources. Natural supports may have minimal or no associated cost.

The leaders of the deinstitutionalization movement in Vermont developed and relied on natural supports rather than developing or redeploying human resources for professional services (Burchard & Burchard, 2000; Nisbet, 1992). The community and families of persons with developmental disabilities in areas where professional resources were not available viewed natural supports as a reflection of the cultural norm. These areas with dispersed populations, far from any metropolitan centers, indeed, have a culture characterized by independence (the ability to survive alone) and interdependence (the mutual need to rely on others for survival). This culture is based on close-knit connections with natural community support. These areas had less highly developed specialization of labor. There were few licensing laws, less educational credentialing, and few professional groups. The rural nature of the environments promoted greater reliance on community as a "natural" way of addressing needs. These areas developed natural supports as a means of meeting family and individual needs early in the deinstitutionalization and normalization movements (Burchard, Burchard, Sewell, & VanDenBerg, 1993; Lewis, 1997).

Communities of this type, such as Alaska (land size half that of the lower 48, with many small and isolated Native American communities, and a total population similar to that of Vermont, approximately 608,000; Vermont Quickfacts from the U.S. Census, 2000), and Western Australia (land size equal to the lower 48 and population four times that of Vermont), had a population that was spread thinly throughout a huge geographical region. Rather than sending children with disabilities away, traveling long distances to special schools or residential settings, these children were included in the existing educational settings. Families were empowered to determine how resources available to them would be used to support the family and the individual with disabilities. With the support of a service coordinator, families were assisted to determine their primary needs and to explore creative ways to address those needs, relying on the people, organizations, and activities already existing in their communities and regions (Burchard et al., 1993; Lewis, 1997). Development of special services, special worksites, and special residences was never an option in regions such as Western Australia, or rare in states such as Alaska, once the movement for community-based services became the Western philosophy of service.

With pressure from families for more choice and the continuing and growing gulf between needs and resources, current best practice philosophy in the continental United States is for the development of natural instead of professional supports for people; natural supports to assist with living, working, and socializing. In Vermont, ways of providing more choice and options to families continue to be developed. Families may now select among service agencies for support, if they are fortunate enough to live in a region with more than one such agency. However, a system for family self-management of supports has been developed in the last few years. Whatever funds are available to support the family are provided directly to the family to do their own services management (Vermont Department of Developmental and Mental Health Services, 2002b). This provides them with more money (no agency overhead costs to support), but a great deal more responsibility and work to find and hire the supports they need.

In rural areas, there are always issues of transportation, housing, and employment. As in the North East Kingdom where Jacques lived, employment is an issue because there are few industries. However, following the normalization philosophy and the policy of family choice and natural supports, through transition planning, the family and team examine "what other people do" in the area to solve these problems. An important question to keep in mind follows: "What is the culture and reality of that environment?" In Vermont, the culture of rural areas is that people share residences, provide care for adults in need of assistance, work on farms or in small stores, or do unpaid "work" around the house or farm. However, there are plenty of opportunities to participate in volunteer community activities—libraries, fire departments, and brief seasonal opportunities for work at ski areas, inns, and bed-and-breakfast operations. Interdependence is the norm. The lifestyle of the cities—apartment living, recreation at health clubs, a myriad of restaurants, and grocery stores, is not the norm. The challenge is to create a viable lifestyle within the culture of a rural setting—such as the North East Kingdom of Vermont. Jacques wants to live independently with a preferred friend (respite worker) while he completes a high school education. According to the McGill Action Planning System (MAPS) process (Forest & Pearpoint, 1992), one of his goals is to have an opportunity to participate in the life of the community, find a job, or gain partial work experience in his rural setting.

THE YOUNG ADULT'S VOICE
THROUGH FACILITATED COMMUNICATION

As part of the movement to assist youth in transition toward their own goals and to aide them in this process of determining their own futures, best practices often now include seeking the opinion of the youth in transition (Sloper & Lightfoot, 2003). Jacques's sole form of communication, other than through behavioral signals of refusal, noncompliance, emotional upset or, conversely, eager approach, pleasure, and compliance, is FC, an accommodation for enhancing the communication of persons with no or very limited oral, gestural, or written communication skills (American Association on Mental Retardation, 1994). This accommodation requires another person to physically assist the person with disabilities to type (computer, typewriter, Canon Communicator) or point (letter board) by stabilizing the person's hand. This technique was developed by Rosemary Crossley in Australia (Crossley, 1992; Intellectual Disability Review Panel, 1989) where, after several court cases over whether the typing represented the client's voice, for example, in requesting to leave a parent's home, it was empirically tested and disallowed (Hudson et al., 1993; Intellectual Disability Review Panel, 1989; Margolin, 1994). Despite several published case studies of persons benefiting from this technique (Biklen, 1993), and a wide following and personal testimony throughout upper New York State and Vermont, controlled studies of FC conducted in the United States, Europe, and Australia, have failed to provide sufficient evidence for the effectiveness and benefit of this approach to communication for persons with disabilities (Jacobson, Mulick, & Schwartz, 1995; Mostert, 2001). No evidence has been found to support that the written communications have emanated from the person with autism or other disability, unable to communicate in any other manner, unassisted by human help (Green & Shane, 1994; New York Department of Health, 1999). Use of FC has led to many court cases based on false accusations of sexual abuse by parents, family members, and care providers. Repeatedly, these accusations have not held up to examination. (American Academy of Pediatrics, 1998), yet they destroyed many innocent families in the process. As a result of these studies and court case findings, professional organizations in the United States have warned against using FC for any important decision making or professional testing (American Academy of Child and Adolescent Psychiatry, 1993; American Association on Mental Retardation, 1994).

Although the school personnel, the interdisciplinary team, and Jacques's family were aware of the criticisms and limitations of FC as a means of communication, Jacques had been using it for 9 years and appeared to be adept at it. In class, he would independently grab his aide's hand and hold it while he appeared to push all the keys without much help. He would occasionally type without any assistance, but the output was limited to a few words or repetitive phrases. Family members said that they could tell when Jacques was "fooling around" and when he was really communicating using FC. Among the interdisciplinary team, there was a range of opinions about the utility and veracity of using FC as an augmentative communication strategy with people with autism and other developmental challenges. Because of its wide use and acceptance throughout Vermont, in schools, mental health agencies, and among family members, it was difficult to challenge its use in a straightforward manner and maintain a family-centered and respectful focus. Direct questioning of Jacques's ability to use FC would have alienated family, and other professional members of the school and community team. It also would have rendered our efforts useless. Everyone was reminded of the cautions against the use of FC, but a direct testing of the youth's communication seemed disrespectful and was not requested by the family or the IEP team.

This constituted a very difficult dilemma for the interdisciplinary team, whose role is to promote interdisciplinary practice by empowering the family to be central to the community team, empowering the community team to initiate collaborative transition planning while honoring the voice and preferences of the person with disabilities. It was not clear what Jacques's true preferences were, especially when different parties reported different preferences all communicated by FC. This was accompanied by conflicting behavioral communications regarding wanting to be at home, at school, or at the respite home. In addition, the community team was at an impasse and members were working at odds with each other, attempting in their own ways to develop and implement transition or "nontransition" plans.

Jacques's mother became his legal guardian and therefore, could legally and unilaterally make decisions about his residential placement and about attending school. The school, however, was moving toward taking legal action to keep Jacques in school until graduation. Meanwhile Jacques's family was working with the community mental health agency designated in Vermont to provide adult services and supports. The agency independently found a semi-independent living situation without the input of the community team including the community mental health services coordinator. Amidst these dynamics, Jacques's parents were counting on the interdisciplinary team to assist in finding resources for immediate transition out of school and for the completion of a General Education Diploma (GED) as an alternative diploma granted for completing work outside of the high school and passing a competency evaluation. This situation led the interdisciplinary team to another set of questions: What is the role of the interdisciplinary team? To whom does it owe its allegiance—to Jacques, to the community team that was fragmenting, or to Jacques's family? And, how is the interdisciplinary team to work constructively? These issues are explored next.

THE ROLE OF INTERDISCIPLINARY TEAMS IN ASSESSMENT AND TRANSITION PLANNING

The story of Jacques and his family highlights thorny ethical issues regarding transition to adulthood for youngsters with special health and developmental needs. It also highlights the need for interdisciplinary and family-centered teamwork so that the needs of the child and family in transition can be identified and met. Interdisciplinary teamwork is essential for children with complex disabilities who often require services and supports from various disciplines. Family-centered care is also important, although challenging in complex situations such as this one. Nevertheless, it may be helpful to review some of the principles of family-centered care, especially those supporting transition. Some of these principles include the following: (a) recognizing that the family is the constant in the child's life, whereas service systems and personnel within those systems fluctuate; (b) recognizing family strengths and individuality; (c) facilitating parent and professional collaboration, at all levels of care including program development, implementation, evaluation and policy formation; (d) assuring that the design of delivery systems are flexible, accessible, and responsive to families; (e) implementing appropriate policies and programs that provide emotional and financial support to families; and (f) understanding and incorporating the developmental needs of children and families into delivery systems (Johnson, 2000; see Chapter 2 for a more thorough review of family-centered care).

In Jacques's circumstance, the family and the school and community team found themselves in conflict and were not availing themselves of effective and collaborative communication. It was unfortunate that the relationships among team members were so broken that the interdisciplinary team felt the need to withdraw, yet the conflict resulted in some meaningful changes toward adult transition for Jacques.

Since its inception in 1995, the Vermont Interdisciplinary Leadership Education for Health Professionals (VT–ILEHP) program has recognized the need for collaboration among the various agencies that serve children with disabilities and their families. This is particularly important as children transition to the adult services. In Vermont, in general, the major service providers identified are from three specific agencies: Health, Education, and Developmental or Mental Health and Social Services. Across these agencies, many disciplines are involved in providing service to children and young adults such as Jacques, including education and special education, psychology, speech language pathology, medicine and pediatrics, nursing, audiology, occupational therapy, social work, physical therapy, and public administration.

Nonetheless, it was not uncommon in the interdisciplinary team to venture out into communities to find that children and families might have service providers and case managers from all three of these networks, with interrelated yet sometimes conflicting goals and service. Indeed, in some areas of the state, the interdisciplinary team found that often these "case managers," including physicians, special educators, and mental health workers, never met to discuss potential areas of support and collaboration. Although all three areas of services, Health, Education, and Developmental Services, are committed to family-centered care, actual practices, such as the inclusive role of family and young adult, on teams varied. Some teams actively seek input and participation from the children and their family whereas others resist, perhaps unintentionally.

As part of its role as a consulting group, the interdisciplinary team is often forced to determine with whom it is consulting. Although referrals and questions might come from any three of these service systems, ultimately the family's and young adult's questions and needs must serve as the basis for the assessment. Rapport with other key team members, including families, is established to determine if areas of desired assessment are in concert with the goals and needs of the child and the family.

The interdisciplinary team realized a need to hold judgment or to recognize that community teams often struggle with the reality of limited resources. University-based teams must also be careful about reinforcing the image that they may be passing judgment from the "Ivory Tower" of academia (a particularly sensitive issue in rural Vermont). The interdisciplinary consulting team can be more effective by sensitively helping community teams to assess their own strengths, challenges, and need for support.

The interdisciplinary consulting team might have done a better job in helping the community team realize that making decisions regarding the involvement of children and young adults in team meetings is complex and challenging, and requires a strengths-based approach toward the child or young adult, as well as some realistic appraisals of the child's disability. When possible, including children on their teams is important. Yet for the child who is severely impaired in cognitive and communication abilities, family members and others closely involved with the child may serve as proxies. For others, there are issues of procedure and legality regarding determining competency or guardianship after the child turns 18 (Dinerstein et al., 1999; Protective Services For Mentally Retarded Persons, 1977).

In the case of Jacques, the interdisciplinary team was placed in a difficult role requiring strong leadership skills while working with the family and school in planning and carrying out the preparation for transition. This role, which led to legal threats by school members of the community team against the family, placed the VT–ILEHP trainee squarely in the middle of it. The difficulty of this role was intensified by the nature of the trainee's relationship with the parents. The family had developed great trust in the trainee and wanted to have him act as their advocate with the school and implement their plans and wishes. This was exacerbated, however, by the foster father's apparent anxiety disorder which resulted in innumerable daily phone calls as the conflict within the community team increased.

Eventually, team communication became so fractious and out of control that the VT–ILEHP team was forced to withdraw from its involvement between the community team and the family, until communications improved. Also Jacques's life circumstances changed dramatically, which made a number of the evaluation questions moot. Jacques's parents chose to withdraw him from school, and developed a service plan with the community-based developmental disability agency. Jacques moved into a supported living arrangement in a nearby town with his respite worker. This arrangement was supervised by his mental health case manager. Jacques's parents became aware of the need to establish legal guardianship for Jacques so that they could make proxy decisions for him. At last contact, the parents hoped to utilize the agency support to pursue work options and training opportunities for their son.

USING PLANNING TOOLS
FOR YOUNG ADULTS IN TRANSITION

The interdisciplinary team has utilized MAPS (Forest & Pearpoint, 1992), which provides some structure to the process of transition. It is also intended to bring teams together in the process for the benefit of the youth in transition. MAPS is a dynamic and creative process that can have a powerful impact on the family and on teams. MAPS is designed to bring teams to consensus in planning transition for children and youth with disabilities.

A typical MAPS involves the student, family members, friends, or classmates, and school and agency personnel involved in the student's life. See Table 7.1 for an outline of the MAPS process. Through MAPS, the team develops a vision of the student's life and comes to consensus regarding what the person needs to reach that vision. All participants are invited to contribute in answering the key questions. By moving from individual answers to group consensus, a description of the person's characteristics, talents, and needs emerge.

MAPS begins by asking the student and family members to share the highlights of the student's life. Next, team members are asked to articulate their hopes and dreams for the individual. The participants are then asked to share their worst fears for the person, for instance, fear of sexual abuse or predation. This can be a difficult yet very important part of the MAPS process.

The last step in the MAPS is to reach a consensus on what the student will need to achieve his or her dreams. After the needs are identified, the facilitators work with the group to establish priority needs and develop action plans toward these goals. VT–ILEHP faculty and trainees trained to facilitate the MAPS process have seen teams go from individualized conflictive positions among team members to teary-eyed expressions of relief. This is particularly so when difficult areas of transition are engaged and meaningful directions and understanding of the child and family's needs are resolved in the process.

Lessons Learned

The story of Jacques, his family, and community team illustrates the complexity encountered in planning transition from childhood to adulthood for children with disabilities, especially when the young-

TABLE 7.1

The MAPS Process

Question 1—"What is a MAP?" The facilitator describes the ways in which a road map is used and links the MAPS process, by analogy, to a road map that will provide directions for the student's life. The result of the meeting will be a chart which will guide that direction, so that it becomes important for participants to answer all questions.

Question 2—"What is (the student's name) history?" Answers to this question describe the student's life, particularly focusing on highlights or milestones. Information is included on medical, educational, communication, and social issues. It is often possible for the facilitator to collect much of this information in advance, to avoid spending too much time on the question, requiring only that group members add anything that is missing.

Question 3—"What is your dream for (student's name)?" Participants are asked to describe their dreams for the student for the next 5 years, 10 years, and as an adult. This will include dreams about where (student's name) will live, work, and about the various relationships in his or her life. Dreams need to be conceived as images of what might be possible.

Question 4—"What is your nightmare for (student's name)?" It is not possible to avoid nightmares if they remain undiscussed. It is important that participants not become despondent if the realities of institutional "care" are raised, or the threat of social isolation or poverty as an adult is raised. Dreams and nightmares are of equal importance to the discussion. Many programs and projects fuel the nightmares, rather than the dreams. The entire aim of the MAPS process is to discuss both dreams and nightmares, so that the former can be realized and the latter avoided.

Question 5—"Who is (child's name)?" This is a brainstorming phase of the process. Everyone is invited to provide words that the facilitator records as a portrait of the person. Not merely good or bad words are used, but also words that convey important impressions of the student's identity. The facilitator might also ask, "What other words have persons, not present here today, used when describing (student's name)?"

Question 6—"What are (student's name) strengths, gifts, and talents?" In this phase of the meeting the facilitator will record the likes, dislikes, preferences, what works, successes, and so forth. The concept of "giftedness" in association with the student is stressed, not in relation to academic ability, but as one of the attributes of the student's personality.

Question 7—"What are (student's name) needs and challenges?" In answering this question, participants must think about the people and resources necessary to make the dreams come true.

Question 8(a)—"What action plans are needed to meet these needs, and avoid these nightmares?" This phase requires the facilitator, working with group support, to pull together finite, specific, follow-up plans. These will include defining who will do what, when, and where. For example, when will the Individual Education Plan (IEP) session be held, who should attend, and when will "Circle of Friends" activities begin?

Question 8(b)—"What would an ideal day at school look like?" Using the information generated in the aforementioned process, a matrix can be constructed for use in school program scheduling.

The entire MAPS "machine" can, if efficiently prepared and managed, take about 90 min to conduct, with none, or few of the participants bored or overly tired as a result. In many instances, the students themselves have sat through the entire sessions. Facilitators have even invited very young children to be present for as long as they like, and have arranged child care if they decide to leave. Many have stayed for the entire session. This particular outcome merely affirms the notion that most people, including those with multiple disabilities, are vitally interested in their own lives. Those who designed the process claim that the best time to use MAPS is as part of the IEP cycle, or at crucial transition points in the student's schooling, for example, from preschool to primary school, primary to high school, or high school to adulthood.

Note.   Adapted from Forest and Pearpoint, 1992.

ster's goals for the future collide with those of the guardian(s) and the school team. All of the core competencies that the interdisciplinary team works to incorporate in its training and service were challenged in the attempt to provide a community based assessment toward meaningful transition outcomes. The section that follows analyzes each of the five competencies—family-centered care, interdisciplinary teaming, neurodevelopmental disabilities, cultural competence, and leadership in the context of Jacques's story—and how they emerged during the assessment process.

Cultural issues were raised regarding the community team members' differences in expectations and directions for his future. School team members, from more urban, middle class backgrounds, were intent on the importance of higher education. Jacques's family members, from rural, agrarian backgrounds, had very different expectations and goals for Jacques's future. Indeed, accepting the developmental disability of autism and its challenges is in itself one aspect of cultural competency (see Chapter 3 for further explanation of cultural competency and the impact on developmental disability). Not imposing one's personal bias based on one's own cultural understanding of transition to adulthood is another consideration for professionals working with young adults in transition.

The concept of family-centered care was challenged by the complexity of this case: a young man in his majority, whose expressed wishes appeared to be contrary at times to those of his parents. Who is the "family" in this case? Renée's mental health condition also added another dimension of complexity to serving Jacques and his family in a family-centered way. Remaining family-centered while supporting the needs of a family member experiencing a mental health crisis was a unique challenge in this story. The practitioners on the interdisciplinary team needed to be tactful and focus on effective, clear communication.

The principle of working effectively in an interdisciplinary model was also severely challenged in this case by the friction of opposing views of the family and the school with regard to the proper educational and transitional future for Jacques. The lack of a clear message from Jacques, due to issues of validity and the contradictory content of the FC to various parties, was at the center of this conflict. There was a perception that the family attempted to co-opt the interdisciplinary team into taking sides against the community team (predominately the school members of the team), whereas the community team was threatening legal action if the family took Jacques out of school. At the same time, community team members were working to use the interdisciplinary team to assist them in maintaining Jacques in school. Each party saw the interdisciplinary team as a vehicle to override the other and to push its own agenda. Each party attempted to work with the interdisciplinary team, through the trainee, outside of the team process.

Knowledge in neurodevelopmental disabilities and, specifically of autism and its communication challenges, was central to understanding Jacques. It was also central to understanding the dilemmas the team was facing in communicating effectively with Jacques and understanding his true needs and wishes. Knowledge of the potential health impacts, for instance, sexuality, nutrition, and exercise, associated with his developmental challenges, was a key component to providing service to this young adult in transition. Making health decisions and working with persons using potentially biased information obtained via FC is a potentially hazardous area of health care management for persons with developmental disabilities.

Leadership in maternal child health is the last competency analyzed through this story. Knowledge of the laws, policies, and best practices associated with transition to adult living for persons with disabilities played an important part in serving Jacques and his family. Understanding these best practice models, for example, family-centered care and MAPS process, and applying them to real-life situations faced by persons with multiple complexities, required a great deal of skill and leadership. Although it was difficult to pull away from this situation, one final aspect of leadership is determining when a situation is unsolvable. It was critical to be clear in feedback, as we were to the community team, our reason for withdrawal.

The interdisciplinary team (the trainees and faculty) learned a great deal from their experiences with Jacques, his family, and the community team. The complexity of issues encountered throughout the assessment process highlights the many issues existing across a number of domains that must be addressed to ensure successful transition for youth with disabilities. Beyond the "routine" considerations facing all youth in transition, this story of Jacques and his family illustrated just how complex the process can be when it involves many people, disciplines, and multiple environmental contexts within systems that lack unlimited resources, and may lack clarity with regard to the youth's voice.

In hindsight, perhaps the interdisciplinary team may have been more successful by identifying certain challenging areas. Team members could have focused their time more effectively to better understand the dynamics of those challenges and find a process to resolve those areas of conflict. Areas that stand out follow. The first area was listening to the voice of the child and the voice of the family and the team, especially regarding an understanding of the FC. Should we have been more direct in resolving this issue? The second are was the legal process. Should we have looked more into the processes at play and asked for more involvement of family court or some other guardianship process to establish the facts of the story? Equally important was to establish the authenticity of Jacques's wishes that were confusing to all parties. The third area was resolving team conflict and developing trust. Should we have recognized this as an issue and pushed earlier for a process such as MAPS to resolve this conflict? If so, a very skilled facilitator would have had to have been identified. We should have recognized early on that the community team was not truly a team because the parents were not effectively involved as members due to the discussed conflict. The fourth area was addressing health care, sexuality, and safety amidst a climate of parents' wishes and fears. Should we have gone further in discussing the nature of their concerns?

Serving families of youth when mental illness affects a parent inevitably affects the team process. This was a fifth area of challenge. Should we have been more direct with Renée to understand his mental health challenges and understand better how we could support him in the process? Issues of confidentiality regarding Renée, and professional boundaries, were perceived barriers. Although we searched the literature on family-centered care, we could not find any specific guidelines to assist us in providing family-centered care to a person with a developmental disability whose parent experiences a disabling mental health condition. Are there guidelines from the mental health community to which we could have turned?

A final area of challenge was recognition of the need for increased interdisciplinary input. Although not involved directly, a physical therapist and nutritionist may have assisted Jacques's pediatrician to develop a plan for him and his family. Such a plan could have included enjoyable physical activities and healthy diet changes to address Jacques's overweight status. Collaboration between Jacques's psychologist, educator, and speech language pathologist may have resulted in more reliable forms of communication and a firmer understanding of Jacques's wishes. A social worker from the Mental Health and Developmental Service Agency may have worked with the school community team at an earlier stage rather than in crisis management as evolved in this situation. An occupational therapist may have been instrumental in assessing the potential for various types of meaningful occupational experiences that might have eventually become work opportunities for Jacques.

CONCLUSION

Utilizing the story of Jacques, this chapter has explored the complexity in dealing with transition from childhood to adulthood for children with disabilities, and their families. It illustrates how complex issues, family circumstances, and ethical dilemmas may emerge while planning transition for youth with complex disabilities. Highlighted issues included authenticity of the facilitated communications, specific legal processes and policies, cultural considerations, unique challenges to family-centered care, interdisciplinary team collaborative processes, including conflict resolution, and knowledge of disability and potential health sequelae that, when collectively understood, may contribute to the leadership skills professionals require when assisting youth and their families in transition.

GLOSSARY

Administration on Developmental Disabilities (ADD)—The U.S. Government organization responsible for implementing the Developmental Services and the Developmental Disabilities Assistance and Bill of Rights Act of 2000, known as the DD Act.

Competency—The ability to rationally understand and act reasonably.

Competent—A person who is competent is free to exercise all the rights and responsibilities of an adult, until determined and declared otherwise in a court of law. Because adults are presumed by law to be competent, the burden of proof is on those who would claim incompetence. Competency is a legal determination and should not be confused with decision-making capacity.

Decision-Making Capacity—This consists of three basic elements: (a) the possession of a set of values and goals necessary for evaluating different options, (b) the ability to communicate and understand information, and (c) the ability to reason and to deliberate about one's choices.

Deinstitutionalization—The term to describe the purposeful and planned-for movement of persons with disabilities out of institutions such as state hospitals and into more community-based supported living situations.

Developmental Disabilities Assistance and Bill of Rights Act of 2000—A bill enacted to ensure that people with developmental disabilities and their families receive the services and supports they need and participate in the planning and designing of those services.

Facilitated Communication (FC)—An accommodation for enhancing the communication of persons with no or very limited oral, gestural, or written communication skills (American Association on Mental Retardation, 1994). This accommodation requires another person to physically assist the person with disabilities to type (computer, typewriter, Canon Communicator) or point (letter board) by stabilizing the person's hand.

Guardian—A surrogate appointed by the court to make decisions regarding an incompetent person's care and custody. The court may set limits on the guardian's authority, including the authority to make health care decisions.

McGill Action Planning System (MAPS)—A dynamic and creative process intended to bring teams together for the benefit of the youth in transition. MAPS is designed to bring teams to consensus in planning transition for children and youth with disabilities (Forest & Pearpoint, 1992).

The Olmstead Decision—This is an historic Supreme Court decision, *Olmstead v. L. C.* (1999), that encourages states to reevaluate how they deliver publicly funded long-term care services to people with disabilities. The court ruled that it is a violation of the Americans with Disabilities Act to discriminate against people with disabilities by providing services only in institutions when they could be served in a community-based setting, and certain conditions are met.

Wrap Around Services Approach—An approach based on a philosophy in which services are highly individualized to meet the needs of children and families. A "facilitator" (a case manager, lead teacher, etc.) may work with a client or family to discover strengths, set goals, determine major needs, and develop strengths-based options. Services and supports are typically community-based, and must be culturally competent and tailored to the unique values and cultural needs of the child, family, and the culture with which the family identifies. Flexibility and ingenuity is encouraged, and services and supports often cut across traditional agency boundaries through multiagency involvement and funding.

RESOURCES
WEB SITES

Adolescent Health Transition Project—Washington, DC
http://depts.washington.edu/healthtr
This project is designed to help smooth the transition from pediatric to adult health care for adolescents with special health care needs. This site is a resource for information, materials, and links to other people with an interest in health transition issues.

The Family Village at the Waisman Center, University of Wisconsin–Madison
http://www.familyvillage.wisc.edu/education/transition.html
A Web site that integrates information, resources, and communication opportunities on the Internet for persons with cognitive and other disabilities, for their families, and for those that provide them services and support. It includes informational resources on specific diagnoses, communication connections, adaptive products and technology, adaptive recreational activities, education, worship, health issues, disability-related media and literature. It provides many links to information on transition to adult life.

Vermont Transition Web Page at the University of Vermont
Center on Disability and Community Inclusion
The University Center for Excellence in Developmental Disabilities Education, Research, and Service (UCEDD)
http://www.uvm.edu/~cdci or http://www.uvm.edu/~trans
A Web site with brief descriptions of transition including a summary of the Individuals With Disabilities Education Act as it relates to transition. Practical information and checklists are included to help teams planning transition.

Tools

Mcgill Action Planning System and other tools for inclusion
Developed by Dr. Marsha Forest and Dr. Jack Pearpoint
The Centre for Integrated Education and Community
24 Thome Crescent, Toronto, Ontario, Canada
http://www.inclusion.com

Books and Manuals

Life Beyond the Classroom: Transition Strategies for Young People with Disabilities (Third Edition)
By Paul Wehman, PhD, with invited contributors

Sexuality

Your Sons and Daughters With Intellectual Disabilities
By Karin Melberg Schwier and Dave Hingsburger, MEd
Both available through Paul H. Brookes Publishing Co., Inc., Baltimore, MD
Phone: 800-638-3775; (international): 410-337-9580; fax: 410-337-8539
E-mail: custserv@brookespublishing.com
mail: Customer Service Department
Brookes Publishing Co.
P.O. Box 10624
Baltimore, MD 21285-0624

Transition Planning for Adolescents With Special Health Care Needs and Disabilities: A Guide for Health Care Providers
By S. Porter, L. Freeman, and L. R. Griffin
Institute for Community Inclusion, University of Massachusetts, Boston
(Funded in part by the Maternal and Child Health Bureau)
http://www.communityinclusion.org/transition/familyguide.html
This booklet has been developed for families to help the adolescent with special health care needs in transitioning to adulthood. Four major areas of adulthood are covered: health, education, employment, and recreation. Each area is discussed and includes handouts and checklists. Also provided are resources for consultants, information on state and federal agencies, organizations, references, and suggested readings. Concluding sections provide a summary of laws related to adolescent transition and a glossary.

Reports

Surgeon General's Conference: "Growing Up and Getting Medical Care: Youth With Special Health Care Needs" (March 1989)
National Center for Networking Community Based Services
Georgetown University Child Development Center
Editors: Phyllis R. Magrab and Hilary E. C. Millar
Sponsor: Bureau of Maternal and Child Health and Resources Development

Conference: United States, Public Health Service, Office of the Surgeon General (March 1989, Jekyll Island, GA)
Publisher: United States, Public Health Service, Office of the Surgeon General
http://profiles.nlm.nih.gov/NN/B/C/Z/S

REFERENCES

American Academy of Child and Adolescent Psychiatry. (1993). *Facilitated communication. Policy statement*. Retrieved May 6, 2003, from http://www.aacap.org/publications/policy/ps30.htm#TOP

American Academy of Pediatrics. (1996). Sexuality education and safety for children and young adults with disabilities. *Pediatrics, 97,* 275–278.

American Academy of Pediatrics (1998). Auditory integration training and facilitated communication for autism. *Pediatrics 102,* 431–433.

American Academy of Pediatrics. (2002). A consensus statement on health care transitions for young adults with special health care needs. *Pediatrics, 110,* 1304–1306.

American Association on Mental Retardation. (1994). Policy statement: Facilitated communication. *American Association on Mental Retardation, News & Notes, 7,* 1.

American Association on Mental Retardation. (2002a). *Mental retardation: Definition, classification, and systems of supports* (10th ed.). Washington, DC: Author.

American Association on Mental Retardation. (2002b). *Position statement on guardianship*. Retrieved May 6, 2003, from http://www.aamr.org/Policies/pos_guardianship.shtml

American Association on Mental Retardation. (2002c). *Position statement on human and civil rights*. Retrieved May 6, 2003, from http://www.aamr.org/Policies/pos_human_civil.shtml

American Association on Mental Retardation. (2002d). *Position statement on self-determination*. Retrieved May 6, 2003, from http://www.aamr.org/Policies/pos_self-determination.shtml

Biklen, D. (1993). *Communication unbound: How facilitated communication is challenging traditional views of autism and ability/disability*. New York: Teachers College Press.

Blatt, B., & Kaplan, F. (1974). *Christmas in purgatory. A photographic essay on mental retardation*. Syracuse, NY: Human Policy Press.

Blum, R. W., Garell, D., Hodgman, C. H., Jorissen, T. W., Okinow, N. A., Orr, D. P. et al. (1993). Transition from child-centered to adult health-care systems for adolescents with chronic conditions: A position paper of the Society for Adolescent Medicine. *Journal of Adolescent Health, 14,* 570–576.

Braddock, D. L. (2002). Public financial support for disability at the dawn of the 21st century. *American Journal on Mental Retardation, 107,* 478–489.

Burchard, J. D., & Burchard, S. N. (2000). The wraparound process with children and families. In G. Burford & J. Hudson (Eds.), *Family group conferencing: New directions in community-centered child and family practice (modern applications of social work,* pp. 140–152). New York: Aldine de Gruyter.

Burchard, J. D., Burchard, S. N., Sewell, R., & VanDenBerg, J. (1993). *One kid at a time: Implementation and case study evaluation of the Alaska Youth Initiative Demonstration*

Project. Washington, DC: Child and Adolescent Service System Program Technical Assistance Center, Georgetown University Child Development Center.

Crossley, R. (1992). Getting the words out: Case studies in facilitated communication training. *Topics in Language Disorders, 12*(4), 46–59.

Developmental Services and the Developmental Disabilities Assistance and Bill of Rights Act of 2000, 42 U.S.C.S. § 15001 (2000, enacted).

Dinerstein, R. D., Herr, S. S., & O'Sullivan, J. L. (1999). *A guide to consent*. Washington, DC: American Association on Mental Retardation.

Edgerton, R. B. (1969). *The cloak of competence*. Berkeley: University of California Press.

Edgerton, R. B., & Bercovici, S. M. (1976). The cloak of competence: Years later. *American Journal on Mental Deficiency, 80*, 485–497.

Education for All Handicapped Children Act of 1975, 21 U.S.C.S. § 1400 (1975, enacted).

Forest, M., & Pearpoint, J. (1992). MAPS: Action planning. In J. Pearpoint, M. Forest, & J. Snow (Eds.), *The inclusion papers: Strategies to make inclusion work* (pp. 52–56). Toronto, Canada: Inclusion Press.

Green, G., & Shane, H. (1994). Science, reason, and facilitated communication. *The Journal of the Association for Persons with Severe Handicaps, 19*, 151–172.

Hudson, A., Melita, B., & Arnold, N. (1993). Assessing the validity of facilitated communication: A case study. *Journal of Autism and Developmental Disorders, 23*(1), 165–173.

Individuals with Disabilities Education Act Amendments of 1997, 20 U.S.C. §1400 P.L. 105-17.

Intellectual Disability Review Panel. (1989). *Report to the director-general on the reliability and validity of assisted communication*. Melbourne, Australia: Victoria Community Services.

Jacobson, J., Mulick, J., & Schwartz, A. (1995). A history of facilitated communication: science, pseudoscience, and antiscience. *American Psychology, 50*, 750–765.

Johnson, B. (2000). Family-centered care: Facing the new millennium. Interview by Elizabeth Ahmann. *Pediatric Nursing, 26*, 87–90.

Kindred, M., Cohen, J., Penrod, D., & Shaffer, T. (Eds.). (1976). *The mentally retarded citizen and the law: The President's committee on mental retardation*. New York: Free Press.

Kugel, R., & Shearer, A. (Eds.). (1976). *Changing patterns in residential services for the mentally retarded*. Washington, DC: President's Committee on Mental Retardation.

Lakin K., Braddock, D., & Smith G. (1994). Trends and milestones. *Mental Retardation, 32*(3), 248.

Lewis, G. (1997). *The operation and subsequent impact of local area coordination and individualized funding on families caring for a family member with disability*. Unpublished doctoral dissertation, School of Social Sciences, Murdoch University, Perth, Western Australia.

Magrab, P., & Millar, H. (Eds.). (1989). *Surgeon General's conference. Growing up and getting medical care: Youth with special health care needs*. Washington, DC: National Center for Networking Community Based Services, Georgetown University Child Development Center.

Margolin, K. N. (1994). How shall facilitated communication be judged? Facilitated communication and the legal system. In H. C. Shane (Ed.), *Facilitated communication: The clinical and social phenomenon* (pp. 227–258) San Diego, CA: Singular Press.

Mostert, M. (2001). Facilitated communication since 1995: A review of published studies. *Journal of Autism & Developmental Disorders, 31,* 287–313.

National Council on Disability. (2001). *Investing in independence: Transition recommendations for President George W. Bush.* Washington, DC: Author.

National Institute on Mental Retardation. (1981). *Orientation manual on mental retardation.* Downsview, Ontario, Canada: York University.

New York Department of Health. (1999). *Clinical practice guidelines: Guideline and technical report. Autism and pervasive developmental disorders. Assessment and intervention for young children (age 0–3 years).* Albany, NY: Author.

Nisbet, J. (1992). *Natural supports in school, at work, and in the community for people with severe disabilities.* Baltimore: Brookes.

Olmstead v. L. C., 527 U.S. 581 (1999).

Protective Services For Mentally Retarded Persons, VT Stat. §§ 18–215–9301 (1977 & Supp. 2001).

Shearer, A. (1976). The media. In R. Kugel & A. Shearer (Eds.), *Changing patterns in residential services for the mentally retarded* (pp. 109–118). Washington, DC: President's Committee on Mental Retardation.

Sloper, P., & Lightfoot, J. (2003). Involving disabled and chronically ill children and young people in health service development. *Child Care Health Development, 29,* 15–20.

Suris, J., Resnick, M., Cassuto, N., & Blum, R. (1996). Sexual behavior of adolescents with chronic disease and disability. *Journal of Adolescence Health, 19,* 124–31.

Vermont Department of Developmental and Mental Health Services. (2002a). *Vermont Developmental Services Annual Report, 2002.* Waterbury, VT: Author.

Vermont Department of Developmental and Mental Health Services. (2002b). *Vermont System of Care Plan, FY 2002–FY 2004.* Waterbury, VT: Author.

U.S. Census Bureau. (2002). 2000 Census of Population and Housing. *Summary Population and Housing Characteristics,* PHC-1-47, Vermont. Washington, DC: Author.

Wolfensberger, W. (1991). Reflections on a lifetime in human services and mental retardation. *Mental Retardation, 29*(1), 1–15.

8

Parent to Parent Practicum to Learn About the Family Perspective: Down Syndrome and Celiac Disease

Jo Yoder
Sara Burchard
Parent to Parent of Vermont
University of Vermont

Questions to Consider

1. What can students learn about a child and family while meeting them in their home versus engaging with them in a clinical situation?
2. Why is it important for the family to set the agenda for student interactions in their home and community?
3. How can students apply to their daily, professional practice what they learn through personal connections with families?

NICOLE'S STORY

When Nicole[1] was born nine years ago her parents, Tina and Scott, and 3-year-old brother, Mark, were excited about the prospect of a baby girl in their family. Their excitement was coupled with the age-old parental concerns about health, adjustment, and a new baby's future. Would she feed well? Would she develop an easy sleep pattern? How would her brother get along with her after the initial excitement wore off? How long would it take for the family to adjust as a foursome? Would the fact that Nicole has Down syndrome influence family patterns and schedules?

---

[1]All family names have been changed to protect confidentiality.

Tina and Scott talked with a few family members and friends when they learned that their baby would be born with Down syndrome. They were surprised when, among their own family members, some felt strongly that a child with a cognitive disability would not fit well into their family. Tina had not expected to hear mixed opinions about continuing or terminating the pregnancy. Tina and Scott had, however, spent long hours talking with each other about their own needs and expectations. They had decided that Tina, who had a degree in graphic design, would go back to work part time after Nicole's birth and Scott would continue his management job in an engineering firm.

There were, however, unexpected challenges. When Nicole was 3 years old, after a long struggle with digestive difficulties, she was diagnosed with celiac disease. This is an autoimmune disease affecting the lining of the small intestine that results in an inability to absorb foods containing gluten. This can lead to failure to gain weight, diarrhea, bloating, loss of appetite, and other gastrointestinal disorders. Celiac disease affects about 10% of individuals with Down syndrome, although it may go undetected. A screening for celiac disease of children with Down syndrome is recommended at age 2 or 3 (Leshen, 2002).

The diagnosis of celiac disease necessitated the elimination of gluten products (wheat, oats, barley, and rye) from Nicole's diet. This had a major impact on the entire family, as it required using less familiar, more expensive foods for everyone, or spending time cooking separate foods. Although Tina spent many hours cooking and baking special foods so Nicole would feel included in meals and celebrations involving food, Nicole longed for the same food she saw her family and peers eating.

By the time Nicole was 9, the family had settled into schedules and routines that answered some of the initial questions they had at Nicole's birth. Yes, schedules had been affected and health concerns were going to be a major issue, but the entire family had made adjustments. They continued to be involved in the outdoor activities they loved, often making accommodations for Nicole's ability level and sometimes finding alternative activities. As care providers were difficult to find, they adjusted group activities to include Nicole. Mark, at age 12, had developed a love of bread and pastries that he indulged at his friend's homes. Tina continued to work part time and Scott full time. They were committed to spending time with Mark and to nurturing an open relationship in which his questions were always welcomed. Most of their extended family welcomed Nicole and they continued the slow process of educating those who were uncomfortable with Down syndrome.

Challenging school concerns became topics of dinner table conversation too many evenings. Children would often tease Nicole, and Mark was torn between protecting his sister and feeling embarrassed about her behaviors. A number of Nicole's teachers had not had a child with

Down syndrome or celiac disease in their class before so they were on a steep learning curve.

Tina and Scott had learned a great deal about Down syndrome in 9 years. They had learned that one in 700 to 800 children in the United States are born with Down syndrome. Children with Down syndrome have an extra or third copy of chromosome 21 in all of their cells instead of the two copies typically present in other individuals. They also learned that children with Down syndrome often have related physical challenges: heart defects (50%), which may require surgery, gastrointestinal issues including celiac disease, upper respiratory weaknesses that lead to frequent colds in early childhood, and middle ear infections. Approximately 60% to 90% of children with Down syndrome have a mild to moderate conductive hearing loss due to middle ear infections, and hearing loss affects language development. Low muscle tone, which results in delayed motor development, is present in all individuals and most have cognitive challenges within the mild to moderate range (Batshaw & Perrin, 1992; Cooley, 2002). Cognitive functioning has in fact increased for individuals with Down syndrome in the last 30 years, as they have been included in and benefited from the social and educational contexts of their communities (Schroeder-Kurth, Schaffert, Koeckritz, & Kernich, 1990).

Nicole experienced her own challenges. Her life was full of physicians, specialists, and early interventionists until she was 3 years old. During this period, she spent time in an Early Essential Education (EEE) program. This program provides special education and related services such as physical therapy or speech and language therapy for children 3 to 5 years old. Although Nicole was a friendly child, her peers in the EEE program did not always accept her overtures of friendship. Establishing friendships became an ongoing, frustrating experience for her. By age 9 she was just beginning to read and she experienced daily struggles in keeping up with academic activities.

THE PRACTICUM EXPERIENCE: FROM A "SNAPSHOT" TO THE "ALBUM"

The family practicum experience in this interdisciplinary model offers a unique opportunity for fellows and trainees to develop a relationship with a family. For 40 hours during a 9-month period, families open their homes and their lives so students can experience a family perspective. The fellows and trainees see and hear about community connections, health care partnerships, school challenges, family interactions, support networks, and the emotional roller coaster of daily life.

A medical student once spoke about how meeting a family in the family's home allowed him to see a broader picture of family life than could ever be possible in a clinical or therapy setting. He likened this to seeing an "album" rather than just a "snapshot." Although a clinical meeting encourages focus on the child and the stated purpose of that particular meeting or therapy session, a home visit without a clinical agenda allows focus on the family, the child as a part of the family, and the myriad interactions that happen there. In this practicum experience, trainees and fellows begin to see the album—the broader perspective of the child as part of a family and a community. In inviting the reader to visit with a family in the various dimensions of the family practicum, the chapter is organized into five sections: (a) a description of the family practicum, (b) the uniqueness of the experience for the trainees and fellows, (c) observation by the trainees of the challenges for families, (d) perceptions of the family strengths, and (e) lessons learned from the family practicum.

FAMILY PRACTICUM: THE PROCESS

The objectives of this practicum experience are as follows: (a) to gain a comprehensive understanding of the daily lives of children with special needs and their families; (b) to learn how existing systems and policies can become more responsive to family strengths, concerns, and priorities; and (c) to identify and show growth in family-centered competencies. These objectives were collaboratively formulated among the interdisciplinary faculty in partnership with families who had offered similar experiences to medical students (see the Appendix).

Families who have children with special needs and who invite trainees and fellows (hereafter called "trainee") into their homes are called "family faculty." They teach a family's perspective by including trainees in various aspects of their daily lives throughout the year. The Vermont Interdisciplinary Leadership Education for Health Professionals (VT–ILEHP) Program Family Support faculty member, who provides supervision and oversight for the practicum experience, recruits families from the Parent to Parent of Vermont network. Within the group of families who participate, children have many different diagnoses and varying degrees of medical complexity.

Families participate in an initial orientation to the interdisciplinary model and training in the logistics of the practicum experience. They receive written guidelines and expectations for both families and trainees and are encouraged to communicate on a regular basis throughout the year with the Family Support faculty member. Throughout the year, times are scheduled for families in the program to connect with each other. These are important times to share family concerns as well as to offer feedback on their experiences with the interdisciplinary trainee. The Family Support faculty member facilitates connections between families and trainees and provides individual support to both if questions or concerns arise.

During the initial training week, trainees meet with faculty for an orientation to family-centered care (see Chapter 2 for a discussion on family-centered care concepts) and to the practicum experience. Written objectives and expectations for the practicum are included in their training manual. At this session, each trainee is given a family match. This is not a "discipline" match as the objectives are not directly about building clinical skills. For example, a trainee who is a speech–language pathologist will not necessarily be matched with a family who has a child with a speech issue. Whenever possible the match is geographically close to save travel time.

The trainee is responsible for initiating the first contact with "his" or "her" family. Thereafter, the trainee and family work together to schedule mutually convenient meeting times throughout the year. The family and the trainee discuss how activities they may do together might address the family-centered specific competencies of this interdisciplinary model. By this time, trainees have already identified areas where they would like to increase their competence in family-centered care. Approximately 20 hours of the practicum experience are devoted to developing a relationship with family members and learning about their life. This is accomplished by spending time with the family: attending medical and therapy appointments and school meetings; visiting child-care settings; and sharing informal times at soccer games, family dinners, or other family activities. The remaining 20 hours are offered as respite time to the family. Trainees suggest options and encourage families to define respite in whatever manner will be most helpful to them.

Trainees write a learning log about the family practicum experience where they reflect on what they learn from the family, how this experience will affect them as practitioners, and how they are developing family-centered care competencies. Learning logs are turned in monthly to the trainees' faculty mentor, the clinical director, the training director, and the Family Support faculty. These faculty members read and respond to the logs, initiating a dialogue that continues throughout the year. For example, a trainee wrote about a mother who was unsure about the trainee doing respite. This mother rarely leaves her children with others and when she has to, she chooses to leave her children with extended family members. The faculty member responded, "They are very fortunate to have such a close and supportive family—not true for some families, [who do] not always [have] a childcare option." This dialogue offers the opportunity to challenge assumptions and consider many perspectives.

Once each semester, trainees and their faculty mentors meet with the Family Support faculty and other available faculty members to talk about issues that may arise from the family experience. Faculty members pose questions such as, "What are you learning from families about the hard questions in 'practicing' the philosophy of family-centered care?" Other questions and themes emerge from these discussions: families might make different choices about treatment than a medical professional would make, involvement of the child in decisions about his or her own medical care, typical parenting issues versus additional stresses around parenting a child with special needs, and the difficulties of scheduling in already complex lives. During these sessions, trainees and faculty members "problem solve" together, learn from each other, and challenge and support each other in practicing as family-centered professionals.

On the one hand, families do not expect compensation for opening their homes to future health care providers through a practicum experience. Their families will benefit, however, by receiving free respite and others will ultimately benefit by the availability of well-trained, family-centered practitioners. On the other hand, it is important to acknowledge the expertise and time these families contribute. In this practicum, families who participate are treated to a midyear "check in" dinner, and are sent a thank-you note and gift certificate at the end of the practicum.

Many families talk about the difficulty of finding qualified, reliable child care and respite workers so the respite hours the trainees provide add a reciprocal component to this experience. Respite, as defined by the family, can range from a "mother's helper" model to doing overnight care when the parents are away. Other creative respite options trainees and families have generated include the following: walk with a child to play in a neighborhood park; play with both the child and his or her sibling while the parent is cooking dinner; spend time with one sibling so parents can spend time alone with another child; stay with children while parents go out for dinner, a movie, or meetings; and join the family on a ski outing and spend one-on-one time with a child so other family members can also ski.

Throughout this process, ongoing evaluation is used to improve the practicum experience and to insure it continues to be dynamic and responsive. Initially, trainees did a policy project with the family. When family feedback indicated that this required too much involvement from them, that project time was changed to respite. As the model was adjusted over the years, the practicum time was changed from 60 hours to 40 hours. The learning log was initiated 3 years after the VT–ILEHP Program started, when we saw the need to encourage regular reflection on this experience.

Occasional difficulties arise. Scheduling is always hard when a busy trainee is trying to match limited free time with an equally busy family.

Liability concerns mean that trainees cannot transport children. This, in turn, limits the range of activities. Inserting one more person into a family's already complex life can create an unexpected overload even when both parties want to make it work. Personalities and lifestyles may be very different. These issues are addressed by providing initial, clear, written expectations, detailed orientation and training, and faculty availability for solving problems. If involvement in the program adds additional stress to a family's life, changes can be made immediately.

Trainees, through the practicum, learn firsthand the model of effective help-giving practice as articulated by Dunst and Trivette (1996). They learn that the three components of effective help-giving are technical quality, help-giver traits and attributes, and participatory involvement. Technical quality assumes professional knowledge, skills, competence, and experience. This is the discipline-specific expertise that, as graduate students or community professionals, trainees will already have. To assure effective help-giving, this expertise will be delivered with an attitude of caring and compassion. If a provider is unable to communicate effectively with parents, speaking and hearing respectfully, his or her knowledge alone will be less than helpful. This is illustrated by a therapist who insists that a parent "must" do a specific therapy with her child a set number of minutes each day, without understanding the impossibility of fitting one more thing into the family's schedule. Participatory involvement begins with respect and commitment to working together. A trainee who was invited to sit in on a meeting with a mother and a case manager who always arrived late gives a clear example of the lack of participatory involvement. The trainee relayed the mother's perception that, "We are all late sometimes, but this case manager is late ALL THE TIME" (VT–ILEHP Trainee Learning Log, 2001). Trainees give numerous examples of the components of effective help-giving in their learning logs. They both observe and exemplify help-giver traits and attributes as they interact with the families.

This practicum offers the families a "gift" of time: it is a trainee who sits with them and hears their stories; it is a trainee who offers to play with their child so they can cook dinner without interruptions; it is a trainee who sits through a meeting and takes time to process it with them later; it is a trainee who is available to remember and build on previous conversations; it is a trainee who will call to ask how an appointment went; or, it is a trainee who brings his or her fun-loving spouse along on a visit. In turn, families give the student the "gift" of their stories. As Susan Zimmerman said, "Our stories shape us. They give us our songs and our silence. When they are full of joy, they allow us to soar. When they are full of pain, they allow us to journey into the darkness of our souls where we meet ourselves, sometimes for the first time. They destroy us and allow us to rebuild. We must share our stories. They are our gifts" (Zimmerman, 1996, p. 1).

In listening to these stories and joining in the lives of families, trainees learn what best practice (see Chapter 1) means for them as health care providers. They open themselves to change, the type of change Myerhoff (1992) described as follows: "If I would tell you my life and you would really listen, it would change you, and what right have I to do that? On the other hand, if I would tell you my life and you would really listen and not be changed, why should I waste my time?" (p. 292).

As the 9-month practicum comes to an end, the trainee has often seen or heard numerous snapshots or stories in the family's album of life with a child with special health needs. These experiences with a family definitely influence their personal perspectives and their professional practice.

UNIQUE INSIGHTS: TRAINEES' "AHA!" MOMENTS

While visiting a family's home, a medical student in a similar family-centered practicum noted the following: "It felt like Grand Central Station. All of the children's friends were coming and going, a neighbor came by to chat, the phone rang, and all the while the parent was cooking a delicious dinner. During dinner one child was excused to rush off to a soccer game." Although families who have children with special needs have additional appointments and caregivers to juggle in their lives, they are often also very active members of their communities. Scott, for example, is a member of the local school board and Tina leads book discussions at the community library. Other families may have to give up some of their community connections when caregiving needs become too time-consuming. One parent could no longer be the organist for her church choir as her son's needs too often interfered with the inflexible choir rehearsal schedule. What better way to learn about these issues than to spend time "hanging out" with a family in their "Grand Central Station" for a few hours? A trainee had this opportunity.

The Child as Part of the Family

The practicum experience allows the trainee to see a child as part of a family, an important difference from the medical model. One parent said the following: "Having Peter realize that Laura is also a sister and daughter to a family and not just a 'sick child' is crucial to having qualified, excellent ... personnel practice family-centered care." A nutrition trainee easily understands the special diet that Nicole needs but now sees firsthand how those needs must be incorporated into the entire family's food plan.

Trainees see a family's concerns over a period of 9 months. By spending 40 hours with a family and seeing many aspects of their lives, it is difficult to discount or minimize concerns. When the trainee arrives at Nicole's home and finds she is ill because someone at school inadvertently gave her a birthday cupcake, she sees the repercussions this has on the family. Nicole misses a number of school days and either Tina or Scott must stay home from work to care for her.

While spending time with a family in their home, a trainee sees a child's behavior within a family context, which may differ from that in a clinical setting. One VT–ILEHP trainee wrote that initially the child did not talk to her when she was alone with him but the instant his family came home he talked "a mile a minute." Seeing this transformation in the home setting was remarkable. She said

> This has taught me a lot about how crucial context is when considering how children behave. If I had never seen Jordan with his family, I might not even know he was able to talk. If I had never seen him completely removed from his family, I might think he was always engaging and enthusiastic. I think all practitioners should have the experience of seeing children in multiple contexts.... In clinical settings, I will have to find creative ways of assessing children in different contexts. (VT–ILEHP Trainee Learning Log, 2001)

Parents as Experts

Trainees learn that parents are experts on their child and on the special needs of their child. Many families spend time researching in libraries and on the Internet, talking with other families, contacting statewide and national organizations, and finding specialists from whom to learn. As they will always be the constant in their child's life, they become the keepers of information. Large binders of reports, letters, meeting notes, and research articles will attest to the hours they spend learning about their child's needs.

The array of resources that families learn about and use is generally unknown to someone who has not walked in their shoes. There are family support organizations, list-serves, and chat rooms available. Funding is available on many levels when families are referred to the right source and learn how to fill out the mounds of paperwork. There are therapeutic opportunities and community organizations available. Nicole has developed a love of swimming and has become involved in the Special Olympics, an organization for which her entire family volunteers. Trainees learn about these resources from families and in turn will have welcome information to pass along to colleagues and other families with whom they work.

In spite of this, trainees see instances when a parent's knowledge is not respected or even considered, as experienced by Nicole's family. They spent hours researching and reading to understand her intestinal problems. They repeatedly talked with the doctor about the increased incidence of celiac disease in children with Down syndrome before he finally took them seriously, did further testing, and proved what they had already suspected. Trainees not only see parents as experts on their child, but also have the opportunity to learn about specific neurodevelopmental disabilities by spending time with these experts.

Honesty is an important component of building a trusting relationship. Families can learn not to view providers as experts who have all the answers, whereas providers can understand that they do not need to have all the answers. It is acceptable, and even necessary, to partner with a family in finding options and planning interventions. One trainee learned this while spending some hours with a child when her mother had gone out. The trainee had all necessary emergency information, phone numbers, pager number, cell phone number, and so forth. Still, she reflected on her discomfort and why she felt that way:

> I felt that I should not be concerned because after all I am supposed to be a health professional and know how to handle these types of things. I had to remember however, that I am not typically alone with children and responsible for their well being in such a critical situation and that it is alright to communicate that something makes me nervous. I do not need to pretend to be 100% confident in every situation. I think sometimes as health professionals we need to feel that we have all the answers, and I am still learning that it is alright to say, "I don't know," or, "I will have to check with someone" or say when something makes you uncomfortable. (VT–ILEHP Trainee Learning Log, 2000)

This trainee learned what parents often wish providers would understand. Parents will respect the honesty of a professional who says, "I don't know, but I'll find out."

The Sibling Perspective

Some trainees found that their respite experience was really designed to support time and attention to a sibling caught in the shuffle of medical and educational appointments for their brother or sister with a disability. They also learned that siblings are affected differentially in families of children with complex health needs. In one family, a sibling may be fully integrated into the assessment and intervention planning of a child with a disability. In contrast, another family may be so consumed with the activities and appointments necessary for the care of a child with special health needs that siblings manage their needs independently or are connected with extended family members or friends who can help out.

Trainees also learned that siblings have different levels of understanding the challenges their brothers or sisters face and require varying levels of support. As they are matched to families of children with special health care needs, trainees often observe the role siblings take, attempt to recognize how siblings "fit" into the family system, and observe how "typical" the siblings' behaviors appear in comparison to other sibling relationships, including their own.

Complicated Daily Lives

Typical daily life often becomes more complicated and demanding for a family who has a child with special needs. One student wrote the following: "Most of the day she 'dances' around him, afraid of triggering his outbursts. It is a strain on their family. This mother is the dumping ground for conflicting advice from well meaning people, who don't live in her shoes. People who don't know what it is like to be his mom" (Vermont Rural Autism Project [VT–RAP] Learning Log, 1998; see Chapter 9 for a description of VT–RAP, a training project to prepare providers to better serve children with autism). The privilege of seeing this difficult "dance" can have a long-term impact on trainees.

Many families say that everything takes longer. Shopping, appointments, transportation, activities, plans for special equipment, and scheduling therapies consume a family's life. Trainees are able to witness and be part of these demanding schedules. One trainee described it in the following way:

> Even simple requests from a provider, "I'd like to see him next month," may be much more challenging for the family.

> For one routine visit to CSHN [Children With Special Health Needs], for a teenager with cerebral palsy [it looks like this]: For the Physician: fresh from his morning meetings, he arrives on time, with his scheduling, nursing, social work and secretarial staff waiting. Medical records, coffee and x-rays are ready. His patients are waiting. He is charming, gracious, professional and concerned about the needs of this child and his family. Within 30 minutes, the physician has reviewed the chart, and x-rays, examined the patient, dictated his note and moved on to the next room.

> For the patient: With his mother [,] personal care attendant and two siblings present for assistance, awaken early, carry to the tub, (he weighs 90 pounds) for a bath in his mesh chair, carry him to the living room floor to be dressed, lift him into his wheel chair, strap him in place, feed him breakfast, start the van, dress him with winter coat, hat and mittens,

cover with a blanket, wheel his chair around through the narrow entry way, over the door-sill, onto the ice covered porch, around, down the slippery ramp, across the frozen rutted yard, wait for the ramp to drop, wrestle his chair up the ramp and into position to be 4-point strapped into place, drive one hour to the [hospital] complex, drop the ramp, disconnect the security straps, wheel him into the building to x-ray registration, wait, park the van, wheel him into the x-ray suite, unstrap him, lift him onto the table, undress him, position him for the needed multiple views, leave him on the table while the quality of the films is approved, redress him, lift him into his chair, strap him in place, get the van, wheel him out to the entry way (with his new films), wait for the ramp to drop, wheel him in, resecure his chair with the four straps, drive 30 minutes to downtown ..., to park in the subterranean Health Department parking lot, drop the ramp, disconnect the straps, wheel him out of the van, down the ramp, to the elevator, up to the second floor, down the hall to CSHN, register, wait, wheel him escorted to the exam room, to wait. When the Physician arrives, after an initial discussion, unstrap him, lift him to the exam table, partially undress him, position him repeatedly for an examination, redress him. Lift him into his chair, strap him in place, (after disposition recommendations) two hours after arrival, wheel him out of the exam room, down the hall, through the waiting room, down the hall, down the elevator, through the garage, wait for the ramp to drop, wheel him into the van, strap his chair in place and drive one hour home, to once more, unstrap his chair, wait for the ramp to drop, to wheel him down over the frozen rutted yard, up the frozen ramp, across the small porch, over the sill, through the entry way ... home! Unstrap him and replace him, his head on his pillow and under his blankets, on the living room floor, most of a day later.

These unique complex common rituals, for a simple routine event, preclude any other opportunities that day, such as shopping, cruising the mall or stopping at Barnes and Noble for a Cappuccino. "Going out to eat" is McDonalds to go, eaten in the van. (VT–ILEHP Trainee Learning Log, 2001)

Privacy was a dream for Nicole's family during the first years after her birth. Tina and Scott were appreciative of the providers who came into their home to offer early intervention services that would help Nicole reach developmental milestones, but they became extremely conscious of being observed. "Was their house clean?" "What was lying around?" "Did the physical therapist notice that they'd eaten fast food for dinner the night before?" Or worse yet, "did the nutritionist spy the donuts and soda that Mark was consuming for his afterschool snack?" "Did the speech–language pathologist hear the argument with Mark about spending too much time at his friend's home?" "Did she think you were conservative, too lenient, or even a snob?" "Should you explain the situation?" "Would she think you were defensive?" "What do these providers think about the way you discipline Nicole?" "When you didn't allow her to eat certain foods before she had an absolute celiac diagnosis, did they think you were being mean ... even neglectful or abusive of your daughter?"

Trainees hear families' concerns about how they are perceived by providers, those who come into their homes, and those with whom they interact in meetings. Families are expected to share intimate details of their lives and to either open their homes regularly or to transport their child to centers for therapy. When trainees see this influx of providers, they realize that they are just one of many. They understand that a family's wish for fewer providers in their lives is not a lack of appreciation for the services given.

These "family albums" that trainees are shown come with a multitude of issues and concerns that families face on a regular basis. Students learn that families are experts, who should be heard. They learn that providers may not and need not be experts on every occasion, and they learn the tremendous time demands that medical and developmental services may impose on families. And, they learn the challenge to families' privacy that special services impose.

TRAINEES OBSERVE CHALLENGING ISSUES

Some of the challenges that families experience are common to most families who have a child with special needs. They include issues around child care, caregiving concerns, and school experiences. Trainees have a unique opportunity to begin thinking about their own participation, as a professional, in the systems that may or may not work for families. They see the role providers must play in advocating for system change, and they often become personally involved in some of these broad, system issues.

Child Care and Demands of Constant Care

When Mark was younger, Tina and Scott could ask their neighbor's 15-year-old son to stay with him for short periods while they ran errands or even went out to dinner or a movie after Mark was sleeping. Finding child care for Nicole has been more difficult. She is an active child who spontaneously carries out an idea with no thought for consequences. On a whim, she will run outside and across the street to see the neighbor's dog. She has difficulty going to bed without following a set routine and teens are reluctant to babysit when they know they will be chasing Nicole and trying to get her to bed, rather than doing their homework or watching TV. Scott and Tina worry about Nicole's ability to discriminate between appropriate and inappropriate shows of affection, especially to strangers. The child-care issue is complicated by the fact that it is difficult to take Nicole to functions that would require her to entertain herself quietly, and now that she no longer fits in the shopping cart, it is impossible to keep track of her in a grocery store.

When trainees spend time doing respite care for a child, they learn very quickly about the demands of constant care. One trainee stayed overnight with a child so the parents could spend time with friends. She described her situation in the following way:

> Well, it so happens Ryan was having a day where he just did not want to be put down. If he was put down he would cry …. So I avoided putting him down. Well, at one point I had to go to the washroom and I obviously had to put him down. So I sat him in a seat right near the door, he immediately began to scream. I was as quick as I possibly could be, but I was so stressed. Just that simple task was extremely stressful…. The rest of the night … was a lot of fun…. My job was to play with Ryan, but if I would have had other things like cook, laundry, run errands, etc. [,] I really can't imagine how I would have done it … everything focused on him …. I left went home and went to bed. I play with Ryan for a couple of hours one or two times each week and we play [,] have fun and then he goes to bed. It was so different with no one else around for the extended period of time. (VT–ILEHP Trainee Learning Log, 2001)

Life can be exhausting for families of children who require constant care. Although caregivers may come into the home on a regular schedule, if they are sick and cancel, the parent becomes the "default" caregiver. A parent can never cancel, even if it is the second or third shift of the day. This has major repercussions for parents' jobs and is often the reason, along with numerous appointments, that one parent works only part time or not at all. In a one-parent family, these challenges can feel insurmountable (see Chapters 5 and 6).

Caregiving Concerns

Parents whose child needs personal care and respite care have few choices. In the best of situations, it can be difficult for parents to leave their child with a caregiver, but if that child has complex health needs, it can be even more difficult. In a 2001 Parent to Parent of Vermont survey, a specific question probed families' concerns for their child's personal safety when they are with caregivers other than the parent. Indeed, 35 of 75 respondents indicated that they had concerns. Their concerns related to caregivers' training to provide specialized treatment, children who could not communicate if abuse occurred, level of supervision required of the care provider, inappropriate touching from caregivers, lack of knowledge of caregivers' past history, and concern that the child would wander off (Parent to Parent of Vermont, 2001).

Respite workers from an agency are not always chosen with the family's input, and there is not always time to build a trusting relationship. During this practicum, trainees and families have time to develop a relationship and parents can see a trainee interact with their child in a variety of situations. One family felt strongly in October that they would not leave their child with the trainee—they were very selective about who could stay with their child and rarely left him with anyone. So they did household tasks like cooking or addressing Christmas cards while the trainee played with their son in another room. After getting to know the trainee and watching him interact so positively with their child in their home, they began to take advantage of a few hours to go to a movie or out for a run, entrusting the care of their child to the trainee.

Although hiring agencies do general training, it is the parents' responsibility to do training specific to the needs of their child and family. It can take a long time to train new respite workers and feel comfortable that they can competently care for the child. Often families lose a caregiver just when they feel he or she is well-trained and knows their child. To deal with this, parents often spend time putting together binders of information and care books so a new caregiver can have a reference for understanding their child's situation. Safety and emergency plans need to be updated on a regular basis. One trainee in this interdisciplinary program helped a family put together this kind of care book.

Funding for respite is another major concern for families. Funds are often not adequate and available funds are rarely flexible enough to give families choices in care. When agencies cannot recruit enough respite providers, that also becomes the parents' job. Parents are sometimes exhausted by the different challenges that come with respite workers. There is the need to locate new care workers, to train them, and to fill in when regular workers are unavailable.

For some families, extended families are a welcome, caring source of respite. Other families choose to live in multigenerational homes so grandparents are available to care for a child while the parents work. In some cultures, this is even an expectation of extended family members, with clear role expectations. Although this can be a perfect solution, assumptions cannot be made that this will work for every family. In mobile societies, family members are separated by distance, but even when extended family members live at a short distance, there are many reasons they might be unavailable to help out with a child with special needs. Some value their independence and want to keep their schedules flexible for personal plans. Others have extraordinary responsibilities of their own or health problems that make it difficult for them to care for others. Family members who do not live with a child can have different opinions about the amount of care a child needs and might be less likely to see the urgency of constant watchfulness. Some members of Nicole's extended family continue to talk about her living in another type of residential setting, alleviating the need for her family to find caregivers. It was obvious to the trainee that these family members felt no obligation to help out with Nicole's care as Scott and Tina disagreed with their suggestions.

School Experiences

Without a doubt, no family would choose to be thrust into a situation that requires learning about the special education process. Once more, in the educational arena, families feel put under a microscope, as though there is an unspoken right to ask about internal family situations. Reports contain summaries of many private family issues. As trainees quickly observe, the school experience can be intimidating for families.

Parents often have an initial unfamiliarity with the Individualized Education Plan (IEP) process and their rights in special education. They may not understand the jargon involved in special education law whereas educators likely have less understanding of the medical terminology that the parents have learned so well. Together they strive to find a common language and understanding. Families face difficult decisions regarding their child's health and school participation. It is imperative that they receive complete information and hear all options regardless of cost, availability, or opinions of providers. One trainee, after attending an IEP team meeting, stated the challenge clearly:

> As several references were made to this upcoming evaluation ... it was clear from the Smith's body language and questions that they were unsure of the purpose for the evaluation and how it fit with Maggie's ongoing qualification for services. The team's reaction to this familiarity, according to my observations, was first not to notice it. Then, when Chris asked a very direct question about what the evaluation was, the team seemed to miss the "cue" that there should be some explaining done about this aspect of the special education process. ... the incident did serve to remind me just how foreign this process can be even to parents that are highly involved, extremely intelligent and well-educated, and exceptionally motivated to learn." (VT–ILEHP Trainee Learning Log, 2000)

The opportunity to observe team functioning before becoming a contributing team member helps trainees gain useful insights. Tina has to go alone to IEP meetings because Scott's work schedule does not allow him to be available until 4:30 p.m. and, in most schools, specialists are unavailable at that time. One trainee observed a well-functioning team: "Again, I want to stress that I was favorably impressed with the functioning of this team overall. Steve and Meghan seem to be happy with things as well, though they continue to be vigilant in pursuing adjustments they feel still need to be made.... These team meetings continue to be an excellent learning opportunity for me" (VT–ILEHP Trainee Learning Log, 2000).

Another trainee, after observing a less than positive IEP meeting, speculated that the difficulties stemmed from system's issues: "... I see that the 'system,' which is beyond the immediate control of the people on his team, is less than supportive. As providers, we need to take action to help make change on the state and national level so that parents can feel supported" (VT–ILEHP Trainee Learning Log, 2001).

Tina and Scott talked about the necessity of getting daily information from school so they could know about Nicole's day and engage her in conversation. Sending a home–school journal back and forth each day would allow both parents and teachers to be apprised of what happened in the other setting and would facilitate follow-up. Their trainee describes what happened with their request at team meetings: "Each time they've tried to suggest a simple system, the school team has tended to think in more grandiose terms, creating some kind of template with a sticker system or something which they will all create together, etc., etc. Meanwhile, the days pass and Tina and Scott can't get just the basic communication they need. This causes frustration (ILEHP trainee Learning Log, 2000).

It is not uncommon to hear parents, when talking about their relationship with their child's school team, mention that they "used to be" nice, not pushy or assertive. Now, they feel they are well-known at the school and that all eyes are on them when they come in the door of the building—"She's here again!" A trainee observed how parents get thrust into the difficult role of "advocate:"

> In school, children are really only provided with the bare necessities. She said she has to really push for anything extra to be added to her son's program. She said it is hard being so upfront, and having to be pushy to get what she needs for him. I can totally see why she feels that way. Not many people enjoy being pushy and demanding, but she especially, does not have that kind of personality. (VT–ILEHP Trainee Learning Log, 2001)

These experiences sensitize trainees to the challenges of participating effectively in the educational system. In this manner, they gain an understanding of the important role caring educators have in working closely with families to make the best possible programming decisions for their child.

TRAINEES LEARN ABOUT FAMILY STRENGTHS

Families' lives can become quite complicated when they have a child with special needs, but they learn countless skills for managing, coping, and living full lives. As trainees are included in a family's life for 9 months during the practicum experience, they have ongoing opportunities to see the pictures of strength in the family album. They observe how families cope with the changes and challenges in their lives and still, in the end, continue to hope and dream (Weick & Saleebey, 1995). They see a family's confidence that the hard work done with a child's team today is building the best possible future for that child, and others.

Trainees watch parents reach out to other families in similar situations for information and support. They observe parents who have well-honed advocacy skills speak out assertively. Some parents are willing to use their expertise to testify at legislative committees. One mother spoke about her transformation from a quiet person to a very vocal leader who ran for local office. A trainee captured the ardent advocacy of one mother in the following way:

> She told me she will go to the ends of the earth to make sure Joshua has every chance in life, every opportunity to grow into a healthy, capable, young man. There are so many struggles along the way though—so many frustrations with society's still prejudice and discriminative attitudes. Joanne wants the best for Joshua ... people often react to her drive as if she is being unrealistic .... Joanne knows she must set her goals high, in order to assure Joshua every opportunity. (ILEHP trainee Learning Log, 2001)

As trainees are shown the family album, they learn that a child's disability is only one piece of the family life. The trainee sees Nicole's family do typical family things: skiing in winter and sailing in summer. When going out to eat, they check restaurant menus carefully, always asking how food is prepared. Although it might be easier to eat at home, Mark loves eating out and his family loves to indulge his wishes. Due to Nicole's requirements for parental time, Mark has become an independent and self-sufficient child. He spends recreation time with a friend's family more than his own. He finds ways to enjoy the food he likes or do the things he likes to do without his family. He knows his sister has Down syndrome and learns there are just some things you do and don't do with Nicole. This highlights another perspective, the sibling's perspective, which trainees capture in the practicum (see Chapter 2 for a discussion of sibling issues).

Parents look for ways to keep themselves physically and emotionally healthy. They use the respite time trainees provide to go for bike rides, to movies, or out for hobby-related activities. These times are wonderful outlets for stress. One parent talked about feeling refreshed and ready to be present for her child once more. Families look for ongoing respite options, knowing this time helps keep their family strong and healthy.

When trainees see the broad picture of family life, they move away from looking at disability as a deficit and begin to see it as one piece of a family's life, rather than as a total definition of the family. Trainees note the strengths of families as advocates, and observe the support they find within the family. Trainees come to admire the resourcefulness and determination they see as families build lives full of typical family "ups and downs."

LESSONS LEARNED AND IMPLICATIONS FOR PRACTICE

Trainees benefit tremendously from the lessons they learn during this practicum experience and subsequently carry with them into their professional lives. It becomes almost impossible for them to work in a situation where collaboration with families is not an accepted practice. They recognize that systems that do not meet families' needs cannot go unchallenged. Trainees have become leaders in interdisciplinary teaming and continue to challenge themselves and their colleagues to grow in family-centered practice.

Educating Preservice Professionals

Throughout this chapter, the voices of trainees and fellows in this interdisciplinary model attest to the importance of learning directly from families. A recent publication of the Institute for Family-Centered Care compiles materials from successful programs all over the country that use families to teach medical professionals (Blaylock, Ahmann, & Johnson, 2002). Vermont had one of the first Parent to Parent programs in the country that collaborated with a college of medicine to add a four-part, Family-Centered Care seminar requirement to the curriculum for 3rd-year medical students. The core concept of that project—families teaching students—has expanded to include pediatric residents, graduate students in communication sciences, nursing and education students, and trainees in this interdisciplinary model. These family faculty programs are not possible without the partnerships with university and medical school faculty members who are committed to the practice of family-centered care. Neither are they possible without the dedication of families to tell their stories so others can learn from them. Lown (1999) wrote of a lesson he learned from postdoctoral fellows: "A story charged with human interest is far more educational than a disembodied fact" (p. v). That is exactly what happens when parents teach students directly and these opportunities must be incorporated into more curricula.

Respite: System Change to Increase Funding and Personnel

Families need access to respite on an ongoing basis. One trainee wrote the following: "Katie said she really appreciated the respite hours I provided, and that they really helped her get through a few tough days" [ILEHP trainee Learning Log, 2001]. The issues with regard to developing and maintaining adequate respite resources for families are immense. How and who can recruit, screen, train, pay, and maintain a flexible workforce of care providers? These are incredibly important yet daunting issues. If families are to be expected to rear and support children with significant disabilities, society needs to address these issues in a very creative way. Responsible care providers must be able to take on respite work while receiving the same benefits and expectations of work and open career avenues as have other health care workers. Addressing this major concern will require some truly "out of the box" thinking.

Teamwork and Collaboration

Trainees learn that the world of services, and especially school, is a complex system with its own vocabulary, institutional practices, deadlines, expectations, family and child rights, and so forth. Not only are these systems difficult for families to navigate, but also, families are often at a disadvantage in achieving parity of opinion when in meetings with professionals. There is a listening factor and an intimidation factor. Professionals might appear to lack the time to listen carefully to parents' opinions and questions. Parents can be intimidated by professional jargon or by a large number of professionals who hold "expert" opinions. Having seen this in operation from the parent's viewpoint, trainees are in a better position to model for other professionals. They have learned to accommodate meetings by using clear, nonprofessional language, explaining services clearly, and listening to and facilitating parent participation. Trainees have also learned, through the practicum and VT–ILEHP community and assessment planning meetings, the danger of having meetings without parent attendance. They are aware of the change in the tone of the meeting, the manner in which opinions are expressed, and the way responsibility is assigned.

This practicum provides an opportunity to see parents as real experts. However, it also should provide practitioners with the view that some parents choose not to be the experts and the need to honor that point of view. The result should be a practice that more fully includes parents as collaborators in the development and implementation of interventions, to the extent that they are able and willing.

Acknowledging the Central Role of Families and Respecting Their Strengths

This practicum has provided trainees with a fuller view of the child as part of a family. It also has provided a context for understanding the disability or the therapy for a disability in the context of families and children. Families are then seen from a holistic perspective. This should provide a basis for greater appreciation of the families and children with whom practitioners work, making family-centered care practices easier to understand and to apply in professional practice.

Trainees see the range of family strengths: knowledge, ability to make adaptations, and normalizing family adaptations. This awareness informs their practice by allowing clinicians not only to appreciate family strengths, but to build on them. It informs their practice by helping them see that parents are the primary source of information, expertise, and support for their child.

Making Accommodations for Children and Families

This practicum creates an appreciation for the full life space of a child. It reduces the tendency to have an instrumental- or disability-focused service delivery practice. The practitioner can now see practice in the context of family and child needs, time and desire. This insight provides motivation to build interventions into and around the family's activities.

This experience provides a greater understanding of the full impact of having a family member with significant needs: the impact on work schedules or ability to hold a job, the related impact on social circles for families and children, the excessive or unending demands on time, and the difficulty in making the many appointments that must be kept. The entire family system is required to make significant adjustments to accommodate to the needs and time requirements of the child with a disability. Practitioners apply this awareness by respecting each family's time and by making every effort to accommodate appointments for families; to find ways for interventions to be accomplished in more normative fashions when possible; to reduce appointments to a bare minimum; to provide child care or child space for other children, including siblings; and generally, to attempt to make modifications that could alleviate the stress and demands on the family. Practitioners can learn to accommodate their practices in a manner that will have an impact on the family system in the least stressful manner possible.

CONCLUSION

This practicum is about trainees building a relationship with families, and becoming part of their lives at whatever level they feel comfortable. Consequently, real learning happens, both planned and unplanned. A trainee's own words speak clearly and powerfully:

> It has been such an incredible experience spending this year with the Lee family.... I have seen Steve and LaShawna get through some scary times.... What I have learned from the Lee family, is that no matter what the challenge, their family continues to love each other, take care of each other, and be strong.... It has been a life-changing experience being able to be with the Lee family over this year, and in the context of getting to know each other, rather than one party providing services to another. I have seen what life is like when a family has a child with a disability and it has made me want to provide family-centered care to such families in my career. Knowing the struggles that families experience when they have a child with challenges, will help me assist families in whatever ways possible, and try to relieve families of the problems they experience with so many service providers. I know I will be a more competent service provider in the future because of what the Lee family has taught me. [ILEHP trainee Learning Log, 2001]

Trainees leave this practicum experience with a deeper understanding of a family perspective and with a raised consciousness of practice issues that will guide their future work experiences. Families have the satisfaction of knowing that by sharing their life experience they have had an impact on the future practice of a provider.

STUDY QUESTIONS

1. How can families and professionals partner to address the respite needs of families who have children with special health needs?
2. How might school staff and other professionals be better prepared to collaborate with families with a child with neurodevelopmental challenges?
3. What are the most effective aspects of a practicum, as described in this chapter?
4. How do true family–professional partnerships evolve in the context of care for children with special health needs?

GLOSSARY

Celiac disease—An autoimmune disease affecting the lining of the small intestine that results in an inability to absorb foods containing gluten.

Down syndrome—A genetic disorder characterized by an extra or third copy of chromosome 21; the presence of the extra chromosome results in physical and mental differences in the persons affected.

EEE—Essential Early Education is an educational program provided for children, 3 to 5 years of age, who have specific developmental needs.

Family match—Connecting students in training with families who have children with special health needs to enhance the students' understanding of and experience with families affected by the complex needs of their children with disabilities.

Help-giver attributes—Those characteristics, such as trustworthiness, meticulous follow-through, caring, and respectfulness, that should be demonstrated in practice.

Participatory involvement—A help-giving practice that ensures families are completely and actively involved in the process for addressing the needs of their children.

Policy project—An assignment developed collaboratively by trainees and the families to whom they were matched that identified and explored a particular policy problem families faced in ensuring services for their children with disabilities.

Respite—Activities generated by trainees and families to provide some rest, relief, or break for families who are challenged on a daily basis to meet the needs of their children with disabilities.

Technical quality—A help-giving practice that addresses the competence of providers, including the recognition of when providers are at the edge of their skill and need mentoring or additional training.

Appendix
Vermont Interdisciplinary Leadership Education For Health Professionals Program (VT–ILEHP)

Parent to Parent Practicum
The Family Experience

This family match offers you a unique opportunity to develop a relationship with a family. This family experience is a required, year-long (40 hour) expectation for trainees/fellows. These 40 hours will include: learning to know your family by spending time with them in life activities (school, health, community) and providing them with 15–20 hours of respite.

Objectives:

1. Gain a comprehensive understanding of the daily lives of children with special needs and their families.
2. Identify and show growth in family-centered competencies.
3. Learn how existing systems and policies can become more responsive to family strengths, concerns and priorities.

Expectations:

1. Within two weeks of the Parent to Parent orientation, you will meet with your family. This is the beginning of building a relationship and should be a relaxed time to get acquainted. You will hear some of the family's story and they might want to know something about you as a person. As you will be meeting with the family very soon, this is an ideal time to schedule your next meeting.

2. Think about what you would like to learn from your family and during your first or second visit with them, discuss some of the competencies that you would like to work on and identify some of the activities you will do together that might address these competencies. These activities could include going along to places where services and supports are provided:
> medical appointments
> school/pre-school
> childcare setting
> care conferences
> Individual Family Service Plan (IFSP) meetings
> Individualized Educational Plan (IEP) meetings.

You might also join the family for informal times: dinner, recreation, celebrations, etc.
Each of these settings offers you an opportunity to learn from your family about their hopes, dreams, their individual and family strengths, interests, priorities and challenges.

3. By the end of your second meeting, write up an account of your interactions with your family. Include: some of their family story, a list of the competencies you plan to work on specifically during this family experience, and the activities that will allow you to do that. Describe family strengths you have identified thus far and include any other reflections or questions you might have. This will be your first Learning Log entry.

4. Plan for respite: You can arrange the 15–20 hours of respite with your family to fit any time during the year, depending on the needs of the family. The family defines what respite means to them and the two of you will schedule it together. Begin to talk with your family about this time immediately and plan the likely times when you will do it. Include a written respite plan, as well-defined as you can, in your first or second month's Learning Log.

5. You are asked to keep a Learning Log to reflect on your relationship with your family and its influence on your understanding of family-centered care, and your growth in the competencies you have earlier identified. Some months, you will be spending many hours with your family, other months it might be a phone call to check in and see how they are doing. You will average 4–5 hours per month with your family. It is up to you to initiate the interactions. Keep in touch on a regular basis (at a minimum, a monthly meeting, phone call or email) and reflect upon all of your interactions and communication with them.

6. On the last Thursday of each month, or more often if you wish, you will give copies of your Learning Log to Jean Beatson, Jo Yoder, and your faculty mentor. We will read, respond and return them to you. You may give us hard copies (clearly handwritten or typed) or send email attachments. These learning logs are confidential and will not be shared further without express permission of you and your family. You are free to share them with your family if you wish and are encouraged to share excerpts with families on a regular basis.

7. Two sessions have been set aside during the year when we will come together to discuss your reflections around this practicum experience, and to relate this to the family-centered competencies. Come prepared to share insights and questions, and to learn from each other.

RESOURCES

Beach Center on Families and Disability
3111 Haworth Hall
University of Kansas
Lawrence, KS 66045
Telephone: (785) 864-7600
Fax: (785) 864-7605
http://www.beachcenter.org

The Family Village
Waisman Center
University of Wisconsin–Madison
1500 Highland Avenue
Madison, WI 53705-2280
E-mail: familyvillage@waisman.wisc.edu
http://www.familyvillage.wisc.edu/ (See "community resources" for
    international and diverse cultural and life style resources)

Family Voices
Post Office Box 769
Algodones, NM 87001
Phone: (505) 867-2368
Fax: (505) 867-6517
http://www.familyvoices.org

Grassroots Consortium on Disabilities
Post Office Box 61628
Houston, TX 77208
Phone: (713) 734-5355
Fax: (713) 643-6291
http://www.GCOD.org (Links to diverse ethnocultural and bilingual
    family organizations)

Institute for Family-Centered Care
7900 Wisconsin Avenue, Suite 405
Bethesda, MD 20814
Phone: (301) 652-0281
Fax: (301) 652-0186
http://www.familycenteredcare.org

Parent to Parent of Vermont
600 Blair Park Road, Suite 240
Williston, VT 05495-7549
Phone: (802) 764-5290)
Fax: (802) 764-5297
http://www.partoparvt.org

Research and Training Center on Family Support and Children's
    Mental Health
Regional Research Institute
Portland State University
P.O. Box 751
Portland, OR 97207-0751

Phone: (503) 725-4114
E-mail: gordonl@pdx.edu
http://www.rtc.pdx.edu

Technical Assistance Alliance for Parent Centers
PACER Center
8161 Normandale Boulevard
Minneapolis, MN 55437-1044
Phone: (952) 838-9000, (800) 537-2237
TTY: (952) 838-0190
Fax: (952) 838-0199
http://www.PACER.org
http://www.taalliance.org

Vermont Parent Information Center
1 Mill Street, Suite 310
Burlington, VT 05401
Phone: (802) 658-5315
Fax: (802) 658-5395
www.vtpic.com

REFERENCES

Batshaw, M. L., & Perrin, Y. M. (1992). *Children with disabilities: A medical primer* (3rd ed). Baltimore: Brookes.

Blaylock, B., Ahmann, E., & Johnson, B. H. (2002). *Creating patient and family faculty programs*. Bethesda, MD: Institute for Family-Centered Care.

Cooley, C. (2002, June). *The young person with Down syndrome: Challenges, opportunities, choices, and decision making interventions.* Paper presented at the annual Summer Institute in Autism and Other Neurodevelopmental Disabilities of the University of Vermont Department of Communication Sciences and the Autism Society of Vermont, Burlington, VT.

Dunst, C. J., & Trivette, C. M. (1996). Empowerment, effective helpgiving practices and family-centered care. *Pediatric Nursing, 22,* 334–337.

Leshen, L. (2002). Pediatric up-date on Down syndrome. In W. I. Cohen, L. Nadel, & M. E. Madnick (Eds.), *Down syndrome: Visions for the 21st century* (pp. 187–202). New York: Wiley.

Lown, B. (1999). *The lost art of healing: Practicing compassion in medicine.* New York: Ballantine Books.

Myerhoff, B. (1992). *Remembered lives: The work of ritual, storytelling, and growing older* [Ed. posthumously by M. Kaminsky]. Ann Arbor: University of Michigan Press.

Parent to Parent of Vermont. (2001). *Parent to Parent Survey.* Unpublished manuscript.

Schroeder-Kruth, R. M., Schaffert, G., Koeckritz, W., & Kernich, M. (1990). Quality of life of adults with trisomy 21 living in mental retardation homes compared with those staying under parental care. *American Journal of Medical Genetics* (Supplement 7), 317–321.

Weick, A., & Saleebey, D. (1995). Supporting family strengths: Orienting policy and practice toward the 21st century. *Families in Society: The Journal of Contemporary Human Services, 76,* 141–149.

Zimmerman, S. (1996). *Grief dancers: A journey into the depths of the soul.* Golden, CO: Nemo Press.

9

The Role of Partnerships in Program Development for Adolescents With Autism Spectrum Disorders

Patricia A. Prelock
Claudia María Vargas
University of Vermont

Questions to Consider

1. How can partnerships capitalize on the resources and expertise of programs dedicated to service delivery for children with neuro-developmental disabilities, specifically children and youth with Autism Spectrum Disorders (ASD)?
2. How important is differential diagnosis to understanding the needs of children and youth with ASD?
3. What are the benefits of partnerships in program development for children and youth with ASD?
4. What challenges do children and youth with ASD and their families face as they address issues of sexuality, transition, and independence?

SAM'S STORY: AUTISM, ADOLESCENCE, AND TRANSITION

Sam was a 14½-year-old adolescent with a variety of previous diagnoses, including obsessive compulsive disorder, nonverbal learning disability, social–emotional behavioral disorder, bone growth disorder, hypernasal speech, and conductive hearing loss. As the youngest of four siblings, who were described as following a typical course of development and having successfully completed school, Sam has been an enigma for his parents, his doctors and his teachers. A referral was made to the Vermont Rural Autism Project (VT–RAP) interdisciplinary team to determine if a diagnosis of Autism Spectrum Disorders (ASD) or some other genetic condition might better explain the challenges Sam has faced throughout his development. The family was also concerned about Sam's future. Knowing what would be available for him during his high school experience and beyond was both a question and a concern for the family. Sam's parents and his primary health provider wondered if Sam's high school was up to the challenge Sam would be presenting in his years there. Because of the nonspecific diagnoses of the past and disagreement among professionals, there was no consistent category of impairment identified beyond "other health impaired." In spite of his health, learning, and social challenges, Sam exhibited an incredible memory, strong reading and decoding skills, and a sense of humor that was unique to him. As is true of any teenager, he desired greater independence and freedom to do the things that other 14-year-olds do, yet establishing and maintaining peer relationships had not been successful. Sam also has shown an increased interest in girls but is challenged in his ability to initiate appropriate interactions and sustain them with girls he knows at school or meets at the local Boys and Girls Club. Sam is aware of his differences and demonstrates some depression around his inability to "fit in." With the family living in a rural community, there are limited services available, particularly social supports and extracurricular activities that would be responsive to Sam's unique challenges and strengths.

INTRODUCTION

This chapter describes the formation of a partnership between the Vermont Interdisciplinary Leadership Education for Health Professionals (VT–ILEHP) Program, the activities of which are the primary focus for this book, and VT–RAP, another federally funded project designed to prepare health care and related professionals to address the special health needs of a particular population—children and youth with ASD. The chapter begins with a discussion of the value of forming partnerships. Through a discussion of Sam's experience, an adolescent with a complex history of diagnoses and a late diagnosis of ASD, the chapter emphasizes the critical role of differential diagnosis, including the value of multiple perspectives and expertise in the areas of social–emotional, communicative, and behavioral development. Both the benefits and challenges experienced by the VT–ILEHP and the VT–RAP programs, in their efforts to form a meaningful partnership that enhanced the quality of service delivery to children and youth with

ASD, is highlighted. The chapter also considers issues of sexuality, independence, and transition frequently facing youth with disabilities and their families. The chapter ends with a discussion of lessons learned regarding the establishment of partnerships among programs with similar missions and how other programs might capitalize, in a meaningful way, on shared visions, expertise, and resources.

FORMING PARTNERSHIPS TO MEET THE NEEDS OF CHILDREN WITH AUTISM SPECTRUM DISORDERS

Partnerships are characterized by cooperative actions and collaboration among two or more organizations in which each stakeholder may contribute any number of resources such as funding, expertise, or personnel to sustain and enhance a particular aim (Vargas, 2002). The partnership that formed between the VT–ILEHP and the VT–RAP programs had a specific aim, that is, to better prepare providers to address the needs of children and youth, particularly those affected by ASD. Although both programs had individual goals and objectives, they shared a common vision for children and families affected by ASD and for the training of individuals who would be providing services to this population. Both programs were training interdisciplinary, family-centered, culturally-competent, and community-based practitioners in the assessment and program planning for children with neurodevelopmental and related disabilities, including autism. A description of the VT–RAP Program is presented below as well as a discussion of the ability of both programs to capitalize on a shared vision, expertise, and financial resources through a partnership.

The Vermont Rural Autism Project

VT–RAP was a 3-year federally and state funded training project with an additional year of carryover dollars designed to prepare early childhood special educators, speech–language pathologists (SLPs), and other related service providers to enhance the quality of their assessment and intervention of children with ASD and their families (Beatson & Prelock, 2002). The overriding goal of the project was to create systems change across the state of Vermont by developing the expertise of community-based teams in assessment, program planning, and intervention for children with ASD. Similar to the VT–ILEHP Program, the assessment and intervention approach modeled throughout VT–RAP reflected a strengths-based (Dunst & Trivette, 1996) and family-centered (Shelton & Stepanek, 1994) framework. Therefore, families who participated in the project were an integral part of the assessment and intervention planning team and were recognized as having inherent strengths on which program development and implementation were founded (Beatson & Prelock, 2002; Prelock, Beatson, Bitner, Broder, & Ducker, 2003). Children's needs, as perceived by their parents and community teams, guided the assessment process. Recognition of the expert knowledge parents bring to the assessment process also supported the family-centered and strengths-based approach that characterized the activities of both the VT–RAP and VT–ILEHP programs.

Families have described the VT–RAP assessment and planning model as an effective approach to not only assessing their children's needs but also facilitating the planning and implementation of the children's educational and community programs (Beatson & Prelock, 2002). VT–RAP would not have been able to provide such a resource to families, particularly in the area of assessment had a partnership not been formed with the VT–ILEHP Program.

Partnership Formation between VT–RAP and VT–ILEHP

The partnership established between VT–RAP and VT–ILEHP was certainly a venture in which both programs contributed significant and critical resources to the other to ensure the quality and sustainability of both programs. Because VT–RAP was conceptualized and funded a couple of years after the initial conceptualization and funding of VT–ILEHP, the Program Director and the Training Director of the VT–ILEHP Program collaborated in their effort to consider ways to improve services for children with ASD. Both had experience and expertise in autism, one as a developmental pediatrician often called on to diagnosis a child with autism, and the other as an SLP who had several years of interdisciplinary team experience in the diagnosis of, and intervention planning for, children with autism. Together, they facilitated interest among state health, educational, and parent organizations as well as school districts to develop a focused effort in the preparation of providers who could address the needs of young children with autism and their families. This negotiation with state and community agencies and the collaboration in decision making about who would be trained and how many would be trained occurred prior to the submission of the grant. In addition, the Training Director of VT–ILEHP wrote the grant and became the Project Director for this newly funded program that complimented the work that VT–ILEHP had begun and expanded an area of expertise. Both she and the Program Director saw an opportunity to address a statewide systems need for supporting the assessment and program planning for young children with, or suspected of, autism. The VT–ILEHP Program provided an interdisciplinary faculty, a structure for community-based assessment, and a process for training, that could be duplicated and enhanced to address personnel preparation for the specific diagnostic, program planning, and intervention needs of families and children affected by autism. The basic principles of the VT–ILEHP Program, including family-centered care (see Chapter 2), cultural competence (see Chapter 3), a strengths perspective (see Chapters 1, 3, & 6) and interdisciplinary practice (see Chapter 1), were integrated into the VT–RAP assessment framework (Prelock et al., 2003; Prelock, Beatson, Contompasis, & Bishop, 1999). The interdisciplinary nature of the VT–ILEHP and VT–RAP collaboration, with faculty representing more than 12 disciplinary perspectives, provided a more expansive view of disability and the patterns of strength and challenge that lead to differential diagnosis.

THE CHALLENGES OF DIFFERENTIAL DIAGNOSIS

Reflecting a strengths-based (Dunst & Trivette, 1996) and family-centered (Shelton & Stepanek, 1994) framework, Sam's family members became an integral part of the assessment team as described for families participating in the VT–ILEHP assessment process presented in Chapter 5 and the VT–RAP assessment model (Prelock et al., 2003). Their perceptions of Sam's needs were prioritized in the assessment process, and they were interviewed before any other team members regarding their areas of concern for their child. Understanding that families also have expert knowledge on their children was an essential element in the assessment process (LaRocque, Brown, & Johnson, 2001). Sam's family participated in all clinical meetings with the interdisciplinary team, which included all of the VT–ILEHP faculty and trainees and fellows as well as VT–RAP faculty and students. The family's assessment agenda was prioritized. They assisted in parts of the assessment itself, collaborated in planning the recommendations, and helped write the report.

Understanding Sam's history of complex diagnoses and working through the maze of differential diagnosis, however, was not an easy task for the interdisciplinary teams of VT–RAP and VT–ILEHP or for Sam's parents and his service providers. Knowing exactly where Sam "fit" was an ongoing frustration for the family. Because of the variety of diagnoses he had received, the category of "other health impaired" seemed to be the only one that qualified him for services. Sam's parents were concerned that such a diagnosis would not provide him with sufficient services, particularly as he prepared for high school, and neither would the pervasiveness of his social difficulties, including his intermittent depression, be recognized or addressed.

The differential diagnosis of children and youth presenting with differences in social and language development and rigid or repetitive behaviors includes diagnoses within the spectrum of Autistic Disorders and Pervasive Developmental Disorders and disorders typically considered outside the spectrum. These disorders outside of the spectrum, however, are characterized by overlapping symptomatology and include specific language impairment, learning disabilities, mental retardation, attention deficit hyperactivity disorder (ADHD), personality disorders, obsessive–compulsive disorders, schizophrenia, and other mental disorders. The overlaps between these disorders and autistic disorder are briefly explored in the following paragraphs, beginning with an explanation of autistic disorder.

Autistic Disorder

The *Diagnostic and Statistical Manual of Mental Disorders* (4th ed., text rev.; *DSM–IV–TR*; American Psychiatric Association, 2000) defines autism by the presence of at least 6 of the 12 diagnostic criteria listed for autistic disorder. To receive a diagnosis of autism, an individual must demonstrate at least two of the social criteria, such as impaired use of multiple nonverbal behaviors (e.g., eye-to-eye gaze, facial expression, body postures, and gestures) to regulate social interaction; failure to develop peer relationships appropriate to developmental level; lack of spontaneous seeking to share enjoyment, interests, or achievements with other people (e.g., failure to show, bring, or point out objects of interest); or a lack of social or emotional reciprocity (American Psychiatric Association, 2000). To qualify for a diagnosis of autism, an individual must also demonstrate at least one of the communication criteria, such as a failure to develop language or a delay in language development, an inability to initiate or sustain conversation, the use of repetitive or idiosyncratic language, or the lack of spontaneous, make-believe play (American Psychiatric Association, 2000). The last criteria that is necessary to qualify for a diagnosis of autism is at least one instance of restricted repetitive and stereotyped patterns of behavior, interests, and activities, including a preoccupation with one or more interests that is abnormal in intensity or focus; inflexible adherence to nonfunctional routines or rituals; unusual motor mannerisms (e.g., hand or finger flapping or twisting); or persistent preoccupation with parts of objects (American Psychiatric Association, 2000). In addition, the identified delay or abnormal functioning in social interaction, language, or play must occur prior to age 3. For clinicians on interdisciplinary teams involved in the diagnosis of children with or suspected of autism, one of the challenges in accurate diagnosis is the use of terms such as "marked impairments," "encompassing preoccupation," and "apparently inflexible." Often, practitioners perceive these terms differently, particularly by those with less experience diagnosing children with autism.

Language Impairment and Autistic Disorder

Distinguishing between the presence of a language disorder alone and the language symptoms of autism is particularly difficult in diagnosing young children. There are many similarities in early language delay and the language impairment described for children with autism; however, the language of children with autism is often more "disordered" in its pattern of expression (Noterdaeme, Sitter, Mildenberger, & Amorosa, 2000). For example, children with autism often exhibit echolalia, metaphorical language, pronoun reversal, and stereotyped utterances (Klinger & Dawson, 1996). Although secondary difficulties with social interaction may be observed in children with language impairment, they can and do use gesture and eye contact to communicate. This pattern of communication and social interaction is different for children with a diagnosis of autism who exhibit significant limitations in their ability to use eye contact and gestures and to initiate communication for the purposes of sharing information and establishing joint attention. Further, children with language impairment alone do not demonstrate the repetitive restrictive stereotyped behaviors typical of children with ASD.

Learning Disabilities and Autistic Disorder

Language disorders and social challenges are also characteristic of children with learning disabilities. Nonverbal learning disability (NLD), although not yet recognized in the *DSM–IV–TR* (American Psychiatric Association, 2000), is characterized by difficulty "reading" the facial and gestural cues of others during social interaction, that results in odd and antisocial behavior (Manoach, Sandson, & Weintraub, 1995; Rourke, 1989; Semrud-Clikeman & Hynd, 1990). Research continues to investigate the overlap of NLD with diagnoses along the autism spectrum (Rourke, 2000; Volkmar & Klin, 1998). A differentiating characteristic of children with NLD from children with a diagnosis of autism may be seen in cognitive testing. Typically, children with autism exhibit a relatively lower verbal IQ whereas children with NLD exhibit a relatively lower performance IQ, although the diagnostic differentiation becomes even more complex when considering children on the autism spectrum with Asperger Disorder. Children with Asperger Disorder represent a higher performing population on the autism spectrum with strong cognitive and verbal skills and poor social interaction.

Obsessive–Compulsive Disorder and Autistic Disorder

The presence of obsessions (persistent ideas, thoughts, impulses, and images) and compulsions (repetitive behaviors) is known as Obsessive–

Compulsive Disorder (OCD). What differentiates OCD from autism is its clinical presentation and manifestation. Typically, OCD presents itself in males at a younger age (between 6 and 15 years) than females (between 20 and 29 years; American Psychiatric Association, 2000). Generally, children and youth with OCD exhibit typical language and social development. Although children and adults with autism may have persistent repetitive behaviors and often appear to be "obsessed" with specific thought patterns, usually OCD is considered a separate disorder.

Attention Deficit Hyperactivity Disorder and Autistic Disorder

There are several differences in the onset, course, associated features, familial patterns, and prognosis between ADHD and autism; however, challenges in attention affect children in both disorder groups (Lord, 2000). Children with autism are reported to exhibit variable attention (Allen & Courchesne, 2001), from highly aloof and inattentive to details in their environment to overly alert and hyper-focused on narrow areas of interest. Often, their attention is characterized by an inability to focus on the more meaningful social information in their environment. Children with autism also have reactions to sensory stimuli that distract them from their tasks or cause them to increase their physical activity. Notably, children with autism have deficits in joint attention. This requires them to direct their gaze and attention to the same object or event as another person and share each other's interest in that object or event (Lord, 2000). For example, a child with autism may be presented with an interesting toy or object but makes no attempt to gain the attention of an adult or peer to share that interest and instead focuses on the object alone. Often, these features of attention are mistaken for ADHD. The pervasive nature of the social deficit in autism, however, should distinguish it from ADHD. When the symptoms of inattention occur exclusively during the course of a Pervasive Developmental Disorder, the *DSM–IV* schema suggest that ADHD should not be diagnosed (American Psychiatric Association, 1994).

Broadening the Diagnostic Lens

In the case of Sam, the VT–RAP interdisciplinary team collaborated with the VT–ILEHP team to enhance the lens from which Sam's reported challenges could be viewed. The VT–RAP team included the disciplines of speech–language pathology, early childhood special education, family support, pediatrics, and psychology. The VT–ILEHP interdisciplinary team added perspectives from nursing, nutrition, occupational therapy, physical therapy, audiology, social work, and public administration. The speech–language pathology, family support, pediatrics, and psychology faculty served both programs.

During the intake and assessment planning sessions (see a description of the assessment process in Chapter 5), it became clear that the collaborating interdisciplinary teams would need to be careful not to view Sam from the previous diagnostic lenses that had been used to provide a piecemeal description of how he interfaced with his environment. The family was asking for a fresh perspective. They wanted some answers to questions that had long-term implications for their son's program planning: (a) Does he have a diagnosis on the autism spectrum? (b) What is a realistic program for him during high school? (c) How can we keep Sam safe and responsible in unstructured settings as a maturing adolescent? The school had similar questions and added one related to the use of technology: How can we use the computer and educational software to support Sam's ability to work independently? The school also added one related to Sam's social life: How can we facilitate positive and appropriate peer interactions in high school? Sam's pediatrician had two critical questions: (a) Is Sam going to qualify as "eligible" for services and funding? (b) Will the school and service systems beyond high school be able to provide a meaningful program with appropriate accommodations that capitalize on Sam's strengths and address his weaknesses? The family, the community team, and the VT–RAP and VT–ILEHP interdisciplinary teams agreed to three general categories in which to focus the assessment process: diagnosis, program planning for transition to high school, and safety.

Although the interdisciplinary teams had full access to Sam's previous records and the array of diagnoses that were used to describe his difficulties to this point, they realized that their observations and assessment should not be clouded by these previous reports. What was critical now was to address the questions asked by the team—the family, school, and primary health care provider—and to capitalize on the expertise within both teams to address the diagnosis, program planning and service system needs, and Sam's safety.

Maneuvering Through the Diagnostic Maze

A variety of methods were used to assess the strengths and challenges of Sam in his home, school, and community environments. These included a review of all previous records and reports, a series of interviews with family members and community providers, and observations and direct interaction with Sam. Assessment tools were also administered. The results of these assessments were then integrated from the observations made, interviews completed, and records reviewed, to answer each question. Finally, three to five priority recommendations were offered for each category of questions. A brief description of the assessment process and results are provided in the paragraphs that follow.

Diagnosis.   Several areas were considered in the category of diagnosis, including Sam's general health, issues of pain related to his bone growth disorder, sensory issues, movement differences, speech–language development, and social skills. Having the expertise of multiple disciplines across the two interdisciplinary teams facilitated the comprehensiveness of Sam's assessment.

The family reported that Sam has restless nights with excessive bruxism (teeth grinding), prefers bland foods, and requires stool softeners because of persistent constipation. Pain was reported as a frequent occurrence because of a number of surgeries related to Sam's bone growth disorder, yet he often had difficulty expressing his feelings of pain and discomfort. In fact, his parents reported an extremely high tolerance for pain in their frequent observations of Sam's injuries or illnesses (e.g., cutting his finger, knee injury, ear infections) and some self-abusive behaviors (e.g., hair pulling and scratching or picking his skin). The family identified Sam as tactilely defensive and often sensitive to warm, sticky, and creamy textures. In addition, they noted he does not attend to the cold (walking outside without a coat) or to body signals (holding his bladder in the morning). Sam also was observed walking with a shuffle-like gait and taking more time than his peers to complete fine motor tasks in his eighth-grade classroom.

A review of previous speech and language testing indicated a range of abilities with relative strengths in expressive language, less efficient receptive skills, but overall language performance within the low normal range. Some articulation and nasal resonance difficulties were reported. Observations by the interdisciplinary team noted significant word finding in Sam's conversational discourse including the use of "fillers" (e.g., um, uh, like), pauses (of greater than 5 seconds), and incomplete sentences. Although Sam did not typically use echolalia and often communicated using complex speech, his communication style was characterized by limited variation in affect, unusual vocal intensity, poor initiation of requests and a lack of emphatic or emotional gestures. The school case manager described Sam as having "black and white tunnel vision" in his social interactions. She reported he does not understand the perspective of others and his emotional response to particular situations is out of line with what might be expected for a student his age and ability level (e.g., getting agitated and emotionally upset when art class ends and materials need to be put away). Observations of Sam's interactions by the interdisciplinary team indicated minimal contact and when interactions did occur they were usually scripted in nature and limited to polite greetings. Adults, such as an instructional assistant, prompted most interactions with peers.

In addition to gaining a historical and current view of Sam's strengths and challenges through record reviews, interviews, and observations, several tools were used to address the question of autism. To determine any early risks or red flags indicative of autism, the family was asked to complete two retrospective interviews, the "Checklist for Autism in Toddlers" (Baron-Cohen, Allen, & Gillberg, 1992) and the "Early Indicators/Red Flags Checklist of Autism Spectrum Disorders" (Prelock, 2000). These retrospective tools provided some historical background on Sam's early behaviors that could have put him at risk for a diagnosis of ASD but were not followed because of other pressing concerns (e.g., bone growth disorder) or his ability to communicate sufficiently to get his needs met. These tools revealed that Sam had limited to no symbolic play skills, failed to share enjoyment around objects or events, and averted his eye gaze immediately after establishing eye contact with another person. In addition, the family revealed that Sam exhibited unusual hand and finger mannerisms and often failed to attend to his name. The "Autism Diagnostic Observation Schedule–Generic" (ADOS; Lord, Rutter, DiLavore, & Risi, 1999) was also used to formally assess Sam's language and communication, reciprocal social interaction, imagination, and stereotyped behavior and restricted interests. The ADOS is a standardized assessment tool used to examine characteristics that indicate a child, adolescent, or adult has challenges consistent with a diagnosis of autism or within the autism spectrum. It can be administered to individuals with a range of verbal ability and because Sam was essentially a fluent verbal communicator, Module 4 of the ADOS was administered. Sam was engaged in a variety of tasks including working with puzzles, playing with toys or figures, looking at pictures, books, and a cartoon, participating in structured conversations, and answering questions about emotions, friendships, loneliness, and other social experiences. His overall score revealed performance within the autism spectrum. Sam exhibited no spontaneous affect and participated in conversations that were prompted through direct questions. Initiations and comments were limited and eye contact with a conversational partner quickly moved to gaze aversion. Sam struggled in his ability to organize his thoughts and often provided literal and concrete responses to questions asked. For example, when asked where he got a book he was reading, he said, "on the top shelf." Attention shifting rarely occurred and although Sam appeared interested and motivated to participate in the assessment, he failed to really engage the examiner in the tasks. Some unusual hand, finger and motor movements were noted during the assessment, including repetitive finger movements, hair twisting, and string pulling on his clothing.

The interdisciplinary team also reviewed the diagnostic criteria for Pervasive Developmental Disorders and Autism as described in the *DSM–IV–TR* (American Psychiatric Association, 2000). Sam's parents and the interdisciplinary team identified impairments in social interaction, noting that Sam demonstrated a flat affect, averted his eyes inappropriately in social interaction, failed to develop age-appropriate peer relationships, and did not show social or emotional reciprocity as demonstrated by his inability to sustain a conversation. Communication was reported as delayed and the parents identified that echolalia characterized Sam's early expressive language. Sam's parents confirmed observations made that Sam demonstrates a preoccupation with one or more restricted patterns of interest (excessive manipulation of beads and string, paper, and clothing), particularly when his anxiety level is high. In addition, he had an inflexible adherence to nonfunctional routines or rituals, for example, having to follow the same route to school and becoming unusually upset when there were any changes in the school schedule.

In collaboration with the family and the school team, the interdisciplinary team determined that although Sam exhibited challenges that some might consider part of his previous diagnoses, that his past accounts of stereotypic and idiosyncratic behaviors and the observations made in various contexts during the assessment affirmed a diagnosis of autism. Sam's failure to develop appropriate peer interactions and his lack of social–emotional reciprocity as well as his inflexibility and focused interests suggested a primary diagnosis of autism. The observed attention difficulties appeared to be secondary to his autism and were most often characterized by his inability to shift his attention and his singular focus on his specific interests. Sam's obsessive–compulsive behavior appeared to be unusual motor mannerisms and sensory patterns often seen in children and youth on the autism spectrum. The retrospective view provided by the historical data the family offered and the record reviews gave the team a perspective of what Sam's behavior had been like and how this behavior evolved over time. Last, the comprehensive look at Sam in several environments using interviews with those most familiar with his behavior, and observations and interactions using formal and informal measures, allowed the interdisciplinary team to differentiate what was and was not characteristic of what they knew about children and youth with ASD. The family asked for a fresh perspective in a broader context, and with their help and that of the community team, the interdisciplinary team capitalized on their expertise to engage in differential diagnosis.

Programming, Transition to High School, and Beyond.   The second category of questions was raised because of the family's concerns that the general education classroom with special education support was too overwhelming and anxiety-producing for Sam. Although he had significant strengths in reading, his math and written language were problematic and the school was struggling with ways to address his weaknesses while capitalizing on his strengths.

Observations revealed that Sam appeared inattentive, or seemed preoccupied with manipulating objects (strings, beads) in his hands or mouth. Interestingly, however, in spite of these seemingly inattentive behaviors, he appropriately asked and answered questions in French and History class. When working in smaller remedial groups, it became obvious that his knowledge level was above that of the peers to whom he was matched.

The "School Function Assessment" (SFA; Coster, Deeney, Haltwanger, & Haley, 1998) was completed. It is a measure that assesses a student's strengths and limitations in performing school-related tasks. The school case manager and the staff working with Sam collaborated with the interdisciplinary team to complete this tool. Results of the SFA indicated that Sam was able to participate in all school-related settings with occasional assistance. Those tasks requiring assistance were eating, toileting, and transitioning from class to class, with inconsistent performance on clothing management and personal care awareness. These were the same activities of daily living that Sam's parents reported as problematic in the home setting. In addition, the results of the SFA revealed inconsistent performance in following social conventions, complying with adult directives, school rules, and task completion. It appeared that Sam had difficulty regulating his behavior and using his language in social contexts. These results confirmed observations and impressions the interdisciplinary team had as Sam's diagnostic profile was considered.

Knowing that transition to high school was a significant concern for the family, members of the interdisciplinary team toured the local high school Sam would attend and interviewed the principal and special education coordinator for high school students. Their observations revealed a highly stimulating environment which could interfere with Sam's ability to focus on important classroom tasks, but there was availability of computers in every room (which could be used to support Sam's written language and associated motor difficulties) and rooms were acoustically treated with wall-to-wall carpeting and low ceiling tiles (which could support Sam's listening difficulties when bothered by his fluctuating hearing loss). There were, however, no resource rooms to support students who were challenged by the academic requirements and this was a significant concern for the family and the current school team. There was also a vocational training school adjoined to the high school that offered an option for noncollege bound students with special interests. Sam's parents saw this as a viable program to prepare Sam for a job that he might enjoy and at which he might be successful, yet the school required completion of a certain level of high school coursework before enrollment.

The insights and experiences of all members of the VT–RAP and VT–ILEHP team were particularly valuable in the discussions that ensued with the family and community team to address Sam's educational needs. The family support faculty on the VT–ILEHP team brainstormed with the parents to identify local resources that might be used to increase friendship opportunities for Sam. Knowing that Sam had some culinary skills and an interest in photography, they discovered there was a Boy's Club program in the next town that offered some afterschool activities in these areas. The vocational training program connected to the high school also had a culinary arts program. The interdisciplinary team encouraged the parents and the school team to approach the high school program and ask for special consideration to develop a combination program (of high school and vocational classes) that would more effectively address Sam's needs. The VT–ILEHP team member with special expertise in special education law offered strategies to facilitate this through the Individual Education Planning (IEP) process for Sam that was up for review.

The family was also interested in initiating a plan for supporting Sam's long-term integration within his community and identifying the skills he would need to be successful in this community integration. The local mental health services program was engaged in the assessment to determine what their agency might provide and how the family might connect early on to obtain funding and support for designing and implementing a meaningful community integration program and supervised living arrangements for their son. It became clear that local resources were limited and that the family would need to begin now to heighten the local mental health services' awareness of future needs. The Parent to Parent of Vermont faculty member on the VT–ILEHP made an immediate connection with her organization's respite coordinator to facilitate some respite dollars and contacts for the family. The Parent to Parent of Vermont organization was also helpful in pursuing greater flexible family funding. For example, a family support coordinator helped the family complete the necessary financial forms to apply for increased funding based on their son's current educational, health, and mental health needs.

Safety. The third priority area of concern for the family was Sam's safety in unstructured social environments. They worried that Sam did not understand safety rules around strangers and that he required supervision in most contexts. He did not have the ability to determine what situations were safe and unsafe or what people could and could not be trusted. The physical therapy faculty member of the VT–ILEHP team recommended that the interdisciplinary team administer the "Pediatric Evaluation of Disability Inventory" (PEDI; Haley, Coster, Ludlow, Haltwanger, & Andrellos, 1992) with the parents to determine what specific areas of social and safety concerns might be identified. Although this tool is typically used with much younger children, specific questions are valuable in determining the level of supervision or modification required to achieve optimal success. Results indicated through parental report that Sam needs maximal supervision to ensure his safety in all situations. Interviews with the school team also indicated that Sam has difficulty interpreting nonverbal social cues and, despite the training he received on the danger of strangers, seems unable to apply what he has learned. Further, the parents, the school team, and the primary health care provider expressed concerns that Sam's impulsive nature, coupled with his intermittent depression and increased social isolation, puts him at risk for suicide. The social work faculty member on the VT–ILEHP team facilitated finding a counselor with knowledge in the area of autism. She had contacts in the local area in which Sam lived and was able to provide two names of individuals who could provide supportive counseling.

BENEFITS AND CHALLENGES OF PARTNERSHIPS IN PROGRAM DEVELOPMENT

Sam's diagnosis of autism had important implications for his service delivery, now and in the future. First, it provided recognition of specific needs, including educational, social, health, and mental health. Second, it increased his access to human resources with specific expertise, including mental health and primary health care with expertise in developmental disabilities. Third, it facilitated opportunities for making community connections. These service delivery needs, however, may not have been realized without the partnerships that evolved between the VT–RAP and VT–ILEHP interdisciplinary teams as well as the school and local community programs. As described in several instances in the previous sections, there were several benefits to the program collaboration between the VT–RAP and VT–ILEHP interdisciplinary teams. In addition, other programs or agencies were engaged in the process of defining a responsive program plan for Sam. The benefits and challenges of these partnerships are described below.

Benefits of the Established Partnerships

Partnerships involve cooperative actions that expand the possibilities of programs affecting positive change (Vargas, 2002). The partnership between VT–RAP and VT–ILEHP revealed benefits at several levels. Broadening the level of expertise available to the families served by both programs was a significant benefit. The VT–RAP team brought a knowledge level in autism that was beyond what the VT–ILEHP team members had been exposed to. Those participating in VT–RAP had at least two intensive graduate courses in autism, focusing on issues of assessment and intervention, whereas the VT–ILEHP team had one 2-hr class in assessment and one 2-hr class in intervention in autism. VT–RAP team members had also been exposed to a variety of assessment tools identified as effective in supporting the diagnostic process for autism.

The clinical expertise of the VT–ILEHP team, on the other hand, was a significant factor in the learning experience for the VT–RAP team and facilitated the assessment process for Sam. VT–ILEHP offered clinical expertise in motor and sensory issues, nutrition, and social work that was absent in the VT–RAP team. VT–ILEHP team members also had established community networks across the state including direct ties with Parent to Parent of Vermont (see Chapter 8 for a description of this relationship).

Fortunately, both the VT–ILEHP and VT–RAP interdisciplinary teams had some shared experiences and a commitment to competencies in service delivery that facilitated their partnerships. They also learned from and improved their process and procedures through their collaboration. Both teams were committed to family-centered care, interdisciplinary teaming, cultural competence, and leadership to facilitate systems change. Although VT–ILEHP worked to establish competency across neurodevelopmental disabilities, VT–RAP focused its efforts on the assessment and intervention of children and youth affected by autism. The community assessment process developed by VT–ILEHP (see Chapter 5 for an explanation) was integrated into the VT–RAP assessment process. VT–RAP, however, expanded its approach to the assessment by requiring family members and community team members to participate in all aspects of planning with the interdisciplinary team, either in person or through videotape or conference calling, to ensure that the family and community perspective on the issues was not lost. This eventually became VT–ILEHP's approach to ensuring family and community presence throughout the assessment process. VT–RAP team members also developed checklists to guide and ensure that expectations for all elements of the assessment and follow-up process were met. Many of these guidelines were adopted and modified by the VT–ILEHP team. The report writing process also emerged as an area in which VT–RAP was able to make a focused contribution. It was determined that generating three to five priority question areas and limiting recommendations to three to five suggestions in each question area was more manageable and meaningful for families and community teams. VT–ILEHP adopted this approach to report writing as well.

A final area of enhanced programming occurred in the development of the Parent to Parent of Vermont Practicum (see Chapter 8). Like VT–ILEHP, the VT–RAP team wished to partner with Parent to Parent of Vermont to ensure that families having children affected by autism would benefit in some way through the VT–RAP project. VT–ILEHP had instituted a family practicum, which VT–RAP modeled. It was decided that offering 40 hours of respite to families who have children with autism would be a significant contribution. This venture was highly successful and lead to meaningful learning reflections by the students and professionals in training. VT–ILEHP then expanded its approach to the Parent to Parent of Vermont Practicum by including a respite component.

It becomes clear that the partnerships established between the VT–RAP and VT–ILEHP teams enriched the learning experiences and services to families at several levels, including the assessment process, the family practicum, report writing, involvement of families, and the knowledge base in autism. These modeled partnerships also facilitated more cooperative encounters by both teams with the school programs, local mental health agencies, and other community organizations. The time and resource commitments to these partnerships, however, were not without their challenges.

Challenges of the Established Partnerships

Although an advantage of the partnership between VT–RAP and VT–ILEHP included some financial support in the form of personnel buyout for both the VT–ILEHP Program Director (developmental pediatrician with expertise in autism) and the VT–ILEHP Training Director (SLP with expertise in autism), this meant that these individuals were committed to twice the number of interdisciplinary community-based assessments in which they would be participating. Both individuals recognized this time and resource challenge when other tasks within the VT–ILEHP Program were put on hold. Neither of these individuals fully considered the extent of their commitments to both projects and later realized the need to make adjustments and prioritize how and in what contexts their role was critical. This lead to expanding the role of some faculty members (adding an assistant training director to the nursing role) and trainees (doctoral candidate in psychology served as a faculty mentor for VT–RAP in her 2nd year as a VT–ILEHP trainee).

In addition, VT–ILEHP faculty and trainees and fellows were at a disadvantage in terms of the knowledge base in autism. The VT–RAP team had a significantly greater knowledge base and understanding of assessment tools and intervention strategies appropriate for use with children and youth with autism. This meant that many team members had critical information that others did not have which compromised the planning sessions between the two groups. Both teams learned, however, that providing tutorials in specific knowledge areas was an effective strategy to enhance the knowledge base of all participating partners. Last, the VT–ILEHP team did not have the opportunity to follow the family and assessment process through to its completion. Neither did the VT–RAP team have some of the needed areas of expertise VT–ILEHP had (for example, occupational and physical therapy, nutrition) on the actual days of assessment. Both teams learned, however, to communicate findings and questions through other means (e-mail, telephone, interview) or offered their direct support. This lead to sustained development of expertise in autism and community networking across the two teams. However, the partnerships required time and effort that was in short supply.

CHALLENGES IN SAFETY, TRANSITION, AND HEALTH CARE FOR CHILDREN AND YOUTH WITH AUTISM SPECTRUM DISORDERS

The educational, social, health, and mental health needs of children and youth affected by autism are significant, and often overwhelming for families and the providers who work with them. Access to human resources with specific expertise to support these needs is frequently lacking, particularly for mental health workers, who can address the social and emotional issues, and primary health care providers, who can manage the health and related conditions affecting children and youth with autism. In addition, access to financial resources, such as respite, and recreational activities, such as school clubs, sports, and other special programs, are limited and often are not accessible to children with the unique challenges that characterize children with autism. This was especially true for Sam and his family. The family had limited funds for respite and Sam had no interest in sports. There was a community Boys and Girls Club in their area, but Sam's parents were concerned about the lack of supervision and Sam's impulsiveness and inability to discriminate safe situations from those that are potentially unsafe. They shared concerns in several areas families frequently identify for children with developmental disabilities. These include issues of safety, transition, and health care.

Safety

For any child with social, communication, and cognitive challenges, safety concerns are paramount. Children and youth with ASD may not develop an understanding of the dangers in society in the same way as do other children. Because of this lack of understanding and limitations in their perspective-taking, they are at greater potential risk for abuse, physical and sexual, and are less likely to be able to describe such instances. Lacking the knowledge of what is acceptable, wanting to be accepted by peers, and having an unconditional trust in others, all contribute to this increased risk for abuse (Sobses, 1991). Families and providers have used visuals and role play to enhance children's awareness of those individuals with whom they can be safe, as was the case for Sam. For example, concentric circles can be drawn with names placed in the center of the circle of those who are closest to the child and less familiar people or those unknown to the child are placed in the outer circles. The child with ASD can then be taught appropriate ways to touch or be touched by those closest versus those who are less familiar. Teaching social and safety boundaries and ways to communicate in unsafe situations is worth advocating for in the educational or developmental service plans for children and youth with ASD.

Transition

Over the last 30 years, special education has experienced dramatic reform. The Education for All Handicapped Children Act, or Public Law 94–142, provided the framework for special education as it is known today (Moore-Brown & Montgomery, 2001). A mandated provision of Public Law 94–142 is a free appropriate public education for children with disabilities, ages 5 to 21 years, in the least restrictive environment. Several amendments have occurred since then to ensure better educational opportunities for special populations, including the Regular Education Initiative. The law (Public Law 101–476) was renamed in 1990 to the Individuals with Disabilities Education Act (IDEA). In these amendments, new definitions for eligibility were provided, including a separate category for autism. The Americans with Disabilities Act (ADA; Public Law 101–336) was also signed in 1990 and it defined those practices considered discriminatory and illegal while ensuring reasonable accommodations for individuals with disabilities. In 1997, amendments to IDEA occurred once again, addressing requirements for transition planning (Individuals with Disabilities Education Act Amendments of 1997). Transition involves the coordination of a number of activities for a student which promotes that student's movement from school to work or other postsecondary education or training opportunities. By age 16, a student's IEP must include transition activities, although transition planning can begin as early as age 14. Also, a student's preferences and interests are to be considered in the transition planning process. This was a request Sam's family was making. Because of Sam's history of health, mental health, and developmental challenges, his parents realized he would require a special plan to ensure his achievement of valued life outcomes such as health, safety, and independence. They also wanted him to have some exposure to community experiences, employment opportunities, and independent living skills. Sam's diagnosis and related problems presented some unusual challenges for the community team, but he had many strengths and his family did not want to lose the opportunity to begin his future planning at age 14 and prepare a program plan that would lead him to a safe, healthy, and independent future life. (For a more comprehensive discussion of transition issues in adolescents and young adults with developmental disabilities, see Chapter 7.)

Health

The American Academy of Pediatrics has proposed that all children have a "medical home" for their ongoing care (American Academy of Pediatrics, 2002). Typically, a medical home is an office-based practice committed to the development of partnerships with families who have children with special needs. Often, practices adopting the concept of a medical home utilize a coordinator of care within their office to facilitate efficient and effective interactions among families, their school teams, and other health specialists. Such practices also develop a medical care plan and a medical information exchange form with schools. These procedural changes and coordination of care appear to make a difference for children with special needs and their families. These are the kinds of changes that would foster improved health care for children with ASD.

Coordination among interdisciplinary personnel, agencies, and specialty health providers is a theme of the medical home concept. Principles of care that guide the concept include the continuity of services, information interpretation, accurate record keeping, and communication among all involved in the child's care. Considering the number of health challenges Sam experienced and the pervasive nature of his deficit, his family sought a health practice that would be effective and efficient in their response and benefit the overall health of their son.

Families, primary health care practitioners, and other providers can develop partnerships to improve the health and quality of life for children with ASD. Some strategies to consider include routine health care maintenance, preventive medical checklists specific to the child's condition (ASD), and maintenance of a problem-oriented medical record to address identified areas of concerns such as those reported for Sam (e.g., bone growth disorder, ear infections and fluctuating hearing loss, inattention, diet). Preventive activities and those responding to identified problems are brought to a care conference that requires interdisciplinary and interagency collaboration and partnership. The medical home concept is one way practitioners across disciplines and settings can collaborate in their efforts to both inform one another and address the health needs of children and youth with autism and their families.

CONCLUSION

Partnerships have the power of engaging a talented group of people in an endeavor that can lead to valued outcomes for children and youth with special needs and their families. The VT–RAP and VT–ILEHP partnership expanded the expertise available to families and at the same time enhanced the training of all professionals involved in the care of children with autism. Although the federal dollars to support VT–RAP ended, the program's training and systems goals were institutionalized in four important ways. First, coursework on autism was established in the curriculum at the University of Vermont. Second, an intensive week-long summer institute in autism was developed and is in its 6th year. Third, several community teams were trained across the state of Vermont to improve the service system for children with autism. Finally, a statewide Autism Task Force was developed to address the ongoing needs facing children, adolescents, and adults with autism. The VT–ILEHP Program continues to collaborate in these efforts.

The partnership with VT–ILEHP was also sustained. VT–ILEHP faculty and fellows and trainees participate in the annual week-long summer autism institute to enhance their knowledge in this disability area. Members of the VT–ILEHP interdisciplinary team who were trained with the VT–RAP team have gone on to take leadership positions as consultants to schools in the area of autism as well as have spearheaded inservice trainings across the state. The Training Director for VT–ILEHP (who also served as Project Director for VT–RAP) is a member of the Autism Task Force and is involved in statewide strategic planning, training, information dissemination, and policymaking affecting children with autism and their families. Partnerships have been established with the Autism Society of Vermont to collaborate on annual training opportunities in autism and with the University of Vermont to identify potential students as respite providers for children with autism. Finally, the VT–ILEHP team continues its partnerships with community teams trained as part of VT–RAP, with referrals for children who have or are suspected of having autism.

Sharing a mission for ensuring the health care of children with neurodevelopmental and related disabilities, particularly those with autism, facilitated the successful partnership between VT–RAP and VT–ILEHP. Training together, sharing resources, and expanding the expertise of both programs sustained the knowledge gained and facilitated new opportunities for establishing relationships and new partnerships within the community, nongovernmental organizations (Parent to Parent of Vermont, Autism Society of Vermont), and government agencies.

STUDY QUESTIONS

1. What is the value of establishing partnerships with community programs, agencies, and organizations committed to serving children with special health needs and their families, particularly those affected by autism?
2. Identify one potential partnership in your community that could be used to improve or enhance the services delivered to children with special health needs and their families.
3. How important is differential diagnosis to understanding and meeting the needs of children with complex health, mental health, and developmental conditions?
4. What is the role of the family, community team, and consulting interdisciplinary team in the assessment and program planning for children and youth with autism?
5. What could be potential problems in establishing partnerships to serve children with special health needs?

RESOURCES AND MATERIALS

Books on Autism for Parents and Professionals

Attwood, T. (1997). *Asperger's syndrome: A guide for parents and professionals*. Philadelphia: Jessica Kingsley Publishers.

Baron-Cohen, S., & Bolton, P. (1993). *Autism: The facts*. New York: Oxford University Press.

Janzen, J. E. (1997). *Understanding the nature of autism: A practical guide*. Austin, TX: Pro-Ed.

Janzen, J. E. (1999). *Autism: Facts and strategies for parents*. Austin, TX: Therapy Skill Builders.

Richer, J., & Coates, S. (2001). *Autism—The search for coherence*. Philadelphia: Jessica Kingsley Publishers.

Satkiewicz-Gayhardt, V., Peerenboom, B., & Campbell, R. (1998). *Crossing bridges: A parent's perspective on coping after a child is diagnosed with Autism/PDD*. Stratham, NH: Potential Unlimited Publishing.

Simpson, R. L., & Zionts, P. (2000). *Autism—second edition: Information and resources for parents, families, and professionals.* Austin, TX: Pro-Ed.

Waltz, M. (1999). *Pervasive developmental disorders: Finding a diagnosis and getting help.* Sebastopol, CA: O'Reilly & Associates, Inc.

Wing, L. (2001). *The autistic spectrum: A parent's guide to understanding and helping your child.* Berkeley, CA: Ulysses Press.

Information on Safety

Davis, B., & Schunick, W. G. (2002). *Dangerous encounters—Avoiding perilous situations with autism: A streetwise guide for all emergency responders, retailers and parents.* Philadelphia: Jessica Kingsley Publishers.

Debbaudt, D. (2001). *Autism, advocates, and law enforcement professionals: Recognizing and reducing risk situations for people with autism spectrum disorders.* Philadelphia: Jessica Kingsley Publishers.

Kahn, R. (2001). *Too safe for strangers.* Arlington, TX: Future Horizons.

Kahn, R., & Chandler, S. (2001). *Too smart for bullies.* Arlington, TX: Future Horizons.

Information on Sexuality

Kempton, W. (1991). *Sex education for persons with disabilities that hinder learning: A teacher's guide* (2nd ed.). Hartford, PA: James Stanfield Company, Inc.

Kempton, W., Gordon, S., & Bass, M. (1986). *Love, sex, and birth control for the mentally retarded: A guide for parents.* Philadelphia: Planned Parenthood Association of Southwestern Pennsylvania.

Kroll, K., & Klein, E. (1992). *Enabling romance: A guide to love, sex, and relationships for disabled people (and the people who can help them).* New York: Crown.

National Information Center for Children & Youth with Disabilities. (1992). Sexuality education for children and youth with disabilities. *NICHCY News Digest, 1*(3), 2–5.

Realmuto, G. M., & Ruble, L. A. (1999). Sexual behaviors in autism: Problems in definition and management. *Journal of Autism and Developmental Disorders, 29,* 121–127.

Schwier, K. M., & Hingsburger, D. (2000). *Sexuality: Your sons and daughters with intellectual disabilities.* Baltimore: Brookes.

Sobses, D., Gray, S., Wells, D., Pyper, D., & Reimer-Heck, B. (Eds.). (1991). *Disability, sexuality and abuse: An annotated bibliography* (pp. ix–xii). Baltimore: Brookes.

National Organizations and Web Sites

Autism National Committee
635 Ardmore Avenue
Ardmore, PA 19003
610-649-9139
610-649-0974 (fax)
www.autocom.org

Autism Network International
P.O. Box 448
Syracuse, NY 13210-0448
www.students.uiuc.edu

Autism Research Institute
4182 Adams Avenue
San Diego, CA 92116
619-281-7165
619-563-6840 (fax)
www.autism.com/ari

Autism Services Center
The Pritchard Center
605 Ninth St., PO Box 507
Huntington, WV 25710
800-328-8476
304-525-8014
304-525-8026 (fax)
www.autocyt.com/aane

Autism Society of America
7910 Woodmont, Ste. 300
Bethesda, MD 20814-3015
800-328-8476
301-657-0881
301-657-0869 (fax)
www.autism.org

Center for the Study of Autism
P.O. Box 4538
Salem, OR 97302
www.autism.org

Cure Autism Now (CAN)
5225 Wilshire Blvd, Ste. 226
Los Angeles, CA 90036
323-549-0500
323-549-0547 (fax)
888-8-AUTISM
CAN@primenet.com
www.canfoundation.org

Federation for Children with Special Needs
95 Berkley Street, Ste. 104
Boston, MA 02116
617-482-2915
617-695-2939 (fax)
fcsninfo@fcsn,org

National Alliance for Autism Research
414 Wall St., Research Park
Princeton, NJ 08540
888-777-NAAR
609-430-9160
609-430-9163 (fax)
Naar@naar.org
www.naar.org

National Information Center for Children & Youth with Disabilities
    (NICHCY)
P.O. Box 1492
Washington, DC 20013-1492
800-695-0285
202-884-8441 (fax)
www.nichcy.org

The Association for Persons with Severe Handicaps (TASH)
29 W Susquehanna, Ste. 210
Baltimore, MD 21204
410-828-8274
410-828-6706 (fax)
www.tash.org

Yale Child Study Center
230 South Frontage Rd.
P.O. Box 207900

New Haven, CT 06520
203-785-2513
203-737-4197 (fax)
www.info.med.yale.edu/childstdy/autism
kathy.coenig@yale.edu

REFERENCES

Allen, G., & Courchesne, E. (2001). Attention function and dysfunction in autism. *Frontiers in Bioscience, 6,* 105–119.

American Academy of Pediatrics. (2002). The medical home. *Pediatrics, 110,* 184–186.

American Psychiatric Association. (1994). *Diagnostic and statistical manual of mental disorders* (4th ed.). Washington, DC: Author.

American Psychiatric Association. (2000). *Diagnostic and statistical manual of mental disorders* (4th ed., text rev). Washington, DC: Author.

Baron-Cohen, S., Allen, J., & Gillberg, C. (1992). Can autism be detected at 18 months? The needle, the haystack, and the CHAT. *British Journal of Psychiatry, 161,* 839–843.

Beatson, J., & Prelock, P. A. (2002). The Vermont Rural Autism Project: Sharing experiences, shifting attitudes. *Focus on Autism and Other Development Disabilities, 17,* 48–54.

Coster, W., Deeney, T., Haltwanger, J., & Haley, S. (1998). *School Function Assessment.* San Antonio, TX: Psychological Corporation.

Dunst, C. J., & Trivette, C. M. (1996). Empowerment, effective helpgiving practices and family-centered care. *Pediatric Nursing, 22,* 334–337.

Haley, S. M., Coster, W. J., Ludlow, L. H., Haltiwanger, J. T., & Andrellos, P. J. (1992). *Pediatric evaluation of disability inventory (PEDI), Version 1: Development, standardization and administration manual.* Boston: PEDI Research Group, New England Medical Center Hospitals, Inc.

Individuals with Disabilities Education Act, 20 U.S.C. §1400. (1997).

Klinger, L. G., & Dawson, G. (1996). Autistic disorder. In E. Mash & R. Barkley (Eds.), *Child psychopathology* (pp. 311–339). New York: Guilford.

LaRocque, M., Brown, S. E., & Johnson, K. L. (2001). Functional behavioral assessments and intervention plans in early intervention settings. *Infants and Young Children, 13,* 59–67.

Lord, C. (2000). Autism spectrum disorders and ADHD. In P. J. Accardo & T. A. Blondis (Eds.), *Attention deficits and hyperactivity in children and adults* (pp. 401–417). New York: Marcel Dekker.

Lord, C., Rutter, M., DiLavore, P. C., & Risi, S. (1999). *Autism Diagnostic Observation Schedule–Generic (ADOS–G).* Los Angeles: Western Psychological Services.

Manoach, D., Sandson, T., & Weintraub, S. (1995). The developmental social–emotional processing disorders is associated with right hemisphere abnormalities. *Neuropsychiatry, Neurophysiology, Behavioral Neurology, 8,* 99–105.

Moore-Brown, B. J., & Montgomery, J. K. (2001). *Making a difference for America's children: Speech–language pathologists in public schools.* Eau Claire, WI: Thinking Publications.

Noterdaeme, M., Sitter, S., Mildenberger, K., & Amorosa, H. (2000). Diagnostic assessment of communicative and interactive behaviours in children with autism and receptive language disorder. *European Child and Adolescent Psychiatry, 9,* 295–300.

Prelock, P. A. (2000). *Early indicators/red flags checklist for autism.* Program. Burlington, VT: Author.

Prelock, P. A., Beatson, J., Bitner, B., Broder, C., & Ducker, A. (2003). Interdisciplinary assessment of young children with autism spectrum disorders. *Language, Speech, and Hearing Services in Schools, 34,* 194–202.

Prelock, P. A., Beatson, J., Contompasis, S. H., & Bishop, K. K. (1999). A model for family-centered interdisciplinary practice. *Topics in Language Disorders, 19*(3), 36–51.

Rourke, B. P. (1989). *Nonverbal learning disabilities: The syndrome and the model.* New York: Guilford.

Rourke, B. P. (2000). Nonverbal learning disabilities and Asperger syndrome. In A. Klin, F. R. Volkmar, & S. S. Sparrow (Eds.), *Asperger syndrome* (pp. 231–253). New York: Guilford.

Semrud-Clikeman, M., & Hynd, G. (1990). Right hemispheric dysfunction in nonverbal learning disabilities: Social, academic, and adaptive functioning in adults and children. *Psychological Bulletin, 107,* 196–209.

Shelton, T. L., & Stepanek, J. S. (1994). *Family-centered care for children needing specialized health and developmental services.* Bethesda, MD: Association for the Care of Children's Health.

Sobses, D. (1991). Toward a scientific understanding: An introduction. In D. Sobses, S. Gray, D. Wells, D. Pyper, & B. Reimer-Heck (Eds.), *Disability, sexuality and abuse: An annotated bibliography* (pp. ix–xii). Baltimore: Brookes.

Vargas, C. M. (2002). Women in sustainable development: Empowerment through partnerships for health living. *World Development, 30,* 1539–1560.

Volkmar, F. R., & Klin, A. (1998). Asperger Syndrome & nonverbal learning disabilities. In E. Schopler, G. B. Mesibov, & L. J. Kunce (Eds.), *Asperger Syndrome or high-functioning Autism?* (pp. 107–121). New York: Plenum.

Building Capacity in Law, Policy, and Leadership: Public Administration in Support of Families and Clinicians

Phillip J. Cooper
Ruth Dennis
University of Vermont

Questions to Consider

1. What kinds of knowledge do advanced clinicians require in order to address the systems challenges faced by families like Allison's?
2. What are some of the contextual factors that are creating systems challenges facing leaders in maternal and child health?
3. How can advanced clinical practitioners make sense of the varied array of factors that constrain or influence decisions they will be called on to make?
4. What kinds of knowledge of public policy concepts and processes are important for advanced clinical practitioners to master to support their efforts as leaders in maternal and child health?
5. Given the fact that clinicians are not lawyers, what kinds of fundamental knowledge is required to recognize important legal issues both to alert families about the need for further assistance and to understand and influence public policy?

ALLISON'S STORY

Some years ago, the Vermont Interdisciplinary Leadership Education for Health Professionals (VT–ILEHP) Program sought to assist Allison and her family. Allison was 18 years old when she was seen by the interdisciplinary team for a community assessment. Her family and those who knew her well consistently described her as sociable, fun to be with, curious, playful, sensitive, and loving. She liked being around her peers and enjoyed camping and other activities. She lived with her mother and extended family.

Allison's greatest challenges were in the area of communication and mobility. She was nonverbal, although she did use idiosyncratic methods to express her needs and discomfort. Allison had cerebral palsy, spastic quadriplegia, and underwent multiple orthopedic and neurosurgical procedures. She had a seizure disorder treated by a variety of medications. She seemed to understand more than she could express and sometimes became frustrated. She used a manual wheelchair. Equipment needs for positioning, mobility, and transportation were consistent challenges. She was dependent for all self-care activities. Transferring and lifting Allison safely was a concern at home and in program settings, and became a greater concern when her mother developed back and joint problems.

Allison's mother, Faye, while helping Allison through all of her challenges, worked at various jobs in the community, cared for her other children, and provided care for her own invalid mother. Faye and her family faced a significant set of challenges, including rural isolation and inadequate housing. Even so, she was known as a formidable woman with strong views and a willingness to express them.

There were times when Faye became frustrated with various service providers and "fired" them. At the same time, Allison and her family needed assistance, because financial resources were limited. Faye lacked trust in all but a few service providers and allowed only one to visit in the home. That social distance was, of course, a serious challenge for those seeking to help the family.

Allison had received educational services through the local school district since age 3 and had attended local schools in special classes and inclusionary programs in her town. Her mother had withdrawn her from school to be home-schooled at one point. She had also missed school due to ongoing medical issues.

The relationship with the public schools had been problematic at times. Although Allison made nice gains in her middle school years, transition to high school at Grade 9 had not gone smoothly. The town did not have a public high school, and contracted for services from a local private school. The responsibility for educating students with severe disabilities was a point of contention between the private school administration, the local school district, and the state department of education.

Indeed, efforts to resolve differences of opinion and assign responsibility for implementation of services under the Individuals with Disabilities Education Act (IDEA, 1997) for other students in the community were before the federal courts while VT–ILEHP was working with Allison. One of these disputes (discussed later in this chapter) eventually reached the United States Circuit Court of Appeals. Legal issues, although never a primary focus with respect to Allison's services, contributed to a climate of caution and apprehension among public and private school personnel and a hesitancy to develop an Individualized Education Plan (IEP) with the range of services the family requested. In fact, Faye did not find Allison's IEP acceptable and she withdrew her from school after the ninth grade. Allison attended an adult day-care program while her educational status was unclear.

Meetings between the VT–ILEHP team and public school personnel clarified several issues. The school district was prepared to educate Allison until age 22. However, because Allison had been withdrawn from school for over 20 days, she had to apply to the local private school or a school in a neighboring town. The local private school provided a segregated program for her outside the regular classroom and ensured support from an aide. Socialization among peers without disabilities happened solely in the hallways.

The VT–ILEHP team first met Allison at the assessment planning meeting. Allison's mother and her aunt attended the meeting in Burlington. Team members were charmed by her playful personality and impressed by her family's pride in Allison. She enjoyed interacting with the team, but her communication limitations were evident.

Between the time of the VT–ILEHP assessment and the community follow-up meeting, Allison returned to high school in town for part of the day. Her mother had asked that, prior to her returning to school in January, an IEP be developed that addressed the family's priorities. With the assistance of the VT–ILEHP assessment coordinator, several letters were exchanged with the school district in response to the need to draft IEPs.

Ultimately, the VT–ILEHP assessment report presented many recommendations. The challenge of addressing that range of actions apparently overwhelmed the team and seemed to further frustrate the family. Recommendations were made regarding medical interventions and supports; respite services, other social supports, transition to adult services, equipment needs, supported employment, and specific suggestions for educational program development.

In part because of all the issues discussed earlier regarding the school, the district, the family, Allison's needs, and the VT–ILEHP recommendations, efforts to coordinate care after the assessment were challenging. The assessment coordinator and her faculty mentor worked to do what they could for Allison and her family. The interdisciplinary team followed Allison for 1 year after the assessment (see Chapter 5 on community assessment and Chapter 6 on care coordination).

It truly was the case that, in a number of important respects, VT–ILEHP trainees, fellows, and faculty felt, as the common expression goes, "dressed up with no place to go" as they tried to help Allison and her family. The problems of many years had created such frustration for the family that there was a reticence to communicate, a desire to insulate the family against intrusion from providers, and ongoing tensions with agencies from the schools to the state. There was little or no trust. Without solid communication, trust, and cooperation, it was difficult for VT–ILEHP to know just what the family's needs and desires were or how best to serve them. There was every desire to help, but a seeming inability to reach across the divide caused by years of tensions to deliver services effectively.

There were frustrations with agencies as well—agencies and institutions that at times seemed more willing to fight legal battles than to cooperate for the good of the young person involved. The fact that litigation was pending only added to communication gaps and distrust. But perhaps most challenging was the recognition that VT–ILEHP needed to look beyond the clinical skills of its faculty, trainees, and fellows and build its capacity in the areas of policy, law, and leadership. It was not enough to provide to those in the community lengthy lists of recommendations, backed by best clinical practice and a caring attitude, and expect things to happen. This was not the first time VT–ILEHP had reached this conclusion, but the question was how to build that capacity in leadership, law, and policy.

LEADERSHIP: INTEGRATING PUBLIC POLICY, PUBLIC LAW, AND MANAGEMENT INTO CLINICAL PRACTICE

In the United States, as in some other countries, services are often offered in a demand-based model. A family calls on a particular organization and presents its challenges along with a request for services. The agency involved first determines whether it is the proper unit of the health or education system to provide those services, determines the eligibility of the family and child for the programs they seek to access, and then selects the types, amounts, and modes of service delivery to meet the need.

As earlier chapters have indicated, however, the system can be daunting, the families may lack resources to access it, and parents often can be frustrated by this group of governments and nonprofit organizations that are supposed to be there to help their child, let alone the family as a whole. In fact, the systems may not only seem to place barriers in the way of meeting a child's needs, but may even become threatening to the family.

Of course, there are often tensions within the service systems themselves, quite apart from anything that grows out of service demands from a particular family. Conflicting missions, overlapping jurisdictions, a tense political environment, and resource shortages can combine to create a host of problems within and among agencies as well as for the families who come to them for services. Some of these problems grow out of design flaws in the policies and programs themselves, whereas others evolve during implementation. These behaviors, and the threats—real or imagined—that they pose for the child and the family, can cause mistrust, impede communications, and create defensive attitudes and behaviors. The families may respond to the service system from these frustrations with an understandable anger.

Unfortunately, all of this can come full circle. Without trust and communication, the real needs of the child may not be identified correctly or in a timely manner. Tensions among participants can become self-fulfilling prophesies, with the family becoming less willing to engage and cooperate and the service providers becoming more suspicious or even hostile. When that happens, clinical professionals find themselves, as the VT–ILEHP team did in Allison's case, all dressed up, professionally speaking, with no place to go. Without the ability to engage the systems and to work constructively with the family, all the clinical knowledge in the world will avail them nothing.

But clinical professionals did not, with few exceptions, enter their chosen specialty fields to be politicians or public administrators. They came to equip themselves with the scientific knowledge, technical tools, and clinical skills to help children and their families meet the challenges of disabilities. The goal is to allow the children to realize their full potential, whatever that may be, and to realize their dreams and those of their family, to the degree that any outsider can support those dreams.

When people with those motivations, that training, and specialty skills must engage a system of care with all of the stresses noted earlier, there are serious problems to be met. Two questions emerge: How has VT–ILEHP sought to equip its fellows, trainees, and its faculty to meet system challenges, to serve the family, and to seek systems change? What lessons have we learned in the process? The answers to these complex questions turned out to be an evolving effort to develop capacity in policy, law, and leadership by infusing the curriculum with different types of system knowledge than those with which we began. At the same time, the effort has been to learn how to fashion those educational efforts to respond to the particular needs of clinicians.

When VT–ILEHP began its working life, it was not at all clear just what role public administration was to play. To be sure, the clinical faculty knew the key federal programs from Medicaid to IDEA and they were certainly going to provide that knowledge to trainees and fellows, both directly and through guest presentations by state program managers. They also had an excellent set of educational experiences designed for students to learn interdisciplinary teaming and family-centered care, including how to work with families, school-based teams, and health care providers in assessments and community meetings. Care coordination and follow-up on assessment recommendations was to be an important focus as well. (These issues are addressed in earlier chapters.)

As time passed, however, two problems emerged. First, the leadership and policy knowledge of the faculty as well as the trainees and fellows tended to focus almost exclusively within the health care and education policy communities (the collection of groups and key individuals with an ongoing interest in a particular field of policy) and the policies of interest to those communities (Cooper et. al, 1998; Sabatier & Jenkins-Smith, 1993). Beyond those policy communities, knowledge of the larger systems at the state and federal levels that produce policies and the budgets to operate them was limited. Second, there was a reticence to engage with politics, law, public finance, and management, all of which have a tendency to be lumped together into that elongated "four-letter" word, bureaucracy.

However, the days when the larger political system would simply give the health care or education communities whatever they demanded had long since gone, and the situation was becoming more difficult with each passing year. Within the state, and beyond it, fiscal and political stresses, even in what purported to be "good times," mounted. Conflict was becoming more common and increasingly intense, whereas consensus seemed to be harder to achieve in almost any policy arena. The stresses felt in Washington and in the state capital were working their way down to the schools, the clinics, and the town halls.

Ironically, the effort to build an interdisciplinary cadre of clinicians who are experts in developmental disabilities and the interventions needed to support children and their families meant new pressures on the system. With more knowledge and skill available, it should have come as no surprise that more diagnoses and more thorough assessments produced more demands for services and financial support. It also meant a need for community providers to become more knowledgeable. The effort to ensure culturally competent clinicians also meant that families in ethno-cultural communities that may not have been engaged in the past now had clinicians who began to recognize their service needs. These are, to be sure, positive and welcome trends, but they present challenges nevertheless.

The more the faculty became aware of the limitations of trainees' and fellows' knowledge in these fields, the clearer it became that the program needed to fashion a leadership education component that went beyond the comfort zone of most clinicians to build the capacity required to engage the system from the broadest perspective, but in ways clearly relevant to the needs of local service providers. The trainees and fellows were, after all, preparing to be both effective local practitioners and leaders for systems change.

While taking advantage of the several leadership components already built into the program and described earlier, VT–ILEHP evolved a series of workshops, seminars, and exercises to better equip the trainees and fellows. It is a component that has grown from what was a relatively limited feature of the program to one that is now an integral and important element of VT–ILEHP. It has three major areas of emphasis, although it is important to consider the other components of the program that contribute knowledge and skill. The three core areas of emphasis are public policy, leadership and management, and public law. Flowing throughout these sets of instruction and experience is an effort to ensure that trainees and fellows are able to sense and understand the decision environment within which they must operate.

Understanding the Decision Environment
Through the Feasibility Framework

One of the great challenges of each leader as a new workday begins is to scan the ever-changing conditions and forces in his or her world. Indeed, almost all organizations have people who are sought out by others, even if they do not hold high rank or title, because they have the ability to maintain a coherent picture of what is happening around them and can make sense of all that complexity. Like an air traffic controller scanning a radar screen, a leader can look at the many blips on the horizon and integrate what he or she sees into a comprehensible picture. That picture provides an understandable context for the work that must be done that day. It offers cautions and highlights possible opportunities in the days, weeks, and months ahead. For a leader, the challenge is to sense his or her decision environment and understand both opportunities and constraints. The leader can then set out to meet the challenges of public policy, management, or legal change.

The particular approach used in VT–ILEHP was developed by Professors Cooper and Vargas in work on sustainable development, involving a number of countries and elaborated in their later work (Cooper, 1998, 2000; Cooper & Vargas, 1995; Cooper & Vargas, in press). Politics has often been described as the art of the possible. For professionals who must not only participate in the development of public policy, but who must also take the lead in implementing policy, the challenge is more complex. Cooper and Vargas refer to it as the "art of the feasible" (1995, p. 206).

The feasibility framework begins from the premise that, for any given task and on any particular day, the professional must ask a series of fundamental questions, the answers to which provide a picture of the environment within which he or she will be making decisions to meet many responsibilities. These questions concern the technical, legal, fiscal, administrative, political, cultural, or ethical feasibility dimensions of the decision environment.

Technical Feasibility.   First, is the task technically feasible? Do we know how to approach the challenge technically? If we do not have those tools readily at hand, can we develop them? Policymakers often adopt what are known as technology forcing policies precisely to encourage research and development in the face of challenges that have not been met with existing technology. This is the area in which clinicians are most comfortable and about which they are the most enthusiastic.

Legal Feasibility.   However, in the public arena, the task at hand must also be legally feasible. The United States operates under the principles of the rule and supremacy of law. Public officials must always be ready to provide the legal authority for their actions. Activity beyond the authority delegated to an agency or official is known as *ultra vires* action (beyond the power) and is illegal. The U.S. and state constitutions did not create a U.S. Department of Health and Human Services or a state department of education, and they did not set out the programs those agencies now administer. The programs were developed in legislation and regulations made in accordance with proper legal processes.

When clinicians are presented with case study situations, it is not unusual for them to assume that they have far more authority than they really possess or that the officials or agencies with which they work can do whatever the clinicians perceive needs to be done. The idea that family members may assert legal rights against what clinicians think is best practice sometimes comes as a great surprise. Thus, it is essential to consider whether the actions contemplated in any given situation are within the legal authority of decision makers and, if so, is there a danger of violating the legal rights of any of those people who are affected by the course that clinicians might have in mind?

Fiscal Feasibility.   There is an old joke about the minister, the political scientist, and the economist who fell into a trap in the jungle set to catch a tiger. As the story goes, the minister fell to his knees and prayed for deliverance and the political scientist argued that they should form a coalition and take group action. The economist is said to have gazed intently at the walls of the pit for a time and then announced, "Assume a ladder." During one academic year, weeks after having related that tale to a group of trainees and fellows, we found ourselves contemplating the challenges of implementing a policy idea that one of them had offered. In answer to the dreaded question about where we would find the money for the program, one trainee instructed, "Assume a budget!"

Unfortunately, neither the families nor service providers can "assume a budget," and must ask instead whether they have the fiscal wherewithal to meet the challenges they face. It seems that some clinicians have only recently come to realize that just because a practitioner writes a prescription, it is not always the case that someone will provide the resources with which to fill it. If they do not have the resources at hand, they must determine where they can find them. That does not mean that they simply surrender to a lack of funds, but it does mean that they do not really understand their context if they are not realistic about the fiscal feasibility dimension.

Administrative Feasibility.   It seems counterintuitive to some clinical professionals, but money alone is often not sufficient. Services and programs require organizations and people to deliver them; and it takes time and effort to build those agencies as well as to find, hire, and train the people to operate them. Indeed, it is commonly the case that clinicians underestimate just how much administrative infrastructure is required to accomplish many of our most common responsibilities. They need to ask, therefore, in any given situation, whether their plans are administratively feasible.

For clinicians who are solo practitioners, consultants, or part of small practices, the idea of administrative development is often an anathema. It conjures up the dreaded "B" word (bureaucracy). Beyond that, disciplinary training often reinforces the notion that administrative structures are problems rather than essential tools for effective service delivery.

Political Feasibility.   One of the most common problems encountered by those who are new to the field is to understand and accept the fact that the right response to a situation, defined in terms of their clinical profession, may simply be politically unacceptable. The newly trained clinician will often look with disdain on older colleagues when he or she sees a problem, the solution to which should be obvious to any well-trained practitioner in the field. It comes as a shock when the newcomer is informed that the obvious solution has been rejected for political reasons. That seems to be the worst possible reason for not taking an action, until one learns enough humility to understand that democracy has a right to be wrong. And, as citizens in the community, so do families, school boards, and community service organizations.

Thus, practitioners should always ask whether the action they are contemplating is politically feasible. A negative answer at the moment does not mean that they will stop their effort, but it may very well mean that efforts will have to be undertaken to build political support to the point where the plans or policy proposals are politically feasible.

Cultural Feasibility. There are two common difficulties that leaders face from time to time. One of the common answers to any problem in the contemporary environment is to write off the difficulties encountered to problems of culture. The other is simply to ignore culture and assume that everyone with common sense perceives a problem in the same way and will respond positively to a solution offered with good intentions by a committed professional. Both responses are not only incorrect, but can lead to serious negative consequences.

Cultural feasibility has two dimensions. The first is the commonly used meaning of the term based in anthropology, concerning the set of values, traditions, and rules of behavior passed on from one generation to the next. The second, and the one less often appreciated by some clinicians, is organizational culture. It refers to the set of values and norms that control behavior within organizations (Ott, 1989; Schein, 1992; U.S. General Accounting Office, 1992). It simply is not possible to provide services effectively, or even to communicate clearly about health care matters in general and developmental disabilities in particular, without an awareness of the impact of culture. It affects everything from the ways in which people perceive and integrate concepts of health, illness, or disability to the approaches that families and children are willing to accept in treatment or services (see Chapter 3). Even in traditionally rather homogeneous, relatively rural communities, it is increasingly common to hear many languages and to have contact with families from a wide range of ethno-cultural groups. Within both dominant and minority ethno-cultural groups, differences are influenced by socioeconomic status, educational background, urban or agricultural lifestyles, and a host of other characteristics. In addition to the fact that cultural sensitivity is an integral part of family-centered care, there are also legal obligations to address issues such as access to programs for persons with limited English proficiency where federal funding is involved (Executive Order 13,166, 2000).

Organizational issues are also important to clinicians in their leadership roles. Thus, the VT–ILEHP teams often encounter very different organizational cultures in schools or in clinical contexts. Similarly, state health agencies often have cultures quite different from state education agencies, and clinicians and the families they serve often need to interact with both simultaneously. Cultural considerations were treated in much greater detail in Chapter 3, but the critical point here is that one must consider cultural feasibility in the processes of assessing one's decision environment.

Ethical Feasibility. Finally, it is important to ask whether there are issues of ethical feasibility. There are occasions when challenges in the public policy arena can present ethical dilemmas. The classic case in recent years has been the difficulties that arise when funding constraints place the clinician in a situation in which he or she cannot provide what the clinical profession considers proper care. Another example arises where the demands of political decision makers require behavior that clinicians regard as inconsistent with the norms of their professions. As policymakers seek to constrain access to some public programs, these ethical stresses can become serious. Another variation on this theme may be present where an organizational culture sets norms in a clinical or educational setting that present serious ethical challenges for clinical professionals.

In the VT–ILEHP experience, there have also been situations in which the desire to be family-centered can sometimes present trainees, fellows, and faculty with ethical dilemmas. Thus, there may come a point where the best interest of the child means actions that might be regarded as less than family-centered. Similarly, there are occasions when problems of communication, perception, or trust require clinicians to take a step back and reevaluate the decision environment before deciding how or whether to move forward.

After some practice, the use of this framework to evaluate the decision environment in which one is operating is relatively easy and not very time consuming. Over time, as one internalizes the process, it becomes second nature. That said, when working with others, it is important to discuss the decision environment to be clear about the challenges it presents, whether the situation involves moving into a meeting with a school-based team or contemplating significant policy recommendations to the legislature.

The program faculty have learned over time that it can be very difficult to get clinicians to understand the need for sensing the decision environment and just why it is important to use a systematic framework for doing so. First, Americans, in particular, as well as many people in other politically active countries, grow up with the idea that they understand politics. After all, they have heard their family and teachers talk about the subject from the dinner table to the classroom all their lives. They have been taught a host of simplistic, and often false, so-called facts about the public arena and the people who operate there. It is common to find that there is a lack of respect, bordering on disdain, for the level of knowledge and sophistication required by public service professionals. Second, for those trained to believe that evidence-based practice is a way to ensure that science prevails in a professional's work each day, it can come as a surprise to learn that decision makers in a democracy, and the people who elect them, often could care less what someone says just because that person claims to be a scientist or medical professional. Beyond that, science, sadly, can often be a competitive, materialistic, and downright adversarial enterprise in today's context (*Daubert v. Merrill Dow*, 1993). Ball (1986) has described the contemporary atmosphere as one of adversarial science. Third, for many years health care professionals were able to obtain what, by the standards of most other areas of public policy, were extremely large amounts of funding not only for service programs, but for research. They are used to getting their way in many areas, but things are changing. Fourth, dominance of the expert professional often meant a lack of public accountability and a general deference to self-regulation by licensing and regulatory bodies largely controlled by the people who are supposed to be the subject of oversight.

Finally, clinicians often see the world one patient, one family, or one program at a time, from the point of service. Although the VT–ILEHP family focus makes that not only a critical but positive perspective, it is not enough by itself. Leaders in maternal and child health must be able to take a broader and more integrative view if they are to shape public policy and play key roles in the operation of the programs serving families and children. That requires not only a broader perspective with respect to maternal and child health or education policies, but a view that is truly integrative and takes into consideration the full range of challenges in the public policy arena facing key decision makers who must set priorities across a wide range of issues with the full context in mind.

At the point at which VT–ILEHP became involved with Allison and her family, the program had not fully integrated this framework into clinical practice and was not adequately addressing the decision environment. As a result, the interdisciplinary team did not develop an adequate picture of the situation confronting the team and the other participants in Allison's situation. In part, for that reason, attempts to implement a host of recommendations for Allison in her home and school eventually became a source of frustration for trainees, faculty, and community service providers.

The failure of otherwise extremely sophisticated clinicians to develop the habit of analyzing their decision environment seriously means they are often far less effective than they might be on behalf of the children and families they serve. It also means that although they regard themselves as seasoned professionals, they may present themselves as extraordinarily naive special pleaders in the political arena at the very time when they need to be alert to the political dynamics that shape the public policies that affect the ability of families and children to access the services they require.

The Policy Foundations of Clinical Practice and Family Support

Clinicians who seek to be leaders in maternal and child health, like the families they serve, engage a host of public policies in a variety of contexts. Those federal and state policies are not static and the process that produces and modifies them continues in operation every day. For these reasons, trainees and fellows need to learn about both the substance of the policies and also the process by which those policies are created and changed. It is that process knowledge that helps them to know where and how they can affect system change. The VT–ILEHP program developed several workshops and seminars in which trainees, fellows, and faculty participate throughout the year to enhance their understanding of the policy process as well as the funding and applications of federal and state policy.

Policy Process. One of the challenges for practitioners in health care is that there are so many different types of people and organizations that operate in that policy arena who come at it from a range of perspectives. Each of these participants approaches challenges with his or her own set of intellectual maps and logic. To be sure, many clinicians come from disciplinary training that emphasizes a scientific or medical model. However, other participants operate from legal, economic, managerial, or political perspectives. Policymaking, of course, requires collaboration with stakeholders who come with all of these perspectives.

Even at the level of service to the individual family, there are limits to the clinical approach. It can be difficult for anyone to step outside his or her perspective and understand that what may be considered best evidence-based clinical practice may lead to recommendations that are not for one reason or another legally, fiscally, administratively, or culturally feasible. Thus, in Allison's case, difficulties of transportation and communication as well as interorganizational, legal, and interpersonal tensions meant that the VT–ILEHP team simply could not expect to achieve what various clinicians thought were the most desirable treatment program and services. Indeed, VT–ILEHP learned that consulting work that results in long lists of recommendations need to be trimmed to a few priority action items if the interdisciplinary team wishes to ensure that something actually happens after they leave.

At the policy level, this awareness of the characteristics of the decision environment using the feasibility framework and sensitivity to the varying perspectives of the many participants in the policy process are essential. It is also, however, necessary to understand that policy process, and to identify some of the most important areas within it that offer opportunities or suggest constraints for leaders in maternal and child health.

To assist trainees and fellows in acquiring this knowledge, VT–ILEHP offers a set of training sessions, seminar sessions, and workshops throughout the year, along with a set of readings and written assignments designed both to assess what they know as they enter the program and to provide what program faculty have found are the basics of policy knowledge.

It is important that they understand the full policy process, from problem identification and agenda setting through policy formulation, adoption, implementation, evaluation, and termination. This dynamic process is always in motion as these clinicians work with families. Their experiences during the implementation of various programs often highlight problems that are important enough to reach the public policy agenda for new policy formulation. In the effort to assist Allison, for example, it became clear to the VT–ILEHP team that team members were encountering a special kind of system problem. It was a situation in which the school district contracted with a private school to provide education for all high school students in the community, but the private school imposed its own limitations on the kinds of programs and accommodations it would provide for Allison and other students with special needs. The effort to implement an IEP developed under federal and state IDEA regulations came face-to-face with unique issues of accountability for implementation in a setting where educational services are provided by a private school under contract. This experience suggested that a new policy might be needed at the state level to fashion a better mode of operation for the future.

A training session on policy concepts and a seminar on the place of policy highlight these broad crosscutting elements of the process. Over time, program faculty have also learned that there are a variety of more specific areas of knowledge that are essential for trainees and fellows if they are to be effective leaders in the policy arena.

For many clinicians who are used to responding to problems one problem or one family at a time, it can be challenging to learn how to identify and define a policy problem such that they can then understand what is needed to move that issue onto the public policy agenda. It is also surprising to some trainees and fellows that, when asked to prioritize issues identified by their colleagues, they often reach very different conclusions. Each year, trainees and fellows are provided with a list of issues identified by former trainees and fellows and asked to prioritize them. The differences are often significant. Similarly, they must come to understand how differently issues are defined and what it takes to encourage key decision makers to not only consider their issues on the agenda, but to press them to a level of priority at which they are likely to get action.

Another of the difficulties has to do with the "problem paradox." The VT–ILEHP family-centered and strengths-based perspectives caution trainees, fellows, and faculty to avoid a focus on deficits and negative language. Yet, the effort to move an issue to the public agenda and to obtain priority consideration for it requires a clear statement of a problem that is sufficiently severe to be the focus of public attention and to command resources that are always in short supply. The program continues to seek effective ways of reconciling this tension, but it is important to be candid with our trainees and fellows about the challenge.

Of course, the stakeholders who are central to decisions about agenda setting and prioritization are members of a policy community. A policy community (also referred to as a policy subsystem) consists of the agencies, officials, for-profit groups, and nonprofit organizations that maintain an ongoing interest in a particular policy arena (Cooper et al., 1998; Fritschler, 1989; Sabatier & Jenkins-Smith, 1993). An understanding of the way that trainees and fellows can identify policy communities and learn their work-ways is essential to effective participation in policymaking. That includes understanding how coalitions are formed and operated among many of the organizations that serve families and children.

To be sure, the identification of problems is only the beginning of the process. The next major challenge is policy formulation and the need to have the policy adopted. Of course, trainees and fellows readily understand from their experience and the training program that the answer to a challenge is often not a single type of policy, but a policy mix made up of a number of different actions. Trainees and fellows try their hand at fashioning such policy mixes, with attention to the feasibility framework.

Once the design is created, advocacy skills are required to move the proposal through the state or federal processes needed to turn it into action. One of the program workshops is designed to teach basic techniques of advocacy as well as to alert trainees and fellows to some of the dangers of poor advocacy techniques. For some clinicians, the types of skills required to persuade or negotiate to a successful conclusion are troublesome. To those who are accustomed to writing a prescription and expecting that it will be implemented, labeling as noncompliant those who fail to honor the expert's order, advocacy can be frustrating and negotiation may seem even to test the boundaries of ethical feasibility. Yet, whether they are seeking changes in state IDEA regulations or attempting to move a school to provide more effective services for a family, these skills are important.

As students consider implementation, evaluation, and termination or transformation of existing policies, it becomes increasingly clear that this is an iterative process that is ongoing and dynamic (Nakamura &

Smallwood, 1980). Thus, they consider the processes by which agencies adopt regulations to implement legislation as well as the basics of the budget process needed to provide resources for them at both the federal and state levels. These workshops are supplemented by other sessions on health care finance and specific programs such as Medicaid. One of the program's efforts has been to teach trainees and fellows how to analyze critically federal and state evaluation reports on existing programs that face reauthorization using the feasibility framework.

Finding and Using Federal and State Policy.   Although it is important for trainees and fellows to understand the processes of system change and to acquire the skills to operate effectively in that arena, they must also learn the existing programs and policies that can be mobilized to serve families and children. As noted earlier, this is done in part by workshops on such key programs as Medicaid with participation by state officials responsible for aspects of those policies, but also by training sessions on IDEA and the Rehabilitation Act as well as a seminar on IDEA issues, all of which are taught annually. The Americans with Disabilities Act (ADA) is considered during a seminar on legal concepts and processes.

However, it is also important for students to learn to access policies directly and to work with them. Thus, there are workshops on legislation and on rule-making in which students not only learn the process, but also access the policies and learn to analyze statutes and regulations. If trainees and fellows are to lead systems change and are expected to advocate on behalf of the individual families they serve, they require skill in accessing critical policies.

Public Management and Leadership: Two Continuing Challenges

Of course, much that maternal and child health clinicians do each day is beyond policymaking. In their interactions with families, service providers, schools, and other public and nongovernmental organizations, they participate in leadership and management activities. Although these two concepts are sometimes used interchangeably, they are in fact related, but different. Both are important and needed to ensure support for families and children. In this respect, there are several different dimensions of these subjects that VT–ILEHP seeks to address, including coalition-building, techniques of public participation, professional leadership, including intergovernmental issues, fiscal knowledge, organizational characteristics and culture, advocacy, and negotiation.

Leadership and management are not closed categories but concepts at different ends of a continuum. At one end, management is classically understood as the efficient use of money, person power, and "materiel" to achieve stated objectives. It is often associated with formal authority. On the other end is leadership, which has been defined as an extremely expansive concept, but one not focused primarily on power. "Leadership over human beings is exercised when persons with certain motives and purposes mobilize, in competition or conflict with others, institutional, political, psychological, and other resources so as to arouse, engage, and satisfy the motives of followers" (Burns, 1978, p. 18). This definition assumes that formal authority alone is not enough and that the leader must work with the followers to identify and continue to modify goals. In contemporary language, the emphasis on leadership is associated with engagement and empowerment.

There is a tendency to view leadership as good and management as bad, or at least to reject management as an outdated approach and leadership, defined in these broad social terms, as the new wave. This is particularly true of people who have made consulting or the generation of self-help books a growth business by advocating that the "new paradigm" (Covey, 1996)—that is to say, whatever the consultant advocates—is all that a sophisticated modern leader needs. Thus, during the 1990s, these gurus spoke of the need for leaders to steer, not row (Osborne & Gaebler, 1992, pp. 25–48). Others speak of the need for leaders to be coaches and not bosses.

The truth, as in most things, is that the relation between management and leadership is not a dichotomy. The trainees and fellows need both leadership and management knowledge and skills. With tongue partly in cheek, and in response to many contemporary advocates, one is tempted to observe that there are two kinds of people in the world: those who dichotomize everything and those who are sophisticated enough to know better.

There is nothing new about this debate over the relation among ideas that span this continuum. It reaches back at least as far as the early 20th century when the scientific management movement burst onto the national and international scene. Those seeking to improve management in the interest of efficiency like Gulick and Urwick (1937) wrote in the *Papers on the Science of Administration* of the techniques needed to achieve public goals in a professional manner, and defined the task using the acronym POSDCORB. That abbreviation described the task of the manager as Planning, Organizing, Staffing, Directing, Coordinating, Reporting, and Budgeting. In many respects, these same tasks describe the day-to-day work of managers from that time to the present. However, in the same era, during the 1920s and 1930s, people like Follett (1937, see also her collected works in Metcalf & Urwick, 1942) and Barnard (1938) were quick to point out that management was not simply an overhead, top-down activity based in power relations and defined in purely efficiency terms, but something more complex and contingent. They argued that narrow definitions of management were inadequate to explain the importance of the informal as well as the formal relationships that are the lifeblood of organizations, states, and even nations. They spoke of authority and leadership capability as something that was yielded upward within organizations. The famous General Electric plant studies demonstrated in the clearest terms the importance of informal work groups (Rothlisberger, 1939). The early texts on public administration warned about the dangers of getting caught up in the semantic debate and the need to recognize the larger picture (Morstein-Marx, 1946).

For anyone who has really had to operate programs and deliver services, it is obvious that the entire continuum is necessary. There are times when clinicians, in their role as leaders, seek to facilitate the development of new visions and work to find ways to remove barriers to the achievement of those goals by those who must operate in the field on an ongoing basis. In this mode, they emphasize relationships and try to support actions by others. This may be policy leadership, professional leadership, or social leadership. On the other hand, there are times when someone in an interdisciplinary team will need to take individual responsibility to make scarce resources count in the most efficient manner possible to get the best coordinated services to the families and their children as soon as possible. Someone has to take responsibility for the POSDCORB pieces, and be accountable for their accomplishment. Organizations must manage themselves effectively and efficiently or they will not be around to engage in the lofty goals of systems change.

Trainees and fellows need to be exposed to the language, structure, and process of management. Their difficulties in the field will often not come from the clinical difficulties faced by the family, but from the management challenges associated with supporting the family, obtaining resources, and accessing programs from the larger health care and educational systems at the state and federal level. There are, of course, times when a family wants clinicians to play a leadership role, but others in which the family has developed its own vision and seeks the assistance of clinicians to help implement the specific elements of that plan.

The VT–ILEHP team's involvement in Allison's life demonstrated quite clearly the reality that although team members may wish to help provide leadership, there are times when the school, the school district, other clinicians, or the family do not particularly want that assistance. Indeed, it was difficult to step into a situation in which there were ongoing legal disputes, tensions between the school and the district, and mistrust by the family of many of the individuals and organizations involved in Allison's life. There came a point at which VT–ILEHP had to put a good deal of effort into identifying precisely what roles the family wanted the program to play and what functions the interdisciplinary team could accomplish given the relationships among the various people and organizations at hand.

What program faculty try to do in seminars, workshops, and written policy and leadership assignments is to build knowledge for trainees and fellows across the continuum. The discussion in earlier chapters of interdisciplinary teaming, family-centered care, intake techniques, community meetings, assessments, and care coordination all speak to aspects of social and professional leadership. The other leadership and policy assignments stress leadership and management knowledge across a range of situations and subject areas. Thus, a workshop and assignment on budget and finance consider both the broad fiscal factors that provide the context for policymaking and the implications of current budgets for specific programs as well as the ways in which those fiscal actions constrain interactions with state and local officials in service delivery. A workshop on advocacy emphasizes both ways to advocate new ideas and to advocate for specific service programs for families, including facilitating compromise. A workshop on agenda setting emphasizes the challenges involved in the management of coalitions of nonprofit organizations that are so important both to policymaking and the operation of programs needed by the families served by the program. The feasibility framework is used throughout not only to help maintain a clear picture of the decision environment but also to help identify specific problem areas that must be addressed.

There are some specific themes within this general pattern of work and learning that the faculty stress. One of these is what is referred to as the levels problem. In the wide range of challenges that advanced clinical practitioners encounter, they must move from very local levels with a family and perhaps a neighborhood school or clinic to state program operations, to federal obligations under IDEA, and back again. For many clinicians, the ability to shift perspective and modes of interaction across all of these levels can be difficult at first, but it becomes easier with time. Put differently, there are numerous problems of intergovernmental relations that are presented both with respect to broad leadership efforts and also more specific management concerns.

It is important to remember that most of the services provided to families have some elements of federal funding to state governments, which, in turn, provide the services to families through contracts or grants to nonprofit or for-profit service providers. In other instances, such as special education funding, the federal funds flow through the state to local schools. At each level, there are different organizational cultures and different sets of rules in operation. It is also the case that the policy community for families who have children with special needs in one state is different in a number of respects from the national policy community or from the policy community in neighboring states.

The effort to understand these differences in programs and context is one reason that the program tries to ensure the use of federal and state materials throughout. It is also part of the reason for the different types of written exercises that the trainees and fellows accomplish through the year.

One of the areas in which trainees and fellows pursue these intergovernmental issues is in an assignment and workshop on budget and finance. They consider issues in both the proposed federal and state budgets in part to understand the kinds of pressures that will affect state officials. Similarly, consideration of the state budget picture helps to clarify the challenges that will be facing the local officials, particularly those in the educational arena with whom clinicians are seeking to work on behalf of families. These discussions also provide some sense of the stresses on service providers and reimbursing authorities.

All of this is very important information as trainees, fellows, and faculty step into their roles as advocates or consultants for families. In advocacy training, the program seeks to ensure that they "remember tomorrow," which is the idea that the actions taken today will shape the situation and constrain options for the future. Decisions are often cumulative and may produce unanticipated consequences, either positive or negative. Assisting trainees and fellows to understand the challenges facing those in the schools or various programs helps them to understand the need to make the effort a partnership whenever possible, which includes the need to make clear what they are contributing to the effort rather than simply making demands. It also involves the effort to educate the decision maker about what the interdisciplinary team has done leading up to the present situation.

It is equally important to maintain a sense of the need to give decision makers choices. Clinicians tend to prescribe what they perceive is the correct answer, but the service providers or educators with whom the family must interact face their own competing demands. The effort to develop options makes it possible to avoid zero sum situations (where only one party wins) that lead to serious conflict. Indeed, it becomes important for trainees and fellows to understand that decision makers often cannot give them and the families they serve everything they want or at least not all at once.

One of the ongoing problems for clinicians who specialize in working with families with children with developmental disabilities is a tendency to assume that the people they encounter in the service system know what the clinicians know. This is a problematic assumption. Clinicians need to be prepared to explain quickly and concisely what they need and why to people with different training, experience, and professional obligations.

Among the challenges clinicians encounter is the need to accept that good advocacy often means negotiation and that negotiation does not mean selling out. The program seeks to clarify the distinction between position bargaining and interest negotiations to avoid adversarial situations. It is often the case that laws provide threats, but if service providers reach the point at which those formal threats become necessary, cooperation often breaks down.

Much of the VT–ILEHP educational experience is designed to help trainees and fellows put themselves in the shoes of the decision makers they seek to influence on behalf of the family. Just as the program seeks to move students out of the standard medical model in clinical terms into something that is more sensitive, respectful, aware, inclusive, and sophisticated, so in the leadership and management arena, VT–ILEHP works to move away from practice based on writing a prescription and expecting action to an approach that seeks to understand and engage those who must not only make decisions about but also do what is needed to support the families. If clinicians fail to take that approach, they may in fact make the situation worse for the family by increasing tension, exacerbating frustrations, or even generating antagonisms that were not present earlier.

In the end, however, there are situations in which no amount of understanding and cooperative spirit can overcome years of difficulties or transform people who are unwilling to make support for the family a priority. Indeed, there are circumstances in which antagonisms toward the family or even discrimination mean that informal modes of interaction do not work. At that point, family members may feel the need to reevaluate the way in which they deal with the service system.

The Law, Politics, and Democracy

When things get to the formal stage or where families consider that they must demand action, it becomes important for clinicians to be sufficiently aware of the law related to children with special needs to be able to communicate effectively about the content of policies and the operation of decision processes with those families. It is also important to know when the parents might want to access formal legal advice with the possibility of legal action. At the same time, clinicians are not attorneys any more than educators are health care professionals. That said, it is important for trainees and fellows to have some basic literacy in the law quite apart from problems presented by parents in part because they are so frequently dealing with public programs and institutions and because they are attempting to build competencies for system change, which implies directly or indirectly a variety of legal concepts and issues. With these caveats in mind, VT–ILEHP builds a number of elements into the program designed to develop basic knowledge and training in how trainees and fellows can continue their learning in the field.

For many clinicians, the thought of studying law and legal process is anxiety provoking. There are many reasons, starting from the fact that people are socialized to be frightened of the law and taught that only lawyers, judges, and law enforcement officers can really understand it. They have generally not been taught to view public law (the law dealing with public officials, institutions, and policies) as something that very much belongs to everyone. At the same time, in part because they rely on others for what they know about the law, they often get partial and many times inaccurate information. Research by scholars of public law dating back to the 1960s has repeatedly demonstrated that information about developments in the law that reach practitioners at the point of service after having been filtered and digested through professional association newsletters, supervisor summaries, and other secondary sources is often inaccurate, incomplete, or, in a number of important cases, simply wrong (Dolbeare & Hammond, 1971; Johnson & Canon, 1984).

Thus, VT–ILEHP seeks to demystify legal materials and processes for trainees and fellows. Over the course of the year, the program expects that they will learn how to access legal documents, to read and analyze judicial opinions, to understand the basics of legislative process and statutory interpretation, and to acquire some familiarity with how administrative rules are promulgated as well as how to read them. The instruction uses both federal and state materials keyed to the specific kinds of issues the trainees and fellows will encounter in the field and are likely to engage as they pursue systems change. There are three recurring issues that arise as trainees and fellows work through these areas.

First, law and ethics are not the same. They can, in a number of situations, be very different, or even be in conflict. Thus, exceeding the speed limit is illegal, but few would regard it as unethical or immoral. By the same token, there are many kinds of behaviors that would be considered unethical when judged by the standards of many clinicians and yet not be illegal (whether or not they should be). Best practices do not constitute what the law requires. That said, there are also occasions when public policy places clinicians in difficult situations because they cannot do what their professional ethics would suggest they should do. That may be either because the law sets boundaries in certain circumstances on what may be done or how it may be done or because the funding constraints in legislation or annual appropriations will not permit it.

The classic example of this problem for a number of the trainees and fellows over the years has been frustration with Medicaid. Because the federal government has not created a national health plan, some states have sought through Medicaid waivers and other devices to make it operate as if it were such a program. It was, of course, developed as a poverty program, and like most such programs in America came with punitive attitudes and demands for accountability to protect against abuses of public largesse. When trainees or fellows bump up against these core principles as they seek to make life easier for families and children, they become frustrated. They sometimes react as if the law ought to incorporate their ethical standards—personal, situational, or professional. Although that may be an attractive idea, it is not the way that democracy or its laws function. Although there is little time to drive home this important truth about law and ethics, the program administrators do at least try to make the point and get trainees and fellows to think about it.

Second, there is the tension between the cooperative spirit of VT–ILEHP and the recognition of the civil rights base that underlies the effort to ensure adequate protection for children with special needs and their families. Many trainees and fellows are young enough that they do not understand the civil rights foundations of many of today's policies and professional practices. Most do not remember the deinstitutionalization movement in mental health and developmental disabilities. Most are not familiar with the effort to use the heritage of *Brown v. Board of Educ.* (1954) to eliminate the segregation of children with special needs in schools. A number of them think that the U.S. Supreme Court established a clear constitutional protection for these children and their families. It has not done so. Indeed, it has specifically rejected the application of the approach used in racial discrimination cases to deal with race discrimination to persons with developmental disabilities (*Board of Trustees of the University of Alabama v. Garrett*, 2001; see also, *City of Cleburne v. Cleburne Living Center*, 1985).

That said, Congress and a number of state legislatures have enacted such policies as IDEA (formerly the Education for All Handicapped Children Act), the Americans With Disabilities Act of 1990, and the Rehabilitation Act of 1973 that provide statutory rights for these children. These laws were needed to ensure the rights that the Supreme Court has not guaranteed and to provide avenues for parents to take action to ensure their implementation at the state and local levels. Most trainees and fellows are unaware that these protections are statutory and that they must therefore be alert to legislative changes to these policies.

Many also have not been aware that federal protections for families are based on grant programs (where funds are provided by the federal government to the states which then contract with nonprofit or for-profit organizations to deliver services) rather than direct regulation (in which federal government agencies control professional practice or service delivery). Thus, there is a complex intergovernmental web of federal statutes and regulations that are then implemented by states using their own legislation and regulations. In some circumstances, parents must take legal action to ensure local compliance. At the same time, trainees and fellows learn that local schools and school districts may be in a box by virtue of the fact that although they are to work with families to develop IEPs, they must work within the constraints imposed on them by federal and state law. (With some states seeking to constrain special education costs, that position between the parents and formal legal constraints can lead to significant tensions.)

In Allison's case, the school district and the private school had been embroiled for some time in litigation brought by other families. Families wanted the IEPs developed in accordance with IDEA to be implemented fully, but the school imposed its own restrictions and insisted that the district, not the school, was responsible for the IEP implementation. The family of one child at the school won a victory in the U.S. District Court for Vermont (*St. Johnsbury Academy v. D. H.*, 1998). However, the United States Circuit Court of Appeals for the Second Circuit, sitting in New York City, overturned that decision, agreeing that the school district was the Local Education Authority responsible under IDEA for the IEP and its implementation (*St. Johnsbury Academy v. D. H.*, 2001). If the private school was to have a responsibility, according to the court, that responsibility was a contractual matter between the district and the school. The parents' only avenue for action was against the district. Of course, the district, which did not have its own school, was facing a private school that was unlikely to agree to accept that responsibility, given its position in the litigation.

While all of this was happening, Allison's family was left with an unsatisfactory situation in which the school would not meet her needs, but the alternative seemed to be to send her away to a school outside her community. Her mother was convinced that was no alternative and that Allison simply could not survive such a course of action. The VT–ILEHP team hit barriers to cooperation and Allison's family was not inclined to join in the legal battles for a number of personal reasons. One of the lessons of this and other family stories is that the interdisciplinary team needs to think more about how to help families who reach the point of litigation to get the advice and support they need to move forward (see Chapters 6 & 7).

At a more general level, there is a third problem that VT–ILEHP seeks to address with trainees and fellows: an awareness of the problem of authority for and limits to official action. When confronted with case studies, some trainees and fellows at the beginning of the year demonstrate a problem that is common among clinicians. They assume that they or others with whom they are working have the authority to do whatever good clinical practice suggests is the right course of action. The general tendency is to assume far more authority than officials may in fact possess. Even in circumstances in which officials do have the legal authority to act, there is a tendency to ignore the fact that there may be procedural or substantive limitations to what can be done.

One of the exercises in which trainees and fellows participate at the beginning of the year is a review of a case, ultimately decided by the U.S. Supreme Court, involving the responsibility for failure to remove a child from a dangerous family situation (*DeShaney v. Winnebago County Department of Social Services*, 1989). The child was ultimately severely and permanently injured. Students discuss the case and are asked to offer policy recommendations to the state legislature. They then discuss these recommendations, using the feasibility framework. Difficulties with legal feasibility often turn out to be the most severe problems with some of the recommendations, many of which are quite creative and interesting. These trainees and fellows who are otherwise very family-centered, often do not see that their proposals implicate important constitutional and statutory rights of the parents, such as the right to privacy and the means they choose for their policies to be structured and operated often suggest serious due process of law issues.

Over time, of course, the hope is that trainees and fellows will go forth to help change legislation and regulations through the democratic process. At the same time, they should be able to carry out evidence-based practice and develop clinical best practice guidelines that fit together better with public policy. However, it is unlikely that clinicians will reach the point where the policy and professional practice do not present tensions or even outright conflicts from time to time.

THE LONG-TERM CHALLENGE: WHAT HAVE WE LEARNED ABOUT WHAT WE NEED TO BUILD ON FOR THE FUTURE?

With all of VT–ILEHP's awareness of the program's limitations and recognition of the need for continuous improvement in educating trainees and fellows in leadership and policy, the faculty still sees a glass half full. The program has learned from challenges over time and has developed a body of knowledge and set of learning experiences in this field that is far better than where VT–ILEHP first began. It is broad-based and aimed not just at training clinicians for the current state of play, but to help them have the tools to remain current, anticipate change, and seek to lead it. That said, program faculty have learned a number of lessons about what should be considered as the program contemplates the future.

Breaking Through the Barriers: Challenging Clinicians to Think in System Terms

Program faculty have learned a good deal about how clinicians deal with systems issues, or, perhaps, do not deal with them. Trainees and fellows often have a significant sense of frustration with systems and administrators who seem to stand in the way of providing better services to families and children. Yet, the truth is that it is important to find ways to ensure that clinicians understand the essential role of administrators as people with whom they must work if service systems are to function at all.

Part of the frustration of clinicians seems to come from discomfort with the ambiguity of systems issues, whether they are the broad challenges of political ambiguity or the most specific difficulties that arise from the complexity of the many policies and institutions that are involved in the service system. There is a sense in which science and clinical practice is clearer, although in truth that may be more a matter of familiarity than an accurate description. One need look no further than ongoing debates over diagnosis of Attention Deficit Hyperactivity Disorder (ADHD) or contemporary arguments over the etiology of autism to demonstrate that there is complexity and uncertainty everywhere.

It has also become clear, however, that there are ongoing tensions between elite clinical judgment and democracy and sometimes even between clinicians and parental judgment. Trainees and fellows, along with faculty members, must continuously wrestle with democracy's right to be wrong and their own striving to deliver the best that evidence based practice can offer to decision making and service delivery. The task is to find engaging ways to keep these challenges before interdisciplinary clinicians.

The other side of this question is helping clinicians deal with what one might call "fear of the system syndrome." Although virtually no clinician would put it in those terms, the program has found that trainees and fellows, when pressed to address significant systems issues, can easily feel overwhelmed and incapable of understanding such a wide range of material. It is often necessary to disabuse them of some of the simplifying assumptions that they acquired over the years from their days at the family dinner table to terrible coverage of public issues by the contemporary media. Partly, the fear of the system seems to be related to the fact that VT–ILEHP asks them not merely to function within their own clinical communities but to operate in interdisciplinary teams, to engage in broad-based community practice, and to reach even beyond that to be leaders in the public policy arena.

In thinking about Allison's story, the program has recognized that the training was not adequate in some respects. These elements in the training program have been expanded and improved substantially since then, but VT–ILEHP still must work harder at challenging clinicians to think in system terms.

Moving Beyond Providing Knowledge and Integrating Systems Concerns Into Clinical Practice

Unfortunately, the program needs to do a better job in moving beyond providing knowledge to ensuring that clinicians actually integrate systems concerns into day-to-day practice. One of the faculty members involved in Allison's case put it this way:

> We didn't back up and look at the situation as a management and systems problem. We didn't evaluate the decision environment. Our clinical bias prevented people from looking at [the situation, in part at least,] as a system problem. Also we were caught up in the clinical process that also steered us in a particular direction. We didn't frame the problems adequately.

Another faculty member, when asked about this situation, began with the idea that the interdisciplinary team had indeed considered systems questions as it began to work with Allison and her family, but, the more she thought and spoke about the experience, the clearer it became to her and to others that the team really had not done so, or at least not carefully and systematically as they always try to do in terms of our clinical work.

In a more recent situation, systems questions were asked at an early meeting, but there was an immediate sense of discomfort among those present. These were not typical, clinically-oriented inquiries and a good deal of processing was required to work through the tensions that grew out of asking these potentially difficult questions. There is still work to be done here.

The program needs to help trainees, fellows, and faculty to integrate an assessment of their decision environment into their normal modes of practice. That includes the ability to recognize clinical biases, step back to a reasonable position, and consider the entire situation, including leadership and systems challenges. If this is done effectively, trainees and fellows will be able to help frame questions in a more comprehensive and useful manner. They can also avoid allowing clinical biases to steer them into trouble.

Developing the Habit of Lifelong Learning on System Issues

Of course, systems are dynamic. Policies and the politics that produce them are constantly changing. It is important to maintain an interest in and knowledge of policy over time. The program has focused a good deal of effort on teaching trainees and fellows how to access information and how to use the feasibility framework to scan their environment for new conditions and changing policy. For example, the program recently assigned students to do a critical analysis of the report of the President's Commission on Excellence in Special Education and later assigned them to try their hand at making budget cuts in programs facing possible reductions in the pending budget proposals. The hands-on approach was used to demonstrate how to work with contemporary news items and policy proposals. Yet, it is important to improve efforts to encourage trainees and fellows to do these kinds of exercises in their professional lives as the years pass. With the demands of their day-to-day practice and the need to keep current with developments in their clinical specialties, systems issues can seem remote or at least less of a priority than many other pressing obligations. At the same time, VT–ILEHP strives to teach trainees and fellows that policy happens in real time and will not wait until they decide they have an opportunity to think about it.

Thinking Carefully About Systems Issues During Critical Stages of Work

At the same time that the program seeks to develop a habit of system thinking for individual clinicians, there is a need to consider more carefully as an interdisciplinary team how to ensure that faculty, trainees, and fellows evaluate the decision environment and look for systems issues at key points in their work. For example, after thinking about Allison's story and a number of other experiences, it seemed apparent that it is important after intake and before the assessment planning meeting to run the feasibility framework and try to anticipate systems issues that might be present. Another important point in the process is the period after the assessment is accomplished but before the report is written. In that period, there needs to be someone who asks about systems issues and assesses the decision environment once again. In Allison's story, for example, the situation changed significantly from the time of the intake to the assessment.

The VT–ILEHP Program is a training program and therefore does not follow families over an extended period of time. However, in the future, trainees and fellows will be in communities and will continue to work with families over a much greater time frame. In such situations, the changes that take place in the decision environment not only are the local issues associated with changes in the family and the community, but also larger policy issues that change as programs are altered or funding requirements change. Hence, it is important to ensure that the practice of evaluating the decision environment is a regular and ongoing activity and not one left only for the critical early stages of work with families and children.

Working Within the System While Trying to Change It: The Facts of Life

The fact of constant change is true not only of the family and its community context but also of the larger policy arena. One of VT–ILEHP's challenges is to try to educate trainees and fellows to work within the system while they are attempting to change it. It is a fact of life that systems change is a long-term project. While it is in progress, trainees and fellows cannot afford to be wasting time and energy fighting unwinnable battles. The families need their help now. The program tries to help trainees and fellows to operate at different levels, from the specific to the general, to acquire some level of comfort with shifting back and forth across those levels. It also seeks to help them be alert to changing roles, from clinician, to consultant, to policy advocate. The program also uses a number of workshops and seminars to try to help trainees and fellows understand the perspectives of and challenges facing administrators and program officers with whom they will work on an ongoing basis. Even while faculty, trainees, and fellows commiserate about our mutual frustrations with the system and consider possible changes, it is essential to work together within contemporary rubrics to ensure services to the families and children who are the focus of clinical professionals' efforts.

CONCLUSION

A look back on Allison's story reminds program participants of how much the families with whom they work teach clinical professionals. They would like to have done more for those families. Yet, those involved hope that what working with Allison and her family taught the program will benefit not only those families with whom VT–ILEHP will work in the future, but also the many trainees and fellows yet to come who may not know just why their learning experiences are crafted as they are but who will take those lessons back to the community, in any case.

The program has come a long way in integrating leadership, law, and policy into the program from where it began with rather narrow discussions of health care administration issues to the much broader and more integrated set of learning experiences that we employ today. Efforts to ensure that VT–ILEHP trainees and fellows have basic knowledge of leadership and management, of policy and how to change it, and of the law and how to continue to learn about it, continue to evolve. There is still much to do and an increasingly complex and challenging context in which to do it.

STUDY QUESTIONS

1. In light of the discussion in this chapter, what are the most important factors on the horizon today that are likely to shape the decision environments of clinicians in the next decade?
2. What are the key stages of clinical practice at which it is most important to consider systems issues?
3. How are intergovernmental relations shaping clinical practice in the contemporary setting, and how are they likely to evolve in the next 5 years?
4. What are the five most important policy issues in maternal and child health?

REFERENCES

Americans With Disabilities Act of 1990, 42 U.S.C.S. §1201 (2003).

Ball, H. (1986). *Justice downwind*. New York: Oxford University Press.

Barnard, C. (1938). *The functions of the executive*. Cambridge, MA: Harvard University Press.

Board of Trustees of the University of Alabama v. Garrett, 531 U.S. 356 (2001).

Brown v. Board of Educ. 347 U.S. 483 (1954).

Burns, J. M. (1978). *Leadership*. New York: Harper & Row.

City of Cleburne v. Cleburne Living Center, 473 U.S. 432 (1985).

Cooper, P. (1998). *Strengthening environmental management and administration in the Asian and pacific region*. New York: United Nations Division of Public Economics and Public Administration, Department of Economic and Social Affairs.

Cooper, P. (2000). *Public law and public administration* (3rd ed.). Itasca, IL: F. E. Peacock Publishers.

Cooper, P., & Vargas, C. M. (2004). *Sustainable development implementation: Beyond policy design*. Rowman & Littlefield.

Cooper, P., & Vargas, C. M. (Eds.). (1995). *Implementing sustainable development*. New York: United Nations.

Cooper, P. J., Hyde, A., Ott, J. S., Brady, L., White, H., & Hidalgo-Hardeman, O. (1998). *Public administration for the twenty-first century*. Fort Worth, TX: Harcourt Brace.

Covey, S. R. (1996). Three roles of the leader in the new paradigm. In F. Hesselbein, M. Goldsmith, & R. Beckhard (Eds.), *The leader of the future* (pp. 149–159). San Francisco: Jossey-Bass.

Daubert v. Merrill Dow, 509 U.S. 579 (1993).

DeShaney v. Winnebago County Department of Social Services, 489 U.S. 189 (1989).

Dolbeare, K., & Hammond, P. (1971). *The school prayer decisions: From court policy to local practice.* Chicago: University of Chicago Press.

Executive order 13166, "Improving access to services for persons with limited English proficiency," 65 *Fed. Reg.* 50121 (2000).

Follett, M. P. (1937). The process of control. In L. Gulick & L. Urwick (Eds.), *Papers on the science of administration* (pp. 159–169). New York: Institute of Public Administration.

Fritschler, A. L. (1989). *Smoking and politics* (4th ed.). Englewood Cliffs, NJ: Prentice Hall.

Gulick, L., & Urwick, L. (Eds.). (1937). *Papers on the science of administration.* New York: Institute of Public Administration.

Individuals with Disabilities Education Act, 20 U.S.C. § 1400 (1997).

Johnson, C., & Canon, B. (1984). *Judicial policies: Implementation and impact.* Washington, DC: CQ Press.

Metcalf, H. C., & Urwick, L. (Eds.). (1942). *Dynamic administration.* New York: Harper & Brothers.

Morstein-Marx, F. (Ed.). (1946). *Elements of public administration.* New York: Prentice Hall.

Nakamura, R., & Smallwood, F. (1980). *The politics of policy implementation.* New York: St. Martin's.

Osborne, D., & Gaebler, T. (1992). *Reinventing government.* New York: Penguin.

Ott, J. S. (1989). *The organizational culture perspective.* Belmont, CA: Wadsworth.

Rothlisberger, F. J. (1939). *Management and moral.* Cambridge, MA: Harvard University Press.

Sabatier, P., & Jenkins-Smith, H. C. (Eds.). (1993). *Policy change and learning: An advocacy coalition approach.* Boulder, CO: Westview Press.

Schein, E. (1992). *Organizational culture and leadership* (2nd ed.). San Francisco: Jossey-Bass.

St. Johnsbury Academy v. D. H., 20 F. Supp. 2d 675 (D.Vt. 1998).

St. Johnsbury Academy v. D. H., 240 F.3d 163 (2nd Cir. 2001).

U.S. General Accounting Office. (1992). *Organizational culture: Techniques companies use to perpetuate or change beliefs and values.* Washington, DC: Government Printing Office.

11

The Pillars, the Process, and the People: An Innovative Approach to Training Health Professionals in Interdisciplinary Practice

Claudia María Vargas
Patricia A. Prelock
Phillip J. Cooper
University of Vermont

The Vermont Interdisciplinary Leadership Education for Health Professionals (VT–ILEHP) Program is a postgraduate training program supported, as are other LEND programs, by the federal Maternal and Child Health Bureau. It is, however, far more than the official description suggests. It is a journey of discovery and growth for the faculty and, we are convinced, for trainees and fellows. That journey, now more than 8 years long, has transformed our understanding regarding what should and could be interdisciplinary practice serving children with neurodevelopmental disabilities and their families. As the preceding chapters have indicated, it is an ongoing process of learning and teaching.

This chapter begins with a look back at some of the significant issues, problems, challenges, and lessons that have been suggested by the analysis provided in the earlier chapters. It then turns to the pillars of the program and the process that has evolved that have helped to shape what we consider to be an innovative approach to interdisciplinary practice. That said, the authors of this book have worked carefully to provide not only examples of efforts that succeeded, but also new and ongoing challenges that the program is striving to address. In addition to these realities, the chapter turns to the nagging challenges that lie ahead. It should be clear by this point in the book that the pillars and the process depend on competent and committed health professionals. The VT–ILEHP program has, in the past and continues today, to enjoy a talented group of professionals and to benefit from engagement with families who not only care for their children but are willing to work to ensure the training of clinicians for the future.

BRINGING IT ALL TOGETHER: INTERDISCIPLINARY PRACTICE FROM THEORY TO ACTION

Some lessons that VT–ILEHP has learned have been sobering. Sometimes what we thought would be the best way to address a particular situation required rethinking. Knowing that was likely from the start, we recognized the need for continuous self-evaluation to improve the process created as well as the curriculum designed for the program. Families, their children, and community professionals have validated our practices, protocols, core curriculum, and processes and they have helped in that learning process.

The Family Support faculty on the team has helped VT–ILEHP implement and not merely espouse family-centered care (FCC). As introduced in Chapter 1, this is one of the five elements that drive the VT–ILEHP model. FC is the focus of Chapter 2 by Yoder and DiVenere. It considers the role of family members, recognizing that family configurations are diverse in size and form, and the impact of disability on parents, the child with the disability, siblings, grandparents, and other relatives involved with the family. An often forgotten person in family systems is the father. The VT–ILEHP Program has made a concerted effort, both within the curriculum and across our practices, to ensure that fathers are considered in all aspects of assessment and program planning for children with disabilities. As single parents, fathers are often equal partners in all parenting responsibilities than was formerly the case, and in some situations, they serve as primary caregivers for the children. It is important that they have a voice that is heard.

A salient feature of FC is transitioning from a child-centered perspective to one that considers the entire family. Such a perspective requires health practitioners to think carefully about the models we employ to understand disabilities, their consequences, and interventions. In doing so, the practitioner can gain an understanding of how the family system is affected and not just the child. As the chapter shows, there are effects in terms of employment for both parents, child-care needs for the child with the disability, time available for leisure activities for the entire family, and the often neglected need for respite, among others.

Another critical aspect of FCC is the effort to engage with the family as a colleague, as a partner, in the treatment of the child with the disability. This represents a departure from the expert model prevalent in modern biomedicine, although the medical model is crucial in delivering sophisticated, technical medical care. In a partnership approach to service delivery, health professionals need to adjust their communication style so that families can be provided complete and unbiased information. It requires open communication with families. This is a dramatic change in the way some health professionals have been trained as "holders" of seemingly secret information (personal medical information).

Family-to-family support, as practiced by parent-support organizations like Parent to Parent of Vermont, or the national organization, Family Voices, can be instrumental in helping a family with a child with a disability break the isolation that is common to such families. They also help the families learn about valuable community resources.

Cultural diversity is equally relevant for FCC. Inevitably, health professionals will interact with families whose racial, ethnic, geographic, linguistic, and family structure differs from that of mainstream society. However, the care needs to be of equal quality.

Although there has been a movement to develop cultural competence in various areas of social services, there is still much to be accomplished in the area of health care to redress inequities in access as well as the quality of care minorities and American Indians and Native Alaskans receive in the United States. Vargas and Beatson, in Chapter 3, suggest implementing various interventions, although they emphasize that the development of cultural competence is a long-term, multidimensional process. It is one in which clinicians must be comfortable with a level of ambiguity and requires negotiation of explanatory models and meanings ascribed to disabilities. Thus, cultural competence may involve adapting health services to the needs of the communities served and not always the other way around as has too frequently been the case.

For health professionals to provide culturally congruent care, several institutional changes may be necessary. There is an expert model (sometimes called the medical model) anchored in the organizational culture of health professions whose assessment of needs and successful outcomes may collide with those of families for whom a disability represents a stigma. Diagnosis and treatment have tipped the balance against minorities who have been victims of the "application error" (Geiger, 2002), especially in the area of disabilities. Reversing this negative sense requires setting aside previous diagnoses. More important, it calls on clinicians to explore the context of the child and the family and then respect their understandings. In that way, we can gain insight into easily overlooked characteristics of the child and his or her needs. There is another important element that we have come to consider and that is the need to integrate contemporary biomedicine treatments with traditional medicine practices. This is often possible and helpful as long as the traditional practices do not pose a danger to the health of the child. This effort can support the trust of the family in the effects of biomedicine. Vargas and Beatson present stories in which traditional practices complemented biomedical interventions. At the same time, VT–ILEHP recognizes the need to help ethnocultural communities understand the ethical and legal implications of dangerous traditional treatments and practices.

In Chapter 4, O'Rourke, Contompasis, and Holland underscore the relevance of early screening and follow-up for premature infants and complications that may be associated with neonatal intensive care (NICU). The screening process alerts families and relevant service providers to potential problems these infants may encounter according to the three categories of high risk infants: low birth weight infants; very low birth weight infants; and extremely low birth weight infants. The stories of the infants in the first two categories illustrate the specific challenges infants may have at the time of the screening. Those born at extremely low birth weight are automatically referred to services. This type of screening is particularly significant for reducing the incidence of long-term morbidity and developmental disabilities. Because it is comprehensive and interdisciplinary (cognitive, affective, physical), it can trigger the services required to help during critical developmental stages, especially when parents are unfamiliar with the kinds of support that are available.

The cultural dimension is just as important in NICU follow-up as in other aspects of care, because there are many traditions associated with birthing and infant care, from nutritional to sleeping practices. Use of an interpreter is critical when the family needs one to ensure that information is accurately conveyed and understood, the voice of the family is heard, and questions or concerns are validated. This chapter also illustrates the diversity of family structures and the need to be sensitive to and respectful of what constitutes a family in any given context. To support the needs of the infant and the family, culturally congruent interactions and communication are necessary, especially in articulating the results of the screening and in making recommendations. Such interactions are needed to support the infant and the family, linguistically, socioculturally, financially, and generally, in terms of specific services they may need. Recognizing the legitimacy of each member of the family as an active caregiver of the infant is essential, whether or not it fits a Western, nuclear family structure, as the story of Edward, the child of a 17-year-old mother, indicated. The story of Dimir exemplifies the story of many refugees who were forced from their homeland, leaving behind a professional career only to find menial jobs and poor housing in exchange for freedom. At the same time that they had to cope with their own stresses, they were as caring and concerned as any other parent, regardless of circumstances. A complicating matter for many refugees is their unfamiliarity with a demand-based service system prevalent in the United States. Fortunately for Dimir, he and his family are receiving the needed services.

The NICU follow-up component has been particularly useful in training health professionals to expand their own horizons. They work in an interdisciplinary fashion as well as in a transdisciplinary fashion administering screening tools typically done by other disciplines. Of course, every aspect of the screening process performed by students is under the supervision of faculty members from each specific discipline. Effective leadership in a NICU follow-up clinic requires the training of pediatricians and other health clinicians who will be alert to interdisciplinary screening and who will think about the "whole" child.

Chapter 5, by O'Rourke and Dennis, demonstrates the value of community-based assessment or a "clinic without bricks and mortar" in several ways. First, the team gets a broader picture of a child and his or her family, and does so in his or her natural contexts. It allows a team to see the child in multiple contexts, which a clinic visit could not provide. Second, it is centered on the family. Indeed, the family drives the assessment as an integral member of the team in every aspect of the community assessment. Third, there is the benefit of an interdisciplinary assessment as opposed to a single discipline. Fourth, modeling interdisciplinary practice to the community teams is crucial as it is not always possible to provide training to the many community teams. For example, the set of protocols and rules that have been established to conduct meetings allow for candid but respectful interactions among the family, the VT–ILEHP team, and community team members. Because the protocols and rules are communicated at the first community assessment meeting, even conflict-ridden team members operate more effectively.

One of the most important lessons learned from the community assessment process has been the need to limit the number of recommendations. Previously, the VT–ILEHP team made numerous recommendations to the community team. The community team left the meeting overwhelmed and frustrated with the multitude of technically sound, evidenced-based recommendations (technical feasibility). However, because we did not consider other issues affecting the decision environment associated with, for example, administrative feasibility, the family and the teams left the meetings, the former full of expectations for dramatic changes, and the latter, fearful on how to make so much happen. As a result, VT–ILEHP now limits its recommendations to three to five key ones.

There are, of course, other challenges that the feasibility framework can help clarify such as political, fiscal, cultural, legal, or ethical dimensions of a situation. As the state of Vermont's fiscal problems became more evident, reflective of the national economic downturn in recent years, the best technical recommendations may be more difficult to implement. The interdisciplinary team began to recognize the need to be more realistic and practical, without compromising the quality of the recommendations. Although the VT–ILEHP Program faculty wanted the best interventions in place, we learned to present alternative plans of action that could meet the technical, fiscal, or political reality. In situations where the team could provide technical assistance to community teams, it began to do so increasingly as a service to the community. In turn, the community team has been a source of tremendous learning regarding the contextual features of the school and the community-at-large that may affect the health care of the children with disabilities. Trainees and fellows who have completed the program have in turn launched their own family support and clinical support programs at the local level.

The community assessment, as designed by VT–ILEHP, also benefits from the perspective of all family members and friends involved in one way or another with the child. Starting from intake at the family's home, trainees and fellows are exposed to not just one family snapshot, but several views. The lenses with which the team conducts evaluations are multiple and diverse, capturing images of the child that may be missed from a clinic-based assessment.

A remaining challenge for VT–ILEHP regarding community assessment is the systematic application of the feasibility framework to help us navigate through the complex and complicated institutional labyrinths of the education and health care systems that families and service providers face (see Chapter 10).

Dewees, Beatson, and Douglas describe, in Chapter 6, how community assessment follow-up, or care coordination as it was originally called, has been an important element of the training. Although it has undergone changes throughout the years, it has taught us critical lessons regarding the perspective of the family, the community team, the faculty, and the students.

As several of the chapters have indicated, the family may constitute a diverse, fluid group. In performing community assessment follow-up, Jane's family (discussed in Chapter 6), which consisted of Jane, a single parent, with disabilities, raising two children, both of whom faced health challenges, presented another family configuration. Although the faculty, fellows, and trainees never hesitated working with this family, Jane's multiple and immediate needs overwhelmed them. In fact, the trainee assigned to this family became so involved that she was receiving regular phone calls to help the mother with a number of tasks, such as transportation for visits to the doctor. Jane was trying very hard to keep her family together, but her interactions with Social Rehabilitation Services (SRS) and service providers became adversarial as her needs intensified. Although she finally found an apartment right before the Christmas holiday season, it was an empty apartment, without food, or presents for her children. She did not even have a blanket to place on the floor when her younger child underwent physical therapy. The VT–ILEHP faculty, trainees, and fellows took a personal interest in the care of this family and provided some support for these needs.

However, as the 2nd year of community follow-up came, the prospects of the family had reached a crisis point. This forced the faculty to really explore what the mission was for a training program the goals of which did not include providing direct services. It is an important lesson for those involved in this type of training programs to understand this distinction.

Community assessment follow-up without any time constraints had to be questioned. The sobering conclusion was that a training program did not have the resources to afford a family continuous, and indefinite, community assessment follow-up (care coordination). The trainee assigned to implement community assessment follow-up became emotionally drained trying to support Jane, a young woman with her own developmental disabilities, who lacked the system support that her family required.

This experience led the VT–ILEHP team to explore the question of how close or how intimately involved the faculty and trainees and fellows can be with any particular family. Thorny ethical issues emerged regarding our obligation: was it to the child or to the family, as in the case of this mother? As the imminent threat of the loss of parental rights loomed, those involved with the program had to confront the conflict between the child's well-being and safety and the program's family-centered care approach.

This experience provided the faculty with significant opportunities to learn as part of a training program. First, the faculty concluded that community assessment follow-up had to be limited to 1 year, except for special circumstances. In the case of continuing follow-up support, the faculty would first have to deliberate the merits of such a decision for the purposes of training. Associated with this issue, the faculty explored the ethical dilemmas when trainees and fellows become too involved with a family, as was the case for Jane. The trainee was driven by her compassion and empathy for Jane's plight and that of her children and found herself experiencing each crisis with the family. This crisis-mode, the faculty concluded, was not conducive to teaching the primary goals and objectives of the program.

Another critical lesson the interdisciplinary team learned was the need to select cases that were effective training opportunities that considered the pillars of the program and objectives of community assessment follow-up. A family's needs would have to be such that trainees could implement effective interventions guided by the family that would ultimately allow them to bring closure at the end of the training period. Although it is apparent that 1 year of community assessment follow-up would not address all the problems of families with children with chronic disabilities, it would be a time during which trainees could get a glimpse of the complex web of services and the multitude of health care providers a family encounters on a daily basis.

A significant challenge VT–ILEHP still faces in the area of community assessment and community assessment follow-up is instituting the use of the feasibility framework. For many clinicians, anything with the words policy, law, or management carries a negative connotation. However, as this story unfolded, those involved in the program had to come to terms with issues specifically in those areas. In retrospect, the challenges were not technical, as the team had the expertise to respond to the needs of the family, and they were not administrative, as the people were in place to respond. They were political, cultural, ethical, and legal, and pushed those involved in the program to face new territory. Political feasibility was at stake because SRS was ready to remove the child from the mother, but VT–ILEHP was trying to prevent family disintegration, struggling with the philosophy of family-centered care for which we so strongly advocate. Cultural feasibility was problematic because Jane lacked support systems to maintain family cohesion. Ethical feasibility brought the program to a head. The interdisciplinary team had to confront the conflictive positions: to be family-centered and protect the role of the mother or to discern to whom the program was obligated. It was a perilous position potentially compromising political feasibility. In response, the faculty concluded that parameters had to be established regarding the mission of a training program. An ancillary realization was that cases selected for care coordination had to be more appropriate to a training program, and that as such, the program was not in a position to provide ongoing direct services. In retrospect, the team learned to look forward with open hearts as well as open minds, recognizing its own constraints.

Transition to adulthood is no easy process for the family, the youngster, or service providers. The Individuals with Disabilities Education Act (IDEA) specifies that schools need to initiate preparations for transition when the child turns 16. However, as every chapter demonstrated, children with chronic, complex disabilities require a great deal from clinicians, family members, and the community. In Chapter 7, Contompasis and Burchard explore the difficulties of planning for transition. These issues are particularly intense when one or both parents have special health needs, as was the case for one of Jacques's parents. Communication barriers were such that the community team was advocating for independent living although the parents opposed it. The communication network became more challenging because Jacques, who has autism, communicated only through a Canon communication device.

On one hand, Jacques was conveying his desire for independent living to the school team and complained that his parents were abusing him. On the other hand, he communicated to his parents that the school team was being abusive. This tug of war placed the VT–ILEHP trainee in the middle of the cross-fire. Although the trainee had a trusting relationship with the parents, he was attempting, in the midst of all this, to foster collaborative teaming between the parents and the school team. Inevitably, the trainee was in an ethical, and potentially a legal, dilemma, and so was the program. The faculty had to address the issue expediently and decided to withdraw the trainee from this care coordination assignment.

Transition can also be complicated by the parents' desire to keep the young person living with them indefinitely. This was so for Jacques's parents and for other parents with whom the program has engaged. Such a situation can be tense for a trainee who may be conveying the need to work with the parents toward transition as advanced by IDEA. However, it is critical, despite a philosophy of supporting independence, to listen to the family.

Equally important is the need to listen to the child's voice, an often forgotten or unheard voice. Jacques's desire for independent living was finally respected. In other instances, such a desire can be compromised, especially when the young person's voice is difficult to decipher, as it is for those with profound mental retardation.

Jacques challenged the interdisciplinary team in various ways. We had to deal with thorny ethical issues such as professional distance (the professional as a friend and the risk of misjudgment), a child-centered or family-centered perspective, and the use and veracity of controversial techniques or communication assistive devices. The professional as a friend is a particularly delicate issue in Vermont, where most people interact with each other on a first-name basis, as opposed to addressing people by their formal titles, as is done in many other states in the United States. Cultural conflict can emerge where professionals act with familiarity, especially when potential ethical or legal complications may be lurking in the background. In the story of Jacques, as well as in the story of Carolina (Chapter 6), we learned the importance of professional role boundary, although it does not have to be strictly dichotomized, especially in a cultural context such as that of Vermont. What is critical is the need to be clear about not misrepresenting or understating whatever issues may be at hand, which would be perilous in any context, including Vermont.

The family practicum, as portrayed in Chapter 8 by Yoder and Burchard, has been invaluable in helping students learn the perspective of the family. The authors noted that one of the trainees captured it in this way: "it is like going from a snapshot to a family album." Perhaps, the practicum is more like becoming one of the characters in a movie, although for families, the movie, better yet the reality, continues. A trainee's narrative typifies the experience in her description of the onerous, multiple, time-consuming tasks required to get a child ready for a doctor's appointment, from getting him dressed, to placing him in the wheelchair inside the van out of the van to move him from the parking structure to the building, into the examining room, onto the scale to weigh him, into the wheelchair, and then repeating all the tasks in reverse, except for a drive-by for a McDonald's lunch.

The family practicum has not evolved without obstacles. It has changed for many reasons, including consideration of potential legal and ethical questions. All VT–ILEHP trainees and fellows and the Vermont Rural Autism Project (VT–RAP) trainees (see Chapter 9) highlighted the family practicum as immensely helpful in understanding the perspective of the family. However, the faculty had to confront legal and ethical matters to be in compliance with university policies. The respite component of the family practicum posed potential legal concerns regarding, for example, the trainees transporting children in their personal cars. Hence, liability issues emerged. To be proactive, the program administrators consulted with the university counsel regarding who is liable in a number of contexts in which the trainees would be placed as part of the practicum. To be precise, the program administrators had to determine whether liability would fall on the program if trainees were driving their own cars in transporting children. Another question that was explored was the potential for a lawsuit in case of allegations of child abuse. Although the program has not to date encountered any complications of this sort, administrators had the responsibility to explore liability and find out who would accord legal protection. It was then necessary to draft policies and appropriate guidelines. These have been useful lessons in implementing the family practicum.

There were other lessons as well. Initially, the family practicum had been drafted as an opportunity for students to engage with families and children with disabilities. As the program progressed, the family faculty identified the need to write specific objectives (see Appendix in Chapter 8). These have been useful in terms of assessing the benefits that students, as well as the family, draw from the experience.

As the literature on social services indicates (Herman & Associates, 1994), it is important to build partnerships to provide comprehensive services as opposed to looking to a single agency or unit, especially if interdisciplinary practice is considered best practice. Although partnerships have been touted as a panacea to solve fragmentation in service delivery, there are cautions to consider in building partnerships or networks (Cooper, 2000; Vargas, 2000, 2002). Nevertheless, Chapter 9, by Prelock and Vargas, exemplifies a successful partnership between the VT–ILEHP and the Vermont Rural Autism Project (VT–RAP). Both organizations improved their assessment process as a result of the collaboration.

First, the VT–ILEHP team was in place ready to support the families served by the VT–RAP. Second, the community assessment model developed for VT–ILEHP was used for VT–RAP and both teams participated in all of the meetings related to community assessment. That is, the structure and procedures for conducting a community assessment for VT–RAP were modeled on those of VT–ILEHP. This included the use of the family genogram and ecomaps (a genogram is a three-generation representation of the family and child served. An ecomap is a visual representation of the school and community supports for the child and the family), assignment of roles to conduct the meetings, and the mentoring or faculty advisor assigned to each trainee and fellow. The preassessment and postassessment on the various competencies expected for the trainees and fellows and faculty, specifically, family-centered care, cultural competence, interdisciplinary teaming and collaboration, and a focus on disability, were shared. This synchronization of mission, goals, objectives, process, and procedures fostered positive outcomes for the partnership.

The family practicum for VT–RAP was modeled on that of VT–ILEHP. This proved to be an invaluable experience that allowed trainees "to live," for a few hours or a few days, the experiences and know the complicated demands faced by the family—from child care to school demands to nutritional issues. However, the VT–RAP trainees, as well as the VT–ILEHP trainees, learned to see the potential and talents of the children with autism or other disabilities that can so easily be missed from a 1-hour school visit or clinical consultation at a medical center. The VT–RAP Program also added a component of respite to the parent experience that VT–ILEHP later adopted.

One important assessment element that was changed in VT–ILEHP based on the experience of VT–RAP was ensuring that family and community team members participate in community assessment meetings. Likewise, the depth and breath of VT–RAP was enhanced from having in place the VT–ILEHP team to consult on the impact of autism in various aspects of the life of the child and the family. The VT–ILEHP students participated in all of the VT–RAP community meetings, benefiting from the specialized knowledge and training required for children with autism. Further, the training director for VT–ILEHP was the project director of VT–RAP, who afforded a strong link between both.

Indeed, this partnership was effective for the VT–ILEHP Program and for the VT–RAP. The principle of collaboration was advanced for both units based on this shared experience. Notwithstanding these successful outcomes, partnerships can be burdensome for any organization providing services to families and children in terms of the time and resources required to build, maintain, sustain, and terminate a partnership (Cooper, 2000; Vargas, 2000, 2002).

Probably the most challenging aspect of the VT–ILEHP Program for trainees and faculty members is the component on public law, public policy, management, and leadership discussed in Chapter 10 by Cooper and Dennis. Guided by technical expertise, clinical in this case, students of the program often want to prescribe the best interventions without consideration of other intervening factors that mean success or failure in the implementation process. Sometimes, as fully committed advocates of the causes of families with children with disabilities, clinicians may overlook the consequences of operating in a demand mode. In this sense, public policy sessions teach fellows how to advocate for the children and families they serve without destroying bridges they may need to cross later. Advocacy sessions specifically focus on learning to develop and present alternative course of actions to the various decision makers with whom they work instead of plainly demanding a single course of action. The public policy sessions include training of basic policy concepts and processes as well as the need to learn to read the political radar, not only at the local level, but also at the state, national, and when necessary, the international levels.

A major barrier in this component has been what Cooper and Dennis label the "problem paradox." Because the interdisciplinary program embraces a strengths-based model, it is unavoidably in conflict with the problem-driven policy arena. To focus attention to the plight of persons with disabilities, the issue has to enter the political radar as a priority, or what the chapter notes is a policy window—or a problem gaining immediacy in the political agenda and an opportunity for action. In synthesis, this chapter underscores that policy, law, and management significantly affect clinical practice, whether or not practitioners want to recognize it. It is an important pillar of VT–ILEHP.

THE PILLARS: IMPROVING THE QUALITY OF LIFE OF FAMILIES AND CHILDREN WITH SPECIAL HEALTH NEEDS

The VT–ILEHP Program is anchored on five pillars: (a) a focus on disability; (b) interdisciplinary practice; (c) family-centered, community-based, care; (d) culturally competent care; and (e) promotion of leadership in the field of disabilities. The challenge of developing a program in which all of these elements are present took a number of years to refine—and that endeavor continues. The effort to ensure that the pillars really function in the day to day life of the program, its faculty and trainees and fellows engage in continuous evaluation and self-reflection, critiquing each component—clinical, curricular, and assessment process and protocols—of the training program. This ongoing, candid evaluation has been possible due to the egalitarian and respectful ambiance of the program since its inception. To many who have participated, this quality has been unique to the program, although its institutional base and the agencies with which it collaborates tend to be command-control and top-down organizations. Notwithstanding the challenges the program has confronted, it has focused on a goal of program improvement to train clinicians to serve better children and families with special health needs. Although this has not meant a tension-free endeavor, it has been one of genuine growth, learning, and advancement for the faculty.

A Focus on Neurodevelopmental Disabilities

From its inception, the program design centered on serving children with neurodevelopmental disabilities, as is the mission of the Maternal and Child Health Bureau. In so doing, the program brings together an array of specialists in pediatric care for children and adolescents. The families and children that the team selects are those with complex health needs, as the stories of the children in each chapter indicate. Karla (Chapter 2) suffered from brain cancer that had been in remission for a time, leaving her with multiple health and learning challenges, until the cancer returned and eventually took her life. In Chapter 5, we met David, who suffers from the most common and severe form of spina bifida, who was born with hydrocephalus and Arnold-Chiari malformation, has a loss of sensation and paralysis in his legs, impaired bowel and bladder function, musculoskeletal deformities, a latex allergy, learning disabilities, and has undergone more than 25 corrective surgeries. Sam's story (Chapter 9) is another illustration of multiple, complex disabilities, autism, bone growth disorder, conductive hearing loss, and hypernasal speech. These are a few stories of the children VT–ILEHP serves. In their current service delivery system, the child and family work with multiple service providers who may not talk to each other about the required care of each specialist or the impact of one treatment or intervention on the care by another specialist—for example, a particular medication may affect a child's appetite, hence the need for the nutritionist to work out a nutritional diet, or the medication may affect mobility, hence physical therapy may have to be adapted accordingly. These children are indeed in need of an interdisciplinary team.

Feasibility of Interdisciplinary Health Care

The health professions have generally operated in isolation from one another. This is often referred to as the silo effect, or operating without consideration of how other disciplines may benefit from or be affected by what each individual discipline is there to do for a child. However, the VT–ILEHP team has been able to maintain a focus on a joint purpose, ultimately serving children with neurodevelopmental disabilities and their families. The commitment of every member of the faculty has been a strong foundation on which to implement interdisciplinary clinical practice. This in no way means that the process has been free of conflict. The norm of respectful disagreement and listening to each other's concerns has served the program well, always with the eye on better serving children and families with disabilities.

The collaborative teaming approach embraced by the VT–ILEHP faculty has been effective. The program brought together a group of professionals whose goal to serve children and families with disabilities superceded potential tensions. Some of these tensions are endemic at the national level as is the hierarchical nature, for instance, of the medical field, which is often seen at the top of the other health or allied health professions. Other stresses originate from the hierarchical value of some professions over others, despite comparable academic training, for example, occupational therapy as compared to psychology. Still others may come from personality, ideology, or philosophical differences. Despite these differences, the mission of the program has been the primary focus of the team, in a manner that is so constructive that it has attracted and retained highly qualified faculty members.

The collaborative feature has been driven and strengthened by the mission that children with complex health needs benefit from an interdisciplinary approach instead of uncoordinated care. Thus, the commitment continues to be to the child and the family with special health needs.

Family-Centered Care

As the program evolved, everyone realized that family-centered care could not be restricted to a traditional middle-class family: the father, the mother, and the children. This was not an easy process because the initial perception was limited to the mainstream concept of a family. Instead, program faculty quickly learned families are diverse, particularly in their needs. The faculty also learned that "family-centered" does not necessarily mean that what a parent does, for instance, is always in the best interest of the child, although that parent may be doing the best he or she can. The important point is that families have a voice, are respected for that voice, and are provided the supports they need

(American Academy of Pediatrics, 2003). Unfortunately, some families are not able to integrate these supports or differentiate the importance of their needs from those of their children. When the safety and well-being of a child is at risk, teams, who have at their core a family-centered philosophy, may face certain challenges. As the story of Carolina and her family illustrated (Chapter 6), a strict, family-centered perspective could have placed the interdisciplinary team in an ethical dilemma, and potentially in a legal conflict.

The story of David, on the other hand, illustrates how a single mother, with low income, and difficult housing situations, was able to maintain her family in a healthy context. There were significant reasons for differences in outcomes for David's family, although both David and Carolina's families lived in poverty. First, David and his family had a strong community team, which demonstrates the positive impact a group of service providers united by a common goal can have on the life of a child and his family. Specifically, David's team supported a smooth transition when the family moved from one community to another. In fact, the team from the first school met with the team of the new school to ensure that pertinent information was shared and that processes were in place to deal with David's special needs. Second, the resource book that the VT–ILEHP trainee had prepared for David accompanied him to his new school. Third, David and his family had a strong support system in the surrounding communities who were willing and ready to help, for example, in building the ramp to the house so that David could use his wheelchair at home. In contrast, Jane, Carolina's mother, lacked familial and community support.

The salient feature that stands out between these two families is the fact that Jane herself had disabilities. That factor complicated her ability to acquire effective parenting skills and to develop judgment about what constitutes a healthy relationship, whether with friends or intimate partners. Jane's poor judgment affected her ability to benefit from the resources and services available. In synthesis, whether right or wrong, the interdisciplinary team confronted the challenges that parents with disabilities face themselves, in addition to those inherent when their children have a disability as well. This experience helped the team see family-centered care in a broader context.

A perspective in family-centered care that seems hidden is that of the father. Although many mothers assume the caretaking role of a child with disabilities, the father often plays an equally important role. The story of Karla in Chapter 2 makes this point when the doctor breaks the news to Karla and her mother about the reappearance of cancer. The father was rightly upset that the doctor did not consider it appropriate to wait to break the bad news until he arrived, as he was a tremendous support to his family. It is critical to consider the father in the care of the child with special health needs, even if he is not directly involved in every aspect of the child's care. It is also important to recognize that for some families, it is the father who attends all the team meetings and who asserts an advocacy role. Often, the father remains the sole provider because mothers often choose to quit their jobs to dedicate themselves totally to caring for the child with special needs, frequently forced to become health insurance and policy experts. Yet, fathers may be treated as if they were outside that formulaic configuration of caretaking. Fathers, indeed, are affected by the child's disability just as much and want to be equal participants in the decision-making process associated with the child's health, as did Karla's father.

Culturally Responsive Health Care

Cultural competence is congruent with family-centered care. As conveyed throughout the book, cultural competence needs to permeate every aspect of a program or organization. It cannot, and must not, be left up to the "multicultural person," but needs to be the responsibility of everyone involved: faculty, trainees and fellows, as well as administrators. In the clinical context, cultural responsiveness is essential to serve all children and families, regardless of their ethno-cultural, racial background. Culturally incongruent health care can undermine the best biomedical treatment. It is also imperative to address cultural competence in health care in response to unresolved equity and equality issues in society. An organization that institutes cultural competence as intrinsic to its clinical practice demonstrates leadership.

Training Future Leaders

The experience of the past eight years has allowed us to gain insights, understand, and learn lessons on what is required of a training program in the area of neurodevelopmental disabilities. Indeed, some of the most important lessons were revealed in the obstacles we faced. One of those has certainly been recognizing our limitations in specific areas such as leadership and management. It has taken several years before becoming aware of the relevance of leadership, law, and public policy concerns. By far this has been the most difficult to tackle, in part, because as clinicians, the tendency is to focus on clinical problems as well as to view them strictly from a clinical perspective. However, in a complex political, economic, social, and cultural context, as is characteristic of contemporary national reality, clinical practice cannot operate in a vacuum. Instead, clinicians serving children with disabilities can benefit from, for example, the feasibility framework to assess their decision environment. Clinicians can use the seven dimensions of the framework, technical, fiscal, administrative, legal, political, ethical, and cultural feasibility, to determine where there may be potential obstacles to the process they may be trying to institute.

THE PROCESS: PROACTIVE, COMMUNITY-BASED CARE FROM INFANCY TO YOUNG ADULTHOOD

The VT–ILEHP Program has gained respect in the communities as families and service providers throughout the state have had the opportunity to work together. Vermont is a state where a person or a program's reputation can be quickly tarnished because knowledge of it travels fast. Although the team has had a few bumps along the way, the program appears to be meeting the communities' needs.

From an institutional perspective, any attempt to formalize a similar program needs to consider that a design like VT–ILEHP is not a turnkey project, but one that will take time and effort to institutionalize. In implementing the various components of the process, and after putting it into practice for a few years, we have learned some valuable lessons described in the next sections.

THE PEOPLE: INTERDISCIPLINARY PRACTICE AT WORK

At the time the program was being shaped, there was curiosity and uncertainty about how it was all going to turn out. Notwithstanding these concerns, there has been, from its inception, true commitment from the faculty. The interdisciplinary team has been integrated by 12 disciplines: audiology, education, family support, nursing, nutrition, occupational therapy, pediatrics, physical therapy, psychology, public law and public administration, social work, and speech–language pathology. The program by itself could not have reached the level attained without the partnerships it established from the start with various government agencies (departments of health and education) as well as nongovernmental organizations (NGOs). Although the program is housed in the College of Medicine, it has engaged the collaboration of various units on campus. Partnerships with NGOs have yielded positive results in serving children and families with disabilities; among them, Parent to Parent of Vermont, the Autism Society of Vermont, the Vermont Parent Information Center, and the Traumatic Brain Injury Society of Vermont. We continue to face the future as an opportunity to advance our clinical practice as well as promote interdisciplinary practice in organizations with which the VT–ILEHP Program interacts to improve the lives of children with neurodevelopmental disabilities in spite of some persistent concerns.

LOOKING FORWARD: NAGGING CHALLENGES

In the area of clinical practice, curriculum development, community assessment, and collaborative teaming, the VT–ILEHP Program has made consistent progress. However, there are some challenging areas with which we continue to grapple. Although the focus of the program is on children with neurodevelopmental disabilities, we have had to learn the perspective of parents with disabilities as well. The other perspective that is really important to recognize is that of the child. As parents enter the maze of the health care system and as they wrestle with the multitude of health care practitioners, the voice of the child often goes unheard. Interdisciplinary team members, especially those who are parents of children with special health needs, have been our beacons to that need.

The international environment related to disabilities also is changing rapidly as globalization affects everyone, and not always in a good way. In the area of disabilities, research is providing new directions. There is also the continuous need to serve refugees and immigrants from very diverse ethno-cultural backgrounds who are now members of our communities. Although many will not be in need of specialized services, there are families with children who have health challenges.

Finally, there is the public policy arena at which many assume to be experts, however, its dynamic and complex nature requires clinicians to be alert if they are to serve well children with complex health needs and their families. The policy arena continues to present the most difficult challenge for the VT–ILEHP team and the trainees and fellows whose tendency is to focus on the clinical aspects as if they were operating in a closed system oblivious to external changes, particularly in public policy, public law, budget, and finance. The tendency of clinicians to zoom into the clinical-specific, microlevel issues will not suffice in the field of disabilities. Clinicians, whether willing or not, will need to expand their horizons to include the interface between macrolevel and microlevel issues, or clinical practice and public policy, law, and management.

Parents With Special Health Needs

Although persons with disabilities and their families have been able to muster political attention to their plight and the need for services in accord with the civil rights model, the attention to parents with disabilities has been less visible on the political agenda. The story of Jane in Chapter 7 epitomizes this in several ways. Unfortunately, Jane did not have family support or friends to shield her from some of the common safety issues persons with disabilities face, including mental and sexual harassment, fears expressed by Sam's (Chapter 9) and Jacques's (Chap-

ter 7) parents. She had been a victim of rape by a family member resulting in a pregnancy and the birth of her first child. Judgment of people
and situations are difficult for persons with various disabilities, such as
autism and mental impairments. For Jane, choosing friends and intimate relationships was difficult. Somehow, she attracted individuals
with problems who compounded the situation for her. Her intellectual
challenges affected her ability to be an effective parent.

The International Environment:
A Dynamic Concept of Disability and Health

Although the VT–ILEHP Program has integrated evidenced-based
practices and tools, such as those used to screen NICU babies, there is a
continuous effort to learn from innovations and research findings in
other parts of the world. Equally important is to learn about the needs of
new arrivals from many parts of the world to one's community. In 2002,
the state received a group of the Lost Boys of Sudan. This year, a number
of Bantu families, a nomadic people from Somalia, arrived in the state.
Currently, there are over 30 languages spoken in the state. Hence, there
is the pressing need to learn about the specific cultural characteristics as
well as the potential needs that are crucial when serving families whose
children may have disabilities.

Looking Forward: Shaping the Future and Being Shaped by It

The policy environment is complicated and likely to continue to be so
for the foreseeable future. That challenging and changing environment
will shape in many important respects the context in which families will
live and seek assistance. It will also shape the institutions, programs,
and resources available to clinicians who seek to support those families
and their children with special needs.

Whatever one's political views, there are certain realities that seem
likely to remain significant for some time. First, because programs such
as the IDEA and Medicaid, which are central to many of our efforts, require periodic reauthorization by Congress as well as implementation
of regulations from federal and state administrative agencies, it is un-
wise to take anything for granted. Second, the reality is that the national
and state financial pictures in the years ahead are daunting and the evidence is that the challenges of budget deficits and growing obligations
will add resource stresses. This less than promising future comes at a
time when many existing policies are not adequately funded. States are
under tremendous stress from rapidly growing Medicaid and Medicare
costs and have yet to see the kinds of federal assistance for special education that are so desperately needed. Third, as Chapter 3 indicates, our

systems of care and support have not provided equality or equity and the effort to remedy this history of unequal access and care, as well as the responsibility to address the needs of an increasingly diverse community, call for increased resources at a time when political demands are focused on tax cuts. For example, federal law requires that social service programs receiving federal funds need to ensure access for persons with limited English proficiency, but efforts have not been made to provide sufficient resources to support those efforts. Finally, although the courts have become increasingly important participants in the shaping of health care and education policy, they have also posed serious challenges. Rulings such as the prohibition of suits against states for violations of the Americans With Disabilities Act and the limits on responsibilities under IDEA for private schools under contract to public systems described in Chapter 10 suggest that we cannot assume stability in the law affecting families and children, even in the near term.

Although clinicians, then, clearly face challenges from a changing environment, we also confront the task of changing that environment. Part of the difficulty confronting clinicians who want to be leaders in maternal and child health is that, as busy as we all are, it is essential to make the task of system change a regular and important part of our efforts. When the immediate demands of seeing children and working with families are vital and pressing, it can be difficult to justify time away to advocate for improvements in the system and, yes, to fight moves that will weaken it. As Chapter 10 points out, this is all the more difficult for clinicians who have never been comfortable with policy, the law, public management, or politics. It is still the case that VT–ILEHP has to work to maintain the kind of attention to systems issues that was described earlier.

Accepting the challenge of systems change requires ongoing efforts that begin with awareness. Understanding the decision environment is a daily task. Political, legal, and administrative feasibility are in many respects as important in shaping that environment as is technical (clinical) feasibility. This need to integrate concern with policy into professional clinical habits is one of the greatest ongoing needs and stresses that many practitioners face.

The task is not merely for clinicians to engage in systems change, but also to undertake the educational role needed to help families build their capabilities in this field. As any experienced practitioner in this field knows, families can be some of the very best advocates for policy change. However, for reasons explained in the preceding chapters, they are often operating under many stresses. Moreover, they can benefit from education about what is changing in the policy environment and with respect to skills such as advocacy or simply learning how to access policies. Thus, changing the environment requires both direct and indirect efforts in capacity building for families. If knowledgeable clinicians and families do not undertake these efforts, other interests in the policy arena will control the future shape of critical programs and policies.

CONCLUSION

The many roads traveled, literally (through the many mountainous, rural roads in Vermont) and figuratively, by the VT–ILEHP team in serving children and families with neurodevelopmental disabilities, have taught us invaluable lessons. The lessons captured in this book are based on clinical practice that the interdisciplinary team has acquired since the inception of the program eight years ago. Although the team enthusiastically embarked on this unique journey in sculpting a program "without mortar and bricks" with the flexibility to take its expertise and services where they are needed in the state, it has also stumbled over important issues. These, too, have been significant lessons. The rural character combined with the harsh winters have not deterred its genuine community-based program. The team, composed of faculty members and students, has traveled to the most remote parts of the state.

The commitment to assess children in their natural contexts, home, school, and community has cemented the notion for a contextualized, comprehensive assessment, as opposed to one restricted to the application of standardized tools. This feature, combined with the **interdisciplinary** practice, has yielded more comprehensive assessments. The **family-centered care** model has certainly expanded the understanding of the family perspective in caring for their children with special health needs. Moreover, it has enlightened the team and the students of the expertise and experience the families have to offer to clinicians. The need to serve all families has strengthened our need to pursue continuous learning in becoming **culturally competent**. This is especially important for clinicians to uphold the oath to serve all persons and to redress some of the historical inequities that continue to affect minority and indigenous peoples and their children. Although these elements have enhanced assessments and subsequent interventions respectful of family choices (when in accord to best professional and ethical practice), the VT–ILEHP team has slowly but surely come to the realization that to afford **leadership** in their fields, clinicians have to be alert and become familiarized with public policy and public law mandates and changes. The dynamic nature of the public policy arena, problem-driven in stark contrast to a strengths-based approach to persons with disabilities, has also turned upside down the assumptions made by clinicians. The faculty and students have had to face the problem paradox, as Cooper and Dennis (Chapter 10) refer to it, and recognize, not always willingly, the place of public policy and public law, to provide leadership in interdisciplinary, clinical practice focused on serving children with **neuro-developmental disabilities**.

The journey has been tremendously instructive and fruitful, although not without bumps along the many roads traveled. The people involved have supported its sustainability, which has only been possible when the mission of the program and a set of ethical principles, focused on serving families and their children with health needs, have been the driving force. Their continuous interaction with the interdisciplinary team has humbled us as we have recognized their strength, their love, and determination to advocate for their children, who have taught us so much about the many challenges for those with complex, health needs.

REFERENCES

American Academy of Pediatrics (Committee on Hospital Care). (2003). Family-centered care and the pediatrician's role. *Pediatrics, 112*, 691–696.

Cooper, P. J. (2000). Canadian refugee services: The challenges of network operations. *REFUGE, 18*, 14–26.

Geiger, H. J. (2003). Racial and ethnic disparities in diagnosis and treatment: A review of the evidence and consideration of causes. In B. D. Smedley, A. Y. Stith, & A. R. Nelson (Eds.), *Unequal treatment: Confronting racial and ethnic disparities in health care* (pp. 417–454). Washington, DC: National Academies Press.

Herman, D. (1994). *The Jossey-Bass handbook of nonprofit leadership and management.* San Francisco: Jossey-Bass.

Vargas, C. M. (Guest Ed.). (2000). Bridging solitudes: Partnership challenges in Canadian refugee service delivery. *REFUGE, 18*, 1–50.

Vargas, C. M. (2002). Women in sustainable development: Empowerment through partnerships for healthy living. *World Development, 30*, 1539–1560.

Author Index

357

Subject Index